THE MEANING OF THREE: BEHIND THE MASK

SANDY SELA-SMITH, PHD

authorHOUSE®

AuthorHouse™
1663 Liberty Drive
Bloomington, IN 47403
www.authorhouse.com
Phone: 1-800-839-8640

First published by AuthorHouse 11/16/2009

ISBN: 978-1-4490-2320-1 (e)
ISBN: 978-1-4490-2317-1 (sc)

Library of Congress Control Number: 2009908943

Printed in the United States of America
Bloomington, Indiana

This book is printed on acid-free paper.

The front cover photograph was taken by Dr. Sandy Sela-Smith at the fire pit in front of her Colorado writing retreat. She had gone out to take photographs of the flames one night hoping there might be a suitable photo for the front cover. When she saw what appeared to be an ominous image of a mask in the flames, she knew this was the right one for the cover.

Processes and procedures included in this book are not intended to substitute for medical advice.

CONTENTS

DEDICATION   vii

ACKNOWLEDGMENTS   ix

FOREWORD   xiii

Chapter One   The Shadow Knows   1

Chapter Two   A Most Disturbing Memory   19

Chapter Three   A Most Disturbing Dream   31

Chapter Four   The Decoding Device   47

Chapter Five   Confluence of Three Stories   65

Chapter Six   I Hate What You Made Me Become   73

Chapter Seven   These Boots Were Made For Kicking   95

Chapter Eight   The Dungeon   119

Chapter Nine   The Forest, The Box, and The Forklift   133

Chapter Ten   Going Back to Go Forward   145

Chapter Eleven   Back at the Beginning   183

Chapter Twelve   A Hole in the Side of My Face   193

Chapter Thirteen   The Boat   215

Chapter Fourteen   Three Levels of Abuse   229

Chapter Fifteen   The Long-Avoided Passageway
                     To The Worse Of The Worst   257

Chapter Sixteen   Dealing with the Residues of 2009   271

Chapter Seventeen   The Rest of the Story:
                     Overcoming the Worst of the Worst   297

Chapter Eighteen   The Rest of the Second Story:
                    Caring for the Causes of Cancer   315

Chapter Nineteen   The Rest of the Third Story:
                    Owning My Place In The Universe   329

Epilogue   A Deeper Understanding of Three   357

DEDICATION

I dedicate this book to all those who have ever been abused in body, mind, heart, or spirit, and as a result came to believe that who they are, deep inside, is not good enough, is not valuable, or is so intrinsically and hopelessly flawed that they cannot ever be wanted or loved. It is dedicated to those who believe they are damaged so profoundly that they can never be good again.

This book is dedicated to those who believed that they had to make themselves into someone, other than who they are, to feel accepted, appreciated, or loved.

I dedicate this book to all who have believed they had to hide or disown parts of themselves, and put on masks to appear to be someone other than who they are, so the world would not turn them away.

I dedicate this book to all the parts of ourselves that still live behind locked doors, in the prisons and dungeons in the darkest places inside us and believe they are separated from everyone and everything, forever alone in an alien world that cannot see, hear, or love them.

And finally, I dedicate this book to the ultimate truth that all of us are loveable, valuable, worthwhile, sparks of the Universal Mystery, and worthy of being loved, a truth that with learning, healing, and growth, we may all someday come to embrace.

ACKNOWLEDGMENTS

Many thanks to William Shakespeare, wherever he is in the Universe, today, for writing *As You Like It* over 400 years ago, which includes the line, *"All the world's a stage, and all the men and women merely players."* It is this insight that can open us to the possibility of putting down the scripts from the well-warn parts that we have played, step out of the dramas, and off the stages that have defined our lives and our destinies for far too long. Perhaps, for the first time, we may be able to experience the depth and breadth of our lives in wondrous spontaneity and authenticity without being trapped within the lines and on the pages of the dramas that have both defined and stolen our lives.

I acknowledge those children, who had the tenacity to reach beyond their circumstances and call out for help, who in their reaching taught so many, including me, to not give up on life. And, I acknowledge all those who had been wounded in childhood, grew into adulthood, and reached deep within to find and free their inner-children who have been held captive within the dramas still playing out behind their masks. For in the process, they, finally, set their own selves free to experience the lives they came to live, which is a gift to us all.

I also wish to acknowledge all the children of the world, through all time, who suffered abuses at the hands of those who were supposed to take care of them and did not survive what was inflicted upon them. Wherever they are now in the Universe, I honor them with a wish that the lessons our species is learning during this time of transition and transformation will make their coming, again, into this world, a far more loving experience, should they return.

I especially acknowledge and honor the many clients who gave me the gift of their trust by allowing me to walk with them for a time while they journeyed on their road to healing. They are an integral part of what has been written on the pages and between the lines of this book. I commend them for their courage to search for truth, for their being open to release long buried memories and feelings, and for their willingness to embrace freedom to what degree they were and are prepared to experience it. Their courage continues to fan the flame of my courage, as well.

I acknowledge the many helpers and friends, who, over the years, walked the often difficult path with me for whatever time was needed, some for a short time, others a long time, and still others who have remained most welcomed and appreciated co-participants in a mutually supporting partnership on the healing journey.

I offer special appreciation to Dr. David Illig, my dear and long-time friend, for his encouragement of my work and his willingness to write the foreword for *Behind the Mask*. His reflections, contributions, and support throughout the writing process were invaluable in the molding of the final product. What a gift it would be to the world if all people could have their own version of a friend such as David in their lives.

Many thanks go to Jeremy Geffen, MD for believing in my work, and trusting me with many of his patients over the years. And a special thanks for his reflective comments, based on his own experience in writing, at the final stages of the manuscript.

Bill from Atlanta is a special person who has continued to support my journey inward to bring healing and find freedom from a difficult past. I offer my appreciation for all he has been to me. I, also, thank therapists Doug in Conifer, Shar in Longmont, and Greg in Denver for their special contributions just when I needed them.

There are people who go out of their way to support others in their projects. Michael Scialfo of Wolf Camera in Littleton, Colorado is such a person. I thank him for his great efforts in polishing my book cover to meet publication requirements. Erin Watson and the SACO design team at Authorhouse, also deserve my gratitude for their hard work in designing the text of my manuscript.

I would like to thank my siblings for providing connection during our childhood years, which gave me the strength to grow into adulthood. Each chose his or her way to survive and I honor them for finding what they needed to live as fully as each could do. And, especially, I would like to thank my sister, Kathryn, for diving into the depths of our past to heal her own self, and in the process, became my greatest ally in my own healing journey.

Though I acknowledged all the children of the world who survived and reached out to life, I want to especially recognize my own child-self, little Sandy, who did not deserve to experience the atrocities that gravely impacted her life and her view of the world. I deeply honor the little girl within me who was strong enough to survive, and waited patiently for decades until I learned how to return to the past and free her to live. Without her, there would have been no adult Sandy, no learning, and no books...at all.

***

And finally...because of all that healing taught me to understand...

I wish to acknowledge my parents for taking on the roles they so powerfully enacted in an age-old, long running play, as they walked through their paces and read their lines in the early stages of my life. They performed their roles in the scripts, and fulfilled the drama so effectively that the mask I put on to play my part became too painful to maintain and finally cracked open, allowing much of it to fall away. The crumbling provided entrance to what was behind my mask, which allowed healing, not only from my childhood, but also, from multiple past lifetimes of wounding, all hidden behind my mask. Without the command performances of both my father and mother, it may have taken many more future lifetimes to heal much of what I brought into this lifetime. And for my being able to accomplish so much in this life, I offer my gratitude to them.

FOREWORD

By Dr. David Illig

I have often asked myself what is the purpose of a foreword? There is a likelihood you have not read this book and, possibly, you have not, yet, purchased it or even decided to read it. Or, there is a possibility you have purchased the book, and do plan to read it. So, the reason for having a foreword can be puzzling. In some of the books, the foreword is simply filled with messages of what the ones who write them have to say about themselves and their own books. Other times, forewords tell about the book, but in a condensed version. However, if the condensation is really good, you probably don't need to buy the book; you could just stop at the foreword. But the purpose of this foreword is to let you know that the magic of the book you are holding in your hands, right now, is not what someone else says about it but is in the process of reading it to its very last page. *The Meaning of Three: Behind the Mask,* and all the others authored by Dr. Sandy Sela-Smith, are the kind that those of us who have read them want everybody to read, even if the people we tell don't know why they are reading them, at least not when they first begin.

Over the years, I have read myriad books and articles and attended many workshops and trainings by a wide variety of experts. As a doctor of psychology, I have been studying the human experience for decades. I enjoy both mainstream scientific psychology and I enjoy ancient healing traditions, and the nontraditional approaches, which often seem the same. I especially have focused on the vastness and immensity of the human brain and complexity of our mind when combined with spirit, consciousness, as well as our body. I especially enjoy recent discoveries that cutting edge science seems to connect with that which, until recently, was considered to be magic, myth, superstition, lore, shamanism, or simply foolish beliefs. An example would be where quantum theory and small particle physics, now suggest the real possibility of the existence of an infinite number of parallel universes, perhaps, infinitesimally close to each other. Time and space are, therefore, closer to what mystics have been saying they are for millennia, than what classical physicists still may be saying. But now, these mystical, magical concepts are science, and no longer considered magic. We forget that at one time in human history, when somebody said if you started walking in one direction and kept on walking to the horizon you would eventually end up right back where you started. Those who made predictions like this were considered to be mystics or nontraditional thinkers, magicians, or perhaps, shamans. Now we call this knowledge science because it is based on the fact that the world is round and of course you will end up where started if you go far enough.

There are many ways of knowing what we need to know. And at the present time, we understand that knowing can come from logic, cognition, thought, and scientific discovery, but also, we know there is emotional and sensory feeling that provides us with what we know. There is "upper" level, or conscious knowing, and "under" level knowing, which is part of the unconscious and involves knowing that is not in upper level, but available at other levels. There are multiple levels of feeling, as well; some are more unconscious than others. And there are even multiple levels of awareness that is neither thought, nor feeling. The interrelated connection of mind, body, heart, and spirit is becoming more scientifically supported each day, where spirit, in this case, has little or nothing to do with what is identified as religion. In time, we may discover that religion could turn out to be more of a code system that allowed humans to entertain the spirit side of our existence until we could come to understand our spiritual essence beyond what is traditionally known as religious.

Modern day neuroscience is showing us more and more everyday that the human being, made of brain, body, heart, and mind, is much more than science used to believe or imagine. A human being is amazingly complex and vast. However, in an age of text messages, twitters, blogs, cell phones, and shortening attention spans, people in our hyperactive society are being told we are actually very simple, easily predictable, and instantly explained. We are told we can be healed by a simple pill or simple procedure, and that simple bugs, simple chemical imbalances, or simple breakdowns in the machine that we are cause our ills and diseases. Solutions can all be simple and clear and straightforward. Or, if something does not respond to our simple solutions, we are told there is no cure or solution. Whether it is by the media, the medical-pharmaceutical conglomerates, or the corporate world, we are told there is an available and simple solution to everything. Recently, it seemed that a flat screen television of sufficient size could fix almost anything. And on a bad day or a lazy day we can briefly believe or accept that we, ourselves, are very simple and can be fixed by purchasing or doing what we are told will fix the simple problem. Or, at least others are simple, and the ones who are inappropriately complex, can eventually get fixed.

Despite what you are being told by all those who profit from your belief in you being simple with simple, purchasable solutions to what troubles you—pills to end depression, bring you love, or let you love yourself by making you appropriately thin or beautiful; cars to make you likeable; huge televisions to bring you joy; food or drink to make you happy—you know there are greater truths about who and what you are than the messages of simplicity. Both new science and our highest selves know that simplicity is a lie; we are, in fact beings of multiple layers and multiple levels on multiple dimensions. These are truths that we have been told we are not allowed to know or which are not safe to know. But you and I know better. The fact of our complexity is a truth that is safe to learn. These are truths that we know but can't quite accept that we know. And the truth of your complexity is what you will be given when you read Dr. Sandy Sela-Smith's work.

This book is about your growth and your healing, and the expanding of your understanding and acceptance of your greater self. This book does not contain some list of how to do something or a set of steps or collection of information that you learn and make use of. *This book is an experience*. It might appear that *Behind the Mask* is about events that happened to Sandy Sela-Smith and how she worked her way through them. And that it is. But understand that what is written here is a teaching tale, or more aptly, a set of tales, which are presented to you, the reader, for the purpose of learning what we all need to learn. Her books each contain a set of teaching tales, which trigger deep and endless healing chains in you, the reader, while you see and hear tales of the experience of the author. Healing stories are more easily hardwired into our nervous system, in our spirit, and inside our body than a "how to heal yourself" sort of book. We are built to respond to stories. The brain, the mind, the body, the heart, the spirit do react to them with healing responses.

This book is much like an experience of deep therapy with Dr. Sela-Smith, as if you invited her into a safe healing place of your choosing and asked her to work with you on your issues, especially ones you didn't know you had. The world has a number of special people like her who are blessed with the gift of supporting others with healing their deep and, often, untouchable wounds. Sela-Smith's belief is that people can be healed very deeply and many more of us can learn to be deep healers of ourselves, and others. While going behind the mask is about finding our deep dark secrets, it is as much about finding out we are more wonderful than we ever knew. And it is about finding out we can and should explore the deep dark secrets, embrace them, survive what we discover, and thrive in the healing process, that finally allows us to reconnect with the wonder of who we truly are.

It is amazing that many in our culture would probably prefer growing cancer than exploring our deep emotional wounds that could cause diseases such as this. We would often prefer dying with cancer to taking healing to those wounds. Do I believe that Dr. Sandy Sela-Smith's work will contribute to preventing cancers and other bodily diseases in those who participate? And can they support healing of those cancers, once they have begun? I truly do. Read this book and you will too, at a feeling level, if not a biochemical one.

This book, her earlier book, *The Mask*, the third book in this series, *Under the Mask*, which is, yet, to come, all allow you, through the process of reading and immersing, to discover that you are much more deep, complex, and wonderful than you ever thought. These three books also convince you that there is a great deal of personal healing that must be done by us all as part of our development. Sandy Sela-Smith is a rare and special healer that is gifted and unique. Her books will inspire your acceptance that you, also, are a healer, who like all of us, has healing work with your self that you must do. She will convince you that no matter the presence or absence of any particular religious beliefs you hold, you have obligations and duties of personal healing that cannot be put off to any religion or any god, for that matter. And if you believe that a loving God exists, when completing this book you will believe that it is a loving God's will that you participate in the healing experience and that you have obligations to become involved in your own growth and healing, regardless of any of God's abilities to save us from ourselves.

Reading this book is a healing experience that, at times, will likely be difficult and at other times seem amazingly simple and easy, and still others times will seem strangely mysterious. It can be uplifting, as well as disturbing, or even depressing, but always, you will find what is contained in these pages to be very close to the truths with which we all need to work, truths that will cause you to laugh, and cry, and live. That is the message I would like to give to you before you read *Behind the Mask* and share its value with others. You will be grateful that you read it.

Dr. David Illig,   *RightMind* and *SuccessWorld*.

www.successworld.com

www.litigationpsych.com

Chapter One
THE SHADOW KNOWS

In a vain attempt to present a perfect image of ourselves to the world, it is not uncommon for us to hide what does not fit that image of perfection behind the masks that we wear. Then, we live in fear that what we have hidden will be exposed, leaving us unloved, unaccepted, and forever alone. We blind ourselves with half-truths and lies not just for others to think better of us, but for ourselves, as well. However, no matter how much we try to hide, we can be sure that deep inside us the Shadow knows.

So many more years ago than would seem possible, my family participated in a ritual that provided a sense of normalcy when normal would never have described the life I lived as a child in the far north country of pre-statehood Alaska. Before TV found its way to our town, radio was the main source of news, information, and entertainment, and sometime in my young childhood, my family got our first radio. The wooden console, made of polished Cherry wood, housed the radio that was taller than I by a few inches, and it had a mesh cloth that covered a very large speaker. It had an open back that provided access to the many lighted tubes and wires that we children were not allowed to touch, though I speculate I must have touched them because I knew from experience that those tubes were very hot. On the upper part of the radio was a glass "window" that revealed a panel with little numbers and marks to designate the frequencies of various stations that required very careful turning of the dial to achieve as static-free a reception as possible.

After dinner, on those special nights, we children assembled in the vinyl-floored playroom to listen to our favorite radio programs, one of which was *The Detective Hour*. As the designated time approached, we pulled up our chairs and gathered around as our father turned on the radio and tuned into a program that always began with an eerie organ prelude to help listeners conjure images of shadowy corridors in haunted houses, or dark city streets, wet with toxic rain dripping from awnings and forming rivulets that flowed into steamy sewers in the even darker back-alley ways. And then the sinister voice of Orson Welles began to speak with slow, determined words—as only *he* could speak—using deep theatrical tones that sent shivers down the spines of millions of listeners, as he said, ***"Who knows what evil lurks in the hearts of men? ... The Shadow knows!"***

All the time he spoke, if you listened very carefully, you could hear what might have been the rustle of a trench coat or maybe the sound of footsteps that seemed to be walking someplace towards that evil. This was followed by wicked laughter that sounded as if it came from someone who had lost his mind; maniacal enough to chill the blood of anyone drawn into what lay ahead. The laughter was accompanied by a swell in the dissonant sounds of the organ, like the music played in old-time films to warn the listener that something terrible was about to happen. This led into the story that would touch our imaginations and keep us all riveted to the glowing lights from inside the radio box that magically brought the sounds from what seemed like another world into our home.

For one night each week, my family listened to a story that nobody even thought of pretending we weren't hearing, and at the end of the program, the evil people were caught because *The Shadow* knew! He exposed the evildoers to the rest of the world, at least to those fifteen million or so of us who were listening throughout the country back then. While *The Shadow* exposed the wickedness of the evil hearts of men on the radio program, a part of me knew there was no one who could expose, much less bring to justice, the people who inflicted much more evil onto children, such as myself, in our town, and no radio program back in the 1950s would have exposed the depths of evil that lurked in the hearts of the abusers. I suspect, that even as the

21st century has moved into its second decade, there is still a reluctance to accept the existence of the kind of evil that was too much a part of my early years. Our culture would prefer to believe that extremely wicked hearted evil is exceedingly rare and belongs only to the few truly perverse among us and on CSI programs or horror films, but not in their own lives, or the lives of people they know. However, my experience has caused me to hold quite a different perspective.

***

From outside observation, we seven looked like a model family, not unlike television families with whom many of us grew up, some of which started out as radio programs and became TV shows later in the 50s and 60s and watched as reruns in the next 30 or 40 plus years, such as the Andersons on *Father Knows Best*, and *Ozzie and Harriet*. Later there were The Cleavers from *Leave it to Beaver* and then Sheriff Andy Taylor on *The Andy Griffith Show*, the *Brady Bunch*, the *Waltons*, the Cunninghams on *Happy Days*, and the Ingalls family in *Little House on the Prairie*. And later still, there were the Huxtables of *The Cosby Show*, and the Keatons of *Family Ties*, all with images that onlookers could easily have attached to my family.

Not unlike Ward Cleaver, Charles Ingalls, Andy Taylor, or Jim Anderson, there was my handsome black-haired father, tall and slender, a popular athlete, salesman, and for a while, not only the local church's lay minister, but also, the town mayor. And there was my mother, a beautiful, shapely redhead—strong, powerful, and independent—who, after graduating from her nurses' training, moved to the last frontier without support of family or friends. She ventured into the cold northern territory all by herself, willing to discover what this unknown life had to offer. But when she married, she became the obedient wife, not unlike June Cleaver, in *Leave it to Beaver* or Margaret Anderson, in *Father Knows Best*, who were dutiful, submissive, and obviously willing to defer decisions to their "more capable" husbands. But any surface appearances that match these characters or any of the others from loved TV families are where the parallels end.

My parents first meeting might have been compared to a comedy such as the old *I Love Lucy* show, when fiery redhead Lucile Ball as, Lucy

McGillicuddy, first met handsome Cuban nightclub bandleader, bongo drummer, and singer, Ricky Ricardo, played by her husband in real life, Desi Arnaz, and soon, thereafter, in the TV series, Ricky and Lucy married and years of comedy followed. Instead of being a comedian taking the role of a musician and singer, as was Ricky, when my parents first met, my father was a Standard Oil man, playing the role of a comedian.

Not long after her arrival to the far northern territory, the young nurse received an invitation to a 4th of July dance that was to be held at the community center in Seward, a small town nestled against Mount Marathon at the head of Resurrection Bay. Her roommate arranged a blind date for her with a guy she was told was very handsome and quite a catch. When she arrived with her girlfriend, they saw the young man who was to be her date for the evening standing on a tabletop, in comedic fashion, holding a Bible above his head, mimicking some generic hellfire and brimstone preacher. He was condemning the partygoers for their sinful, drunken ways, all to the delight of his friends. Despite the frivolity of it all, the young woman who was to become my mother found his behavior to be rude and irreverent. She was sure she would never have anything to do with a man she considered unacceptably disrespectful and irreligious. Six months later, she walked down the aisle to marry the man she found abhorrent a half-year before and was ready to begin another exciting chapter in her life.

Very soon thereafter, the beautiful redhead became pregnant with her first child, and, upon hearing the news, her husband sent the young mother-to-be to his parents' home in Washington State, to give him time to build a new home for their family in the Alaskan wilderness. All this could have become a pilot for a family oriented TV series, but the next events would have had to be left on the cutting room floor.

For a number of months, the young man didn't communicate with his bride. She wrote weekly, and sometimes more often, but in all the months she was gone, she never received a single communication from him. She waited and waited for a letter or a wire telling her that their new home was ready for her return, or maybe a note saying that he missed her, but nothing ever came. Less than nine months after her wedding day, and shortly before the child was to be born, the beautiful redhead made a decision to return to Alaska. Without telling her young husband of her intention, she booked passage on the Baranof, a passenger and cargo ship that departed from the Port of Seattle, crossed the Gulf of Alaska, and headed to the far north territory. And as fall was making its way toward the cold and dark of winter, the very pregnant young woman disembarked from the ship onto the dock at Seward to reunite with her dashing husband and their new life together.

But instead of finding her new house completed, or at least under construction, she found that her husband of less than 9 months was living with an Alaskan native woman. The details of what happened immediately afterward never became a part of the family story; the indiscretion of her husband was mentioned only once to me, and then it was put back in the box of unacceptable memories, never to be brought out into the open again.

A few weeks later, when the redhead came home from the hospital with her infant daughter, the three of them lived in a small apartment until her husband completed remodeling a slightly bigger home for the young family to live. Buried in the other clippings of unacceptable footage would have been the scene at the hospital in which the young grief-stricken mother sobbed with heart-breaking disappointment when she was told she had given birth to a lovely little girl. The redhead wanted a boy.

The next episodes would likely have included the births of the next four children, one girl after another and another, with the last being the long awaited boy.

And later episodes would include camping trips in the summers, retreats to the cabin on the Kenai river, and blizzards in the winters with images of the young family of seven making its way through the normal challenges of life in the cold north, maybe something like the stories of *Little House on the Prairie*. We four girls even began singing together, and if we had the right opportunities we might have given Lawrence Welk's Lennon sisters reason to be concerned about the competition.

But unlike the TV episodes in which everything was depicted as good and problems were solved in the allotted half hour or hour, all was not well behind closed doors of my family home. And as a sidebar, it is interesting to note that the people in the TV families were fighting demons of their own behind the scenes, but, in either case, such things were not made public back then.

Much of what happened in the icy cold territory disappeared into the unconscious of most all of my family members' psyches. While some of the darker events were dismissed as being uncharacteristic of an otherwise wonderful family, they were seldom discussed, even to this day. However, the extremely dark events that happened to little Sandy, and perhaps, to others in my family were not only *not open* for discussion they were *not acknowledged* as ever having happened at all by everyone but my oldest sister and me.

***

Explaining to anyone what it was like being little Sandy growing up in a household of abuse has never been an easy task because most of my adult life I had almost no recollection of being little Sandy. A few scattered memories, like tiny puzzle pieces, fit the preferred picture of the perfect family, but most of what I call the very difficult "always" memories didn't fit in that perfect puzzle; they just couldn't be made to match the image we wanted so much to claim as real.

The preferred picture did exist now and then. I recall building snow forts and snowmen with my siblings, as well as experiencing blizzards in 40 degree below zero temperatures that kept us out of school and all bundled away in our little home for days at a time keeping warm against the oftentimes treacherous winters. I remember camping trips in the summers, encounters with moose and bears, and feeding baby deer by hand from the garden behind the old log cabin on Kenai Lake at the headwaters of the Kenai River. My heart smiles when I recall listening to stories told under the stars around the crackling, sparking campfire. On one of those memorable log cabin nights, my father made his famous fudge, and while it was cooling, he made popcorn for all seven of us. My parents seemed truly happy that night, and at least a part of me felt safe and loved. Every now and then, when I get into a dismal mood, I have a longing for fudge and popcorn.

These were the good things that made it easier to forget the not so good things and helped us bury the really bad things so we'd never have to remember them at all.

***

Just after I turned 9, around Thanksgiving time, my family moved from Seward to Anchorage and life changed dramatically for us. The truly terrible things that happened in our birth town stopped. We had the most extravagant Christmas we'd ever had that year and even got a television set and later, a new automobile.

Lowell Thomas Jr., the famous film and television producer, who's home was *over the river and through the woods* in a very different neighborhood than our house, arranged for a gigantic children's Christmas party. It included a sleigh ride through the snow-packed streets, as children were picked up along the way to join in the season's festivities. There was real hay in the sleigh, and horses had bells that jangled when the magnificent animals shifted from trotting to dashing through the snow, just like we were living the Jingle Bells song. We sang Christmas Carols, like something from the movies, and I remember having hot chocolate and cookies in the biggest living room I had ever seen. We were living out own version of the famous *White Christmas* movie.

That first Christmas in Anchorage, one of my gifts was an exquisite pair of ice skates that I wore constantly that winter. With blade guards, I could wear the skates to school instead of shoes so I could skate to the bus stop and back home again, and of course, I was able to skate on the huge ice rink outside Northstar Elementary School, for recess, gym class, and lunchtime. For just a little while, I dreamed of being a professional ice skater. About that same time, the neighbor girl taught me the words to *Silent Night* in German, while we made angels in the freshly fallen snow and tried to sing the lovely version even more beautifully when a neighbor boy we both thought was so handsome walked past us. That was a storybook winter.

There was such magic when spring came, which meant that jackets, scarves, gloves, and boots could be put away and we could run, unencumbered, wearing canvas shoes, t-shirts, and corduroy pants. The most "spiritual" experience for me in my Alaskan childhood was the first day the tiny green buds opened on trees, a sign that life was returning after what seemed like an eternity when all life was gone.

Just a bike ride away, there were excursions to the cliff, overlooking the fjord, where my older sister and I believed we actually discovered an island that no one had ever seen before, and we found our way through the forest to a place of beauty unmatched by any place I have ever seen in this world, before or since, that my sister named Happy Valley and another we called Pine Valley.

All of these memories fit the picture that would be acceptable, not just to us, but also, as a showpiece to the world about our family. And, I suspect that some of my siblings hold tightly to this picture, choosing not to open the doors that go into places where other images might be remembered for fear they will loose these wonderful memories.

***

I remember getting my first pair of glasses when I was in the second grade, and I felt so upset that I had to wear them. Perhaps as a gesture to take away the pain of children's taunting me with "four eyes," or some other reason that I never understood, when I was six years old, my parents bought me a burgundy bicycle. I was so excited about learning how to ride it, until my father ran over it with his car. When he came into the house, after having *accidently* run into my bike, he was in a rage, screaming that he had told the kids not to leave their toys outside. I knew there was something else going on under his anger, but as a small child, I didn't know how to say what I felt when I stood in front of an unrecognizable clump of metal.

Even though I was only in the second grade, I knew that the bike had to have been run over, again and again, for it to look like it did. If he had been driving up to the house to park his car out front, he would have been going slowly and would have seen the bike and avoided it. But, if for some reason he hadn't seen it, a parking kind of bump might have knocked the bike over or misaligned it a little. Whatever else was going on inside my father turned the bicycle into something that would never be a bicycle again. This part of the bicycle memory didn't fit the preferred puzzle, unless we all chose not to notice how bent up the bicycle was and focused on blaming the kids who left their toys outside for their insubordination.

There was a time my mother had become very sick. I remember my father had to carry her to the dinner table because she couldn't walk. Her legs were covered with huge red bumps that looked really awful. Her condition worsened, and not only could she not walk, but she began having trouble breathing. It was terrifying to see her struggle for breath and not be able to do anything for her. We all thought she was dying. I remember being in the kitchen looking into the living room through a door with windows in it. Two doctors were standing over my mother, examining her to find out what was causing such bizarre symptoms that were sending her into hysteria. It was obvious that she was gasping for breath, and at one point she reached for one of the doctors in desperation because her breathing had stopped. My sisters, brother, and I were all crowded around the glass watching this terrifying drama take place a few feet away. And as my heart was breaking, I prayed, "*Please, Jesus, don't let my mommy die,*" while my father sat in a chair, with apparent total disinterest in what his young wife was experiencing. My child-self knew that something was very, very wrong. But I had no words to say what my heart felt was true.

***

After my parents left Seward in November of 1953 with 5 kids, a dog, a cat and a few possessions, the old car that helped me in my attempt *to go to sleep and never wake up* when I was 8—something I will talk about later—became our second car as my father brought home a brand new, shinny black Nash. I remember how excited my father was when he stepped out of the car to show it to us, and I, also, remember my mother standing on the front porch with a scowl on her face asking where he had gotten the money for the car and how he expected to make payments for it.

Less than two years later, our move from Anchorage to Seattle was unexpected, and so heartbreaking because this time, we left our dogs behind, something that took decades for me to heal. We left Alaska because my father needed to have an operation. He didn't trust the doctor who would have performed the surgery on him if he had the procedure done in Alaska. On more than one occasion, he expressed his belief that because he had differences with the surgeon, he was sure the Alaskan doctor would have killed him during an operation. But after his recovery, instead of us returning to Alaska, my father announced that we would be living in Seattle. Like our move from Seward to Anchorage, we had to buy new clothing and new furniture, but this time, what we purchased was not quite as extravagant as the previous move. My father seldom had a job after that. He had tried to reestablish himself as an insurance salesman, but failed to make the right connections. My mother became a delivery nurse at a Seattle hospital; however, her salary was not enough to support the seven of us, and money was always an issue, which created ongoing tension.

As we got older and ate together as a family, dinnertime was a very mixed experience. There were times we had plenty to eat, and other times the cupboards, literally were bare. A small mom-and-pop grocery store allowed my mother to buy groceries on a tab. She often rode the bus from the hospital where she worked as a night nurse, beyond our stop, to get to the store where she picked up five pieces of fruit so we would have something to take with us to school for lunch and, perhaps, she would get something for dinner when we got home. After she got her paycheck there was money for food, and for a little while, things were good. Some of the evenings during the abundant times were filled with animated conversations about what we learned at school or the news of the day, which included politics, economics, or whatever else was of interest at the time.

Other dinner times were torture. When my father had no money, and there was little food for us, he would sit at the head of the table and refuse to eat while my mother would make attempts to put what little food we had on his plate or pour milk in his glass. It was not unusual for him to explode in rage when my mother's insistence that he eat became intolerable. This was followed by an exit, accompanied by threats of killing himself by driving off a cliff. I can still hear the squeal of his tires as he pulled away from the curb, barely making the hairpin turn at the end of our street that took him to the main thoroughfare and to wherever he was going. After one of these traumatic departures, he would be gone for hours and occasionally far into the night.

During most of those Seattle years, there was not enough money to pay the bills and to eat, so sometimes we ate and other times the bills were paid. One pair of shoes had to last for the school year, whether the heels fell off, the soles separated from the tops, holes grew into the bottoms, or how much our feet outgrew the shoes. While all this was going on, my father stole money from my mothers file drawer when he ran out of his allowance for cigarettes, gas money, or whatever else he needed. The drawer was where she kept cash to pay for the month's bills and necessities; they couldn't have a checking account because my father had written too many checks that bounced. With each paycheck, my mother cashed her check at the grocery store, and on returning home, counted out the cash for each bill, put the money into separate envelopes, and later, she hand carried payments to the companies on the due dates. But when it was time to pay a bill, it was not uncommon for her to open the envelope and find some portion missing. She demanded that all of us come into the dining room for interrogation, while all the time, we knew it was our daddy who took it; but none of us told on him.

On one occasion, while we were experiencing worsening financial troubles, my father's parents came to our home with a trunk full of jars of food that grandma had canned. They had learned about our situation, probably from my mother, and took fruits, vegetables, and beans from their storehouse to supply us with enough food to get us through the difficult time. After they left, my father went into a rage and destroyed the jars, kicking them and breaking them into many splintered pieces; he believed the handout was his mother's attempt to humiliate him, something he could not handle.

My mother attempted suicide two times that first year we were in Seattle. The first time she locked herself in the bathroom and slit her wrists. Her blood covered the sink, floor, and walls before my father kicked the door in, leaving a broken door-jam and wood splinters everywhere. Her second attempt was by overdosing on sleeping pills. My father found her in her bed with a nearly empty pill bottle next to her, and though he tried, he was unable to arouse her. My oldest sister tried, as well, but our mother wouldn't wake. My sister and I positioned her limp body between us, holding her arms over our shoulders and walked around the living room to see if she could be revived, but she didn't respond to the movement.

While this was going on, my father took the time to brew coffee and tried to get her to drink it, but the hot coffee spilled out of her mouth and onto my sister's hand, scalding her. Many years later, my sister told me what a shock it was that our father would try to force our mother to drink coffee that burnt my sister. When that attempt failed to revive her, he piled us all in the car and drove to the hospital on the other side of town where she worked instead of calling an ambulance that would have taken her to a much closer hospital.

On arrival, he got out of the car and walked into the main entrance but was redirected to the emergency room, instead. As he reentered the car to go to the correct entrance, he raged at no one in particular, saying that if she died he would kill the people for not admitting her in the first door. But his rage didn't seem authentic, and he didn't rush to the emergency entrance, as would someone whose only focus was on keeping his wife alive. I knew there was something wrong about his raging and with his slow responses, as if his intention was to forestall any help for as long as possible. But I had no words at the time to express my feelings. I was in the sixth grade when all this happened. This entire event was filled with puzzle pieces that didn't fit the picture of the perfect, loving family, and though no one denies that it happened, talking about it has remained unacceptable.

My father had developed a long-term affair with a woman, resulting in his fathering a child, and apparently left both my mother and this other woman to live with a third family when I was in my early 20s. Several years later, when he returned to my mother, she never asked why he left or why he returned. His affair, his leaving, and his return, as well as the son he fathered, were known by all but not discussed.

Before there was any knowledge of his other families, we wondered where my father went for such long periods of time, but none of us challenged his excuses that he was attempting to make sales or was looking for work, even though there was never anything to show for it. After his excuses of looking for work wore out, he claimed that he had gotten a night job, but for some reason, his boss didn't seem to remember the checkbook to pay him. Finally, my mother demanded the phone number of his employer so she could order him to pay her husband, but my mother accepted my dad's promise to bring home the money the next day.

He walked in the next afternoon with a roll of bills that he dropped on the table in front of my mother. When she saw what he brought home, she threw the money across the room with violence, raging that no boss would pay a man in a roll of bills. I remember wishing that she would just accept the money and stop trying to force him to say what she wouldn't have wanted to hear anyway. After a few more years, when my little brother was in junior high school, he did challenge my father, giving the name of the woman my brother discovered our dad was visiting instead of going to work, but was punished for being disrespectful. Decades later, after my father died in 1996, I was told that thousands of dollars were found in numerous rolls of one hundred dollar bills, wrapped tightly by rubber bands and hidden away in the strangest of places all over the basement where he had lived like a hermit for the last years of his life. Though I am sure there must have been many questions in the minds of family members, I don't believe anyone ever tried to find out where the money had come from; I am sure it would have been impossible to find out.

A few years before my father died, my mother had been hospitalized sometime in the early 1990s with a bleeding ulcer, which had eaten its way into her aorta and internal bleeding nearly killed her. While she was hovering near death following the operation, I went to the hospital cafeteria to get something to eat and my father joined me since neither of us had eaten anything for many hours. As we sat across from each other, my father told me that he believed God did this to stop her from interfering with his vision to transform the tax system in the US, which he believe would be the only thing that could save our country from an inevitable economic collapse. He believed God had called him to be the messenger to bring about this change and he blamed my mother for its failure because she tried to control him in everything he did. I remember being dazed by what I interpreted as his deranged thinking process, that God would take the life of my mother so the Almighty's plan to save the US through the wisdom of my father's tax plan would be fulfilled.

She survived, but when my father died a few years later, there was no funeral, no memorial service, and no death announcements sent to relatives or friends. His own sisters didn't hear about his passing until after he was cremated. There was a simple obituary in the paper, like so many others that appear every day, naming the spouse, children and grandchildren, and a simple statement of what he had done in his life, of course, including only the acceptable puzzle pieces, meaning only we five children were mentioned, not the son who was over 30 years old. I remember reading his obituary, noticing the others, and wondering what remained hidden in the other life stories.

I, also, remember how baffled I was about the decision to cremate him because I understood this was not what my father wanted. Years before his death, my parents invited me out to lunch to discuss their will. After talking about her wishes related to the house and property, my mother told me that they decided on cremation. I noticed that my father looked very disturbed but said nothing. I just couldn't pretend that I didn't notice, so I asked him if cremation was his choice. My father told me that he hated the idea of being burned up in a furnace, to which my mother responded with a firm, controlling voice that let both my father and me know she was extremely displeased with his challenge. With that clenched teeth posture, she indicated it was her understanding that *they* had decided on cremation. For the first time in years, I heard him challenge her by saying, *"No, You decided."*

***

These were just some memories, which were a part of what I call my *forever* memories that didn't fit the beautiful image of the loving, happy, Christian family. The other ones that were too dark, too overwhelming or too shattering to remember were hidden away in back rooms behind locked doors and down in dungeons, all behind the mask that I wore, covering everything up, along with the parts of me that had experienced the unspeakable. It wasn't until I began therapy to try to save my crumbling marriage that the agony of my, then, present life, cracked open the protective mask I wore, which was created to keep me from knowing what was cut out and left, not just in those back rooms, but in the dungeons and basements of the family's unconscious, all kept separate from the recollections of what I wanted to believe was my *ideal childhood*. These dungeon memories included all that I hid from myself behind my mask, afraid that if I knew what was there, the very knowledge of it would destroy me. It took many years of uncovering to discover that *not knowing* what was in the shadow behind the mask was really what would have destroyed me had it remained hidden.

The buried memories and the known but unspoken memories held the patterns that kept me separated from knowing who I truly am. The belief that I was unwanted, not valuable, unworthy of love, and undeserving of being treated with respect or care, created patterns that lasted through most of my life. They caused me to be terrified of speaking the truth or speaking up for me. These patterns caused me to believe that it was my job to make things right even when that was impossible, but that I would die if I didn't do the impossible. The fear of having what was hidden exposed caused me to not only avoid looking in the direction of what remained hidden, but also, it caused me to deny the existence of all that had been buried in the shadows behind my mask. For the first four decades of my life, I lived as if everything was perfect...until it became very clear that it was not, when my shadow side emerged.

***

I, certainly, am not the first to suggest that we all have a shadow side where we bury what is not acceptable whether we are willing to admit it or not. And it is not a new idea that we are all capable of doing anything that is human in our efforts to protect ourselves from what we have hidden deep within, including committing acts of evil, whether we believe we are capable of doing such things or not. This understanding does not suggest that all of us live from the place of darkness, but it does acknowledge that the potential is there.

The best of what is human, as well what we call the worst exists as a potential in every one of us. The fact that both are there, allows us choice, and our choices are what determine how we experience our lives. You might recognize that I am communicating something you have come to accept as true, or you might resist this idea, perhaps feeling afraid of what it would mean to accept that you are capable of doing what you hold to be the most reprehensible behaviors. Or perhaps, you might be disturbed that I would suggest that there is darkness lurking in your heart or in the heart of someone you hold with high esteem.

***

As my own story unfolds in chapters that follow in *The Meaning of Three: Behind the Mask,* you may come to a deeper understanding of the person you want to think you are, as well as the person you may be afraid to think you are; but most importantly, you may come to discover the *Being* that you truly are underneath all that is behind your mask

Reflections

Allow yourself to peer into your childhood…into your life to notice what you might not have let yourself notice before. Do you have blank spots where you don't remember pieces of your childhood? Do you have memories but little feeling associated with your growing up years? Do you recall feeling as loved when you did something wrong as when you did something right? Do you sense that there are scattered pieces of your life on the cutting room floor that cannot be discussed when you visit members of your family?

When you look at your current life, do you notice that you feel safe? Loved? Good enough? Do you feel free to speak your opinions in your relationships? Are others able to speak their opinions and ask for what they need from you? Are you living a life that is fulfilling? Does what you do in your life reflect who you are? Can you handle being with other people as well as being alone? If you have times when you are alone, do you need to fill the time with sound, with activity, with entertainment, anything to distract you from really being alone? Do you like yourself? Do you love yourself?

Have you read these questions over quickly, avoiding feeling into the answers? If the answer to this last question is, yes, are you willing to go back to the questions and read them more slowly, allowing yourself to really think about the answers? Are you willing to let the questions take you behind your mask, at least for a few minutes? If you decide to look at the questions again and to let yourself search for the answers, remember that you don't have to do it all at once. You can always come back to this page, or you can take the time with all of them, now, if you choose.

We all have surface awareness, which often contradicts what is below the surface. Some would prefer to live on the surface suggesting that what lies beneath is better left buried in the past. The problem is that the unhealed past will continue to invade the present. When parts of your personal story or your family story have been cut out, they are not really gone. These parts will draw to you what you have avoided knowing because what has been wounded seeks healing, and the only way whatever part was wounded can be healed is when what you have hidden, finally is known, and truth is allowed to enter with love.

Chapter Two
A MOST DISTURBING MEMORY

Healing the deepest of wounds is not easy, but it is possible. If we are willing to face what we have resisted for years, for decades, or for a lifetime or more, we will need to reconnect with what felt non-survivable. The part of self still hiding from the wound needs to know that we survived. We need to bring love, truth, and forgiveness into whatever hurt us and to forgive ourselves for what we have hidden so long behind the mask. If we choose not to do this, the painful effects of the deep wounds will continue to impact our lives.

It was almost springtime of 2009 when I began to write what has become this second book in the trilogy, *The Meaning of Three*. The first book, *The Mask* had been out in the world for a couple of months, and I was anxious to get going on the next, but I felt so stuck, unable to move forward in the writing of this one. Despite my intention to find and release what was still hiding behind my mask, I'd been resisting accessing an experience I had avoided dealing with for decades. Though I had made numerous attempts to start writing possible chapters, even as early as the summer of 2008, I couldn't feel the beginning, and every attempt felt disconnected and meaningless.

So much had happened within me that opened to the dark side as I was writing *The mask and* revelations continued to emerge following the completion of book one. It may take several chapters, or maybe even the entire book for me to fill in missing pieces, to find and understand the meaning of what remains in the shadowed darkness behind my mask and to release the patterns of hiding that have affected my life.

As I explained in book one, the mask is the front we put up that fits the roles we play. Masks cause others to believe we are what we want them to think we are or they present what we think others want us to be. We use masks when we feel who we really are would not be accepted. Most of the time, our wearing of masks is unconscious and most of us don't even know that we are wearing them. While book one did include the dark side, its focus was on the mask most every one of us wears, which covers the dark side, hoping that both others and ourselves will not know what we don't want to face.

The intention of this book, however, is to *focus* on what is behind the mask. What is about to unfold in the pages that follow—revealing more of my story, the story of the dark side, and the human story— foretells the choices that have been laid out in front of us; and all of this will open in its own time, and in its own way. And whatever that will be, I have no idea as I begin. I have always been aware that what I write is really the writing, writing me, and I don't know where it is going or what it will be until it is finished.

***

Two operations for cancer in less than a year and many back and forth trips for medical treatment between my home in Florida and my writing space in the foothills of the Colorado Rockies had made the period from the spring of 2008 to the spring of 2009 a financially depleting and physically exhausting time. My bank account was nearly empty and my body felt more out of shape than ever before. Despite the fact that I have been overweight for many years, I was strong and had great stamina, but the struggles of that difficult year had cost me both my endurance and strength. Familiar, old body-pain patterns had begun to return, which included muscle cramping and stiffening, and difficulty breathing.

One frigidly cold Colorado morning in early 2009, my little dog, Jenny, and I went out for a walk in front of my carriage house, when I noticed a car backing up toward us. The driver seemed not to have noticed us, and as it approached, I leapt toward the car to hit it with my hand as a warning for the driver to stop. In the moment, that seemed to be the only way I could protect Jenny from the possibility of being run over. But as I took the leap, I slipped on the ice and badly pulled the calf muscle in my right leg. Immediately, I knew significant damage had occurred. The painful contraction of an already cold and contracted muscle made walking back to my carriage house difficult. In spite of my best efforts of icing and heating my calf muscle for several days, the contraction got worse. This pulling in and stiffening of my muscles seemed to hold a metaphor for what was happening in the rest of me, on many levels.

Many years of working with life pulse taught me the necessity of maintaining a smooth, equal flow in both extension and contraction in bodies, in muscles, in organs, in breathing…in everything that is alive…to maintain health. If I began to experience a greater pull towards contraction and much reduced extension—not just in my leg, but in my life, as well—and did nothing to bring the pulse back into balance, I knew I would begin to age and die sooner than necessary. I was not willing to shut down.

***

Many people live their lives not consciously considering the depth of commitment they have to life, taking blows, figuring how to get back up and do it all over again, until something happens that causes them to approach a tipping point, and they don't know how to move back into an upright position and continue on, or they might give up efforts to find the way to re-engage in life. Whatever that something might be—the loss of a relationship or the death of a loved one, an illness, a financial defeat, a betrayal, a humiliation, an intolerable situation that seems unchangeable, getting knocked down one time too many, or myriad other life events—the experience of it offers a *choice point* regarding life or death. If our choice is to give up on life, life begins to withdraw from us. Taking in life becomes less and less an intention; the world becomes smaller and smaller, as what is outside begins to match the inside. Vibrant life-filled people, fully engaged in the world, can reach a tipping point, and without working through it, they can find that life has become a metaphoric rocking chair in front of a television set watching reruns with nothing new entering into their world as they wait for death to close the door on life. The light goes out of their eyes, and the wait can be a matter of days or weeks, or it could be decades where a flicker of life continues on without real connection to life.

We can continue to open to life until its completion, even if we have been diagnosed with some incurable illness, since life as we know it, now, is eventually terminal anyway, or we can withdraw from life and invite its ending. For as far back as I can remember, I have been a person who has always chosen to get back up again, though some times it took a while to figure out how.

***

Following the slip on the ice, stiffening spread throughout my body, letting me see a possible future of limited movement and pain, something I wasn't willing to accept. So, I signed up for a few one-on-one Yoga lessons to regain the ability to extend my body and counter the contraction that was in process. Just a few days before beginning this chapter, I had my first lesson, which caused me to be aware of being in my body in a very different way than had been usual for me. The healing processes I had experienced in recent years caused me to feel being alive, countering my former pattern of being in my body as something I thought about in my mind, rather than something I experienced physically. However, when the current life struggle around cancer in 2008 consumed me, I went back to the old pattern of thinking about feeling life, not actually feeling it. But Yoga drew me into *feeling* being in my body, *feeling* being alive, again.

In the middle of that first lesson, I remembered why I had stopped practicing Yoga 25 years before. Back then, every time I felt myself inside my body in that deeply experiential way, I would cry, not with physical pain, but with overwhelming grieving. That kind of deep sadness was just too much to deal with when my life, my marriage, and my world were all crumbling, at the same time, so I stopped.

During the second Yoga training session, the tears showed up again. When I reconnected with the intensely tight muscles, especially in my neck and shoulders, experiencing the tightness from the *inside* rather than observing the tightness as I had before, tears spilled down my cheeks. This particular pattern that caused my muscles to be stuck in contraction had been there since childhood, and they had resisted release through two decades or more of deep-tissue body therapy, arising every now and then, making me feel like I might be dying. It felt as if the contraction pattern had been reawakened by the slip on the ice and was still resisting letting go.

The pain of this pattern was not present all the time, but when it showed up, an unbearable contraction would begin in the middle of my back, where several vertebrae would feel as if they were fused together, creating stricture of movement and burning pain. The muscles from this place in my spine attached to my shoulders and neck, as well as into the muscles in my legs. The muscles in my groin felt as if they turned into steel cables being drawn tighter and tighter, pulling my body into the fetal position. All of this was related to painful burning in my forearms and lower legs, a burning that went deep down into my bones, and once it began, there was nothing I could do to make the burning stop. I had not been able to figure out the cause of this constellation of contraction patterns or what would make them dissipate. But when they decided to come, the burning pain would make me feel like death would be the only relief.

What had been so frustrating was that I had worked with memories related to this pain so many times in so many ways, but somehow, this particular body response just hadn't let go. In all the years I have worked on my own tissue memories, and those of clients, it has become clear to me that this kind of experience often is embedded in multiple levels and layers in body and mind, and it often takes many journeys inward to, finally, bring healing release.

One recent morning, I was in particularly intense pain from all the contractions as I walked Jenny, my sweet little dog, through the expansive acreage surrounding my carriage house. With hundreds of tall Colorado pines rising above us, I sat down on a metal chair by the fire pit, very aware that every part of my body was in agony. It felt as if all my joints were made of rusted gate hinges, shrieking in determined resistance to being opened. As Jenny wandered off in exploration of the grounds near the frozen stream, sniffing and searching for evidence of any critters that might have walked that way recently, I examined thoughts about quitting. All the while, I was leaning back and forth, stretching the steel rods in my legs, pulling on the rusty gate hinges inside me, and pushing into the pain to see if I could alleviate it, just a little. With tears welling up, I asked myself whether or not I really wanted to keep moving toward expansion and growth or if I was just too tired to keep up the struggle.

The thought of being in a room with a fireplace in it, curled up in a rocking chair and wrapped in a soft fleece blanket, quietly releasing all resistance to contracting into the fetal position and slipping into forever sleep, sounded attractive. I knew this was another one of those *choice point* times; in that moment, letting everything go seemed desirable, though on a deeper level, I knew I would not quit. I knew I would not curl up and go away forever, at least not now. There had to be a way to reconnect with the expansion energy. I knew I had to find it; I couldn't let the tipping point win.

***

The pain in my right shoulder and neck, which was related to back and groin muscle contraction, had been there, on and off my whole life, but the reawakening of the pattern began in the summer of 2006 as I was preparing to leave Florida for an unknown destination. I had just sold all of my furniture and most of my belongings to an auctioneer for the paltry sum of $600. At the time, I felt as if the woman who took my furnishings off my hands for such a small amount had stolen from me; but there was little I could do about it. In reality, it didn't make sense to keep everything in storage when I had no idea where I was going or how long I would be gone. And despite my feelings, it made sense to save hundreds of dollars each month in storage fees, which would add up to more than the value of the furniture if my away time lasted as long as an intuitive part of me believed it would last. I moved my personal belongings to a dear friend's home and that became my permanent Florida address while I began my life as a wanderer, in search of something I didn't know.

After the "sale," I put the remaining boxes of books, non-furniture items, nearly 15 years of client notes, and business papers on a flat-bed dolly and wheeled a number of very heavy loads from the two large units to one much smaller unit. I remember feeling defeated and angry, not only for feeling ripped off, but also, for having to do all this heavy work by myself, even though both situations were created by my own decisions. But something inside didn't feel that having to do it this way was my choice.

While pushing a heavy load down the long hall, the wheels abruptly turned, causing the cart to come close to go crashing into the wall, so I quickly pulled the cart away from the near collision and, in the process, pulled the muscles in my right shoulder. Later, when I raised my arm to lift something, an explosion of pain ripped through my shoulder, neck, and arm. I lost movement and nearly all strength in my right arm, making driving nearly impossible; I was unable to leave Florida for another month, waiting for enough healing to occur to let me drive. Ever since that time, my right shoulder had been weak and would become painful if I tried to lift it too high or carry too much. Much later, I found out why raising my right arm was so traumatic. Yoga stretching put me back in my body, causing me to feel both the emotional and physical pain locked up in that right shoulder.

Without a doubt, I know that when there is unexpressed anger inside and I am doing something physical, my body is in rigid contraction and injury is far more likely than if I were doing the same task while relaxed and happy. The truth is that my mind had decided selling the furniture made sense, but my heart had not been in agreement. I had not released the furniture emotionally, which caused an inner war between my angry heart and my practical thinking mind, especially when the auctioneer offered such a small amount for furniture that I dearly loved. My heart felt justified in turning against my mind for making the decision to sell everything without working through what my heart wanted. This is not unlike what happens when one person in a relationship makes a unilateral decision that affects the other without exploring options and sharing the decision-making process.

The inner war created contraction in my muscles, and when I pulled on the cart to keep it from crashing, the forced expansion tore the contracted muscles and ligaments. Because the pain had remained for over two years, I knew there would be work ahead with the deeper roots of this inner war.

***

The yoga stretching made it clear that my shoulder was incapable of supporting me. And, as I was mimicking the poses of my teacher, I began an internal conversation with my shoulder. Over the years, I have learned that my body can and does communicate with me when I take the time to listen with focused attention. To my surprise, my shoulder told me it didn't think it would ever be good again, and when I heard these words, tears began to spill down my cheeks. I knew the voice from my shoulder was coming from a child part of me, still stuck in a most horrible incident, and the tears were hers. From that communication, it was clear that despite all the other parts that had released deeply buried emotions and embraced healing, this part did not believe that she would ever be healed or reconnected.

I knew, both in my head and my heart, this conclusion that healing wouldn't happen was not the truth, but the dissociated child-part stuck in my shoulder, believed neither my heart nor my head. All the work I did with the shoulder pain since my reentry into Yoga in early 2009 kept bringing back a horrible incident from my childhood, when I was barely six years old, an event that embedded itself in those same muscles that had been wrenched just before I left Florida in 2006 and was reactivated with that incident on the ice in Colorado a little over two and a half years later.

Writing about this, even now, takes me into the place inside that feels so deeply dark. As much work as I have done over the last two decades, I can still find myself dropping into that darkly hopeless place. The difference between my going there now, unlike years ago, is that I know being there doesn't last forever, and if I want out of the dark, I can usually find my way back to the lighter side fairly easily. I know what remains buried in my shoulder is something I have to work through and I know that I will, but I am in a place where the part of me still stuck there doesn't believe what I know, which is that healing is possible, even from *the worst of the worst.*

Because that event from so many years ago is deeply rooted in the dark side, I know that as I write this book, not only will I see what I have resisted, but I will, also, bring healing to this decades-old trauma that I have avoided for far too long.

However, in this very moment as I write, something very deep has been triggered. I am experiencing the part of me stuck in the past in the most horrible event and I can't stop the tears that are streaming down. As I connect with what my shoulder is remembering, I am aware that what is coming out of me is beyond crying...it is a silent howling, a grieving that goes back so far, and is so, so huge that it feels bigger than my whole body. It feels like the howling is flowing out of the very center of the earth and exploding through me like volcanic lava made of a fiery, red-hot sound that engages all of the pain in every bone, muscle, and fiber. And, if I were to fully release it, it feels like the sound would melt the world. But nothing is melting around me, just yet, though writing this has left me feeling somewhat melted and exhausted.

As I was experiencing the writing in the above section, the event that kept flashing in my mind was the worst thing that ever happened in my childhood. It was worse than not being wanted when I was born, and worse than being raped in the forest when I was 4 years old and then buried in the box afterward as punishment for telling the truth. It was worse than seeing a man murdered in an Orphanage. It was worse than the shattering rape when I was six, an event I wrote about in *The Mask,* and worse than being left in the hold of a boat with a dead man. It was worse than seeing the murder of a child and being raped in the playground when I was 8, and it was even worse than being strapped down to a chair and having electrical shocks rip through my body, though I think that was a close second. All the things I couldn't talk about were not as bad as the *worst of the worst.*

It was worse than all of these things, because most were done to me; *I didn't do them.* When I was forced to watch what was being done to others, *I wasn't doing it.* Even when my body was overpowered and forced to participate in the horror of unthinkable sadistic acts, it was other people's energies that were fueling what was happening, not my energy. *I didn't do it.* The event that kept coming into my thoughts after

I began Yoga was one where the fueling energy came from me; *I did it!* And that is what has been stuck in my shoulder and in my buried memory forever; that is what made the muscles and tendons in my legs turn into what felt like steel cables pulling me in and makes me want to curl up in the fetal position, and go to sleep…and never wake up. This is what has been so, so hard to release because I have carried the guilt that has a way of drawing me back into the dark side, with all the beliefs of being so, so bad that I will never be loved and forever will be alone…and I'd never be good again!

Reflections

You have your own version of whatever was the worst experience you lived through that has contributed to molding your view of the world and feelings about yourself. What happened to you does not have to be a horror story like ones I disclosed in book one, *The Mask*, or that will be revealed in the pages that follow in *Behind the Mask*, for them to be damaging. Any experience that caused you to lose trust in your caretakers, any physical, emotional, or psychological pain that caused you to recoil in fear or strike out in anger, or any event that caused you to feel unsafe or unable to trust the universe you live in, even if what happened seems insignificant in comparison to other people's experiences, could have caused you to separate from your essence. This separation created patterns in you, which became your way of life, your mask.

It is likely you have no idea what the original separating experience was, and you may not know what your worst experience might have been. It is, also, probable that you don't recognize the patterns you created to keep yourself safe because they are normal to you. But the patterns exist, nonetheless. Because what you have buried has a way of being acted out, and you keep drawing evidence of that worst experience to you, you have a pathway to the original cause…and a pathway to healing.

As you continue to read, allow yourself to notice your patterns and what you have drawn into your life, including any of your reactions to reading passages in this book. Somewhere, in all of this, is what is disturbing you and is likely causing you pain; it is shouting out for your attention because it is ready to be healed. Ask the part of you that may be shouting now, even if the shouting is silent, to help you find out what happened that caused you to separate from who you are, as well as from the universe, the Great Mystery, the creator of all that is, to help you see what is needed for your healing.

Chapter Three
A MOST DISTURBING DREAM

As long as we pacify ourselves with the idea that we don't have a dark side or convince ourselves that we don't wear a mask, and as long as we keep telling ourselves that bad things never happened—or, if they did, they really were not all that bad—it is likely that we will resist any internal drive to heal our separations and will continue to experience the dark side of what is human.

A number of years ago, I wrote a story about a most disturbing dream, or more aptly, it should be called a nightmare. In that nightmarish dream, it is late at night. I am in a confined place, standing with my face pressed against what seem like bars, like I am in some sort of a cage. I'm aware of loud sounds everywhere around me and many people are nearby, but don't seem to notice that I am there. The people are moving strangely, but it's hard to see them clearly because there is a smoky fog everywhere. An old woman I think I know approaches me and gestures in a way that seems to be her way to calm me, and then she leaves. There is a pungent smell in the air that makes it hard to breathe. In time, the noise stops and all the people go to sleep. I am very tired and so relieved that everything is finally quiet. It seems in the nightmarish dream I fall into welcome sleep and experience a dream within my dream.

In the dream, I wake in the middle of my sleep by a sound. I look up to see very large hands reaching for me. I am terrified. The hands pull me up and away from where I have been sleeping in my cage. I am frightened because the hands are rough and don't hold me carefully.

I want to cry out to wake the people who are sleeping, but the hands cover my mouth. The huge hands are carrying me over people, who are sleeping on the floor. I am being carried through a doorway into the darkness of the night. I see the image of something that looks like a car silhouetted against the night sky. I hear what I think is the sound of a car door opening.

I feel helpless; I'm unable to move. Something I cannot understand has completely overpowered me. I hear a loud sound, like a door shutting and hear the sound of an engine. I think I have been put in a car, but I am not sure. Everything is so dark, and I seem to have no control over my body; I am frightened. I can see lights and dials flashing above me. There is a man sitting next to me. I cry out in fear, but no one comes to help me. The man's hand pushes hard against my chest until I can no longer make any sound.

It seems like a very long time has passed, and then, everything stops. There is no more engine sound; there are no lights. There is only the sound of the man breathing. The rough hands pick me up and I am powerless to resist. I hear the slamming of a door. I am being taken into the darkness of the night, again, and I am so afraid.

I feel my body being jostled, moving up and down quite rapidly, but I cannot see because the man who has abducted me is holding me against his large body, with my face shoved up against his chest. I can tell that the man is running very fast; he seems to be running and climbing, running and climbing, and I am helpless to break free, as if my body is limp with fear. It feels like my head is going to disconnect from my body, and his hand is pushing so hard against me it feels like my bones will break from the pressure. I scream.

The hands begin to shake me so hard that I stop screaming and then, the running continues. I feel my body being hit by something that stings me. Cold, sharp, cutting feelings slap against my back and head. I can hear the breathing of the one who holds me too tightly. The breath is heavy and hot, the hands are wet, and they press me against his sticky wet clothing. The smell is so horrible I want to vomit. I feel my clothes being torn off of me and I am even more terrified. I am so cold, as the wetness from the man touches my skin and the night air makes me shiver.

I am thrown on the ground in leaves and grass, as if I were being thrown away, like some piece of trash. I didn't know my body could hurt so badly. But then, I feel something that is even more horrible; too, too awful. I am being torn into pieces. I try to keep the feeling from cutting deeper into me and I hold my muscles tightly, but the painful feeling tears open the holding muscles. I think I am going to die. It feels as if he is shoving something all the way through my body and it rips me all apart inside.

Hot and cold, smells—horrible smells, blood and sweat, breath and holding breath, sharp pinpricks on my skin, the tearing feeling deep inside, and the night all are one. Pain—more pain—I cannot stand the pain. Hands grab my throat and squeeze tighter and tighter, so hard I can no longer breathe; I can no longer cry. The pain in my throat makes me forget about the pain in my body, and the darkness on the outside becomes darkness on the inside. I believe I have died. But I don't wake from the dream; I drop into a deeper sleep...maybe I *am* dead.

And then in that deeper sleep, I have still another dream. Everything is quiet. I seem to be outside in the daytime. It seems like something very bad has happened, but I can't remember what it was. I am lying on the ground in a pile of leaves and I cannot feel much of my body. I am not sure if I even have a body. There are branches and leaves on top of me, as if I have been buried alive...or perhaps, I am dead. But maybe I am not dead, because I can feel my skin. I think something is biting me... little stings...and tiny tickling movements that make my skin itch; I can feel something is crawling on me but I cannot make it stop. The sun is shining through the brush that covers me. It is getting so hot...I think I am hungry, but I am not sure.

I am feeling very weak. I am not sure if I can cry. I want to cry; I try to move my arms, my legs, but noting seems to be connected, and my thoughts of moving don't allow me to move. My mouth is so dry. It feels as if the hot sun is making my mouth turn to dust and my lips stiffen and crack. I have no idea what has happened. I don't know why I am here. This does not seem to be where I am supposed to be, but

I don't know where I am supposed to be. I remember having legs. I think I used to stand on legs, but I don't feel them and I don't think I could stand even if I could feel them. Maybe legs and standing were just dreams.

It feels like I have been here for so long. I think there was something before being here, but I don't remember; maybe something before was a dream. I don't know. My throat hurts. It feels like something is wrapped around my throat; when I put my hand to my neck, nothing is there, but I can't make the feeling go away. I realize that I can move my hands, my arms; I lifted my hand to touch my throat. Can you move your hand if you are dead? I wonder if I am dead. Could I feel things if I were dead? Silence is everywhere. And then I can hear the sounds of birds.

Birds are near; I can hear them. A squirrel looks at me. I can see him through the twigs and brush that seem to be covering me. I can see the birds and the squirrel. I wonder if you can see birds and squirrels if you are dead? There is silence, only silence except for the sounds of the birds chirping and the crackling of the squirrel walking on the twigs…this is a silence that seems to have always been and always will be. I think I can remember a time when there was not this kind of silence and burning heat, and when there was not stillness, but maybe that was just a dream.

Shhhhhhh. Do I hear a sound? Voices—they are coming closer? Oh, please voices be good; see me under the branches—I am here—please see that I am here; everything hurts and I don't want to be here any more. Please help me to wake up from this terrible dream. I am filled with terror that they may not see me…that they will pass by and I will be left here, under the branches, trapped in this nightmare. Please see me between the blades of grass. I can make my throat cry. I know my throat is supposed to cry. I hope crying is not a dream. If I can cry out maybe I can make myself wake up. I open my throat, I breathe, and I make a sound.

Oh no, it is too quiet. It is not loud enough. My whole body is filled with terror. They may pass by and not find me, and I will be forever alone in this dream from which I cannot wake. The voices might not hear the sound. I am filled with desperation, exploding with a panic that fills every cell of my body. Perhaps I can lift my arm...yes...I can lift my arm and push it through the grass that covers me. I am strong enough to hold it up. Please voices...please see my hand that reaches for you. Please wake me from this terrible dream.

One voice seems to hear me; maybe it sees me. I feel both terror and hope because the voice is coming closer, getting louder; it sounds like a good voice. I see hands above me, hands connected to the voice. They are removing the branches that are over me, dusting off the dry leaves. The hands touch me. Now I remember hands from before, huge rough hands in my dream. The voice is connected to gentle hands that lift me from what felt like it might have been my grave. They lift me up carefully, and I feel safe. There are tears on the man's face. He seems happy and sad at the same time. His face is covered with wet tears and his hands hold my face against his face, and I feel love pouring out for me, as I have never felt love before. This wetness in the light feels different from the wetness of the dark before the horrible thing. The good voices come around me and the hands that hold me let me know that I am safe. My fingers find cloth that is connected to the good voice and gentle hands. I cling to the cloth. I can't let go. I can feel the good hands; perhaps, I am not dead. Perhaps everything in the darkness was just a dream. It was just a dream.

***

How I wish that this had been *just a dream*, but it wasn't. This is a story created from the details of an actual kidnapping and rape of a 9-month-old infant in Tampa, Florida, on September 21, 2001 as told from the compiled information provided by the 21-year-old rapist, the grandmother of the infant, and police officers. The facts of what happened, from adult perspectives, appeared in the Tampa Tribune, written by Jose Patino Girona and Lindsay Peterson. It was reported on all the local stations for several days after the horrible event. After reading the story, I decided to write the "dream story" from what may have been the baby's experience, a perspective that most of us usually don't consider, or more likely don't want to consider when we read about something so unbelievably awful that happens to children, such as this. We try to distance ourselves from the horror by telling ourselves that the infant will not be damaged by this incident because she will not remember it. And we try to pretend that she was *too young to know*. But if we conclude this, we would be so very wrong.

A Tampa police officer explained that little Mooka, the 9-month-old baby girl was snatched from her crib early in the morning by a 21 year old man who had been partying with a number of others in the living room where the little girl slept in her crib. Sometime in the night, according to the reports, the man, Randolph Standifer, who is now serving life in a Florida prison, took the baby girl from her crib, put her in his station wagon and drove down a dead-end road. He parked the car and headed toward a forested area. While holding the child against him, he then climbed two iron gates and entered a wooded area where he brutally raped the infant, strangled her, after which he covered her body with branches and other debris, and left her for dead.

Meanwhile, after a night of partying, everyone had gone to sleep and the grandmother didn't wake until about 9:10 AM. Grandma went to the crib to feed the little girl, but found her missing. She reported the baby missing around 9:30 AM, and a police interview was conducted. The officers spoke with the baby's grandmother who explained that she had tucked the little girl in the previous night. Her story, together with interrogations of the others who attended the party and spent the night, revealed that one person in the group of partiers, Standifer, who remained afterward, as well, was missing when the others woke in the morning. He was traced to his home. After being questioned and failing a polygraph test, the man admitted to raping the infant, strangling the baby to death, covering her with leaves and brush, and leaving the tiny body in the woods.

The officer, who was reporting the story on television, very shortly after the rescue, was nearly overcome with emotion as he related what happened next. When the officers went in search of the body in the location that Standifer described, they first found a diaper in the woods, and then one of the officers heard a whimpering sound, something that he said sounded like a bird. Then he saw a tiny hand reaching out through the grass and tree branches. He ran over to her and removed the debris that covered the infant. The baby was naked, dehydrated, and covered with insect bites. When the officer picked her up, the little girl reached out, grabbed his shirt, and wouldn't let go.

Two weeks later, the child with the nickname of Mooka was released from the hospital, but instead of being returned to her home, she was placed in the custody of the court. Though the story of the events of the kidnapping and recovery filled the airwaves and press for a number of days, the baby's own story was not told; she could not tell it.

***

Without extra-ordinary loving support from family and very wise therapeutic support as this child grows into womanhood, a baby such as little Mooka would most likely grow up never being able to know about, much less speak of her story. What happened to her occurred before she developed language skills, and once learning to speak, her conscious awareness would revolve around people and events connected to her verbal language, while memories not connected to words would likely not remain in conscious awareness; but instead, they would be unconscious. This does not mean the story is not recorded. It is recorded in the cells of her body as somatic memory, and will become a part of her inner structure from which she will interpret the world and her self, as well as live her life. One of the greatest mistakes we can make is to assume that because someone is too young to have words to describe what happened or because they don't appear to remember what happened, that horrible experiences such as what happened to little Mooka, do not impact their lives.

Years from now, she may have nightmares that contain tiny pieces of that horrible September day, on that first day of fall, 2001. She may dream in tiny pieces because she would not be able to withstand remembering the horrible night and day as a single event, at least, not for a very long time.

In the intervening years, between that fall horror and the beginnings of her disturbing dreams, she might lead a life filled with many symptoms that reflect the world, as seen from the eyes of the raped infant, who was left for dead. She may be terrified of the sound of a particular car engine, or become anxious at the opening and closing of car doors and react in unfathomable ways. She may hate the smell of perspiration, even her own, and may not want to do anything that would bring on body sweat.

She may hate the smell of musty forests and dislike going outdoors, or decide to attack the outdoors, by engaging in high risk-behaviors. She may relate to life with a vengeance, but never feel connected to life, to the outdoors, or any wonderful outdoor experiences. She may be fine in relationships with men, longing for them to reach for her in the day, but she may resist any man that reaches for her in the night; she may avoid anything that leads to sexual intimacy, or she may enter sexual relationships only when she can be the dominatrix.

She may try to distance herself during intimacy while pretending to be involved; or she may respond to any sexual advance by becoming frigid or violently angry when a man gets "too close" to her.

As a woman, she may attempt to recreate the circumstances around the horror as a way to tell her story, reenacting all the parts of the event by becoming a helpless infantile woman-self unable to protect herself from the abuses of "Randolph" kinds of men. She might have a whole series of relationships with similarly wicked abusing men with rough hands who treat her like garbage to throw away, and she may experience mistreatment, rapes, and attacks at the hands of these men. If she stays with one abusing man, and keeps returning to him after he hurts her, the psychiatric world would say she has battered wife syndrome or dependent personality disorder. She may spend her life reaching out to be freed by gentle men, only to feel unsure of the safety, developing a come here, go away style of relationship, looking for the nice man to save her from a violent relationship, but leaving the nice man for another "bad" man because she is unconsciously compelled to act out what happened to her before she was a year old.

She may play the role of her grandmother and the other party-goers by not protecting herself from people who have no regard for her own self, by not caring for the safety of other people's children, or not showing proper vigilance for her own children. She may long for closeness and safety, professing her love for any who comes close to her, emotionally grabbing on to them like her infant self clutched the shirt of her rescuer, but as soon as they get too close she goes into anger and fear, viciously pushing them away as she wished she had the power to do when Standifer began his vicious assault and she would be labeled as having borderline personality disorder. It is possible she might grow up to become an over-protective mother, hyper-vigilant, unwilling to allow her offspring normal independence, teaching them to fear the world as much as she fears it, without knowing why. If she seeks help, she might be labeled a person with anxiety disorder and given medication to curtail her fear.

She may take on the part of the vicious perpetrator, attempting to be the one in control as a way to avoid being helpless. Or, perhaps, she may spend her life trying to cover herself up, replicating Standifer's covering her up by the leaves and debris, using any number of means. She might live a quiet, withdrawn life in silence, even within a relationship, until a part of her can no longer stand to be isolated. Then, she may reach out for help, or she may scream to be set free, causing those around her to believe she has literally gone crazy.

Perhaps she may find herself running and running in whatever she does in her life, not know why, and labeled obsessive-compulsive. She may become a person who has gentle hands that rescue others as a way to hold on to the idea that rescuing is possible and be identified as a hero. And she may become all of the roles, switching and changing, from one part in the drama to another throughout her life.

If trauma continues through her childhood, similar to what happened when she was an infant, she may be diagnosed as having dissociative identity disorder. This could be her way to reveal to someone—to anyone, perhaps, even to herself—her untold story, a story for which there are no conscious words or memories, yet, one that must be uncovered and released if she is to become free of it.

As a result of the role or roles she takes on as an expression of what happened, her life may be filled with conflict, with disaster, with unexpected shifts and turns that are difficult to understand on their own. She may live her life as a successful person, accomplishing amazing things, but inside she may feel a quiet desperation that she is a failure without knowing why, or she may find herself in institutions such as hospitals or prisons as a result of acting out the story. And no matter what role or roles she takes, she will not feel connected to herself or to her life. She will feel as if she is acting in some play, reading a script that is disconnected from her authentic self, and in her heart, she will feel as if something so very important is missing. If anyone would be willing to study her life, as if it were a drama, a metaphor telling a story, he or she might be able to see the horror hidden behind her mask being played out on the stages of her life.

Another part of this story is what may well happen to her body years later, as it, too, expresses the damage that was done so many years before. She may not be able to have children because of all the tearing and scaring that was done to her reproductive organs before she was even a year old. Intimate relations could be too painful, or she may be so disconnected from her body that she is unable to experience orgasm. Sexually transmitted disease, long dormant, could erupt in her body in her adult years. And she could develop cancer of her ovaries, her vagina, her cervix, or her vulva, all places that experienced the ripping apart. Her skin might become extremely sensitive to any contact with the outdoors, or she may experience skin rashes, which look like tiny bug bites that break out in times of sexual intimacy, times of stress, or they may simply appear as autumn comes. She could develop chronic or seasonal problems with her throat, even life threatening illnesses, such as throat cancer.

This little girl could grow into a woman that vacillates between bouts of depression and anger, and the medical world would label her bipolar, giving her medication to correct what they interpret as a chemical imbalance never addressing what they don't know how to access. She could lead an anxiety-filled life, afraid of living and afraid of dying, suspended somewhere between the two.

It is, also, possible that as she grows from child to adulthood, she could develop what is often called seasonal grief, or seasonal depression. Every September she might drop into deep, dark sadness, without explanation, unless someone figures out that on the first day of fall, not only did she experience what no child in the universe deserves to have experienced in that brutal attack, but Mooka, also, lost the only family she had known, dysfunctional as it seems to have been, when she was made a ward of the court and released to the foster system two weeks after this incident. Most of us don't want to ever touch that degree of grief in our own lives and do all we can to avoid being reminded of what deep loss feels like. That kind of grief from the loss of family, perhaps more than any other emotion can feel even worse than one's own dying. To numb the pain, Mooka may turn to drugs or alcohol in her teen years or become addicted to pain killers, legal or otherwise, in her adulthood.

***

For hundreds of years, our culture has comforted us by rejecting the thought that babies have feelings, perhaps, so we could accept what happens to them without feeling the shame, guilt, and grief that would likely oppress us if we let ourselves know the truth. The idea that little children and animals don't feel pain the same way adult humans do because their brains are not fully developed, allowed scientists to do vivisections on animals. Researchers cut into bodies of helpless animals while they were alive, but not sedated, because they wanted to study nerve responses, while discounting the screams and looks of terror in the animals' eyes. In the early years of psychology, babies underwent psychological testing that would be considered damaging by today's standards but were accepted because of that same unconscionable belief that small children were too young to know or to feel.

Current research has verified what people connected to their hearts know without needing research findings to support their knowing, which is that animals and babies do feel what happens to them. Babies are intelligent; they remember what they have experienced even in the womb, and they often block out and then act out what was too painful just as older children and adults do. They, also, create a picture of the world and live from that picture in later life, based on what happened to them in their formative months and years.

Part of that early picture includes beliefs, not just about the world, but also, about the self, and because these are pre-verbal, they can be much harder to access, much less transform. An incident, like what happened to this 9-month-old baby girl, could cause her to believe she does not possess value because she wasn't protected from the rapist. She may live

41

from that belief, without ever knowing that she believes such a thing. But everything she creates or draws to her, including her relationships will have embedded in them the belief of her lack of value. The words she hears inside, whether consciously or unconsciously, are a constant reminder that she is not good enough, not acceptable, not lovable, or worthy of love and not valuable.

She may spend her life doing everything she can to cover up her low self-worth, pretending to others and to herself that she thinks highly of herself. But deep inside, she may not be able to shake the feeling that she doesn't matter, even when she pushes herself to accomplish great things in her life, and she could feel that whatever she does can never be enough.

The likelihood is that braided together with great fear and grief she will, also, feel overwhelming rage for what happened to her when she was too little to have words that could identify its cause. Because of her gender, she will most likely suppress the rage—rage is not an emotion that is approved of for girls in most cultures—and those energies, more likely, will be turned against her instead of the outside world. Such rage often shows up as depression, as self-destructive behavior, or in the form of physical ill health.

Unexpressed energies inside us have a tendency to push themselves up to the surface for expression and release; but when the cause is unknown, the feelings attach to current circumstances unrelated to the original experience, similar only because the event in the present touches deeply buried feelings very close to the present feelings. If she does express any of the rage in later childhood, as more boys do in comparison to girls, it could be in the form of bullying or physical assault on other children, but without releasing the original cause.

She might go through her entire life with rage dripping out of her pores, while she smiles sweetly, never knowing that she is filled with seething anger. Since our culture approves of anger in boys but not sadness and pain, which are interpreted as weakness, boys who experienced damaging childhoods, more often than girls, become angry and express violence toward the outer world. Girls who carry childhood wounds more often than boys end up in hospitals or therapists' offices, while boys damaged in childhood, more often, become men who fill the prisons. It was no surprise that Standifer had been sexually abused when he was a child.

Little Mooka may bury herself in other people's lives rather than experience her own, but as she grows into her middle years, she may feel so separated from herself it is possible she could give up on life or she may begin a journey to find herself. No matter what path she chooses, if she does not find a way to reveal and release her story, her middle years will be a challenge. If she does not find the way to allow healing before she grows old, the likelihood is that she will spend her senior years living the pain of the her infant self in her muscles and bones.

And her mind, which began the pattern of forgetting what happened to her so many years before, may begin to show increasing signs of forgetting pieces of her life and eventually her whole life, built on patterned responses to an infancy and childhood…and later on, her adulthood that she can no longer remember.

***

What might be a surprise to some is that people can experience similar patterns as described in this scenario without having to have gone through what baby Mooka suffered on that first day of fall in 2001. Any experience that causes an infant or a child to feel unsafe or unloved, especially when brought on by those who are supposed to provide safety and love, can result in patterns of defense. As a protection, they put on masks that not only separate them from others, but also, from their authentic selves. And behind those masks, are the hurts, the pain, the fears, the angers, the rages, the wishes to inflict pain equal to the pain they felt, and the hate for others, as well as for themselves. Behind the mask is the shadow, the darkness, and the capacity to commit any or all of the "deadly sins" that few of us are willing to acknowledge exist in us.

Since we humans have a need to feel accepted and loved, as well as to feel that we are significant, we begin to identify with the masks that cover up anything that would make us seem unacceptable, unloved, and insignificant. Because we, also, seem to be wired inside to want to contribute to our social group, we may push ourselves to do something worthwhile with our lives. But when our contribution is generated by fear of not being good enough and if what we create is to prove our worth, not only what we experience ourselves to be, but also, what we create, will feel counterfeit.

To feel that blissful expansion of joy in what we do with our lives, *what we do needs to flow from deep within us as an expression of who we are*; if it doesn't, we are left with disconnection and emptiness, and the feeling that something important is missing.

***

I wish I could say that Mooka's story is so unusual and that very few infants and little children ever experience such horrible life-destructive events. But, unfortunately that is not true. Far too many infants and young children in our own country and around the world are violently treated, and sadly, many do not survive. We have only to read the newspaper or watch Television to hear the stories of so many missing children, whose bodies are later found with evidence of being brutally assaulted and murdered, to know that this kind of cruelty, born out of unhealed rage and the unaddressed dark side of the abuser, does happen. And many, many more children survive the treachery of abuse, but bury it behind their masks, living lives from the emptiness of disconnection.

Whatever occurs that causes us to feel separate, unsafe, unacceptable, and unloved is bad enough at the time it happens. But, what is even more devastating are the long-term effects of what is hidden behind the mask that we put on to make ourselves appear to be worthy when parts of ourselves don't believe we are worthy, even when that belief is unconscious. The mask we put on to recreate safety covers not only the lie we believe about ourselves, but also, separates us from who we truly are, much deeper inside, under the mask.

Reflections

Like most of us, you are very likely incapable of seeing all of your patterns without having something reflect them to you or someone in your life tell you—or shout at you—what is in you, and even then, it is not an unusual response to minimize or reject what life or others reflect. Once you really get it that you draw to yourself what is in you, you can open to the people and events that cross your path or the people or circumstances that accompany you on your path, as the Universe's way to offer guidance to help you see the patterns that have been controlling your life.

A willingness to see what you draw into your life, and your reactions to what you draw, will help you greatly if you choose to begin the inner search for what is within you that needs to be healed. Until you learn to enter your dark side and embrace, with love, what you find there, you will continue to experience a life that reflects back what has remained separated within and hides behind your mask.

Let yourself observe your life and notice how you relate to the world. Look at anything that disturbs you or seems to possess you, and become aware of experiences that seem to keep happening to you. Just notice. Then ask your wise self to help you to see the story that has been covered by a mask. Once you discover the story, you can re-connect with the part of yourself that remains stuck in the story, bring truth to whatever lie that part believes and allow this part of you to embrace love and truth, which will allow that part to become free to join you in the present.

Chapter Four
THE DECODING DEVICE

In our journey through life, when mind, body, and spirit are connected to the love that resides in our essence, we flow in harmonious balance that allows us to experience freedom, personal empowerment, authenticity, and spontaneity. Or, if we've disconnected from love, we experience our lives from the prison of protective patterns, intended to make us safe, but instead, cause us to feel imbalanced and guarded against love and all the wonder and joy that our connection to love creates.

My intention for writing *The Mask* was to support the reader in discovering that healing is possible, no matter how great or deeply buried the trauma. I wanted to convey that we humans are capable of creating balance within us of mind, body, and spirit. These three aspects of us—three in one and one in three—represent our *Being*, our *Doing*, and our *Experiencing*; all three contain each other, and are braided together. They create our wholeness, and when balanced in the braiding, these three aspects of ourselves allow us to experience living from our true selves. If one of the three aspects is not healthy, and is, therefore, not in balance, then all three aspects will be out of balance. Since what is going on within us is what we draw to us in the outer world, when we are out of balance inside ourselves, our lives will reflect back to us the same imbalance in experiences such as painful relationships, frustrating disturbances, problems, catastrophes, conflicts, weakness, accidents, illnesses, and troubles that seem to keep coming into our lives.

Internal disturbances occur because imbalance in the interactive flow of mind, body, and spirit creates undue stress on the body, and over time, such stress decreases the effectiveness of our immune systems to protect us. We can become physically or mentally ill or experience a loss of our strength, our endurance, our thinking processes, and our coordination of our selves and our lives. Internal imbalance can also lead to external disturbance because we are unable to tolerate stresses coming in from the outside, and we react. This can result in short tempers, aggressive behaviors, making poor choices, intolerance, and so much more that impacts our relationship with everything external.

***

Not only do major life-traumas create imbalance in the internal flow, but what we might consider little incidents in childhood can create imbalance, as well. Just like major events, these little things can take a lifetime to overcome, even if we convince ourselves that what happened was nothing important. As an example of how a little thing can have a big effect, consider the following scenario. A child is delighted to get an ice cream cone, but when he takes his first lick, the round scoop falls off the cone and onto the dirt. The loss causes the child to feel shock and grief to which he might respond with inconsolable crying or he might throw a tantrum. Depending on what follows, the child could heal from the pain of his loss, accept what happened, return to balance, and remain in connection with his world and himself, or he might experience unresolved pain that results in imbalance, disconnection, and the formation of another pattern in his mask that, without healing, lasts the rest of his life.

If the parent feels embarrassed that the child is hysterical in public he or she may condemn the child for crying or for throwing the tantrum by telling the boy to quit making such a public fuss or he will be punished and really have something to cry about, or the parent could shame the child by saying *"big boys don't cry!"* The parent might feel angry the child was so careless that he wasted the money spent on the cone, declaring the little one will not get another ice cream, maybe never again. The parent might not have the money to replace the cone and could tell the child that he will just have to accept the loss, without offering any compassion. Or, the parent may choose to respond in an empathetic way, explaining to him that if they had more money, he would surely get another cone. The parent may pick up the crying child and hold him with love. When the child responds to being comforted, the parent might begin laughing at the colorful mess melting in the dirt. Parent and child could play a game of what the melting ice cream looks like and then point out how the ants will be so very happy to receive an unexpected dessert, thus, transforming tragedy into comedy and loss into gain. The child could discover that even when something does not turn out as expected, what is received can be wonderful, too.

There could be a thousand, thousand responses to such a very small incident in a child's life, and each one, forms the growing structure of the child's interpretation of the world, along with myriad meanings attached to that world.

The child could conclude that he is not worth an ice cream cone, or that he is incapable of preventing painful loss from which there is no healing. He could conclude that he is not good enough to deserve love and understanding or he is incapable of doing things right. He could become afraid to express his emotions, or believe that his emotions are bad; he could conclude that the expression of what he feels is unacceptable, even to him. These would not be conscious thoughts; they would be unconscious conclusions that can form a significant part of the child's self-identity and his worldview.

Any of these conclusions would cause the child to separate from his essence and experience disconnection and imbalance, something he could carry his entire life. His world would appear to be one that is unloving, uncaring, and out to punish him for being so unworthy. Even though loving, caring energy comes his way later, he would likely not notice it because he only experiences what he expects and only sees what his experiences, over time, have programmed him to see. Even if his conscious awareness might not believe he sees the world from this pain of his childhood, an aspect of himself holds the dark world view, and if he experiences a loss in his adult life, he may find his world collapsing because of the meanings he unconsciously holds about loss.

Or, if the parent reacts to the incident from acceptance and love, the child may conclude that the world is a loving place, and unplanned things happen in the flow of life. He can know that even something unexpected can have a bright spot if you look for it. Whether or not he gets a replacement ice cream in that moment, he can know that what happened is not a picture of what will happen; and above all, he can know he is loved, which re-establishes internal and external connections, and balance is restored. The world in which he lives is experienced as one that supports him and loves him; it is safe to venture into and embrace his world. He might notice when unloving, unsafe energies exist, but he does not focus on them. This child may learn not only how to see the *silver lining* that exists with any dark cloud, but will be able to see beyond the cloud, altogether to see the expansiveness of the universe, instead of being swallowed up by the darkness.

***

The physical body, the house of the will of our feelings —*our will to live, our will to feel love and be loved, valued, and appreciated, our will to feel connected and independent, safe and uniquely significant, our will to experience joy, peace, and bliss, as well as our will to live a life free of shame and guilt, apathy and grief, fear and longing, anger and pride and so much more*—too often holds the pain of having some aspect of the will dashed. But resilient as we are, most of us find a way to move past the pain by splitting off from the hurt of our dashed will and pushing it away from our conscious mind and self-image. We learn to carry on with our lives as if the painful, dashing event never happened.

The problem is if we don't move through the pain by discovering the lies embedded in it, an aspect of ourselves is left along the way to hold the pain and keep the meanings that were attached at the time. Years later, deep within the man, there is still a little boy grieving for the loss of the ice cream, feeling as if he is all alone and unloved. This pain is attached to an even deeper inner structure that grieves for the loss of a loving world that supports and cares for him, and perhaps the rage at what he experiences as a world that hates him. He could take a path that seeks revenge against the world and all who cross his path, or he might turn the rage against himself for being so flawed that the world would reject him, as it seems to have done. He may spend his life trying to prove his worthiness to the world, doing what he believes those in his world would approve instead of what his heart and soul want to do. Without healing this part of him, he will not be able to connect to *feeling* love; even if he finds abundant love in his later life, being loved does not fit his worldview structure. He may know he is loved as an idea but not feel that love in his heart or in his body. He may spend his entire life not knowing that he does not feel loved, he believes that his thoughts of love are the same thing as his feeling love, and…they are not the same.

***

When there is unresolved and unhealed trauma, the inaccurate or false beliefs that were first constructed from the event still cause us to feel as if we are separate, unsafe, not good enough, or any of the other oppressive conclusions we made long ago. These constructs remain in our unconscious minds, buried deeply within, behind the mask, which is formed, in part, for us to not have to face the pain of what happened. We also want to escape the meanings we attached to the event, and want to keep other people from seeing what we believe is the horrible or unacceptable truth about us. Over the years, as we walk the path of our life's journey, more and more parts of ourselves can be scattered in burial plots along the way. As we get older, we have less and less of our energy from which to draw to keep us healthy, happy, and alive because too much of it is trapped and buried in the past, along with those dissociated parts of us.

Too often, we resist going into the pain to heal the broken will and instead pretend that we are whole and balanced, when behind the mask is the evidence that we are not. What has seldom been taught to us is that if we can acknowledge, at least to ourselves, that we are in pain and are experiencing fear, anger, grief, jealousy, hatred, shame, guilt, or anything else that causes us to be unbalanced, we create the possibility of releasing these heavy emotions. Then we can reconnect with the disconnected parts of us and heal whatever was damaged, resulting in restoration of balance in body, mind, and spirit, and reconnection to the essence of our life force.

The man who lost his ice cream when he was a child, but was not comforted, would need to metaphorically experience his separated little boy-self in his arms, feel the separated feelings, empathize with the loss, discover what the conclusions this dissociated part of him drew from the experience, and expose the lie of separation by bringing in love and truth. The man can become the loving parent that was not there when he was a child, and in bringing love, he also brings a new worldview to his child-self, which means he, as the adult, *experiences this new worldview*, as well. The separated child, buried somewhere in the past, now joins the man in the present, bringing back all the life force that became separated from him when he buried the pain so long before.

Even if the child's carelessness caused the loss, the loving adult-self can help the child uncover the cause of the carelessness. If the child's anger caused it, the adult-self can bring loving teaching to help his child-self look under the anger to find the original pain that created the emotion and action, which resulted in the incident. By bringing care and healing to the pain, anger will melt, and connection with love and balance can be reestablished.

When the internal-self experiences healing, the external effects of the internally held lie will dissolve. This transforms the experience of the outer world, as well. When a man who lived his life from the belief that he was unworthy of love finally releases that belief, he opens his life to knowing and feeling that he is worthy of love. Perhaps, for the first time, he is able to see what was always there but was invisible to him because his worldview had not allowed him to see it.

Our ability to experience worthiness comes from connection to our essence, which is the unique mystery within us that is connected to the Great Mystery in all things, a concept that will be more deeply explored in book three, *Under the Mask*. We create our lives, either from the protective patterns formed from the belief in separation from our essence and our world, or from that place of balance, love, compassion, joy, spontaneity, authenticity, and so much more that comes from experiencing our essence.

***

We often hide what we are afraid to face in ourselves, but our lives have a way of exposing what is hidden. As a case in point, while I was making one of my many attempts to begin this second book, my sister called after having had what, to her, felt like a horrible drive to work. Shortly after leaving her home, she was in an entrance lane to the freeway when traffic came to a dead halt. As she approached the problem, she saw a man who appeared to be unfamiliar with the nuances of entering freeways and had come to a complete stop. Apparently, he was attempting to find a break in the traffic to safely enter. But anyone who drives on freeways knows that finding a break in rush hour traffic is something that, most likely, is not about to happen from a stopped position; the driver needs to ease out and merge. It seemed as if he didn't understand how much more difficult it can be to enter the flow of freeway traffic from a stopped position, and it appeared that he didn't know how to trust that in moving forward, a space would open up for him. By stopping, he likely caused, not only himself, but also, all those behind him, to experience a much more difficult time merging with the forward flow.

Not long after making her way past that experience, my sister noticed traffic was slowed to an almost dangerous pace on the freeway itself and observed many drivers in her lane were swerving out into the HOV lane to avoid a car that was moving far too slowly for safe travel. As she moved up behind the slow moving car, she saw the driver and passenger were immersed in a conversation that seemed to take precedence over driving. After a great deal of frustration, my sister finally found an opening on the right and merged into that lane. But as she passed the slow moving car, the passenger turned her head to the right, screwed up her face, and stuck her tongue out. My sister was shocked by the obviously insulting expression and explained to me that she had not honked or acted in an aggressive manner toward the two women. Since she was extremely frustrated with the apparent lack of concern the women showed for others, her frustration might have shown up on her face or in the way she changed lanes.

After these two disturbing incidents, a third situation happened, one too many for my sister to come out of her drive to work unscathed. She was in the process of making a lane change to the right and was nearly two thirds of the way into the lane when a man began to move from the far right lane into the lane, now, almost fully occupied by my sister. She had to brake to prevent him from sideswiping her; she flashed her lights to let him know that she was there, and she honked her horn. Instead of acknowledging his "invasion" of her claim of the space—as in possession is 9/10 of the law—he responded by aggressively taking the space in front of her and when he was directly in front, he stepped on the brakes and then instantly sped up, which nearly caused her to get into an accident with someone else to avoid rear-ending him. From an external observation, his actions could easily be seen as road rage and my sister was the victim, or someone might see her honking her horn as a milder form of road-rage, and his "over the top" response was to get even for her honking and light flashing.

So rattled by these three morning experiences, my sister called me when she was off the freeway and could safely talk. She didn't want to go into her office feeling so frazzled and hoped that a phone connection might ease her stress. As she was relating the incidents, it was clear that she had brought into her life three energy patterns that were about both the outer world and about her inner world, as well. The man who had come to a stop before entering the freeway traffic seemed to be living in and representing the fear that so many of us feel, whether consciously or unconsciously. Many of us don't know how to move forward in our lives, so we come to a standstill because of fear of making what could be a disastrous mistake. But what we can't understand is that fear-based hesitation often leads to situations that can be as damaging, if not more so, than what may happen if we risked moving forward.

Many of us live in patterns, like the two women talking in the car. Our distraction on the metaphoric *road of life* might be like theirs, talking without noticing what is going on around us, or it might be drinking, text-messaging, being glued to our favorite entertainment, obsessive working or playing, stirring up trouble, dating or creating partnerships to make sure we are not alone, competing, or using sex, porn, volunteering, gambling, drugs, or anything else to avoid having alone time to notice what is going on inside, or avoid what is going on around us.

When something happens that makes us shift our focus from our own distractions to the needs of others, we can become angry. Like the passenger in the car that was moving slowly, who seemed to be unconcerned as to how her behavior was affecting many other drivers, we can decide that other people's distress with us has nothing to do with our behaviors and either literally or figuratively "stick out our tongues" at them if they express any displeasure with our actions. Or, we can become even more aggressive like the man who slammed on the brakes endangering his own progress to shake up someone else. An alternative might be that we could intentionally drive five miles under the limit on a one lane road to anger a person driving close behind us, obviously in a hurry, as a way to get even with his attempting to put pressure on us by driving too closely. I am sure we all have had experiences on both sides of these troubling patterns.

As my sister completed telling me about the three people that crossed her path on the way to work, she was approaching the door of her office, but didn't want to go in while she was carrying all the stresses from her morning commute. However, the trip to work was not the only concern that morning; she was, also, carrying another stress that had to do with her work.

For over a year, she had planned to retire from a job she had not enjoyed. She wanted to discover what she would do with the rest of her life, but so many things kept getting in her way. At first, she extended the time before retirement because she felt she needed more money to feel safe on a limited income without a paycheck. Then she decided to buy a car, which she wanted to pay off before she quit her job so she wouldn't be forced into making such a purchase when she had less income. But, then she needed to regain the money she had spent on the car, so she decided to stay longer. As a result, her timetable for departure kept changing.

Any or all of these decisions could have been fueled by her lovingly taking care of herself or by fear of what it would mean to actually leave and begin another chapter in her life, something she both wanted and feared. What can make understanding experiences such as this one difficult is that the decisions we make—or are afraid to make—can originate from a blend of both love and fear.

She believed that new workers, as well as some of the older ones who depended on her to help them when they became stuck, would likely be helpless without her direction. One, in particular, whom she deeply appreciated, had been begging her to not leave as she had planned. As a new employee, he knew there was no one as qualified as she to help him maneuver the system as effectively as she could. Her concern for and loyalty to him was pressing her to reconsider her decision to retire. But she found herself feeling forced to do what she didn't want to do. Just going to work caused her to feel as if she would be stuck indefinitely helping people who weren't becoming independent in their jobs and she would never be able to move on with her life. It was clear that her trip to the office was a metaphor for what she was experiencing in both her professional and personal life.

***

The morning my sister had experienced this "series of unfortunate incidents," she was participating in an expression of several drama triangles as proposed by Steven Karpman in the 1960s and later was popularized by the Twelve-Step Program as the codependent triangle. This triangle explains the complicated relationships that develop among people within dysfunctional systems, where one person is identified as the "needy" person, who is the victim, the addict, or the helpless person, and another person is the rescuer of the one that is needy. The needy person is seen as dependent, and the rescuing person is codependent because the rescuing person needs the needy person to be needy in order for the rescuer to have someone to rescue, thus making them feel needed and, therefore, important. (Whew!) The needy person then feels taken care of by the rescuer.

The rescuer feels important when he or she rescues someone. But, one of the requirements, whether directly spoken or subtly expressed through guilt or shame-inducing actions, is that the victim properly accept being rescued and correctly express appropriate dependence and appreciation. This allows the rescuer to feel superior, "in charge" or "in control." The victim can feel taken care of and free of having to be in charge of solving whatever is happening, and for a time, might feel safe.

However, most people dislike the disempowered position of the victim for extended periods of time, and often they "rebel" against what feels like control coming from the rescuer, instead of love. And most rescuers eventually feel unappreciated and used by the victim. When either the victim or the rescuer becomes dissatisfied with the relationship—as when the needy one is not performing the "needy role" correctly, or the rescuing person is not acting out the rescuing role to the satisfaction of the needy one—whichever one is unhappy can move into a third position and become the persecutor by being passive aggressive or outright aggressive toward the other to force the other into "doing the original role correctly." So there are always three roles in any dysfunctional relationship or family: The Rescuer, The Victim, and The Persecutor. Together, they form the codependent or "drama" triangle, and from these three roles, all other dysfunctional roles emerge.

The purpose of all the roles is to control the other or others in the relationship to get needs met without considering the effects on the other. The rescuer wants to appear to be a significant person, the victim wants to feel important enough for someone to take care of him or her, and the persecutor wants to appear to be powerful and in charge. And it is not uncommon for both or all people in a relationship to take any of the roles, depending on the circumstances. This is why someone, who believes she is madly in love with another, can transform into the *wrathful woman scorned* as her "loving feelings" turn into wishing for or inflicting all manner of pain or evil on her beloved. The man who feels betrayed may find ways to hurt or even destroy the woman he claims to have loved.

Though most people likely believe this complicated and dependent relationship-form occurs only in dysfunctional families or in couples' relationships, in fact, it can exist in interactions of otherwise healthy people, and is likely, the most common way we humans have of relating with each other. We can be in triangles without knowing that we are in them, and we can be in them with people we are not close to or people don't even know. Certainly, co-dependency can show up in relationships with co-workers or people with whom we share freeway space. We might become addicted to the conflicts among the roles because they produce the adrenalin rush that makes us feel alive, so we stir up codependency conflict to avoid feeling dead.

Since these three roles are not exactly attractive, most of us try to camouflage our codependent/dependent/aggressive behaviors by hiding them behind masks, and pretending to be interacting with others from a more socially acceptable place. However, we are still trying to get others to do what we want them to do, or to make them stop doing what they are doing. This "drama-triangle" is central to many of our life-stories and it literally blocks us from healthfully moving forward in our lives and being closely connected to those with whom we share relationships.

What might be an even more significant understanding is that not only do we experience living out this kind of triangle with other people, but also, these same behavior patterns are going on inside us, among the multiple parts of ourselves, usually completely out of our conscious awareness, and operating behind the mask.

The only reason my sister felt pressure from her co-worker to stay beyond her planned retirement was that despite her wish to retire, a part of her didn't want her to go, either. A part of her was much like the frightened man who didn't know how to leave the entrance ramp and move onto the freeway. She, herself, was afraid to leave the safety of her work and enter retirement as a woman moving forward by taking a new road in her life.

Another part of my sister was like the woman and passenger in the car, so involved in the moment, that this part could "stick out her tongue" at the part of my sister that wanted to move on in her life and begin to find and pursue her deeper life's purpose by deciding to buy a car, collect more savings, and help out her co-worker. And a third part of my sister was angry with her inability to move forward, causing her, too often, to turn on herself and figuratively put on the brakes in her life, with self-sabotage. That angry sabotaging part of her may well have been partially involved in frightening another part of her enough to make the decision to buy a car and fully pay for it, and then replace the money she spent before leaving as a socially acceptable way to resist retirement, though another part of her might have made that decision as self-care in a most healthy way.

By not owning these parts of herself she had hidden behind her mask prior to that morning drive to work, they emerged in the outer world in her freeway experience to reveal to her what she had hidden. Because the hidden energies under the mask are activated by similar external energies, she was able to see herself in the reflections of those people who crossed her path that morning.

When we don't own what we are experiencing internally, we project whatever is disowned outward onto other people, believing these others are causing our disturbance. After the projection, we usually fall into the triangle and become either the victim of those others, the rescuers of them, or we become angry; as the persecutor, we want to find a way to punish them for creating trouble for us. However, with insight into the workings of human patterning, we can take any external disturbance as indication that there is something unresolved internally and begin a healing process to resolve the conflict within.

The gift of that difficult morning is that it provided my sister with a pathway into these unknown parts of her self, so that she could bring them together, to get to know what had caused them to feel separate, angry, and frightened. In her connection with these parts, she could bring healing and integration within herself, which in turn, would allow her to make the decisions she needed to finalize her moving forward in life. It is only when our whole self is united in its forward movement, when our desire is connected to our energy, can we feel the special exhilaration, which results in experiencing joyful bliss in our lives.

Had my sister not been experiencing a struggle behind her mask with various internal parts related to the question of moving forward, either she would not have found herself in the traffic situations that morning, or she would have not reacted to the situations, and they would have come and gone without them showing up on her radar. And had she not had her own reticence about quitting her job, her co-worker's plea to stay longer than she intended would not have made her feel obligated to stay or disturbed her. Likely, she would have expressed her understanding of his plight and let him know that she planned to take care of herself, while helping him as much as possible as long as she was there. If she failed to take responsibility for herself, she would bring negative energy into her staying to help him anyway, and that would not help either of them in the long run.

At the time I was sharing these thoughts with my sister, I was in my Colorado writing space, making one of the many failed attempts to write the introduction to this, my second book, while waiting for the corrected galley of the first book. I was, also, watching hummingbirds fighting with bees that were in conflict over access to the feeders hanging outside my window. It was past the middle of August, when many of the tiny birds had already headed south for the winter. However, some remained, getting the last of the nectar, but the bees were making feeding difficult for the hummers.

So, while my sister was telling me about her difficulties with moving on in her life, I was watching birds that were not, yet, ready to move on, experiencing nature-wars as a result. I explained to her that what I was observing in that moment was a pathway for me to look at what was preventing me from moving on, as well, and why I might be willing to put up with struggle to keep my life safe where I was, instead of moving on to whatever was ahead for me, including writing what has become this book. I could look at what was right there in front of me as a way to see the metaphors being presented outside my window and in what my sister shared with me about her morning, both clearly reflecting what was happening inside me.

My sister asked if I believed that all the things that we experience in our lives represent metaphors for things inside us, and I answered by saying I have come to see, in my life, that absolutely everything that I draw into my experience—including her call, as well as the warring hummingbirds and bees—contain metaphors that I can use to discover more about what is inside me. Because I am connected to all there is, whatever crosses my path is a reflection of something in me that is like what I am seeing or experiencing in outside events. And when my attention is draw to something from the outside that I find disturbing or unbalancing, for me, this is an indication that there is something inside that wants to be healed.

I mentioned to her that other people might not choose to see life this way and that was perfectly okay. But it has made my life experience richer because I have come to know more of who I am and what I want in my life's journey. This perspective helps me release the stress caused by the "conflicts or disturbances" that drop into my life, from time to time, by seeing them as opportunities to bring healing to their counterparts within me. It is like having a secret formula, something like a powerful *decoding device*, to understand unfathomable cascades of otherwise indecipherable information present in the myriad events moving through my life...and it works.

When I allow myself to see troubles in my life as providing pathways to greater understanding of all the aspects of myself, the stress I feel from events dissipates and is replaced by a calmness that happens when I finally recognize and reconnect with parts of myself that are reflected in the disturbance. I can only work with these parts—most of which are not in alignment with other parts of me—when I am conscious of them. In the embrace and acceptance of the previously separated parts, and by going through the process of understanding by actually hearing their previously unexpressed wants and needs, I can create balance and inner harmony as is possible with any external conflict, as well. When I experience inner harmony, I am in my most powerful and creative self and I can more effectively deal with any outside event that occurs in my life.

Certainly, there are times I would like to say that I have mastered this, and I have learned enough to remain in inner harmony reflected by a life that is flowing and harmonious all the time; but, like you, I am still learning, something that will likely be happening up until the moment I take my last breath in this lifetime. My sense of it is that we are all on a path of learning about our inner universes, and like the outer universe, as long we and the universe are alive, both will be in a continuously expanding process. This means something new will be always coming into existence with which we will interact, and with it, there will always be something new to learn about our world and ourselves.

***

My sister noticed how much more relaxed she had become when she was able to recognize the frightened part of herself that really was afraid to move on; so afraid that she would allow her co-worker to seem to be keeping her from leaving. And she could see how her angry self was so critical of her reluctance to allow her life to move forward that she often self-sabotaged her own life by doing to herself exactly what frightened her in the outer world, aggressing against her self in a way that kept her from moving on. All the parts, played by others in her outer world that morning, reflected what was inside her, and for the first time, these parts of her felt noticed and were given a voice. Just noticing parts of ourselves can be calming…because they know they are being heard.

As she gets to know them, and work with them to discover what caused them to separate and resist what is her desire, she will be able to move out onto the freeway of her life with ease, at least until the next hidden part needs attention. In our 15-minute conversation, my sister had shifted from a person, so stressed she couldn't go into her office, to being a calm and relaxed person, who felt hope for herself and her future, wherever it may lead.

After the call, I walked out onto my front porch, and got stung by a bee; I smiled. The sting didn't swell up or create any damage. It was as if the bee was prodding me with its stinger to notice the part of me that wanted to push me forward in my life, even if it means stinging me, and also, to become aware of the part that wants to be safe with the nectar and not move on.

Most of us have no idea what causes us to live the lives we are living. We may have convinced ourselves that we know, but knowing is seldom the case. There are so many levels and dimensions of us that influence what we do, and most of it comes from unconscious places within us. There is so much that we don't want to know, causing us to hide from our own selves all that motivates and fuels our behavior, leaving us to blindly wonder what has gone so wrong when what is behind our masks begins to draw their likenesses to us from the outer world. The content of our lives offers a pathway to understand the universe that exists within us…if we would only garner the courage to look beyond the safety of our protections and discover what is not in harmony behind the mask.

Reflections

When Socrates was on trial for encouraging his students to think for themselves, to challenge the accepted beliefs of the culture, and was accused of corrupting the youth of Athens, he was given a choice of being sentenced to death or of living out the rest of his life in prison or exile. He chose death with the statement, *"The unexamined life is not worth living."* We are fortunate that we don't have to make such a literal choice of life or death; but we are continuously being given an opportunity to choose to look within. On some not so metaphoric level, it is possible that this choice may really be one of life or death.

If you truly want to become as conscious as possible and make choices in your life that are an expression of your highest and best self, instead of living out patterns, make a decision to look at the quality and character of your life and all who reflect back to you what is difficult for you to see on your own. If you are unhappy with a significant person in your life, ask to see the part of yourself who is like that person. If you are experiencing a conflict that has not been resolved, ask for the parts of yourself that are like those with whom you are in conflict to communicate with you so you can understand them. If you didn't have a part inside you like the outside person with whom you are in conflict or someone who reflects a belief you hold about yourself or your world, you would not be experiencing the conflict.

Take the time to examine your life. Even though facing the truth about yourself and about the world in which you live can be difficult and is often painful, the toll that is taken on you when you don't face the truth is far, far greater.

Chapter Five
CONFLUENCE OF THREE STORIES

Most of us have stories, like long running plays, that keep coming back to us, stories we just can't quite release. Either we relive the story over and over with the same people or we play it out with others who take on the old familiar roles. We play our part in the drama, which continues hanging onto us, forming our experience of life by maintaining the conclusions we once drew about the world and ourselves. By bringing truth and healing into the story, we provide a pathway out of the drama and into true life, finally freed from the patterns.

Back in September of 2001 and the dreadful attack on the Twin Towers in New York City, the Pentagon in DC, as well as the plane that crashed in Pennsylvania, like many other people, I became very despondent about the direction our world seemed to have taken. It felt as if humanity had made a choice to head down a path of destruction and there was little any individual could do about it. Just ten days later, that horrific story of the kidnapping of Mooka broke in the Tampa Bay area. I recall feeling immense sadness and empathy for the tiny child, and was aware that I was feeling disgust, not only from the details of the terrible event—I knew too well that this kind of thing happens to children all around the world—but also, because of the response that came from so many circles.

People from the media, the family, and the community seemed to be comforted by the fact that the child was so young that she wouldn't remember what happened to her. Time and again, reporters and news anchors reminded us of the resiliency of children. My heart broke because it seemed as if clinical evidence indicating that aftereffects of these kinds of events are extremely destructive with life-long impact, didn't register with those who were trying to make a truly ugly story seem not so ugly. They acted as if all would be well after they washed the infant off and the bug bites on her skin healed. Everything in me saw this response as coming from a mask that society has put on itself to avoid acknowledging the truth of what our species can do.

In my depression, I felt as if I wanted to give up trying to change this limited perspective in the world that refuses to see what is really happening. But the tiny child who clung to life through the horrific rape and strangulation, the isolation, the insects, dehydration, and everything else touched something deep inside me. She pushed her little hand through the debris, apparently trusting the goodness of an outer world when there was little indication such a world existed. Because of her courage, I knew I couldn't give up.

Without realizing it, my despondence was also coming from what was hidden behind my own mask that could be deeply shaken by an event that contained so much pain. Mooka's story touched what had not been healed within me, the part that was still disconnected from my essence who believed she would never be saved from her pain.

The decision to not give up on the world was only one commitment I had to make. I had to not give up on my own personal journey to heal what had been dashed, broken, and pushed behind my mask. Despite all the work I had done in the 20 plus years of processing inner pain, and all of what I uncovered and wrote about in the first book of the trilogy, there was more uncovering ahead. Pathways to my story had been provided in the two very different and unlikely stories of Mooka's attack and of my sister's drive to work.

***

Each of us can become aware of the pathways that open for us by noticing what we hold onto, and by what thoughts, images, feelings, and stories linger. The first time I heard the idea that I draw to me what was inside me, I didn't want to accept it. I became defensive and angry because there were so many defensive, angry people in my life. I didn't believe I was either defensive or angry, but there I was, demonstrating defensive anger to myself. It takes time to see what is difficult for us to see, especially when we have identified ourselves with the mask. And the mask I was wearing was not an angry one. Also, I didn't believe there was any thing about me that needed to be defended.

For many people, 9-11 recorded the images of the first tower with smoke coming out of it as the one that has remained, while others see the second tower exploding in a fireball from the second plane, which has remained in their heads ever since, and for still others, it is the collapse of the towers in the mushrooming dust cloud, with people running in terror that has been imprinted in their minds, returning in flashes even to this day.

But for me, what has remained in my body and soul is not so much September 11th as September 21st. I didn't write an experiential piece about a person who died in the tower or was a passenger on one of the four airplanes who perished on that September morning, but I did write the story of Mooka, a story that has stayed with me for the years that have followed.

When I bring Mooka's story together with my sister's story, I can easily see that there is something I still have not dealt with from my past, something still behind my mask, likely related to the abuse in my childhood. Something in my story continues to hold me back, preventing me from moving on in my life, reflected by my sister's story…and…the prodding reminder, by way of the bee sting, that I needed to continue on in my journey. These two stories, Mooka's and my sister's contain rich sources for my finding the pain, healing it, and finally, becoming free to live my life from wholeness instead of from my mask or from fear of what is behind my mask.

***

The likelihood is that most all of us have stories that keep coming back to us, things we just can't quite release like long running plays. Either we relive the story over and over with the same people, or with others who take on the old familiar roles, as we play out our part in the drama. The story continues hanging onto us, forming our experience of life while maintaining the conclusions we once drew about the world and ourselves. By bringing truth and healing into the story we provide a pathway out of the story and into freedom from the patterns.

One such story, though very minor when compared to some of the other incidents of my childhood, is the one my mother told, for as far back as I can remember. Every year, I could count on her retelling how my being born was such a disappointment because my arrival three days before my older sister's first birthday ruined the family celebration for my soon-to-be one-year-old sibling. Though its unlikely that this caused pain for my sister, it is more likely that it was my mother who was hurt.

If my mother wanted to bring healing to this for herself, she would need to stop projecting her pain into my sister and onto my birth, and return to her experience as a young mother to find out what was so painful about having her second child's birthday missed. The greatest likelihood is that sometime when she, herself, was a child her birthday was either missed or forgotten and her heart broke. It might be that as a little girl, she believed that the forgetting meant she was not loved, not important, or, possibly, not wanted. She might have believed that she was not worth being remembered. Whatever is her story contains the doorway to healing, which might help her see that despite what happened to her, she was, is, and always will be a being of value and worth who is eternally loved and not forgotten, even if her family forgot her.

But, the retelling of that story was not just about my mother, because I, too, continued to play my part as the child who was born at the wrong time and created family pain. Not only was I the one who came "early" but also, I was the one that literally kept hearing the story, every year, for my entire life, and for most of those years, felt hurt by it.

It wasn't my coming three days "early" that was painful to me but it was my being reminded of the pain I caused my mother and my family, year after year, which, in turn, caused me pain. Hearing her words when I was a child caused me to believe that my very coming into this world was a bad mistake, a disappointment to others, that somehow I must have been insufficient, not valuable enough, and not wanted. Because my sister's birthday seemed more important than my birth, I concluded that while she was important, I was not.

Every time my mom repeated the story, I would momentarily hold my breath, and I could feel my heart withdraw; until one time, not that many years ago, I decided to tell another story to my mother. After she "read" her expected lines in the drama, I explained that my coming three days before my sister's birthday was such a great gift, because the two of us were able to tell a story that we continued to repeat to each other even into our adult years.

For three days every year, my dear sister and I were the same age, something that seemed magical, both to us and to our little friends, which was that we were not twins, but we two were 5 or 6 or 7...or whatever was our age that year. Now we joke about how my older sister is preparing the way for me to become the age that she would soon be leaving, and on one of those three days when we were the same age, I usually would ask her how her last year went, so I could know if my next year would be something to look forward to. I can think of only one time that we didn't talk to each other during that magical time when we were "both the same age" and that was when I lived in China.

That reframed story changed my attitude about my mother's telling of the disappointment. Her story no longer disturbed me, but despite the fact that I gave her another way to look at my coming early—as a gift instead of a disappointment—she continued to live in the story of disappointment and likely will continue to do that until old age causes her to forget, she passes on, or she heals whatever it was that was painful to her, perhaps, as long as 90 or more years ago.

***

So now, like my mother, I have an opportunity to receive another story about other aspects of my childhood, including the meanings I gave to the *worst of the worst* that has held me captive in a prison of patterns since I was 6 years old; I can find another way to interpret it.

But I have not yet found the new way. Somehow, holding on to the original story has strapped me down and held me back from living fully into my life, experiencing what I know in every cell of my body is what I came to this Earth in this lifetime to do.

From the time I was a child I knew I would be a teacher, and for years, now, I have seen images of myself giving presentations all over the world. I have been a teacher all my life, but the visions go beyond what I have done, thus far. I believe that I will teach what I have learned from my own healing journey in a way that has not, yet, been fulfilled. As of this writing, I have done very little to make that happen. In fact, I have resisted going out into the world, providing myself with all the excuses, not unlike my sister's excuses for why retiring was not good. And without a doubt, I know what makes me resist doing what I came into this world to do can be understood in the meaning I attached to the *worst of the worst* that, in some form, still remains behind my mask. I know this story needs to be released—and in the releasing I know that I will discover how easily I will be able to move forward. I am also aware that this will likely come in the evolutionary process of writing *Behind the Mask*.

Reflections

You will benefit if you take the time to look at the stories that you continually live or the ones you continually tell yourself. They may show up as complaints that never get resolved, as hurt feelings that keep happening, as roles you keep playing that cause you distress, and more. By staying in the stories instead of living life, you do harm to yourself by creating more of the same in your life. The reason they keep coming back to you is so you will not just notice them, but decide to do something about them. To change a pattern, you need to bring love and healing to the part of you that holds the pattern, transform the beliefs that grew out of the pattern, and then, do something different.

The stories not only hold you back from experiencing the life you came to live, but they, also, reflect what you hold onto that needs to be healed. Even stories that seem to hold a promise of power, fame, safety, or love can be unhealthy if they entice you into living patterns instead of living life.

Enter the story to find the part of you that keeps spinning the same drama, and embrace that part with forgiveness and love as you bring in the truth. Whatever it was that caused the pain, will stop having power over you when you allow yourself to find the meaning you placed on the event and work with your inner wisdom to help you discover the higher meaning. Your experience can be transformed. And then...you, yourself, can open to the transformation. You can heal.

If you don't have contact with your inner wisdom, simply send a message inside that you are aware that you don't have connection and want to experience it. Simply ask your wise self, even if you have not been aware of that part of you in the past, to bring whatever message you need to hear. Then, notice what happens. Contacting your inner wisdom will bring you peace.

Chapter Six
I HATE WHAT YOU MADE ME BECOME

There is no such thing as unexpressed anger, though there is such a thing as unacknowledged anger. If the cause of anger is not acknowledged or given voice, it will be expressed indirectly and become destructive of mind, body, heart, and soul, and the destruction will be turned towards others or towards the self, and at times, it will be turned against both.

The Tattooed lady from Manitou Springs, Colorado I wrote about in my first book, who predicted I would write three books, was correct. Almost immediately after her psychic reading, I began writing *The Meaning of Three: The Mask*, not because of the prediction, but because what she said rang true to me, and hearing her words was the catalyst for me to start doing what I knew was in me to do. In that same reading, with a warning in her tone, she reminded me about paying attention to my health. Not long after that warning, I made an appointment with a skin doctor who froze a number of skin lesions and he advised me to see an oncology gynecologist about what turned out to be vulva cancer.

After I had been diagnosed with cancer in the fall of 2007, I ended up falling through the cracks of the medical system. I didn't have medical insurance and for some time was unable to find a doctor who would be willing to work with me, either on sliding scale, or with making time payments. I left messages detailing my needs at a number of doctors' offices, but promises that doctors would get back to me were not kept.

After a couple of months of getting no answers, I decided that this lack of response from traditional medicine was a message that the universe wanted me to do more extensive natural healing by doing cleansing, eating alkaline foods, and taking remedies recommended by naturopaths. I made the decision to continue doing my natural healing for a while and then try again to find a doctor who might work with me. My expectation was that an examination would reveal that the cancer cells had returned to normal tissue.

Disturbance in vaginal tissue was not new to me. As I wrote in my first book, which was not a part of this trilogy, *E Pluribus Unum: Out of Many...One*, in 2004,

My body had been revealing the childhood secrets throughout my life, but I had not been attuned to its messages. I had developed endometriosis when I was still a teenager, which caused menstrual periods that left me nearly incapacitated. In early adulthood, I had five miscarriages. I had the beginnings of uterine caner that required D & C and freezing procedures called cryosurgery on more than one occasion, and both vaginal and uterine infections were ongoing. Kidney and bladder infections were constantly a part of my life, causing urination to be a painful, burning experience from the time I was five years old.

All of this taken together is a strong indication of childhood sexual abuse, but I didn't know it at the time. From my 30s to the present, I had positive pap smears that resulted in scraping, snipping, and cutting, and recommendations on more than one occasion for a complete hysterectomy. But I resisted. I felt a need to keep what the medical world seemed all too eager to remove. Without knowing there was a much deeper purpose for not having such an operation, I believe an aspect of my unconscious intention was to hold on to the evidence of what happened to me as a small child, to prove what no one in my family acknowledged was true. On an even deeper unconscious level, it is possible that I wanted to prove to myself that it is possible to heal a physical disorder with psycho-spiritual healing.

***

After I had begun therapy in the mid 1980s to see if there was a way to repair my crumbling marriage, the process of digging deeper within caused me to discover what had been buried inside me for 4 decades. In that process, not only did I learn to listen to the parts of me that had been long split off from my conscious awareness, but also, I discovered that it was possible to talk not only to parts of me, but also, to the cells of my body. I studied with Matthew Manning, the renowned healer from London, as well as with other healers and shamans who held a very different view of illness and healing than the Western medical perspective, and developed my skills in body language.

I discovered that by communicating with my cells and apologizing to them when they were damaged because of my carelessness, I could heal faster. Even a broken bone in my foot healed at a speed that astounded the doctor who first examined the break. And a surgical procedure that a surgeon expected to be accompanied by a significant amount of bleeding had almost none. I was told that I would likely experience extreme swelling and bruising and there was a potential that I would be left with scaring; however there was no swelling and no black and blue discoloration. Three days later when the stitches were removed, there was almost no evidence of the incision and no scaring formed. The doctor asked what I had done, and when I explained about talking with my cells, his facial response indicated that he couldn't take my answer into his world-view.

These experiences led me to see a universe inside me that I had not experienced before and allowed me to understand that by recognizing my connection to this immense and magical internal universe, I could influence what was happening inside me. I could also listen to my cells and change my patterns based on what they needed. There were times, however, that I couldn't bring healing or experience wholeness until what existed in the deeper levels within were accessed, revealed, and released.

The experiences following the diagnosis of vulva cancer were a part of what I had included in the last third of *The Mask*, which reflected the need to go deeper to find healing. In early March of 2008, as the first book was very close to completion, I was on my way from Denver to Tampa to undergo an operation to remove the cancer.

***

I truly believed that all the work I had done over the years, as reflected in *The Mask*, to rescue a badly damaged part of me, and all the visualizations with the Earth Child and the Mountain Lioness had healed the cancer, and there would be no need for an operation. But that didn't happen. Up to the last minute, I struggled with canceling the surgery, wondering if I had made a mistake to approve having a part of my body removed without trusting inner healing to make the necessary changes. I was worried that if I didn't have the cancer removed, it might spread to other parts of my body before my internal work could provide healing. In retrospect, it is clear that the fears around the operation, as well as the fears around canceling the operation were what really needed to be healed. I opted for the operation, having decided that healing could incorporate both the traditional and non-traditional methods, and to risk my life by stubbornly holding to the non-traditional ways was not a kind and loving thing to do to myself.

The pre-op process to ready me for surgery was uneventful, but after being wheeled into the operating room in a very groggy state, the attendants moved me from a gurney onto an operating table. The last I remember was feeling movement in my left arm, tipping my head in the direction of the movement, and seeing someone strap my arm down to the table. Then everything went black. The next moment, I was in the recovery room throwing up all over myself.

Prior to surgery, I had talked with my cells to explain what was going to happen and asked them to cooperate with the surgeon's knife, by allowing the blade to separate the cells that were leaving from the ones staying. I had explained that some of the cells would be experiencing their existence outside my body and the other cells could release them and wish them well. I reminded them that when the knife first touched my skin, that was the cue for my blood vessels to stop the flow of blood and for my tissues to allow the separation of those leaving from those staying; when everything was sewn back up, and reconnected, the flow of blood could begin again.

Following the operation, I asked the resident doctor about bleeding during surgery, and she told me there was very little, much less than normal for this kind of an operation. She speculated that it might have been less than a quarter of what would be expected. Somehow, that seemed to make all of what happened more tolerable because it meant my cells listened and cooperated.

During the weeks of recovery that followed, I kept seeing flashes of my arm being strapped down, but it was not my adult arm, it was the arm of my child-self. And every time I saw the image, I became dizzy and felt sick.

During the recovery time, I was, also, keenly aware of my genital area because any movement at all pulled at what I was told were the three levels of stitches: external stitches that were somewhat cosmetic to allow what was left of my vulva to look as normal as possible, ones below the surface that felt like chicken wire poking holes in me should I move too much, and others that were deeper inside that I could not feel, ones that would melt away in time when the healing was complete; and these many stitches on each level kept me together. I had to smile at the metaphor of three levels of stitches just like what I was writing about in the trilogy: the surface mask to make us look good, what was behind the mask below the surface that was not unlike the chicken wire causing pain if I didn't stay confined to rigid patterns, and finally, what was under the mask, too often so deep inside that we are unaware of it, but will reconnect with the rest of us when we are healed. Life is filled with amazing parallels!

Both the flashes of the image of my arm and the physical discomfort that kept me focused on a part of my body that I had avoided nearly my whole life, kept me in touch with my child-self in a way that nothing else could. I knew there was more work to do with all of this.

When I returned to have the stitches removed, the resident doctor informed me that lab results had come back and shown that despite the extensive amount of tissue removed, the tissue edges were not clear. It was possible that I still had cancer. Though I tried to be upbeat, I began to feel a depression that was sapping any fragments of joy I'd been experiencing. And though I wouldn't wish to ever have to go through something like that again, it helped me to understand what many of my clients who had struggled with cancer felt when they went back for post surgical exams or after going through rounds of chemotherapy or radiation, only to find that the cancer had returned or spread.

The recommendation was that I return in a month for observation of the tissues, and depending on what happened there, perhaps another appointment would be necessary in three months. A short time after that August visit, I began experiencing vaginal bleeding, and then a little while after that rectal bleeding began. I returned in November for another exam, and the vaginal bleeding was determined to be coming from my uterus, which, according to the doctor held an extremely high likelihood of being uterine cancer in postmenopausal women, such as myself. The doctor explained that I would need a second operation, but this time, I would be in the hospital for several days because they would most likely perform abdominal entry surgery to remove my vagina, uterus, ovaries, and they would look again at the edges of the vulva to decide if it would be necessary to do a complete radical vulvectomy. Possible recovery time was from two to three months. I was devastated.

When I found the Earth Child and brought healing to her by way of the Mountain Lioness energy, as I wrote about in *The Mask*, I had only worked with the "victim" and the "rescuer" parts of the internal codependent triangle and transformed them into the vulnerable child and defender parts in healthy internal relationships. I had neglected to notice that I had not, yet, worked with the ragingly angry parts of me, the parts that remained in my body when all of the damage of my childhood was taking place. I needed to discover those angry parts that wanted to do damage, not only to the abusers, but also to the child aspects of myself, from whom the angry parts had separated. These angry parts had long since decided that these child aspects were responsible for what had happened in my childhood. The discovery of the angry parts of me was about to happen.

***

For years, now, I have understood that dreams are very important gateways into the deepest levels of our selves. Dreams can help us to see parts of ourselves that we normally do not recognize as being in us. One hundred years ago, Carl Jung suggested that all the people and images in our dreams are parts of us, and we can learn the most from our dreams when we engage those parts to discover what beliefs they hold. When we have parts of us that struggle with other parts, not only do we experience internal disturbance that can show itself as physical, psychological, emotional, or spiritual illness, but also, we find the same patterns of struggle in our outer worlds with other people in our lives that reflect these inner parts. Just as all the people who cross our path in the outer world and trigger us in some way can be interpreted as examples of parts in ourselves, like in my sister's experience on the freeway, I knew a dream that came to me provided valuable insight into an extremely angry part of myself. I titled the dream, *The Maniac Masculine.*

In my dream, my dreaming self woke from a deep sleep state, feeling almost as if I had been anesthetized. I felt disconnected, disoriented, and dizzy. I looked out the window to be sure my car was still there, and it looked as if it had been towed away...apparently there was a question as to whether or not I parked in a handicap zone, which I hadn't. I had parked to the left of the zone, but my car was still gone. I felt shocked, very disturbed, and didn't know what to do about my missing car.

It was very near time to leave for a camera class that was being held downtown, which I had registered to take some time before. I turned to get dressed, when I noticed that I had been sleeping on a mat on the floor. I looked out the window again, and saw that my car in fact was still there; it was just parked in another spot to the right of the handicap space.

I pulled my bathrobe around me and headed toward my bedroom so I could get my clothes, get dressed, and hurry to my class, but when I entered my bedroom, everything was different. A woman was in a bed that was not my bed, though it should have been mine, and the room no longer looked like my room. There were all sorts of items scattered about, and the room was very disorganized. Just then, another woman came in, after having worked all night, and wanted to get some sleep; she didn't want to talk to me about rooms, beds, or clothes.

Since the room was mine, but didn't look like mine, I decided to walk toward the place where my closet should have been, and there was no closet, only boxes, and drawers with other women's clothing in disarray. It looked more like a college dorm room where none of the residents put anything away. There seemed to be three or four young women living in my space.

It was getting closer to the time of the class, and I was concerned that my dog hadn't been walked yet, so I handed my puppy to my sister and asked if she would take Jenny out while I got dressed. My sister was hesitant to take on the job, and I was feeling more and more panicked.

Returning to the bedroom to see if I could find what happened to my clothes, I discovered that I was not alone; I seemed to be with my two elder sisters. Then Jake walked into the room...but he looked like some perverted villain instead of my X-husband. He walked over to me and put his right arm around me as he told me that he had been taking classes to improve his sexual ability. Acting more like a sleazy biker or gang-member than Jake, he asked if I wanted to get a little action with his new abilities. He, then, began to bump and grind his hips in a way that felt demeaning of me. Then I noticed that his penis was hanging out of his blue jeans as he was demonstrating his skill in front of my sisters and me. I was so embarrassed and asked him to stop. He acted like his antics were a big joke.

I looked at his face and saw that he had a number of nose and cheek piercings, and a very thick piece of wood penetrated his lower lip from the left to the right, like something one might see in a National Geographic photo of aboriginal tribesmen. As I looked closer, I could see that his lip was swollen to nearly twice its natural size and the outer part of his lip had many vertical scars, as if they had been purposely cut in some *coming into manhood* ritual.

He seemed to be the image of some ancient tribal macho masculine, disconnected from everything and everyone, but proud of his strong, aggressive nature. I told him that I really needed my clothes and asked what he had done with them. He pointed to an adjoining room, so I hurried into that room, and was astonished to see everything upholstered and covered in velvet brocade cloth, even the walls that went up 20 or more feet were covered in silk brocade wall covering. It looked like a gaudy mansion from the 1920s…with lots of over-stuffed furniture, high ceilings, and a strange mixture of brocade patterns in various shades and hues of red and gold, none of which looked like they went well together. I was directed to go into another room, only to see what looked like a warehouse filled with old Victorian furniture, lots of the pieces were broken, and sawdust covered the floor. When I peered into an open door beyond that storage area, I could see that rooms kept going on and on.

Jake must have been following me, because when I turned around, he was there. I asked for help in finding my clothes because they seemed to have been buried very deep, somewhere in the back rooms of this mansion house.

He pointed to still another room that I was sure had no promise of having my clothes. But I went in and looked around anyway, and sure enough, my clothes were not there. I returned to the room where he had been earlier, and he was sitting at a computer doing something I couldn't see. I was very concerned because it was almost time for my class, and I needed to leave as soon as possible. I tried to get his attention from whatever it was that he was doing.

Jake became very angry and slammed down the computer. He headed back the way we had come, by way of the warehouse, where I saw a man on a forklift shuffling some of the Victorian furniture around from place to place in the storeroom. For some unknown reason, Jake went into a rage, and stormed toward the man on the forklift. He kicked the steel-lift very hard and then pulled the man off the forklift seat, which frightened the man, who then ran away. Jake was seething with anger and I was nearly in shock from watching this person that I thought I knew, but obviously did not know.

In that moment, I realized it was too late to make it to the class on time. I woke feeling as if I had been drugged. My head felt dizzy and I was disoriented, just as I had been when I woke inside the dream, and then a shock went through me that I had slept too late and missed the class I actually had in this three-dimensional world.

I looked at the clock and it was 7AM. I hadn't missed my 10:00 class, after all. Through the morning, I kept getting flashes of this very angry, pierced Jake, that I knew was not my x-husband, who I had never seen go into such a rage. While Jon-Luke, who I wrote about in *The Mask*, is the loving masculine side of me, this angry man, who I recognized in my dream as my former husband, even though he didn't look or act like him, represented the out of control, dangerous, shadow masculine side of me. I knew that he was the part with whom I would be working in the days or maybe weeks ahead.

***

At about the same time I had dreamed this dream, I had begun to experience bleeding from my anus, as well as from my vaginal area, again, and I knew this was all connected to the dream. In spite of all the work I had done in releasing the negative energies, I began to experience oppressive self-doubt about being unable to bring healing to myself. That *not good enough feeling* was pervasive. *"How could I teach others that healing is possible if I can't even heal myself?"* was a question that attacked me almost as aggressively as the dream image of Jake attacking the forklift and the forklift driver.

While I was struggling with this painful situation, my friend Bill called and very soon, we began working with my dream. When I got to the part about the "angry Jake" who was being irreverent with his sexuality, Bill identified him as my dirty boy-self and asked, where is the dirty girl? His question sent a shock wave through me, because I couldn't imagine either the dirty boy or dirty girl being parts of me, though with all of my dream work, I knew both of them existed as very separated parts of me.

My inner-child was deeply upset by Bill's question because she didn't want to acknowledge a dirty boy or dirty girl. Bill suggested that I bring in protection for the child, and almost as soon as he said that, Jon-Luke, my inner-mate and a collection of shamans and angels appeared to help the child. She clutched onto Jon-Luke as tightly as Mooka had held on to the policeman, and I discovered that my little child-self was filled with sadness. Through her tears, she explained that she couldn't be protected from the dirty boy and girl because they were in her, but if she were to see them, she believed they would destroy her.

Little Sandy believed that the destructive dirty energy belonged to her mother and father, and it was in her because she was carrying their DNA, along with what they had done to her. Bill suggested that I call for a team of transpersonal surgeons, nurses, and doctors to pull her parents energy out of her, and then change the vibration of her DNA. The medical people arrived and began to apply special lotions, gently removing all dark material as the child lay on a mystical healing table made of light.

I was aware that the immense anger was related to the pain, which was held by the dark side male in my dream. Though I wanted to remove my parents' energy, I didn't want to remove this part of me from myself, I wanted to talk with him to try to understand him...I wanted to ask him what made him become so angry that he would attack the man on the forklift with such violence.

The angry male told me he was hurt very badly and hates the world for hurting him. When I asked him who hurt him, he spit out the words, *"Your father hurt me...I hate him, I hate him...I hate him."* I was aware that this angry male was a part of me, but also, noticed he didn't claim my father as his father. Bill asked me to suggest to the angry male that he could show my father a rock or a boulder that contains all the hate and hurt inside him, but instead of a rock or boulder, the angry male wanted the image of his anger to be the forklift. It was then that I noticed that the forklift had a long 12-foot carpet prong at the end of it instead of the more usual 4-foot double flat pallet board prongs that forklifts usually have; the phallic symbol of the prong did not go unnoticed. This very angry male said he wanted to destroy the forklift to show my father how angry he was for what happened.

In my inner vision, this part of me climbed onto the forklift that was from my dream and began to destroy the room with the Victorian furniture in it, and then he destroyed the rest of the building by smashing the forklift into walls, ripping holes into everything with the long, steal prong and then he began slamming into walls tearing them down, and reducing them to rubble. After the destruction, he turned the forklift toward a cliff. I could see his intention was to drive it off the cliff so it would crash onto rocks below, and I was in total disbelief. I sent my thoughts ahead of him to try to eject him from the forklift before it came to the edge where it looked like he was headed. But no matter how I tried to make it different, this raging part of me stayed on forklift and drove it over the cliff. Everything smashed into a fireball and melted into what looked like bubbling lava. I was in total disbelief that a part of me chose to kill himself in such a horrible, horrible way because of his rage. Suicide made no sense to me. This part of me killed himself to express something to my father, a man who would not understand, much less care about something as huge as this crash and suicide that was a fruitless attempt to catch his attention. I felt such overwhelming grief for the loss of this part of me.

As I looked over the cliff, I could see that the forklift not only melted, but so too, had the rocks, and the whole area down below, which had become a sea of molten lava that must have burned up the part of me that hated my father. To my surprise, the orange-red bubbling liquid began to flow back up the side of the cliff and then past me, towards my father, who was standing in the rubble of that building with many rooms. Just as the lava began to approach my father, the angry male separated himself from the hot burning liquid rock, and returned to human form. He looked at me for a moment, turned, and walked toward a large boulder a few yards away from me, one that had been unaffected by the returning lava flow, and he sat down. In that moment, I understood what I had written nearly sixty pages before:

I am aware that what is coming out of me is beyond crying...it is a silent howling, a grieving that goes back so far, and is so, so huge that it feels bigger than my whole body. It feels like the howling is flowing out of the very center of the earth and exploding through me like volcanic lava made of a fiery, red-hot sound that engages all of the pain in every bone, muscle, and fiber. And, if I were to fully release it, it feels like the sound would melt the world. But nothing is melting around me, just yet, though writing this has left me feeling somewhat melted and exhausted.

Without knowing it at the time, I was writing the feelings of my inner masculine-self that had been so wounded by my father, the part of me that tried to protect me from my father's attacks, but failed. His rage has been inside me all these years, like a volcano filled with lava...and it took the dream and then working with the dream for all this to finally erupt.

I turned my attention back to my father; it felt as if I was watching some horror film of the worst kind. It was clear that my father was terrified of burning fiery liquid that was coming closer and closer to him, but he was trapped by the rubble of the fallen building, and there was no place for him to run. I watched in stunned amazement as the lava flowed into my father's penis and began filling his body. The glowing red-orange liquid was consuming him, inch by inch, while he was looking down at his melting body. I was completely frozen in shock and was unable to do anything for him.

The angry young man began to sob with a grieving that shook his entire body. He was sitting on the boulder, totally engulfed by the emotions that poured out of him. I walked over to the rock and I put my arms around the young man. Seeming to be more like a little boy than an angry man, he raised his arms and wrapped them around me as if to seek comfort from the pain of a wound that appeared to be so deep it could never heal. My embrace was what this broken and sobbing, angry, boy-man needed.

Bill surprised me with his next question. He said, we know where the dirty boy is, but where is the dirty girl? Without my even having time to answer his question, I saw a girl emerge from behind the boulder where the now grieving young man was seated. She had spiked raven-black hair, black make-up and nails, and wore a nose ring. Her very short and tight clothing was made of black leather.

She walked toward my father, and wanted to hiss her seething rage at him. An intense body vibration filled with hate for what he had done to her erupted out of her, like the rattle and hiss of a thousand snakes ready to attack. Her eyes were focused directly into his eyes as she told him he stole her femininity and turned her into a vengeful person she knows she is not...but she had to look and act like that to protect herself...she said she hated him for what he turned her into. The hatred felt the same as when the angry man was smashing the forklift into the walls turning everything into rubble.

As she spoke, I was filled with deep grieving sadness for what this part of me lost. Though I never expressed myself as she did, I knew she was a part of me.

Bill spoke on her behalf when he said to my father, *"I am not your little whore!"* Floodgates opened as this girl in black leather and I became one. I began to sob more violently than the young man seated on the rock had sobbed, just moments before. Somehow, Bill knew that my father had made me feel like I was filthy. I hated my vagina that often leaked noxious liquid, even when I was a small child. He had used me like a man might use a prostitute, someone that existed only for his needs. If he needed pleasure, he used me for that. If he wanted to pour his anger into me, he did that in ways few people would believe a parent could ever do to a child.

Bill told me that these parts of me could send all the dark energy they held, back into father. In that moment, I remembered my father used to call women he found disgusting, *dirty underwear types,* a term for most all women. If they weren't in that category, he said they were *uglier than a mud fence.* For the first time in my life, I realized that it was his filth that made my underwear dirty…with infection, feces, urine, blood, and drainage after his rapes. I remember how ashamed I felt my whole life about my underwear. I used to scrub them before they went into the wash to be sure there was nothing in them anyone could see. I recall one of my sisters used to boil her underwear in bleach, though none of us ever asked her why.

The girl in black began to throw her soiled underwear at my father and all the sticky mess that was in them stuck to him. In a short period of time he was covered in a pile of noxiously stinking dirty underwear.

Bill asked me to bring my mother into this scene where her husband was filled with seething lava on the inside, and on the outside he was covered with hundreds of pairs of very dirty underwear from all the times he every used and abused his child, as well as so many other girls and women in his life. Bill spoke directly to my mother and pointed out that since my mother had supported my father and professed her love for him, despite what two of her children had told her he had done to them, this was the time to show her love by embracing her husband.

But she was reluctant. She didn't want to touch the filth that covered him.

Bill insisted that since she believed her husband was so good and whatever might have happened was all her little girl's fault, she should show her acceptance of him by embracing him. Though she tried to approach him, she could not force herself to touch all the filth that was on him. As I watched her responses, I realized that all of this reminded her of her childhood in which she felt so very ugly and believed her sexuality was as repulsive as filthy rags. The filthy rags were those mentioned in the biblical scriptures, which described the culturally reviled and unclean rags used to collect menstrual blood, something detested in ancient cultures. My mother believed that this is what God sees when he looks at us and is repulsed by our filthiness, an understanding she made sure we heard many times in our growing up years.

There were times in my childhood that I sensed she was jealous of me; she thought I was pretty, while she thought she was not. She believed my father's raping me was evidence that he preferred me, to her. I believe that because of this, she didn't care what happened to me, and on a deep unconscious level, she wanted me to be hurt by him to assure her that he really didn't have a preference for me.

Bill, then, suggested an appropriate punishment for my mother, the woman who had allowed her husband to cause her daughter such great suffering. He proposed that she be sentenced to a year in a nudist colony, where she was not allowed to cover herself at all. As soon as he said that, I knew that was absolutely appropriate. She would be forced to face her own hatred of her nakedness and her sexuality, which she projected onto me and then decided that my father's raping me was my fault because she believed I was his "pretty little girl," his little whore, his dirty underwear girl.

I saw her as she was being escorted into the colony by guard-angels. She looked so very uncomfortable, as she searched for any place to hide, but there was no place. There were naked men and women doing all sorts of things: reading, playing tennis, swimming, sitting by a pool and doing what people do on vacation, and some couples were in their open rooms making love. At first she saw her nakedness as abhorrent, but in time, she came to see that it was not as awful as she thought it would be. Bill asked me to return to the colony when the year of her sentence was very close to being up, and I was surprised to see that she was now like all the others, very comfortable in the nakedness of her own skin—and she had no shame. She wandered around talking with people, so relaxed, and actually seemed happy.

Bill suggested that my father could now come to the colony and observe his wife in this very unusual setting. He was astounded at how relaxed and at ease she was, and something in him knew that he had spent his life not seeing her for who she really was. He seemed sad at the loss. By seeing her through the eyes of a sexually deranged man, he had been incapable of seeing who she really was from the eyes of love.

Though I am aware that these were my visions about my parents, in fact, they were also about parts of myself, specifically my angry masculine who had taken on energies and beliefs of my father, and my prudish, disconnected part that, like my mother, had blamed me and my sexuality for the atrocities committed by my father against my child self.

***

I intuitively sensed that similar atrocities that happened to little Sandy had happened to my mother when she was a child. Whether it came from sexual abuse or from some other source, she found sexuality to be repugnant, and I often wondered if she had been abused when her father took her on overnight train rides when he was a conductor in the very early years of her life.

When my mother was a small child, she was deeply wounded by comments from her mother about her appearance, but she was hurt even more by her father. When she was in primary school, she was to play in a piano recital and her father had decided that she needed to look as pretty as possible, so he paid for a hairstylist to come and curl her hair. Afterward, she took a bath and put on her prettiest dress. When she entered the living room, her father exploded in an uncontrollable rage, beating her with his belt until her body was covered with welts.

The bath had taken out the ringlets that he had paid for to make her look reasonably pretty, and now his daughter would embarrass him at the recital with straight hair. She told me all she could remember about her first recital was feeling the burning welts on her legs that were oozing fluid causing the sores to adhere to the piano bench. She had no idea whether or not she had done well in her recital.

When she was a young woman her father, who had remained critical of her appearance, told her that she would look better if she would wear makeup to cover up her face and put color on her white brows, lashes, and pale skin. Her feelings were so badly hurt, that with a raging heart, she swore that she would never wear makeup. I guess she saw herself as being *uglier than a mud fence* and decided not to cover up her ugliness to be accepted. Deep inside, she hated anyone that was not ugly, and believed that anyone who she saw as pretty was probably a *dirty underwear type,* just as my father believed. So if I was a pretty little girl, I was the type that deserved to feel the pain of punishment.

My mother had grown into quite a stunningly beautiful woman with fiery red hair and beautiful skin, but she continued to believe she was ugly. And then, she married a man who could only see women as either dirty or ugly.

After visioning all of this, I was surprised to see that my grandparents entered this scene. Tears were streaming down their cheeks as they expressed such remorse; they had no idea that so much generational harm would come from how they treated their daughter. They asked all of us for forgiveness.

In that moment, my mother became a small child as my grandmother became a young woman. They both looked into each other's eyes and it was clear that they were finally able to see each other's beauty, as well as their own. My mother's child-self, then, turned and looked at little Sandy and the two children embraced each other with obvious love. They began to play dress-up, both curling each other's hair, and painting each other's nails. They were putting on pretty clothes, and slipping into pretty white anklets with pink flowers on the top, and buckled up their shiny black shoes. All of this seemed to be a girlish ritual to embrace their beauty. I smiled when the two girls piled up their tomboy pants, her brown lace-up shoes and my shoepack boots and the unattractive shirts we both wore, and lit them on fire. In this ritual it was clear to me the two girls were burning up the idea of being ugly.

Bill directed my attention back to my father, by asking how he was doing. He was still covered in dirty underwear and in the moment that I looked at him, I saw his parents enter the space. It was clear that he hated his mother for hurting him, but he, also, hated his father for not protecting him from his mother.

Bill reminded him that he could send all their hatred back into his parents. But despite the anger he felt toward his father, he didn't want to hurt this man who, on so many levels was so sweet. He was just a broken man, a coward, when it came to his wife. Perhaps he felt so defeated because he had let his wife down by not becoming a wealthy man.

Grandpa was afraid to challenge his wife for fear he would lose her like he lost his mother, and that was just too painful for his little boy-self. There were lots of tears, so much pain for that loss, and then parents, grandparents, great grandparents and all those who came before, were able to see how abandonment of their children created such horror. A river of tears, from myriad generations back, flowed down through time, washing through the generations of pain.

Bill suggested that I could send light through the river of tears to heal all the past generations and then my mother's family reappeared and light flowed backward from me into my mother, and to her parents, into great grandparents to all the generations as far back as there was pain. They all received light. I was in awe as I watched the profound healing that was taking place in my multi-generational family, and in the DNA in me that connected all of us together.

I knew something monumental had just taken place. My body was shaking with energy and light that I could see with my internal vision, and I knew extremely significant transformations were in process. The work with Bill was complete. We wished each other a goodnight, and

I hung up the phone feeling much gratitude for my very good friend from Atlanta.

***

Not until I was almost finished with this chapter did I realize that my child-self was far more disturbed than I had imagined about the difficult "forever memories" that I wrote about earlier. My father treated me with monumental disrespect, but a part of me aligned with him and had great disrespect for me, as well. When the man in the dream drove the forklift over the cliff as an expression of his anger, he was reflecting to me the densely dark energies I had taken in from my father's threats to drive off the cliff and kill himself all those years we were growing up. This part of me was willing to kill himself, too, and adult Sandy along with him to express his anger towards my father, and on another level, towards myself.

As a child, and later in my reflections on my childhood, I was able to acknowledge my terror of the sounds of the screeching tires but not my fierce anger that my father would treat all of us so, so badly. While my conscious self shivered in fear that we would find out that he had, in fact, carried out his threat, deep inside, I hated him for one more thing he did to keep us all in a state of terror so he could do what he wanted away from home. Much, much later, we discovered that what he wanted to do was to go to one of his other two families when life with ours was too unpleasant…and apparently he returned to my mother's house when life with the other people became too difficult. At my mother's house, my father had his own space in the basement where he could escape whenever he wanted to be alone. And as he got older he spent more and more time down in his own dungeon, all by himself.

The dirty girl, who hated my father for turning her into someone she didn't want to be, was my child-self who was made to feel like a whore by my father. While my ashamed-self covered the whore's body with bulky clothes and later excess weight, another part of me searched everywhere for her identity, by way of the search for clothes in my dream, but was unable to find what had been buried, and still another part seethed with hatred for my father for making her hate her own body.

When terrible things happen to us, we learn to express the emotions that are acceptable, and hide the ones that are not. Those emotions that are buried deep inside are there, whether we know it or not. They will remain inside creating pressure and stress in our bodies and on our minds until they are given expression. If these emotions remain unreleased, they fill us up like lava or spew from us like poisonous toxins, taking a toll on our bodies and minds, as well as on the people around us.

***

Not until I did the third editing of this chapter, following the completion of *Behind the Mask*, did I notice that I had not fully embraced the dirty boy and dirty girl parts of me. I understand that because of what was inflicted upon me sexually, in my childhood, I had rejected what I would call raw sexuality, but others not abused would consider natural sexual feelings. I embraced these two shadow masculine and feminine aspects and let them know we all had much to learn about accepting and loving Sandy, and opening to expressing love to others. This seemed to be something, not for another chapter, but for another book in the near future. That seemed to be okay with Vincent and Carol-Victoria. I didn't know they had names until this very moment. Vincent came immediately, and so did Carol, but something was not complete; when I asked again, she said Carol-Victoria. Since the meaning of a name is something significant for me, I did an Internet name search, and found out that Vincent and Victoria both mean conqueror, and Carol means "free man" or in her case, free woman. How appropriate!

Reflections

Ask inside for contact with parts of yourself who have been altered because of something that crushed you, perhaps something you can recall, or maybe something that you cannot remember. When you had such an experience—*notice I said when, and not if*—it created separations within you, and at least one part of you, and maybe many parts were split off and suppressed. Even if those separated parts appear to be nothing like you, they are a part of your vital force, your energy, and without them you are incomplete. Ask for these parts to come forward and share with you their feelings and the meanings they hold about the world and about you. This will provide the opportunity for you to give new meanings to what happened.

When we are strongly defended against knowing shadow aspects of ourselves in waking life, they often come out in dreams. Consider dialoguing with those who show up in your dreams. Pay attention to everyone including those in your dreams that do you harm. If dream characters show up as someone you know in waking life, look inside yourself for characteristics of those people that might help you find hidden parts of yourself. Find out what motivates the behavior in these parts of you.

You might notice that you can do the same thing you do with dreams with events in your waking life by looking at these events as if they were dreams and looking at the people as if they were parts of yourself; dreams and events provide mirrors for seeing yourself. This makes sense when you see that you draw to you experiences and people that are reflective of what is inside, just as your dreams reflect what is in you.

Without embracing these parts of you, you are incomplete and your world will continue to reflect back to you what you won't let yourself see.

Chapter Seven
THESE BOOTS WERE MADE FOR KICKING

We were neither created to live in pain nor were we created to inflict pain on others, but once the back and forth pain pattern begins, the inflicting and receiving of pain can become entrenched in our behaviors and go on endlessly. Everything that happens to us that involves pain provides an opportunity to forgive ourselves and to forgive others, ending patterns that may have been in place for as far back as our souls have memory.

All that had happened in the healing session with Bill put me in a very good place for several weeks. I was sure my vaginal concerns had been healed, so I was not bothered by the fact the doctor hadn't returned my calls to schedule what might have been a potentially unnecessary second operation. However, bleeding rectally continued and I was sure it was coming from some other angry energy I had not resolved, perhaps, a part of me that felt the pain of being anally raped and wanted more than just to stop what was happening. This part wanted to destroy the people who had damaged me so badly, as expressed in the forklift dream. Not long after the anal hemorrhaging had begun, bleeding from my vagina returned, as well, causing me to be frightened. I wondered if my body was manifesting cancer in both my anus and my vagina because some part of me blamed little Sandy for what happened to so many years before.

***

While working with alternative healing methods to deal with what might be another expression of cancer inside me, I began talking with the cells that might be holding the idea of cancer. I explained that I wanted them to transform so they wouldn't have to be cut out, as I continued sending love and visualizing healing taking place. A short time after I had done what felt like a powerful visualization, I began working on a project while the TV was on in the background, and I was only half watching some program when the hour changed and another program began.

Because I really wasn't paying attention to what was on, I had not noticed that it was one of those CSI programs that show scenes usually too disturbing to me to continue watching. I normally would turn off a program like that but my work distracted me from it. I heard lots of heavy music and unidentifiable sounds, which caused me to look up from what I was doing, just in time to see a scene of a gang of maybe a dozen or more teens wearing dark grey *hoodies*, walking down a city street at night. They were in several rows, walking shoulder-to-shoulder like a single entity, with hoods pulled over their faces so that all you could see were dark shadows instead of faces. They were seething with negative masculine energy, like raging, snarling bulls out to kill anything that crossed their path. The fact that the scene was at night, along with the dark hoodie jackets concealing their faces made what was happening seem even more sinister. While the background music intensified, the gang moved as one, knocking over street stands, bumping into people with an intention of frightening them, damaging people and property along their way. There was something about the angry masculine energy of marching youth that became permanently etched in my mind, and I could viscerally feel something going on inside me that was both terrifying and hard to explain.

The next scene was of a body in a morgue being examined. It looked like there was no skin on the corpse at all, and then the scene went inside the dead person's body showing all the damage to the tissues, bones, and organs. Apparently some street person had been kicked to death and the inference was that it was this group of hooded gang members who had done it.

I was so sickened by the violence they were depicting that I quickly turned off the TV, but the image of the angry hooded young men viciously kicking the man on the street, which viewers saw as a corpse in the morgue, remained in my mind.

The next time I did a visualization to bring healing to my vaginal area, I saw the angry hooded males instead of my cells. When I tried to talk with them, they seemed unapproachable, as I imagine would be the case for young men such as these in three-dimensional reality. I knew these cells were my angry masculine energies, but I had no idea how to let them know they were loved. Or, maybe the truth was that I didn't love them, and what I really wanted was for them to just stop hurting me by causing me to have cancer. I knew they were part of me, not something external, so I tried to reason with them, that if they kept doing what they were doing, they would have to be cut out and they would suffer from their own behavior, or if I died from the damage they were inflicting on me, they would die, too. They seemed totally uninterested in what I was saying. I couldn't figure out how to connect with such defiant anger.

I knew from the previous work I had done that there still could be very angry places on the inside of me. I had dealt with the part of me that was willing to crash and burn over the cliff in order to carry out his revenge against my father. This rage, in the form of the gang of hoodies, was being expressed as cancer in the place where I had been hurt in the violent rapes of childhood. This made sense, as well, because it is very common for victims to blame themselves for what was done to them, creating huge self-rage for the deeply buried pain.

Over time, my visualizations and inner work reflected a reduction in the number of angry, young men, but they hadn't all gone away, so I told the remaining ones that I needed to take care of the rest of me, and if they didn't transform, I would need to have them removed by an oncologist surgeon. My request turned to pleading because I didn't want to remove parts of my body in such a violent way.

But phone calls to the oncologist were not returned and I wondered if maybe the doctor didn't want to work with me because I had no insurance and if he were to find an extensively advanced problem he would be ethically obligated to provide services with a likelihood payment would have to be over a very long time. I wondered if the way to avoid this responsibility was to ignore my calls in hopes I would go somewhere else.

Confused as to what I needed to do to either remove or transform the recalcitrant cells, I began visualizations again; but, instead of feeling like I had to do it right, which for me meant that I had to find a way to heal whatever was going on inside me in the natural way instead of using surgery and the medical system, I surrendered. I finally got it that whatever was needed is what I would do to take care of me and I would let my higher self direct what was right. All the worry seemed to fade when I surrendered.

***

I decided it was time to get outside assistance to handle this negative male energy that was living in my vagina and anus, as well as in my right arm, right leg and my right knee. Again, I called my Atlanta friend Bill, and we scheduled a time for the next Friday night. In my inner work over the years, I had reconnected with my positive feminine energy, letting her emerge into the world in both her light, and dark aspects and have even worked with the negative light and dark feminine, though there is likely more work to do there. I worked with reconnecting with the positive, light masculine energy in the image of John-Luke as presented in *The Mask*. I had worked with the angry masculine who was willing to self-destruct in order to force my father to see the destructiveness of what he had done to me, but I had never worked directly with what I would call the dark evil masculine energy that lives in a walled off room with a sealed door, which opened only briefly when a client asked me about how parents pass on evil energy to their children. The awareness of the presence of this place in me, and the raging energy it contains, was devastating, and I never fully addressed it. This is the angry male that wants to do damage to anyone, to the world, for being complicit in the wounding, and to damage or destroy the innocent child for being innocent. This angry masculine energy wants to do damage for the sake of damage, but also, as a way to release the volcanic pressure inside. This is what I brought to Bill when we started our work that Friday night.

***

After explaining what was going on with the cancer situation and seeing images of the hooded young men inside me, I mentioned I know when people are hurt, there is an almost knee-jerk response to want to hurt the other back, at least as hard as they were hurt. But as children, we seldom are capable of challenging the energy from powerful adults who hurt us. Until we heal and release it, we continue to hold the unaddressed fear and unacknowledged anger inside us. It is not uncommon for that angry energy to attack the more vulnerable parts of ourselves, because these angry parts had first split from the fear by seeing the frightened aspects as separate, and then they blamed the frightened parts for whatever harm came to us.

Following my description of the "hoodies" most vicious attack, Bill mentioned the word *lechery* to describe them, which surprised me. I didn't see their viciously cruel attacks as sexual in nature, and this threw me off a bit. So I asked him to define the word for me, as he was using it. He said lechery is a product of weakness; it abuses, operates in excessiveness, is exploitive, and sees people as sex objects. It, also, has a fear of intimacy while having sexual addiction and is an expression of low self-esteem. It really did seem to fit the image from the TV show of the angry young men in hoods, as well as the energy of my father who inflicted so much damage on my child-self.

Though it was disturbing to accept the presence of such cruel energy inside me in the cells of my vagina, it made sense that cancer cells could contain such energy, and those cells would, likely, represent the repressed parts of me that were filled with rage from what happened when I was too little to defend myself. I could understand how the angry parts of me still held the hurt of the attacks in both the anal and vaginal rapes and blamed the little girl for what happened. After all, the angry masculine energy could presume, if she had not been a girl the pain wouldn't have happened. These disconnected parts could decide they wanted to hurt or even kill the girl for making them hurt, without realizing in killing her, as well as me, they would be killing themselves.

When I focused on the raging *hoodie* cells and the energy my body was feeling, I could feel the vibration of the angry masculine energy in my lower rib cage and back into the middle of my spine. It was quite uncomfortable…and it was an energy that wanted to explode. I asked the body-feeling to take me to the first time I felt it and I was taken to one of those horrible little houses in the red light district of Seward infamously known as *The Line*. I couldn't have been much older than six. I was wearing only underpants, lying on the floor with my knees pulled up toward my chest, attempting to protect myself, and then I saw a boot kicking me between my legs. It was a very hard kick that made my whole body writhe in pain, but I was too scared to cry out. It was such a vicious kick, that I am sure blood vessels must have burst everywhere in my whole pelvic area and I think my pelvic bone must have been horribly bruised. The force of the kick and the resulting pain reverberated through my body and was stopped where my back met the floor and where my lower body was pressed against my ribs.

Bill asked me to rescue the child, but she seemed to be in an energy field that did not allow me to enter. It was like the whole scene was frozen and I couldn't move into it as I had done so often in previous rescue missions into the past.

I realized the child believed no one could rescue her. Bill asked if I could bring one of my warriors to protect the child, and as soon as he said those words, a larger than life winged being appeared. He wore animal skins, clothing a caveman might have worn, and on his head was a helmet similar to those worn by Vikings with horns coming out of the sides. He had gigantic muscles and was one of the really tough-guy angels. He lifted the kicking man up by the shirt and held him in the air—just held him up there—sending energy daggers directly into the man's eyes.

Bill asked what the child wanted to do or say to the kicking man, but she was terrified to say or do anything. She believed that if she said anything he would hurt her even worse afterward. But I assured her that he would never be able to touch her again because I was taking her away from that place. She could tell I was saying the truth and began to trust me enough to let me hold her, probably because she saw that I could bring in protection in the form of the Viking angel. With my guidance, she gave the kicking energy back to the kicking man, letting the force of his blow leave her body and go back into his foot.

More healing angels came and began to care for the little child. They put healing salve on the whole area between her legs, which quickly absorbed into her pelvic bones, vulva, vagina, and uterus. The salve helped the blood vessels heal and it healed the bruised bone. The salve also created a passage for the release of the energies that had been held in her body up to that place on her back that was pressed against the cold floor and abdominal area where her lower body had curled up against her upper body, blocking the upward flow of pain at her ribs. While the healing continued, the angels dressed her in very soft pajamas, which she turned into a soft pink floor-length nightgown with ribbons.

After they provided all this care, I took my little girl-self to an outdoor children's hospital in alternate reality that had very lovely hospital beds for little children, but instead of being in a room or a ward, the beds were in an open grassy area, surrounded by beautiful flowering plants and tall trees. In the center of the grassy clearing was a healing pond. Without us saying anything to each other, the little girl and I went into the water. Though it was similar to other healing ponds from past sessions that required deep healing such as this one, I knew this pond was significantly different, though I was not sure how I knew.

While the angels and spirit beings were caring for little Sandy, I returned to deal with the kicking man, and when I entered his energy field where I could see into his past, I discovered that he had been brutally kicked when he was a little boy. In fact, such kicking was an ongoing abuse from his father and older brothers. Kicking was the major punishment in his family. And, since he was the youngest, he got it from everybody. I saw his mother watching and, like in many families of abuse, the mother didn't make any attempt to intervene in what was happening to her little boy; she was too scared to help him.

I felt it was necessary that the kicking man be required to watch what had happened in the past to his child-self as a reminder of the pain he felt when he was too little to defend himself. In this way, he could see he had done to little Sandy exactly what had happened to his helpless child-self so many years before. After I told Bill what I was seeing, he asked if the man was sorry for kicking the child and I got more of a sense that he was filled with confusion rather than with sorrow. So, Bill suggested it was time to call the police and social workers to send him to prison for child abuse and then my Atlanta friend said, *"You know what they do to child abusers in prison."* The man became terrified. It was as if he was now a little boy who knew he would be kicked and even worse would happen to him. He would live in a brutal world without end.

The kicking man seemed to get it and was ready to say he was sorry for doing the same thing to the little girl that he had experienced as a small boy. But his confusion made it difficult for me to know if he was sorry because he was about to go to jail, or if he was really sorry for what he had done.

Bill suggested that the man could give the kicking energy back to his father and brothers; but, his child-self, just as little Sandy had been earlier, was afraid that if he gave the kicking back, the older brothers and men in his family would become even more brutal. Bill reminded me that the little boy has a warrior like little Sandy has, and the warrior could be called in to protect him. The boy understood and accepted his warrior's help. Finally, the man that had so brutally kicked little Sandy seemed really sorry.

Just then, the police showed up to take him off to jail and I became upset. It didn't seem right that he would have to get punished just when he had a change of heart and he now could live differently. It seemed wrong to put him into the brutal world of prison since he had softened. Bill asked me if I was trying to rescue the man, and I could see that I was trying to protect him just like I had tried to protect my father that time he had such a frightened little boy look on his face when he thought my mother would do something terrible to him if I told what he had done. The man who had kicked little Sandy was confused and scared and told his warrior that he needed help. The message the warrior gave him was to *stop…* to *just stop this pattern of kicking.* His guide seemed to be talking to both of us; though I didn't know why he would be talking to me, since as far back as I could remember, I had never kicked a single person, an animal, or even stomped my feet in anger on a floor or the earth.

All of a sudden, an image of pair of black boots came into my mind, which were not the man's kicking boots from that painful event in my childhood. Instead, when I looked at who was wearing them, I saw a person who looked very much like my grandmother. But that image was only a flash, and I wasn't sure if it was my grandmother, or a woman far back in my ancestry...or, even me in a past life.

Then I saw a pair of knee-high military boots, and when I described them to Bill, he suggested that boots are a symbol of power. In my mind I was remembering the two most recent past lives that I wrote about in *The Mask,* when the sound of military boots terrified me in my childhood in China when the Japanese soldiers entered my house and in the next life when the German soldiers entered the hiding place where my family and I were trying to escape cruelty and death at the hands of the Nazis.

But these knee-high boots in my inner vision were from at least a few centuries ago. The boots looked like they belonged to a military leader, maybe riding boots of someone in the cavalry. The more that I looked at them, the more I knew they were mine. When I allowed myself to see the person I was when I wore them, I saw that I was in charge of many men, and to my chagrin, I saw one of the boots kick a soldier. It was a vicious kick...as wicked as any of the kicks the hooded youths inflicted on the man who died in the TV program. In that life, for some reason, I was treating this subordinate in a vicious inhumane way.

When I looked closer at this event, I could see that the man I kicked had disobeyed me. I ordered that he be stripped naked and I kicked him hard enough to do major damage to his penis and testicles. I was devastated that in that long ago past life, I could have done such a viciously horrible thing.

Bill asked me if I was willing to apologize to that man, and without hesitation, I told him I was so sorry the person I was back then was so unconscious that he could treat anyone with such cruelty. I told him he didn't deserve to be treated so horribly, no matter what he might have done. I let him know he had guardian angels who could come help him heal, and he could give back to me the energy I had given to him in that cruel kick. As he did, I saw me of that past life give the energy back to the one who had given it to me, and I became aware that my father in that past life was, also, a military man. He disciplined me, his son, by kicking me when I did something that displeased him. This seemed to be a family pattern that went back as far as I could see. And this pattern was the reason I used my riding boot to kick a man who I determined had been insubordinate to me.

I saw myself as the kicking military officer turn to his angelic guide and then my officer-self cried with such remorse for what he had done. The man that I was, then, knew how painful and terrifying it had been to receive his father's boot, and when he grew up, he did exactly what his father had done. His guide put loving arms around the kicking man and allowed the "me" of so long ago to feel comforted in the forgiving and being forgiven. The soldier broke down and cried like a small child, finally letting go of kicking and being kicked. It was a powerful, humbling experience.

***

Then, Bill asked if I would be willing to invite all of the souls of everyone I had kicked in any lifetime to assemble in front of me. Immediately, I saw hoards of people. Bill asked if I would be willing to apologize to the souls from many lifetimes, where such brutality was used as a common way of punishing. I stood on a wooden platform in front of all of them and told them what the angel had told me, that this kicking had to stop. I owned the fact that I had kicked all of them, at one time or another, and I knew they were hurt and angry enough to want to kick me as hard as I had kicked them. I, also, told them that the likelihood was that at some time in their incarnations, they had kicked me, too. I explained that if they decided to continue kicking, this would not stop the brutality. As I looked through the massive crowd of souls, it was very clear that every one of them had not just been the recipient of cruel kicks from me and from others, but they had, also, been kickers. Children who had been kicked grew up to be parents who kicked their children. Military officers, like me in that past lifetime, who had kicked their men as I had, had been kicked by their fathers, their mothers or their siblings and they, in turn, kicked those who were subordinate to them, even their animals. It was a vicious cycle that had to stop.

I asked the kickers, if they would be willing to ask forgiveness of the ones they kicked…and I saw all these people asking for, and giving forgiveness to each other and the field was filled with massive waves of healing energy. The men, and even the kicking women seemed to be giving "man hugs" to each other filled with strength and love, celebrating this victory…this freedom. At Bill's suggestion, I invited them to notice that all of them had guides right over their shoulders. They all turned around and saw their powerful guides were right behind them all along. Because they had been so focused on living life from the place of attack or be attacked, kick or be kicked, kill or be killed, they only saw what was in front of them; they had never noticed what was right there behind their backs all the time, ready to help and protect, ready to open them to their higher consciousness.

One after another fell into the guides' arms like little children, who had been lost for far too long, embracing beloved fathers or mothers after the long separation, sobbing, rejoicing, feeling the love in being hugged. I have never seen anything more beautiful than this field full of people who were receiving love, forgiving, and being forgiven.

This insane pattern of dark-negative masculine energy, which really reflects weakness, not strength because it uses force to overpower someone weaker, seemed to melt away. These souls in the field stepped into their strength. Everyone seemed to feel relief to finally be free of this pattern of treating people in such an intolerable way and being treated that way, as well.

For anyone who might not understand my use of *masculine energy* here, it is because the masculine—not the same as male or man—contains outgoing energy, in that it contacts or interacts with the outer world by extending itself. Feminine energy—not the same as female or woman—is inward flowing; it draws what is outside into itself and nurtures what it embraces. And all of us contain both masculine and feminine energy. In order for us to experience life in a powerful, balanced way, we must embrace both energies. Much more will be said about this in book three, *Under the Mask*.

Bill, then, suggested that each of the souls in the field who had kicked others not here in this field, could go to their own stages and call all those they had ever kicked in any lifetime and repeat what had just happened here. And in a moment the field was empty. I am sure that there were stages all over the universe where souls gathered and were given opportunities to make the same transformation.

Then Bill recommended that we go to the hall of the Akashic records and ask for a video of what had just taken place on the field so we could bring the recording into current reality in this lifetime. And we did.

***

I felt as if a very profound shift had happened in me, down to my DNA, related to my masculine energy, freeing it from such a negative energy pattern. I am sure I kept aspects of my masculine energy in internal prisons preventing them from being expressed in this life, for fear they would do harm. But, I couldn't experience my wholeness with parts of me locked away. Then, Bill asked me to return to the red light district and that awful shack where little Sandy had been kicked. He had me notice that the police were there in that terrible place ready to take the man who kicked my child-self to court, and we would show the judge what had transpired in the field. Again I protested, as if with all the changes, a judge wasn't necessary. Bill, however, reminded me to trust the process. So we stood in front of the judge who gave the man a choice. He could go to prison and teach what he had learned to the inmates or he could become a free man, teaching what he had learned in the outer world. The man chose to become a counselor to prisoners. My felt sense was that would be what he does in his next lifetime.

What an amazing outcome. I told the man I would send messages to all the places in the universe to support him in getting whatever training he needed, and almost as soon as I spoke the words, Bill reminded me that the man had his own guides. On reflection, I was able to see how I felt I needed to be in control of the healing process of someone else to guarantee for myself that outcomes would be good. This was a well-intended pattern, but it was harmful because it was based on fear, not trust. The frightened Sandy wanted to make sure the man got his training so he wouldn't create any more negative energy that could turn on her. I realized I needed to do just what Bill had advised... trust

106

the process…trust other people and their guides and trust my newly freed and transformed masculine energy to protect me, thus, ending my need to be in charge to create safety, because I am not in charge, anyway.

In that moment, I remembered a prayer I had prayed while in a Lakota Indian *Inipi* sweat lodge in the mountains of Colorado a few weeks earlier. Prayers prayed in this place seem to have so much power in them, perhaps, because of the depth of the intention and, also, because they are prayed with the support of everyone else in the lodge, as well as the grandfathers and grandmothers and spirits that join us in the ceremony. My prayer was that I could learn to wait for my turn and then be willing to take my turn when it came, and, finally, let it go when my turn was over. To be honest, I was not 100% sure what I meant when I prayed that prayer. But it was what emerged from deep inside me when it was my turn to pray for myself. This really was a powerful prayer to learn to trust the process and let go of needing to control. What I had prayed for in the lodge was being answered while working with my dear friend from Atlanta, and I knew it would be a transformed way of living, as well.

Bill directed me back to little Sandy to let her connect with her guide and then asked me what guide I had been working with. I sensed it was Sela—the one I joined when I took her name over a decade ago—so he asked me to ask Sela if I was ready for the next step. And she said, yes.

Bill said that Sela could take me to a healing temple in a high place, and almost as soon as he spoke those words, I found myself in the courtyard of a grand palace made of a shimmering golden white marble-like material. Everything, the palace, the courtyard, the pool, and gardens looked like what I imagine a Greek Temple must have been like, but even more exquisite. Instead of being made of marble tiles, I was surprised to see the amazing substance that formed the temple and courtyard was made from a perfectly smooth, seamless marble-like material. There were beautiful columns at the far corners of the courtyard that supported a seamless glass ceiling, which opened to the most radiantly blue skies.

The tropical looking plants that surrounded the courtyard and other plants set in huge vases near the pool and temple entrance, were perfect, unblemished, and radiant like everything else there. They were the most beautiful shimmering iridescent green I have ever seen. Some of them were flowering plants hosting a rainbow of hues, brighter and deeper in color than any in the 3-dimensional world. The pool, filled with the most beautiful clear water, was made of the same seamless marble-like material as the temple and courtyard as well. There was quiet music that seemed to be everywhere, but it didn't feel separate from the forms or the shimmering. I was dressed in a sleeveless robe, which was made of a material like nothing I have ever seen. It was white, but it glistened with a golden color, the same as in the temple. I was aware that I was slender and felt vibrantly healthy.

Little Sandy and I stepped into the pool and to my surprise the water seemed to buzz. It felt like it was alive with electricity, but it wasn't shocking. Maybe it was what people who invented carbonated drinks were trying to duplicate, but completely failed. This water was alive.

Bill asked me to scoop up the water in my hand and pour it back into the pool, and as I followed his direction, I saw that same shimmer that was in everything in this place, but the more I looked, the more the shimmering looked like tiny angels, and then the angels looked like they were some kind of a vibration, a very, very high vibration. I felt my body relax into the water—water that I later noticed was not wet, but nonetheless was water—and I felt the tingling of the shimmer enter my body and flow into every cell. It was a profoundly trance inducing experience.

While I was in this deep state of consciousness that allowed total release, Bill asked me what message my guide had for me, and I heard the word, "Receive." In that moment, I understood why that word was so important for me. Receiving was something to be feared in my life experience, because to simply receive opened me to being vulnerable and vulnerability was something that brought with it so much pain. Instead, I became very good at giving but not receiving. I was definitely out of balance.

Taking in all of this, I knew letting myself receive was so significant. Somehow I knew my ancestors had a hard time with receiving, as well. They could take, which didn't require surrender to vulnerability, or they could give as in sacrificing, but simple sharing and receiving were not practices the generations before me could do.

Bill made a simple comment, *"We are our parents."* And I remembered the fractals I first learned about in graduate school, where there is a core pattern and everything that follows the first form replicates the pattern with only tiny differences based on the interaction of time, space, and movement. We focus on the tiny differences, see them as profound differences, and believe we are nothing like our parents when we are, really, near duplicates of what came before us. But like all of nature, there are moments in time when major transformations happen as old patterns dissolve and brand new patterns emerge. In times such as this, the iterations that follow are remarkably different from what was before. This was one of those moments in time.

***

This powerful work that Bill and I did together, allowed me to make a monumental shift in the core energy within myself and my DNA, which, also, transformed the patterns in all the generations that came before me because all my ancestors' patterns had been in me, as well. And on the higher planes, all the souls who embraced their guides and released the kicking and being kicked pattern, changed their DNA for all who went before them and those who came after, too. Those people, alive today in another incarnation, who, as souls, were kicked by me in some distant past life or had kicked me in another, have been changed, as well. And they can decide what they are going to do with this change. They can choose whether or not they will follow the old ancestral, past-life patterns or open to the new one that may have been activated in their energy fields for the very first time because of the transformative work Bill did with me.

***

My dear friend asked me if I would be willing to look at the man who I kicked when I was the military officer. I thought he was leading me to see that it was Jake; however, I knew it wasn't and told him so. But in that moment, a shock wave washed through me as I saw that the *insubordinate* soldier I had kicked in that past life was my father in this current life. In that life, he had done something to disobey an order I had given. I kicked him with such fury with an intention of doing great damage to his manhood, likely because I interpreted his disobedience as challenging my manhood.

I felt such remorse for what I had done. Bill asked me if I could ask my father for forgiveness for what I had done to him in that life. I felt like I was talking to both incarnations: the soldier from that past life and my father in this life. I stood in front of this wounded soul as myself in this life, and told him how deeply sorry I was that I had treated him with such cruelty in that incarnation when I was his superior officer. Even as I am typing these words, tears are coming to my eyes, because that man didn't deserve to be so, so damaged…and for the realization that over time, what had begun there had turned him into a metaphoric hoodie in this life as he so cruelly attacked my body, not with kicking this time, but with actions that were far more cruel. As I am writing this, now, I feel such grief for this whole pattern that has done such profound damage in his life, my life, and in human history.

I asked my father's soul to forgive me, and as I spoke the words out loud, I felt my father's soul embrace me with tears as he forgave me. Bill asked if there was anything my father wanted from me, and I broke into sobs when his soul asked if he could be taken to that same high temple of healing that contained that most magnificent pool. I was so deeply touched by his request. His guide appeared and took him to be healed. It was so, so beautiful. Then I saw the guides and the souls of all those who had been released from the "kick and be kicked" energy playing in the pool, as well. They had all come to experience this ethereal palace of healing, where the water was not wet, but was still water…living water.

Bill then asked if my guide and my father's guide had anything to say to me, and I heard the word, *"Speak,"* as in *"Communicate this in the world!"*…Bill heard an additional word, *Truth*. Long before I had begun to write, I knew that I was being directed to communicate to the world the truth of what I have learned in my experience of wounding and healing, and, at the time, I knew this would be a significant part of what has become this second book about what is hidden behind the mask.

An hour and a half had passed, but somehow it seemed as if an eternity had come and gone since Bill and I began this session. Bill's last words, just before ending the call, were that what happened in the session was *Beyond Ananda*. Later I learned in the Buddhist way of thinking when we experience connection with the Self, or the Great Mystery, we are in a state of bliss, or Ananda. But when we no longer identify with the even the Self in our individual personhood we become a part of eternal peace, not just connected to it, which is beyond the feelings of bliss and we flow as one with the One, beyond Ananda.

***

The next day, reflections of the session were flowing in my mind, and I realized I didn't work with the old woman with black boots, the one I thought might be me in a past life, perhaps a grandmother of my grandmother, but the more I looked, the more I knew she was my father's mother. Then I remembered something my father told me years and years ago.

***

In one of the rare moments he shared anything about his childhood, my father told me that when he was in primary school his mother had treated him so badly that he came to hate her. Before she married my grandfather, she had gone to *normal school* to become a teacher so she could create a different life for herself. As a middle child in a family of 16 children, she had been a caretaker of younger siblings and had learned to hate that responsibility. She didn't want to spend her life as a chore woman, and she determined that teaching could be a path out of such a life. She received training to teach primary school children, but never actually taught.

Before she was to begin her first official job, she met and decided to marry a handsome young man, instead. At that time, a woman could only teach as long as she was not married. My grandfather was considered a good catch with lots of promise because of his position in a surveying company, and, it was probable that he could provide her with a better financial foundation than living her life as a spinster schoolteacher. Soon after beginning their life together, her husband's investments crumbled when his business partner cheated him out of everything. As a result of this loss, she was forced to take in laundry, becoming a chore-woman for others to earn money for her new family, the very thing she had loathed from her childhood.

My father told me that when he was a little boy, his mother often tied him to the ironing board stand and made him recite his school lessons while she pressed cloths on the board above him. If he made a mistake in his recitations, she kicked him with her pointed black "old-lady" shoes. I can well imagine that her kick contained all the anger she felt toward my grandfather for ruining her life and toward her son for being the product of her bad choice. But also, that kick, most likely, held the anger she had felt toward herself for marrying a man who had turned out to be a failure in her eyes. On some level, though she was kicking her son in the 3-dimensional world, she was kicking herself for marrying. Her kicks covered his body with bruises, and I speculate may have done harm to his stomach and abdomen. He died of a ruptured abdominal aorta many, many years later, and she died from a rare disorder of her vascular system that resulted in bruising all over her body.

As I remembered what my father told me, my inner vision saw the first vicious kick my grandmother gave my father as a child and saw how that kick wakened the place inside his soul that carried the kick I gave to him when I was his officer lifetimes ago. So when I was born, not only was there an unconscious energetic link to that past life that was made, but also, I was a female, the gender that had done him great harm in his life, beginning with his mother. The hatred he felt for women, together with that place of rage inside him, wanted to do harm to me that was greater than the harm I did to him as the officer, and the harm his mother did to him as a child.

On another level still, an angry, judging part of him wanted to harm his own child-self for making mistakes in his homework, which then caused him to get kicked so viciously by his mother. And that angry, judging part of him must have evolved into a more adult part of him filled with self-condemnation for the pain he felt as a result of being so deeply hurt by the women he most wanted to impress in his young years, which were women from the best families. These women rejected him for "not being good enough" because he came from a working class family. I could see how he picked this self-hatred up from his mother who hated herself for making life choices that turned her into the chore woman laundering cloths for the rich families that she had so detested. The repeating of patterns is astounding.

***

I had done major damage to his genitals in that long ago lifetime, and in this life during that vicious rape in the forest when I was 4, and all the rapes he later executed, my father did tremendous damage to mine. But that was not enough for him. He needed to cause more pain than what he had received. And he managed to do that very effectively. This need to inflict more on the one who did harm than was done seems to be a part of the pattern of getting even, which is not just getting even; it seems to be more about regaining a position of superiority than evening the score. Despite all of this, I was able to see how we all were carriers of age-old patterns, and I found compassion for him, as well as for me.

Postscript to Chapter Seven

Very near the end of chapter one I wrote, *"It took many years of uncovering to discover that not knowing what was in the shadow behind the mask was really what would have destroyed me had it remained hidden."* While on a flight from Denver to Florida in August of 2009, I was looking back through what I had written in *Behind the Mask*, and I copied that statement from the text and placed it on a separate sheet, thinking that it would belong in a future book that had been playing itself on the inner pages of my mind. But what I didn't know is that I needed to include it in this book, in spite of the fact that I had already submitted the manuscript to the publisher.

The evening after I arrived in Safety Harbor, my friend Esther and I decided to see a movie after dinner. The one we had selected was the Brad Pitt film, *Inglorious Basterds,* one that I had heard about but had no idea as to its content. I discovered it was a Quentin Tarantino film that might be called a fantasy about a Tennessee Hillbilly and a group of American Jews who went to Germany to kill Nazi's by becoming as viciously murderous to the Nazi's as Hitler's followers had been to millions of people during the reign of the Third Reich that preceded and continued through World War II.

Perhaps there are no people on the face of the Earth who deserve to inflict revenge on those who massacred their forefathers as the Jews for the heinous crimes and heartless torture the followers of Hitler inflicted on them during that terrible period in world history. One might call the film a journey into the past to right what had been so wrong, not unlike psychic rescue missions people take into their personal pasts to retrieve some damaged aspect of their child selves, still stuck in the prisons of their minds suffering from some atrocity of the past. My own wounded male self came to me in a dream, using a forklift to destroy the walls of his prison, and in the post-dream visualization, murdered himself by crashing over a cliff, exploded into a raging fire that turned into vengeful lava, only to return to my father and burn him alive.

I can understand millions of Jews in the 21st century holding the pain and hatred of their parents, grandparents, their uncles and aunts, relatives and friends of loved ones who were so brutally snuffed out, and I can understand hatred of many more millions, whose relatives were killed because of that monster, who today, would like such a film depicting the power of revenge. And I could see how many non-Jewish people wronged by others who abused, bullied, or humiliated them in their growing up years would feel vindicated by such a film. Despite that awareness, I was deeply saddened by the numbers of people in the audience who unconsciously joined the vicious acts of violence that were being depicted on the screen as demonstrated in their laughter and applause during particularly gruesome scenes of Nazi's being brutally murdered. I suspect that without knowing it, some of the people who were watching the Tarantino film that night with me were reflecting an aspect of themselves in the very same images from the film that depicted Nazi's in occupied France delighting in a film they were watching showing Allied soldiers being killed.

The Nazi film being shown in the movie we were watching, which was a significant part of Tarantino's story, was of a young Nazi war hero, who played himself in the film within a film. As the war hero, who was perched in a tower, killed hundreds of Allied soldiers, the Nazi audience laughed and applauded with each Allied death. But the fatal switch was that the Nazi's and Nazi sympathizers depicted in *Inglorious Basterds* were finally slaughtered by their own mirror image version of the hero in the tower by Brad Pitt and his group who had trapped the Germans in the theater, and the Germans not shot were burned to death in the raging flames set afire by a huge pile of very flammable films, likely depicting other stories of never-ending dramas. Leave it to Tarantino to create in his writing and direction such a profound collection of multi-leveled metaphors about the dark side of human nature!

As the credits rolled at the end of the film, I tried to imagine how I might find the way to speak throughout the world to communicate a different message than one of revenge as I experienced in my life and as depicted in *Inglorious Basterds*. I could hear a response that in the *real world* there are times the only way to stop the worst evil is to turn on the evildoers with their own medicine. I heard, *"When someone such as Hitler and his Nazi's are inflicting such damage, airy-fairy love-not-war messages are meaningless."* I wanted to shout out that despite the deep human need to punish those who violate the humanity of others, there is such a great a cost when to do so turns the hearts of the righteous into the very people they have come to hate. All the great teachers, prophets, and sages have reminded us to love our enemies…but how do we do that when our enemies are so, so cruel?

After seeing that powerful film, it occurred to me that it is not my job to find the way to stop evil by preaching love to the millions of people who want to attack the attackers and shout to the world that no one can ever be allowed to inflict such damage on others, ever again. It is not my job to stand between the wicked and those seeking vengeance to shout loud enough to be heard over the explosions of gunfire and the screams of victims imploring them to end the wars that have the potential to go on and on forever in the insidious patterns of the dark side behind the collective masks. My job is to stand, or perhaps walk in my own truth, knowing that I no longer choose to hold the pattern of revenge. What I embrace is trusting love to create another universe for me, despite the universe that may be swirling all around me in the commonly held world. Mother Teresa proved it is possible to walk through the middle of a war with a trail of orphans and not be shot by either side. She created her own universe in the middle of a violent universe exploding just outside the boundaries of hers. Without such clear demonstration, there would be no model, no idea that a peaceful universe can exist in the midst of a violent one. The amazing truth is that those who choose to live centered in peace will live there, and in time it is possible that more and more people will choose the universe of peace, making war obsolete as the old patterns melt away.

There are practical answers to living in the midst of violence without becoming another actor in a long-running play of violence, which will likely be a part of a future book that was playing itself out in my mind during that August '09 trip to Florida.

Reflections

One of the most difficult understandings to grasp is the connection between innocence and guilt and to recognize that both exist on the same continuum. Within every perpetrator is deeply buried innocence and within the innocent victim is a potential perpetrator, if not against someone else, then certainly against the self. When seen from the highest plain, there is no difference. These polar opposites arise out of pain, and all of us have experienced pain at one time or another in our lives. Ending the pattern of perpetration requires intervention in the here and now to prevent further pain. Healing comes when we move above the continuum that assesses blame, to discover the higher truth that releases giving and receiving pain, which then, opens the way for us to find forgiveness for the pattern we carry in us and forgiveness for the pattern carried by the other.

If someone has hurt you, ask inside to see how you have contributed to the pattern of hurt. Notice what you have done to others that may be similar to what is being done to you, even in subtle ways. Commit to releasing your pattern of inflicting or accepting hurt. Become aware of what you need to do to prevent others from causing pain to you. If you are the one always receiving the hurt, ask inside what beliefs you hold that cause you to think you deserve to be the recipient of this pain. You might need to give yourself a voice. You might need to seek assistance from some outside authority for your protection, or you might need to surrender to Spirit, which is not the same thing as giving up. Be willing to see what you have not seen before and act upon your insights in the most loving and caring way possible.

Chapter Eight
THE DUNGEON

Parallels between the outer world and the inner world exist everywhere if we allow ourselves to see, and once we can see them, an opportunity opens to expand our perspective far beyond what it had been before we saw the parallels. With this new vision, the patterns can become visible, and once seen, they can be changed.

In the spring of 2008, the world was stunned by the news coming out of Austria, that a 72-year-old retired electrical engineer, Josef Fritzl, had held his daughter in a basement dungeon for 24 years, raping her thousands of times, and fathering seven children from those rapes, one of whom died because Fritzl refused to get medical treatment for the infant soon after the baby was born. Three of the six children had never seen the light of day their entire lives. At the time of their release, the dungeon children were 19, 18, and 5. The three other surviving children were taken when they were infants to live upstairs, and were adopted by Fritzl and his wife, claiming that their daughter had abandoned them on his doorstep on three separate occasions, shortly after each of their births. He told police that his daughter had become a member of a cult and didn't want to take care of her babies; no one questioned the story.

The Monster—as he was dubbed by the European press—spent 18 months in jail in the late 1960s for what the Guardian newspaper in the UK, said was a brutal rape of a 24-year-old woman at knifepoint in 1967, but after he was released from jail for that heinous crime, his wife accepted him back into her home when the daughter he later imprisoned was only 2 years old. Because Austria removes criminal records after 15 years, no information about the raping incident was available to prevent the adoptions of the three babies in the 1990s. (But his wife knew he had raped and knew he was dangerous!)

While he was in prison for 18 months, serving time for the rape, Fritzl made plans to build a dungeon under his house. Nine years following his release, he began sexually abusing his little girl, beginning when she was only 11 years old, and a year later, when she was just 12, he began building the underground cellar he had designed while in prison. After suffering 5 years of being raped by her father, his 16-year-old daughter tried to run away from home to escape his torture, but he caught her and dragged her back home. Two years later, when she was 18 and legal age, he thought the girl was planning another escape, so he decided to imprison her. As a way to justify his wickedly inhuman behavior, he claimed that he decided to put her in the dungeon to protect her from her bad behaviors. The truth was that if she had managed to escape, he had no legal right to force her to return home, and he would have lost his last chance to implement his wicked plan. His psychiatrist told the press that; *"He decided to lock up his daughter in the cellar so that he could 'live out' his 'evil side' while leading a seemingly normal life in the flat upstairs."* And the truly sickening thought is that he planned to build this dungeon prison when his little girl was just an infant.

The monster father asked his daughter, then 18, for help in the basement to install a heavy door, but, after she helped him, he chloroformed her, drug her body to the other side of the door and down into the dungeon, that was 200 square feet at that time. He locked her in that horrible, tiny space without windows. The dungeon space was accessed through a series of eight locked doors with the last one being the one she helped him install, which opened from the outside by an electrical lock that could only be activated by a code that he alone knew. The door was made of reinforced concrete and steel. After she regained consciousness, he told her the cellar was rigged with explosives that would blow her up and gas her should she try to escape.

For the first 9 months of what was to be a 24-year sentence, she was tethered with a 5-foot dog leash around her neck, and then, when he raped her he chained his daughter to the wall. After the children were born, the youngsters were not far away, so they were able to see and hear what he was doing to their mother.

Later on in the captivity, after raping her, he played with the children while she cooked meals from the special food he brought in as a treat for all of them. He believed this reflected a harmonious family he had created. In April of 2008, the oldest of the underground children became extremely ill. The severity of the girl's condition caused the mother to finally stand up to her rapist father and demand that the girl be taken to the hospital. When it was clear that she would die without medical intervention, he agreed to let the young girl be taken to the hospital. And later, he allowed his captive daughter to leave the dungeon to be with her daughter when the local news reported that the girl was not expected to live. Once out, the woman who had been prisoner for 24 years, revealed her story. After telling the authorities what had happened to her and the children, an investigation was begun, soon followed by a discovery of the dungeon. Fritzl was arrested shortly thereafter, and then he was convicted nearly a year later, which finally resulted in his incarceration for life.

He told his lawyer that the cellar belonged to him and to him alone. It was his kingdom, and no one else could have access to it. In addition to the rapes she endured for all those years, according to the judgment against him, Fritzl's daughter and her children suffered "deprivation, humiliation, starvation, threats, beatings, and torture," yet, according to the *Scotsman*, a Scottish newspaper, Fritzl considered himself to be a good father to his underground children because he gave them gifts on their birthdays and provided food and clothing for them. After all, he said, he could have killed all of them and no one would have known, but he didn't kill them.

In her testimony, the 42-year-old daughter said about her experience, *"No one heard me scream down there. No one heard me cry out to God, to the heavens, why me...why, why, why...I was forsaken by the world."* At his trial, she testified that he often turned off the power if she or the children disturbed him in any way, and they lived in darkness for unknown periods of time while food from the freezer melted causing flooding and breath-stopping mould to grow in their underground prison. Along with the rancid air, rats and other vermin were constant visitors, reminiscent of medieval dungeons. The space was ventilated by a pipe and was lighted by a track light. When investigators entered the dungeon, additional air holes had to be drilled because the air that this woman and her children breathed for years, was not breathable by these others.

Neither his neighbors nor the rest of his upstairs family seemed to have noticed that the monster had brought in building materials to create additions to the dungeon including huge amounts of insulation to prevent the leakage of sounds from beneath into the upper part of the house. He brought in other building materials, such as cement and tile, and he installed a sink, toilet, shower, kitchen stove and refrigerator, and a bed, all in a space with a ceiling height of 5 feet, 6 inches. Very narrow halls led from one small room to the next. There was, also, a padded cell where he punished any of his dungeon family who upset him.

Apparently, he added rooms in the dungeon as the family grew, eventually covering a space of about 600 square feet. His daughter and the children had to dig out the dirt with their bare hands to create what would be their added space. And none of the outside people questioned his having a kingdom in his cellar that no one else could enter…just because it was *his, and his alone.*

But even before all this took place, no one seemed to be concerned that he bricked up the upstairs bedroom windows where he kept his mother imprisoned for the last 20 years of her life. Apparently, Fritzl experienced extreme child abuse at the hands of his mother, and he claimed he did all of this as revenge. And, a few reporters noted that he grew up just a few miles from a Nazi concentration camp where the smoke from the death ovens would have infiltrated his childhood, doing who knows what psychic damage to a little boy.

Like in so many houses of abuse, no one surrounding Josef Fritzl dared look any deeper than the surface, an uneasy parallel to his earliest years when so few people dared to look into what the Nazi's were doing just a few miles away, or, for that matter, what his mother was doing to him, when Josef was a child.

Fritzl's family chose to believe he was a good man and the neighbors believed that he was a kind father who loved his children. Perhaps, because people prefer that others don't look very deeply into their lives, they do not look very deeply into other people's lives either, and when *out of the ordinary* events occur, they don't let themselves ask questions or notice.

If this one story weren't enough for people to see how abhorrent this was, the media soon reported several more cases of fathers who committed similar acts of cruelty against their daughters. Not far from Fritzl's "double" home—a supposedly normal home above ground and an evil dungeon below—another Austrian father kept his daughter in prison for 24 years, as well, raping and fathering children. A father in Sheffield, England raped his two daughters over a 27-year-period and fathered nine children, and still another from Poland kept his daughter in a prison for 6 years and fathered two sons. And, a woman in Turin, Italy was imprisoned and raped for 25 years from the time she was 9 years old by her father, a man the press called Italy's Fritzl. The girl's older brother was accused of not only raping his sister, but later raped his own four daughters, as well. According to the BBC, *"investigators say the case is unusual in that most of the other members of the large family of the accused - he has eight sons and two daughters - defend their father and have told police that they worship the ground where he treads."* What does seem to be common, however, is that the families often claim no knowledge of what took place when it seems that there were clues scattered about if people were willing to see.

The importance of the Fritzl story and the others in the context of *Behind the Mask* is that they are a present-day depiction of the *evil that lurks in the hearts of men*, with men referring to humankind, not just males. The Fritzl story also represents a metaphor that points to the fact that while everything can look good on the outside, deep within the dungeons of people's lives, there are hidden places behind locked doors where so much goes on that no one discusses. While these hidden things occur in families and among people in the external world, they also happen within human beings, where parts of the self experience torture, and other parts inflict the torture on those victim parts, while still other parts of the self find ways to believe that there is no torture, there is no conflict, and there is no dungeon.

***

At one time or another, most of us have acted in ways that were damaging to ourselves, even life threatening, without seeming to care about the outcome, all the while defending our actions as our right or an expression of our freedom. These actions are the evidence of our having dungeons within, in which one part is torturing or threatening another part. Acting in reckless ways, drinking and driving, becoming addicted to dangerous substances, remaining in abusive relationships, working in environments that are unhealthy, participating in unsafe sexual activities, and so much more, are all examples of dungeon treatment in which one part is threatening or actually doing harm to another part of us. The risk-taking part's attempt to explain away the torture of another part, in fact, reveals our inner splits and our inner dungeons. Even though it might not seem like it on first glance, our depressions and more-so, our suicidal thoughts are examples of one part of us threatening another part with entrapment or murder, not so unlike Fritzl's treatment of his daughter. When we allow ourselves to be treated in disrespectful or cruel ways without speaking up in our own defense to end such treatment, or remain in abusive situations, part of us is keeping another part of us in a dungeon.

Unlike Fritzl, we might not have built our inner dungeons to inflict pain on other parts of us; more than likely, they were originally constructed as places of hiding to protect ourselves from what was happening in the outer world. A child who is suffering abuse can find a crack in the wall, a hole in the ceiling, or maybe a light bulb, or sound, into which his or her mind can escape to not feel or know what is happening in the outer world abuse. Over time, the child internalizes the external hiding places, to recreate hiding places inside.

The child might, also, hide pain someplace inside where it can be walled off to prevent the rest of the self from having to experience what would be too overwhelming to consciously contain. In time, the internalized hiding place—or places—can become not just a place of protection for the frightened inner-child, but also, storage places for vast amounts of memory, shock, pain, inner conflict, and rage. The rage may begin by being focused on the outside source that is causing the pain, but, in time, it is not uncommon for the rage to be turned inward by finding cause to blame some aspect of the self for what happened. The raging part might blame the abused self for not being able to stop whatever was happening, for being "so stupid" to be in a place where the abuse took place, for being a girl or a boy, or whatever was the unacceptable gender in the family or community. The blame turns to judgment, declaring the vulnerable, wounded part guilty for causing what happened and the declaration of guilt leads to inflicting punishment, which shows up as self-sabotage.

***

When we experience pain, a normal response is to either confront or attack the source to stop the pain from continuing, or to distance or run from the source to avoid experiencing more of it. These are the options in the *fight or flight response*; but, there are times neither of these options are possible. In those cases, we hold back both normal, biological responses, and experience an internal war. The *freeze response* results, when a person splits between one terrified part that believes striking back will cause more pain or death and another terrified part that believes running away will result in greater pain, if not death. This is, very likely, what happened to Fritzl's daughter. She could not fight her father when she was tethered and chained and was unable to get out. Likely, when she was, finally, unchained, she believed that to try to escape would kill her. After her children were born, she had to consider them, as well. Her solution was to go into the freeze mode, to numb herself, become robotic, and cook his meals when he came to the dungeon to give her food and play with her children.

Even after her release, the inner wars between various parts of herself will probably continue until all parts of her, not just her rational self, come to understand that what happened was not her fault. These inner wars, originating in the dungeon, will very likely continue to affect, not just her mind, but also her body. Even though she has been set free as far as the rest of us are concerned, her internal world and the world she has learned to see for most of her life as the real world will likely continue to be experienced within as a confluence of opposing muscle responses, when both contraction and expansion are activated and resisted simultaneously, resulting in a freeze in movement that can become tighter and tighter over time.

On the physiological plane, when tissues remain stuck in this frozen, tightly constricted state, blood does not move normally through the muscles, which brings a halt to nutrition and oxygen flowing into the tissues, and natural cell elimination is greatly reduced, creating a waste backlog of unreleased toxins, as noxious, if not more so, than the vermin infested dungeon Fritzl built. The inside becomes a reflection of the outside, even after the outside has changed.

It is not uncommon for this frozen state to continue far beyond the time of the trauma, and generally continues for years, if not decades, until deep psychic healing finally allows release of the war between expansion and contraction impulses, when the normal pulse of life is finally able to re-engage. If this healing is not found, the warring muscles and toxic build-up can overwhelm the immune system and weaken the part of the body that holds the hiding place. Over time, the compromised part of the body, lacking the oxygen and nutrition for health, is unable to fend off bacterial, viral, or parasitic invaders, and ill health or death can result.

Psychologically and emotionally, the painful event creates behavior patterns that become rigid responses to the outside world, paralleling the rigid frozen muscle patterns on the physiological level. Not only is there a sense of separation within the self as the presence of the internal dungeons makes it feel unsafe to travel very deeply within, but also, fear of being uncovered by the outside world creates a need for external separation, as well. Others are seen as potential enemies who can recreate the hurt or as persons who might discover what is hidden inside, bringing awareness to what is believed will cause death if accessed. The result of these rigid patterns is the creation of toxic relationships, as in codependency that are based on control instead of loving connection, or in resistance to relationships, fearing closeness of any kind with anyone. If there are external relationships, no one is allowed to intimately know the defended person.

Over time, because both the mind and the body are affected by the inner dungeons, the toxins from unreleased painful energies create not just an energetic festering, weakening the psychological balance, but also, a physiological festering, weakening the immune system, tissues, and organs. In times of stress or during times when defenses are down, what is hidden within—fear, self-doubt, hatred, anger, rage—rises to the surface and invades behaviors in the outer world, much like a boil on the skin, which is evidence of an infection much deeper inside the body.

The psychological toxins, bubbling up from the internal dungeons, slip out and into the three-dimensional world in unusual behaviors uncharacteristic of the person, such as emotional explosions, revenge, and damage inflicted onto others or onto the self. However, this expression only relieves the pressure; it does not relieve the pain of what has been hidden because the original cause does not get addressed. The misinformed, frightened or angry self, that created the hiding place, unfortunately believes that facing the original pain and its cause will bring death, when the truth is that, over time, not facing the pain is what causes death in some form.

There is, also, a parallel of the mental/emotional responses to what is hiding behind the mask with the biological/physical responses, since both are affected by what is held within. The body can, also, explode in myriad physical illnesses mirroring psychological anger or fear-based disturbances creating what Chinese medicine calls diseases of heat or diseases of coldness.

***

For many years, while working with the deepest places inside me that held the shock wave vibrations of excruciating pain, I worked not only with several gifted psychotherapists, but also, highly skilled physical therapists who used both Eastern and Western methods to assist my body in accessing my internal hiding places and releasing long buried memories. The psychotherapy coupled with the physical therapy allowed memories to be revealed, usually in bits and pieces over the years of intense recovery work. When the memories came back, they were often in single flicks of pictures, sometimes there were just sounds, sometimes there were turbulent, reverberating emotions that exploded as the memories returned, and other times there were no feelings at all to accompany remembrances of events.

Each part of me that split off during these exceedingly dark events carried only what that one part could hold. The full memory was like a box full of puzzle pieces, none of which, alone, would be too much to handle for any one part when no part was capable of carrying or experiencing the whole picture at one time. Some events were so heinous that many multiples of shattered parts were necessary to carry the tiny pieces of the full occurrence. There was not a timetable for or sequencing of reconnected memory puzzle pieces. A first-time emerging memory might come from the middle of an event, followed by a last memory puzzle piece and months later the first might be revealed.

When a majority of the previously dissociated, splintered puzzle pieces were brought into consciousness, an internal shifting process drew all of the pieces together in proper order, and finally, within a microsecond, some magnetic-like energy created order that emerged from the chaos, and I knew what had happened to me. If feelings had been expressed all along in the retrieval process, the assembling of the final picture would be accompanied by a great sense of relief with the understanding. But, if the emotions had not been experienced along the way, the final picture could result in an eruption of grieving sadness or howling pain that could hit all at once, or wash through me in waves of energy, for months or years following the full picture emerged. There were many times I wanted to die while this process was going on, and other times, I thought the memory would kill me even if I didn't want to die. Just as the gift of dissociation allowed me to survive my childhood, the gift of deeper understanding of the human condition and reconnection with my true Self under the mask, allowed me to survive the process of reclaiming memories and the reconnection with lost parts that were hiding or trapped in my own internal dungeons.

***

The best way I can describe what happened in the splintering might be compared to a mirror that is hanging on a wall, reflecting the room in which it hangs, as if it were taking photographs every millisecond. This special mirror retains the image that it reflects deep inside itself. Now, imagine that someone comes into the room where the mirror hangs, raises a gun, and shoots a hole in the mirror that shatters the glass and causes the mirror to crash to the floor, hitting a table on the way. With each impact—first from the bullet, then the table, and finally the floor—splintering occurs. Every piece of the shattered glass carries a portion of the image at the moment of impact. One shard of glass might carry the image of the gun barrel, another the sight attachment on the gun. Another contains an image of the approaching bullet and a dozen, dozen pieces might carry tiny parts of the shooter's face. Because the incident occurs over time—the moment of the impact from the bullet, the moment the glass falls onto a table and the moment it falls onto the floor—some pieces experience one impact and some experience all of the impacts, it may take a very long time to pull together all of the pieces, not only in space, but in time, in just the right sequence to know what happened. If we increase the capacity from a mirror that reflects an image to a child who sees, hears, smells, tastes, feels, thinks, and forms meanings about an incident of monumentally shattering trauma, you might have an idea of how difficult it can be to pull together a horrifically traumatic memory that cuts into the fabric of a mind and a life. Because recall occurred over several years and one memory was not always fully recovered when I was working on others, it is not possible to relate the memory retrieval in the same order it came to me.

As much as possible, in the chapters that follow, I will tell what I finally came to know about events in my childhood when they came together in complete puzzle pictures, or at least ones that are as complete as possible to date. These belong to the memories I refer to as the ones in the shadow, *behind the mask*. These hidden, shattering events carried such a painfully shocking vibration that they scattered my psyche into many, many pieces, and it took something far beyond the efforts of *all the kings' horses and all the kings' men* to put me back together, again.

***

The likelihood is that you are not in any way like Fritzl, and you may not have experienced anything as shattering as I described in the mirror metaphor. But there may be many parts of you that have been chained up in your internal dungeons, without you even knowing that you have these parts, or that dungeons exist in you. Little boys often chain up their soft and sensitive parts, fearing what they will be called by their peers if these gentler aspects became known. Little girls often chain up their angry parts, fearing that they would be rejected, not only by the society, but also, by their families and by their peers. Girls might, also, chain up their adventurous or intelligent parts, fearing that letting these parts see the light of day would end their chances of being accepted in a world that often rejects girls who possess these qualities, even in the post-women's-liberation era. And though our social system is in process of making changes related to these gender biases, it can take generations for the changes to take place at the grass roots/DNA level where people live.

When we go on diets that rob us of our health to receive public approval, or when we take steroids or any other physically enhancing drugs that have dangerous side effects to win acclaim or recognition, we have put part of ourselves in chains in some internal dungeon. And when we eat out of sadness, fear, loneliness, or anger to repress some aspect of ourselves, we are putting a part of us in a dungeon. When we are with people involved in tearing apart another and we feel badly, but say nothing, some part of us has been relegated to a prison. When we force ourselves to go to places we don't want to go, or to do what we don't want to do because of peer pressure or our need to please others, or even prove something to ourselves, we are subjugating parts of us to chains and abuse.

There may be parts of you that were deeply hurt by uncaring people in your life and you were afraid to allow yourself to be vulnerable in front of anyone. So the wounded parts went into hiding, and in the process, separated from you and from connection to your essence. If there were lots of hurts, there is a possibility that other parts of you built walls around the hiding places to be sure that no hurt could ever come in again. Parts of you stand guard to be sure the vulnerable parts never come out and, in time, a hiding place becomes a dungeon just as horrible as the underground bunker Fritzl built to keep his daughter imprisoned. I believe that so many people were deeply stirred by this story of the father who imprisoned his daughter for 24 years because parts of so many of us have experienced being both the captor and the one held captive. If we are to experience wholeness, we must set all parts of us free from the dungeons that exist behind the mask and we must discover what caused a part of us to become the captor of another part of us, so we can bring truth and healing to set both sides free.

Reflections

We all have splitting or shattering experiences that are unique to us. Some have far more than others, but internal splitting is universal. Each person develops his or her own internal strategies, hiding places, and dungeons, based on perceived needs for self-protection, along with the stories we hold about the self and the world. If you know the events that caused you to build such places on the inside of you, and if you would like to find healing and reconnect to your wholeness, you may want to send in a message to whatever parts of you that live in the separated or walled off places that you love them, or if you are not sure you love them, you might tell them you are willing to get to know them, to listen to their story, and learn how to love them. Ask them to come out so you can hear their stories and bring comfort where comfort is needed. Ask your higher Self for guidance in knowing how to bring truth to the lies these parts of you hold about themselves, about you, and about the world. Ask your wise Self to provide guidance or to bring you to someone in the outer world who can give you the direction you need to connect with your truth.

If you are unaware of any hidden places inside yourself, send in a message to any part of you that may be hiding from some unknown event, or is locked up and cannot communicate with you. Let any unknown parts of you know that you are open to discovery. Ask any hidden parts to communicate with you what happened that caused them to go into hiding or to be locked away by another part, and let them know that you will listen when they are ready. Then allow yourself to be open to see parallels that come into your awareness from the outer world and be open to see any patterns within the parallels that you didn't notice before. Any automatic response you have to a person or an event is an example of a pattern. Under the patterns are parts of you that are in hiding or that are locked in inner dungeons, and want to be set free.

Chapter Nine
THE FOREST, THE BOX, AND THE FORKLIFT

There are times we can handle our knowing only one piece at a time. If we are willing to continue to seek becoming conscious, eventually we will be able to see a whole picture...like the reminder from the Biblical love chapter that suggests: "For now we see through a glass darkly, but then face to face; now I know in part, but then shall I know even as also I am known." 1st Corinthians, chapter 13 verse 12

I have no idea why most of the abuse in my childhood took place the way it did, or why some of the experiences, especially the ones that seem so wickedly bizarre, happened. I would imagine that much of what you will be reading in the next few chapters might be difficult to take in, because it was difficult even for me just to contemplate writing it. And certainly, there were events that were difficult for me to accept as having happened, long after the memories first returned. But when I finally stopped resisting the memories and accepted what various parts of me revealed, I found that after working through the pain, and grieving, transformational healing occurred.

I know when I was born I was not wanted by either of my parents, though my mother would say that was not true. My father once told me, himself, that he resented having children and had never wanted any, and my mother often spoke of how much she wanted a boy, until her later years, when she decided it was my father who wanted a boy, not her. She wanted to believe she loved all of us equally, though that was not my experience. She cried when my oldest sister was born, and expressed her disappointment when my second sister was born, something she recorded in my oldest sister's baby book. I was her third disappointment, and by the time there was to be a fourth child, she had an agreement with the doctor that if the baby was a girl, she wouldn't pay for the delivery, but if it was a boy, she would pay double. This was a story we all knew as long as I can remember. And the take-home message was that girls were not worth paying for, but boys, they were worth double the going rate, which is a message replicated millions upon millions of times throughout the world. The fourth child was my little sister.

Though there were no words directly spoken to us saying that we girls weren't wanted by our mother, we didn't need explicit words to experience the initial response to our births. An infant interprets the world at the beginning of its life through energy feelings-tones, which become the first communication the infant has with the outside world. Too often, after we learn language, we cut ourselves off from the truth of our feelings and accept verbal statements as truth, while our visceral experience drops into our unconscious knowing. Not only did we know our mother's feelings about girls from our own body feelings, but on innumerable occasions, my mother verbalized how much she had wanted and waited for her boy. We grew up knowing that he was the special child, an unquestioned and accepted truth in our family. The corollary to that truth for me was that as a girl, I was not of value. The family joke was that the girls ought to thank the boy for waiting to come, because if he had been first, none of the rest of us would have been born. Translated, that meant we did not matter. I have long since learned that the Universe wanted me, as did myriad people and souls who have always loved me. However, the path prior to learning that truth was painful. Without a doubt, I was deeply wounded by the body awareness that I was not wanted, but what happened in the forest outside my house cut me even more gravely.

As a small child, one of my favorite activities was clearing off fallen leaves from the ground in a patch of forest that separated our house from town. I enjoyed scraping the debris all the way down to the rich black earth to make paths on the forest floor. It was easy to get absorbed in path building and forget about the world that belonged to the whitewashed tin covered house on the other side of the trees. I placed stones along the edges of the paths and felt that something magical was happening as I transformed the forest into a place others could enter and find their way from magical trees to sitting rocks, and beyond to the other side of the forest.

One afternoon, while I was fully engrossed in my work, I must have missed or dismissed the ringing bell that indicated I was supposed to come home. While in my magical place, I heard a noise, looked up, and turned my head to see my father standing behind me. I felt so happy to show him what I had accomplished on my path, when I realized that he was very angry with me, and I felt myself freeze in fear. I noticed the belt he was wearing, and then he unbuckled it and unzipped his pants. I felt his very big hand push me to the ground and onto the stones that lined the path's edge. The very hard stones penetrated into the muscles of my back...and...then...I began to feel the terror of his attack. While the torturous pain ripped through my body, I tried to turn myself into a stone...

Everything that happened that day, and most of the following days of my childhood were put away in hiding places so I would never have to look at them or feel them again. I, like many children who suffered shattering abuse, learned to separate from the horrible events, to hide them in myriad places within, and to grow up as if nothing bad ever happened. Living in the learning part of my head was the safest place for me, so that is where I remained, identifying myself with my mind and my education. After getting my BA degree, I married my high school sweetheart, but only a small part of me was connected to the relationship, and in time, like most anything that does not fully engage all aspects of us, our relationship began to die.

***

I had started going to psychotherapy sessions in the spring of 1986 to save my marriage. It was falling apart from the inside out, and I had decided that I couldn't live with the crumbling. So to my reasoning self, it seemed logical to decide that either I had to kill myself because what I was sure was about to happen seemed un-survivable, or I had to find a way through therapy to prevent the crumbling from happening.

While I was struggling with the problems of 1986, child parts of me began to surface, something that was most disturbing to me at the time. During a session with my therapist, the man I called Seattle David because I had so many men named David in my life, I was talking about my wishes and dreams, when it was apparent that a child part was present in the session. Something we were talking about must have touched something that affected this dissociated aspect of myself and she began to talk with my therapist. After a little while, he asked my child-self what she wanted; but, instead of sharing what she wanted to happen in my marriage, as my adult-self had been discussing, she started to tell him what she wanted in her time, decades before, but the connection between David and the child didn't go very well.

I felt something inside me shut down, but couldn't explain what had happened. Both the child and I wrote about the experience in my journal that day, and six years later, I included my journal notes in *Melting the Chains,* a book that I never published, explaining in the passage what had happened after David asked me that question about what the child wanted.

She thought for a short time and in the voice of small child, began to tell him she wished Daddy wouldn't hurt her and Mamma would make everything better and Daddy would be sorry for what he did. As she was speaking, David stopped her and reminded her that what she wished for should not be dependent on what other people might do. That was too much for a four-year-old to understand and she went away. A couple of hours after the session, I was in a very distraught place. I felt as if the session had not gone well that day, but didn't know what to do about it. It was clear that my child-self wanted me to call my therapist to tell him that she was very upset because she thought he wanted to hear what she really wished for, not what he wanted her to wish for.

I made a call from a telephone booth—that was in the days when there were no cell phones, and people used telephone booths when they were away from home—*and when he answered, I explained my dilemma. David asked if the child could hear him, and when I said, "Yes," he apologized to her and asked her to write down what she really wanted. She and I felt better. After that conversation, I drove to Alki Beach, found a comfortable place to sit on the grass, took out a pen, and asked her to write what she really wished for.*

A very strange feeling overcame me; I felt as if I had lost control of my hand and something on the inside had taken over, and whatever that was, was moving my hand. I knew I was not in control. The child responded by writing in large and irregular letters. My sense is that my 4-year-old self allowed a slightly older part to write what she wanted to tell me.

I couldn't tell cause Daddy would get in trouble and Mamma would say I lied and she would see me out of her mean eyes and she would hate me and maybe kill me cause no one would love him and its not right to make him hurt and Mamma wouldn't love him anymore and it would be my fault. If I could tell and it would be good, then Daddy wouldn't hurt me any more and Mamma wouldn't get mad. They maybe would talk and say they were sorry and Mamma wouldn't have mean eyes anymore or think I was so bad and it wouldn't have to get dark inside and the angels would stay with me when it got dark outside and I wouldn't have to hide under the pillow to wait for morning.

Turning into a stone didn't hurt. That was really easy. Breaking the stone hurt. I couldn't be there if the stone broke cause I was the stone and if it broke I must have to be dead because stones doesn't break.

I wonder if other little girls hide in stones. Maybe I can protect them from being broken if I pick them up. Then no one will see that they are pretty and break them. I will keep the stones and they will be just fine. They must be very pretty and very different from other stones because they have little girls in them and they must be held in my hand to make them warm so they will know they are inside the stone and they will not be broken. Maybe if they are held long enough and looked at and made warm they can stop being stones and they can breathe again and it won't hurt to be a little girl. But it does hurt. It keeps hurting and I want to stay a stone.

Once the writing had begun, my adult self was not connected to what this child part of me was writing. When the child completed what she had to say, she lay the pencil down and went away. Unaware of what she had written, my adult self read her words and became very angry. I was angry with my therapist for therapy that was going in a direction I had not intended. My purpose for going for help was to find a way to repair my marriage, not to go digging into places inside that I believed were not real and saying things that were not true. I wasn't prepared to handle what I had buried so, so long before. And I was terrified that my body was doing things over which I had no control, like writing things I didn't consciously know I wrote.

I called Seattle David and told him I thought something was wrong with what was happening in communicating with inner parts. I didn't like what little Sandy wrote. I refused to accept her incriminating statements regarding my father. Though I did not have any idea why, I thought I must have been making it up somewhere in my mind. It took nearly two more years for me to believe her and understand how lonely my child-self felt when she "became a stone." It seemed to me that every time I tried to make contact with internal parts at the beginning of my therapy, like this first time, I rejected what they told me. I cut the parts off and refused to accept what they knew.

When I cut them off, they became silent and sad, which showed up in my adult life as being withdrawn and depressed. My adult self became frustrated because of what I saw as a lack of progress in finding solutions for my marriage and my life. I didn't realize that the problems in my then current life were directly related to all that I had buried in my past behind my mask and that my resistance to opening those buried places was frightening these parts, which made telling me what they held so much more difficult. And I had no idea that what had happened to me as a child had literally created the patterns in my marriage that led to the crumbling of it. The mask I wore, which presented a happily married woman who was successful in life and a part of a very loving family, covered the little child parts, the pain they experienced, and the beliefs they held about me. Moving forward, required that I go back to heal the past, something beyond my understanding back in the mid 1980s.

After much work in opening to and communicating with the hidden parts that had experienced that forest rape, the puzzle pieces fell into place and I was able to see what had been too frightening to know for nearly four decades. I had to face what the little child wrote me after that difficult therapy session.

***

Being inside my house was not a good thing when I was little, or for that matter, it seldom was a good thing. Being outdoors was one of the gifts of summer and fall, and I often went into the nearby woods to play. I loved to talk to the trees and feel the special places around the trees and big rocks that seemed to be magical.

When I felt the stone in my back and felt the pain of my father's raping and tearing into my tiny body, I hid in the stone that was under my back. My child-self believed she could be protected from his attack by becoming a stone, because she had never seen anything so hard and had never seen a stone break. My child self concluded that perhaps my father must have been able to break the stone and that is why he was able to hurt her. She must have tried to reconcile what she knew and what had happened, because it didn't make sense.

After he finished with me, he left me lying on the forest floor in the middle of my path, broken and in pain. I don't know how long I remained there, but in time, a dazed and shattered little girl part used the leaves to wipe away the mess between her legs and pulled her pants back up. In great pain, she walked back home, terrified of what was going to happen. I must have been the only one of us children who didn't pay attention to the bell, so my child-self reasoned what happened was her fault…and that conclusion became a major theme in my life…*Whatever happens is my fault.*

My mother must have noticed the blood on my clothing and in my underwear, because I remember that she demanded that I tell her what happened. Her question was angry; it didn't feel compassionate. She didn't seem concerned about the obvious trauma I must have experienced. I told my mother that daddy had hurt me down there, and it was very clear that her mean eyes were on fire. She grabbed my wrist and pulled me to where my father had gone, and demanded that he tell her if what I had said was true. For the briefest of moments, he had a look on his face that made me feel so, so sorry for him. It was a look that was begging me not to tell on him. He looked more like a frightened little boy than my father. And then, a look of anger and defiance appeared on his face, and he denied that he had done anything. My mother, still holding my wrist sent the fire from her eyes into me and ordered me to tell her what really happened. Terrified to tell her what she didn't want to hear, I told her that an Eskimo had hurt me in the forest. She turned me over to my father to punish me for lying.

My father took me someplace; I don't know where it was for sure because my focus was totally on him as he dragged me toward the terrible thing that was about to happen. It is possible that the place might have been in the space under the house that was big enough to be an entire room but had a dirt floor. He tied my hands and feet, and put me into a wooden crate that had cracks between the boards and put the crate in a hole in the ground. He began to shovel dirt over the box. I was in total terror as I peered between the cracks and watched each shovel full fall on the box. I panicked when a cracking sound caused one of the slats to break. Not only did more dirt fall against my face, but also, something sharp stabbed into my right leg, causing excruciating pain.

I lay in the box, with my face partially covered by dirt and everything was dark. I had been buried alive. I was terrified to scream out, for fear that making noise would cause him to become even angrier; he would leave, and I would die. But also, I was terrified to be silent for fear if he did not hear me he might forget that I was there, leave, and I would die. I must have lost consciousness from a combination of the total panic of not knowing what to do and the lack of oxygen, because I don't remember how I got out of the box, but I remember my mother dusting me off, and telling me that it was just a joke.

Memories coming back during those difficult years of therapy in the mid 1980s, especially when they had physical side effects, put me in deeply depressed states for long periods of time afterward. In one of those desperately *alone* moments after the pieces of the box memory fell into place, a wave of panic flooded me and it became difficult to breathe. Still feeling the residue of overwhelming feelings coming up from that incident, I felt I would never heal from all that happened to me as a child, and while all this was going on, I wrote in my journal:

I feel so empty. I know there are tears in me, somewhere, but they have gone to an underground river and there is no wellspring for them yet. Oh, Father God, I am struggling to breathe. I ask myself if what I am doing is worth it? Why am I worth it? What difference would there be if I suffocate and die? The wind will not know or care. The sky will still have clouds and stars, and the sun will keep setting over the ocean and waves will continue to crash against the shore. No matter how I try to pretend that I can be, too much has happened in my lifetime that teaches me that I am only a reflection. I tried, but I can't be anything else. I have given up the illusion of the dreams. If I can't live without them, I can always make the last choice. I think, in reality, this is really the only choice I have. I should have accepted long ago that I was never meant to belong or to be. I need to be free from the chains, the bondage into which my soul was born. Please someone see me. I am going away and no one will have ever seen me. It hurts too much but no one knows.

Now they are coming, and I can't stop the tears. Please stop the tears.

***

As long as I felt there was no place for me to be, I looked for ways not to be. My own internal self had too many hidden rooms and unsafe places, so even my inner sanctum didn't seem like a safe place anymore. I felt as if I were absolutely alone with no place to go.

It took weeks of therapy to work my way through the desolation of that memory and the longing to end it all. What I didn't know when I was locked into this post-memory recall depression was that the emptiness I was feeling, the difficulty in breathing, the mournful sadness of not being anything but a reflection, and not being seen was what my child self had felt while she was in a the box, frozen between the decision to scream out and remain silent. My 1980s adult-self put the words on the soul-crushing feelings of my 1950s child-self without knowing that was what I was doing.

When I did a shamanic journey many years later to better see this whole event, I saw little Sandy near death on the dirt floor and angels were breathing into her lungs bringing life back into the child, into me. Since then, I have worked to be aware of the presence of angels in my life instead of believing I was left in the dark places where life seemed to be gone. The truth was that I wasn't stuck in the winter; spring had come and leaves of life were budding. The child in the box needed to see that she did, in fact, survive.

Although I thought the work I had done had unearthed the whole forest rape and box memory in 1988, there was still another piece that had not, yet, been connected. Just before I finalized my divorce in 1989, and as I was preparing to go to China, I noticed what looked like a very small pimple midway down on my right shin. I scratched at it to let it open so I could clean it out, but within a very short period of time, the tiny opening turned into a small hole in my leg. The hole grew from the size of a pea, to the size of a dime, and then to the size of a quarter. The wound opened all the way down to my bone. It became difficult to walk. I went to several doctors, each one sending me to another, unable to tell me what was happening to my leg. Each doctor filled the still-growing hole with gauze to keep the wound clean, and the next removed the pack to peer inside. I was told to stay off my leg, and crutches were ordered. After looking at the wound, another doctor told me he thought it might be from a recluse spider bite, but if so, the tissue around the bite should be turning black and dying, which wasn't happening. The wound was simply opening, exposing the tissue inside, and there was no infection showing up. Another specialist told me that it might be something that could result in the loss of my leg if the hole didn't stop opening, but gave me no advise about what to do for it.

Despite the orders to not use my leg, Sara, the little dog I had at the time, desperately needed to get exercise, so I found a way to hold on to both the grips of the crutches and her leash. During a walk, that first night I was able to get out since the wound opened up on my shin, I began to see images of the box again.

The sounds of walking along the dirt road, coupled with the pain in my right leg reconnected me to the rest of the memory. After being revived from the burial place, my father grabbed my wrists and forced me to walk from the box area to another place where he inflicted a most viciously painful sodomy attack on me. While he was dreadfully injuring my body, he warned me to never tell anything to anyone ever again. I worked through the pain of that incident in therapy, and immediately afterward, the hole began to close. Healing went very quickly and all that was left was a tiny scar, about the size and shape of a staple.

The retrieval of the full memory in 1989 that revealed my father's anger in his vicious thrusts into a little girl so long before, matched what I saw in the 2008 dream, where my masculine self was ramming the forklift prong into the walls and turning the building into rubble. This masculine part of me was demonstrating my father's sadistically angry and damaging attack, as well as my own unexpressed anger at being so viciously violated, but was far too terrified to express.

I had retrieved the memories of the forest and box in the mid 1980s, which reconnected me with the terror and the emptiness of dying alone, having never been seen or known. In 1989 I felt the pain, the fear, and the deep sadness that accompanied the memory of the sodomy, but I hadn't felt the anger. That connection came to me by way of the 2008 forklift dream I wrote about in chapter six. After my struggles with vulva cancer and bleeding from my uterus in 2008 that were connected to the first part of the memory, I had the forklift dream, which soon was followed by rectal bleeding.

Because of that childhood experience, I lived my life frozen between choices. Behind nearly every decision I had to make was a belief that if I made the wrong choice, I would die. The only ones that didn't throw me into that frozen state were not really decisions between two alternative actions, they were the choices of whether or not to follow the deep calling of my spirit, and that choice was simple. Follow the calling. If I chose against that call, I knew the light in my eyes would go out, and that was not a choice. But also, I lived my life terrified of connecting with anger. To be angry seemed as if it would make me be like my father, and to be angry could have caused me to die. Later, I discovered another deeply buried reason I feared accessing anger. So I stopped anger before I could even be conscious of feeling it.

My body had been screaming as loud as it knew how, for all of my life to tell the world and me that really bad things had happened, but I was unable to hear it for over 40 years. As I write this, I can better understand the woman who had been held captive in her father's basement for 24 years when she cried out, "*No one heard me scream down there. No one heard me cry out to God, to the heavens, why me...why, why, why...I was forsaken by the world.*" My child-self locked in the inner dungeon since she was four years old had screamed out, as well...and finally, both of us were heard.

Reflections

It is not uncommon for people to ignore the messages sent to them by their bodies. What they can't ignore, they numb with some form of painkillers, or they find some way to cover over what is being sent because of conscious or unconscious fears that they can't handle what is pushing itself into consciousness for healing.

When you don't listen, your body begins to speak louder and louder, and eventually the only way that is left to send the message is illness. If you have any body pain, talk to that pain as if it were a person. Ask it when it first came, and invite it to show you images of what caused the pain to appear. It might not be what you think it is, so let go of preconceptions. If you have an illness, talk to the illness. Ask it what message it is sending to you and ask it to take you to whatever it was that caused it to believe what it believes about you and about illness.

Take a moment to be very still, and ask your body to talk to you to let you know what it needs you to understand. Let your body know you will listen…and then listen. Once you hear, send love to the part of you that is communicating its message.

Chapter Ten
GOING BACKWARD TO GO FORWARD
The Unfolding Of A Story

There are times that the best way to go forward is to go back to the beginning, and once there, the beginning becomes clear, allowing us to move beyond where part of us has been stuck in the past into the present, and then we can finally allow ourselves to move into our future.

THE PRESENT

After writing about the dungeon in the eighth chapter, I knew I needed to write about my own dungeons, beyond what I experienced in the burial box, but there were so many of them, on so many levels. The one that held the *worst of the worst*, required entry through a passageway that I thought would likely be difficult for you to read because I was sure would be difficult for me to write. I tried to figure out how I could explain this most terrible incident without having to go into what was in the passageway. But I couldn't figure out how to do it.

When we hear horrible reports such as one like the Fritzl case, we all go through our own reactions that could include shock, anger, rage, or disgust, and maybe there would be some who would respond with doubt, disbelief, and denial. Some might focus on Josef, wanting to understand what could possibly have created such a monster or imagining what kind of punishment he would deserve to pay for the horror he committed against his daughter and the seven children that resulted from his rapes.

Others might focus on the daughter to try to figure out what could have led to her being trapped in this horror for so long. They might try to find holes in the story or look for how the victim might not have tried hard enough to escape, or maybe they would scan for ways she could have freed herself. In my own mind, when I read Fritzl had used a pipe to vent the dungeon to at least allow some airflow, I wondered if there could have been a way to scream into the pipe so the outside world would know of her plight. When I read that there was a trap door through which the monster father handed down food and necessities to his growing family, I wondered why she couldn't have figured out how to use that as an escape route. Some part of me wanted to know that she had truly exhausted all the possibilities for escape, and if she didn't maybe, just maybe, there could have been a way. I imagine that whatever part of me identified with her, needed to know that if something similar had happened in my life, I could have found a way to escape.

The report stated there were times Fritzl joined his daughter and the children to celebrate birthdays and holidays. She cooked for him with the special food he brought down into the dungeon, while he played games with the children. I wondered why she didn't boil water and throw it in his face and escape. The doors had to be unlocked, and the heavy concrete and steel door to the outside must have been unlocked because the locking device was on the outside. Anything would have been better than spending 24 years in hell. But then, by the time the cooking was happening, she had already been there for years, which had to have affected her mind. She didn't know it would be 24 years, and she believed what he had told her that the place was booby-trapped, which would blow up and send gas into the space, killing her and the children if she tried to escape. It took no stretch of the imagination to figure out the source of his idea of the gas threat.

When I first heard the story, without knowing what was happening on deeper levels, a part of me blamed the daughter for not trying harder to escape. Part of me identified with her as the victim, and another part of me wanted to make her responsible for what happened. By making her responsible, she was elevated to being in charge of what was taking place and if she was in charge, she could save herself. The thought of her not being in charge, meant that she was powerless, and feeling powerless would, to me, feel like her life and death were totally in the hands of someone who literally was a monster. That was too intolerable for my own internal child parts to accept. A part of me still hiding behind my mask wanted to believe Fritzl's daughter could have found a way to escape. If so, there would be hope for this trapped part of me to experience having power over her life and escape from her dungeon, as well. In order to hold on to hope, it is not unusual for victims to accept blame for not trying hard enough to stop what is happening to them. This belief allows them comfort in believing that someday they will be able to regain power and stop whatever is happening.

***

After he was arrested, Josef Fritzl complained that the European press had dubbed him *monster*, a title he would not accept. He said if he were a monster, he would have killed them all and no one would have ever known. The fact that he didn't kill them, in his mind, meant that he was a good man. On some level, the daughter had to have known that he did have the power of life and death, and had no idea how to counter it. That thought could be totally destructive.

All of this touched places inside me that caused me to hesitate writing about the *worst of the worst* and the passageway to get there. I was terrified of judgment, not just of the world in the form of you, the reader, but also, from judgment from myself that I didn't try hard enough, which meant I was responsible. Probably the hardest for me to deal with for years, was the belief that I drew my own version of the evil monster father to me so it really *was* my fault. Daring to speak the unspeakable and reveal what had been hidden so long, incurring what I suspected would be wrath of those who would doubt or deny the truth of what I spoke, or perhaps even blame me for what had happened, was overwhelming. Our history is replete with examples of denial of truths, where we would rather say nothing bad happened than to accept the truth, which would then require us to figure out how to handle the truth. As a way to avoid all this responsibility, killing the messenger has been far too common a response.

***

In a socioeconomic and political system that was present for most of our national history, children were identified as being property of the father and the father was the king of his castle; few concerned themselves with how a man chose to treat his property, something that was seen as no one else's business. However, there was a social taboo against incest. The solution to what could have ended up being two opposing social constructs was the old version of *don't ask, don't tell,* to avoid noticing when anything like incest was occurring. In 1896, when Freud presented a paper based on clinical findings related to his patients, which suggested that sexual abuse in childhood resulted in hysteria in adulthood—hysteria was the name given at that time for neuroses and psychoses—his medical peers literally booed him from the stage. They refused to accept that both men and women had hysteria, something they saw as a female illness only, and rejected the idea that Austria's most prominent citizens, whose daughters were Freud's patients, had violated such a well accepted, but clearly, not honored taboo.

A few years following that humiliating experience, Freud recanted his position and presented the concept that it was not incest in childhood that caused the hysteria in his patients, but rather, the child's unrequited fantasies toward the parent that caused the mental problems in adulthood. Instead of being identified as the victim of incest, the child became the perpetrator, accusing the innocent adult with claims of incest, and we have been living with that culturally created mask for over 100 years. Despite the evidence that explodes in front of us every day, there remains massive denial of rampant incest, as well as childhood sexual abuse in our culture and the voices are still strong that claim such incidents are rare. With a culture that too often makes the innocent appear to be guilty of something related to incest, I felt fear about a subject that might be considered worse than incest, whose veracity has been challenged even more adamantly in today's society than Freud was challenged over 100 years ago.

Another problem I faced was that I didn't know how to open the door into the dungeon that held the passageway to the *worst of the worst.* There were so many threads to the fabric of this story, which meant that if I told one thing, I would have to explain something else that in time would lead to something else that needed explanation, and I would get caught in a tangle of threads that would be too difficult for any reader to follow…because it has been difficult for me to follow, as well. The only way I could figure how to get to the story of the *worst of the worst* and the patterns this experience created in my life was to go backward through various stories that would lead to what felt nearly unapproachable.

1992

In the early 1990s, I wrote a book I referenced earlier, that was never published. It was an autobiography of sorts, created, for the most part, for myself as a way for me to pull together my own story so the many scattered and shattered parts of myself would be able to see the whole picture, although at the time I had no idea that it was still only a partial picture. The catalyst for writing *Melting the Chains* was a letter my oldest sister had written and sent to the whole family about experiences from our childhood. My mother responded to my sister, with copies sent to everyone, as well. I felt my mother's letter was an unjust attack on my sister, and I couldn't sit by and say nothing. For two weeks, I agonized about what should be my response. Finally, I decided that I needed to write a letter in support of my sister. In February of 1992, I wrote to my parents and siblings, letting them know that I was no longer going to remain silent about the life our family had lived in pre-statehood Alaska.

My Dear Family,

It is a sunny Saturday morning and "fall" has finally come to Florida. I am sitting in the backyard of the my little house watching leaves fall, enjoying the dry cool breeze and reflecting over the feelings that have been swirling inside me for the past couple of weeks. Our sister's letter set off a whirlwind of feelings, especially fear, because she dared to express anger. Then, I received Mamma's letter a few days ago that turned my internal energy into a tornado and I felt as if I was in the still, uneasy calmness of the eye of the storm, knowing that there was tumultuous thrashing and churning all around me. I wasn't sure what to do as sadness grew. If I did nothing, I sensed that I would lose touch with the last six years of my life, leaving me uprooted and scattered by the gale force winds brought on by painful and angry words typed by my sister and mother in Seattle.

In the middle of this family storm that has come to the inside of me, I attended a meeting of all of the college faculty and staff on "sexual harassment" because of the Hill/Thomas hearings. As the legal definitions, rights, and responsibilities were bantered about, I realized that the most significant factor contributing to this social evil is silence. I raised my hand and began to speak. I said I believed that silence is generated by fear of something worse happening if the truth is spoken, and another fear that speaking truth will not produce the hoped for good. Silence, which makes it seem better to ignore or deny the truth, is based on an erroneous belief that if words are not spoken, the horrible things will not need to be addressed. Silence can appear to be right when speaking truth would require something to be done about it, and those who see or know are not prepared to make the necessary sacrifices that may have to happen as a result of knowing. When I raised my hand at that meeting to be recognized, and commented about the poison of silence, I knew I was talking to myself, not just the faculty and staff who had collected in the lecture hall.

Our family has chosen to live in silence for so long. I can no longer hold it all back. I have justified silence as a noble act, but that seems now to be hollow, unloving, and ignoble. Your daughter—our sister—alluded to events of her childhood that have long been silenced, but when finally spoken they were dismissed as fantasy or hallucinations. She spoke, in spite of the pain of being left uncomforted, both as a child and as an adult. I too, have been struggling with memories that were buried deep inside me, of rape, brutality, seeing people murdered and many other unspeakable atrocities that wreaked havoc on my inner self all my life. I learned to separate myself into parts and closed off those memories, covering them under layers and layers of protective walls that prevented me from knowing about or dealing with them before I was prepared to handle all of this.

I have no need to prove to anyone the things that I know in my own heart and mind. I have no photographs or videotapes of the events. And I have very little external verification, except a life that reflects what the textbooks indicate result from extreme childhood abuse. I know what I know. I know that growing up in our family was a painful experience. I felt extremely isolated and afraid to have my own thoughts and opinions. I felt I had to be a reflection of those around me instead of being the "me" that I was on the inside. I had a gnawing feeling that I was unforgivably bad and somehow, a possession of Satan who had power over me, and would keep me from ever being one of God's children. I believed no matter what I did I would still be as filthy rags, with no value, no worth, but I, also, hoped that if I could do one truly great thing, God might change his mind and I would deserve to be alive.

The only problem was that I knew that no matter how good other people thought I was, the hidden truth was that I was bad, bad, bad. So even if I did something good, it would be tainted by my badness; even my best good would be bad. I lived my life believing that I was a fraud. People saw me as loving, intelligent, and accomplished. I saw myself as something that was vile, stupid, and a failure; I saw myself as successful only in tricking people into believing my goodness. I could find no substance in myself. I had no one that I could tell about how I felt. I was isolated, lonely, and silently sad.

I was afraid of upsetting Daddy; I was afraid of making Mamma angry. I was afraid of being condemned forever by a wrathful God. I was afraid of my thoughts, my feelings, especially my sexual feelings. It seemed that there was always tension. It pressed heavy on me as long back as I can remember. Tension meant something horrible could happen at any moment. My responsibility was to be sure that the tension never exploded, and I failed.

I always had to project far ahead to see all the potential results from any word I might say or action I might take to be sure what I said or did would not make a bad thing happen. It was like playing mental chess with human beings and I was a pawn that could be sacrificed. The most important job was to maintain the family, at all costs. This was not a tension that existed only for a few economically distressing months in Seattle; it invaded our family sometimes overtly, sometimes subtlety, but none-the-less existed, always. I remember it in every place we lived.

My memories of Alaska are entrenched with sadness and tension. Even our camping trips that had good times had an undercurrent of stress when Daddy left to conduct business. There was an aura of abandonment that seemed to emanate from Mamma and that feeling was there in spite of her attempts to be calm and involved with us while hiking or reading mysteries around the campfire. Our moves all over Alaska were entangled with unspoken anxiety that I felt on the deepest of levels.

Our first year in Seattle was devastating with Mamma's suicide attempts that left me desperately terrified that if I did one thing wrong, I would be the cause of her death. Daddy's unspoken threats of leaving, his continual threats of killing himself by driving off a cliff, and his dark moods permeated all my memories of our family. Daddy never seemed happy to be at home. Mamma never seemed to feel at peace. We did have what I have come to call our "fudge and popcorn" nights when there seemed to be a truce with calm peace, but those days were so scattered, unpredictable, and ended so quickly, without any known reason.

I didn't grow up with a sense of being loved, of being nurtured, of feeling wanted, secure, or safe. What I wanted or needed seldom crossed my mind and certainly didn't seem important. I was afraid to have friends, to allow anyone to get too close or know me too well. I haven't maintained many conscious memories of childhood, but one that always puzzled me was the time I was recovering from the asphyxiation incident. I remember Mamma stayed with me the first night, on the porch of the cabin. Her arms were around me and I heard her whisper: *"I don't know what I would have done if I had lost you."* The words were etched in my memory so clearly she could have spoken them yesterday. But also, I remember feeling numbed by the words and didn't feel the loving warmth of gentle arms. I remember wondering why Mamma said those words. They didn't seem real to me. For oh so many years, I wondered why I felt that way. I should have felt close and loved by those arms and comforted by those words, but I was not. This lady beside me seemed to be a stranger.

When I say these things, I am not saying that Mamma didn't love me or didn't mean what she said. What I am saying is that I didn't feel loved or comforted. It was much later in my life that I asked myself, why?

There were lots of things that made me decide to see a psychologist six years ago, but the most pressing one was that I had decided to kill myself and I wanted to find out if there might be a way out of it. The sad thing is that suicide didn't seem to be a bad thing; it seemed logical. I knew I had not ever truly lived. Whatever it was that I was experiencing, that appeared to be life but was not life, was too painful to continue. Because of that decision to seek help, I chose to look at truth no matter how frightening or death-threatening it appeared. For 4 years, I struggled, sometimes wishing I had never started the process, but none-the-less, I continued on the road I had chosen.

When I pulled back the layers, and re-opened the sealed, but unhealed wounds, I found horrors that made death seem more palatable. There were times that I thought I must have been going crazy. One such time, in tears, I turned to our sister with a flashback that was too powerful for me to handle alone. To my dismay, I discovered that she too had struggled with an identical memory a few years earlier in her therapy. We had witnessed the same event, but from a different vantage point, in the basement of the Jesse Lee home. We made a pact, for our own good, not to reveal any details of memories regarding events until we could be assured that the other had already had her own memories clear enough that the telling would not cause distrust of our own recovery process.

She had memories that I didn't have and vice versa, but there are a number of events and circumstances we both separately recalled during the therapy sessions. I don't doubt the truth about the traumas that were inflicted upon me, nor do I need to defend my knowing them to be true. I don't need any one else to accept my truth. I have learned to stand on my own, hold my own truth and heal my own wounds as I find them. I have learned to love my life and myself and let go of my sense of unworthiness. I know that God loves me and is protecting me and I look forward to whatever years we have planned for me to be here contributing to the world that we both love. I don't need to convince anyone of my goodness or my worthiness, and the need to prove something no longer is the fuel behind my actions.

The silence I have maintained around the wounds from growing up in our family has been unhealthy. I kept silent because of the fear of hurting everyone. I, also, feared being attacked because I have no "acceptable" proof. Even as I write these words, I feel tears in my eyes and a tightness in my throat because I will hurt Daddy, I will make Mamma angry, I will make some of you angry that I would dare say anything to hurt our parents; and you might never forgive me for hurting them: I will make some of you sad and I will have to answer things for which I have no answers. I have even been afraid that I have included our oldest sister in a letter that should have belonged just to me. I have been afraid of being isolated, without a family and of being condemned for what I am saying. I have been afraid of loosing you all. But the truth is that if I live in "pretend," I have lost everyone already, and more so, I have lost myself.

In the personal work I have done over the last six years, I discovered that naming truth, feeling it, knowing it, and releasing the pain of it is what has set me free. Pretending has just kept me in a prison of silence that I choose not to stay in anymore. I no longer hold hatred, and most of the anger has been cleansed. Even few regrets exist for what has happened in my life. With each painful experience, a gift was given and I now have the privilege of sharing those gifts with other people who have been wounded. I am living an exciting, challenging life and look forward to more open doors leading me to many new places and experiences. In many ways, I feel like I am just starting out with a whole lifetime in front of me.

I love all of you. I will be fine if you choose not to talk to me about what I have written; though I hope we will someday be able to talk about our lives and what we all felt in the years we spent together. I hope we can feel free enough to open our hearts and souls, exposing who we are, what we have needed and missed without any need for pretending or for judgment—only needing truth.   Love, Sandy

In this letter, which seems as if I had written it lifetimes ago, I didn't accuse my father of anything, though to those who knew, it must have seemed as if I had implied it. And my guess is that most of my family knew. If I had thought of it at the time, I might have added a P.S. and that would have said, *"If you are feeling afraid or angry with what I have written, I wish you would look at what is happening inside you that is making you feel that way."*

In early March of 1992, my mother responded to the letter I wrote. While I interpreted the letter I had written to my family members as a statement of freedom from the family lies, my mother took it as—as what? I'm not really sure, possibly the letter of a misguided child who had no way of knowing her own thoughts or feelings because she was being controlled by therapists who wanted to make money convincing her that her parents were bad. That was the attitude she had taken about the statements in my eldest sister's letter.

My mother's letter didn't address much of what I had written except to challenge what I felt as a child as being impossible for me to have felt, followed by an imperative to "forgive and forget" the past. In all of the responses she made over the years, she usually began with the statements, *"No children were ever loved more than you were loved."* and *"Nothing bad happened to you,"* followed by a pleading that I forgive and forget.

She didn't like it when I asked what she thought I ought to forgive and forget. One phone conversation was powerfully significant when she begged me to forget the past and live for the future, *"…because the future is all that really matters anyway."* She said, *"Honey, why can't you just forget the ugly past? I did."* So for her, with that statement, the books were closed and *"Nothing Bad Happened To Me."* But she never could explain what was so ugly about the past that had to be forgotten.

***

In an early March letter, she responded to what I had written:

Dear Sandy

Your letter came on Monday and it's taken longer than I thought it would to answer it. I was shocked and deeply hurt to learn that you felt you weren't loved when you were little. Of all our children, honey, you were the most obedient. I've said this many times before: I don't believe you ever had a spanking. Just saying your name and shaking my head "no" was enough to keep you from doing something wrong. I don't understand how you could feel I didn't love you, honey, when I held you in my arms after you had been overcome with carbon monoxide. I'd have been completely devastated if you had not revived. I mean that, Sandy! When I looked at you kids in the back seat, on our way to Anchorage, and saw our cat, Archie, slobbering on your blanket and you suddenly rearing your head out from under the blanket--I cried out: "Oh my God! Daddy, stop the car!" Your brother may remember that because later he told me I had sworn God's name! I told him I wasn't swearing-- that I needed God's help in a hurry!

How can you say you weren't loved, Sandy? Daddy and I loved and wanted each one of you. Why is it you and your sister don't seem to want to remember any of *the good times we had together? Why do you think Daddy built the swings and teeter-totter in our back yard?....Surely you remember the little pink stuffed doll with the happy and crying faces...Daddy picked that dolly out for you. <u>No</u>, <u>Honey</u>, I <u>just can't believe you felt unloved, because your Mamma and Daddy loved you very much.</u>* (Text was underlined in red.)

I wish you'd read Elizabeth Loftus' book--"Witness for the Defense." There is such logic in it, I think, you with your wisdom, could see how memories can be influenced and changed to be very different from the truth. Elizabeth Loftus conducted many experiments that prove this. I have noticed that my sisters and I have different versions of the same happening in our past. Who is to say which is the truth? Does it really matter? The past is the past-----It can't be changed. Today and all the tomorrows ahead are what really count!

I have a mini-book called "Forgiving and Forgetting" which was written by Charles Swindoll. He's a radio minister that Daddy and I listen to almost every day. I copied a few pages that sort of represent the theme of the book. I'll enclose them with this letter. Honey.

We want to help you, Sandy, far more than your counselor does! Please listen to the <u>Biblical Counsel</u> of Charles Swindoll and <u>look to the future, and forget the past!</u>

Love, Mamma

My mother focused on the one thing that she allowed herself to know, and that was that she loved me. I never doubted that and didn't say I believed that she didn't love me in my letter. What I said was that I didn't feel loved. For her, because she felt it, I had to have felt love coming from her, too. And she didn't address any of the other comments about our lives together in Alaska related to memories, "*...of rape, of brutality, of ...murder...and my thoughts of suicide,* all dismissed as false without saying anything about them. Nor did she comment about the unhappiness and tension we lived with or my statement that, "*I learned to separate myself into parts and closed off those memories, covering them under layers and layers of protective walls that prevented me from knowing about or dealing with them before I was prepared to handle all of this.*" I speculate that she couldn't address them because to say anything about any of these things would touch the truth that she really did know, but she didn't know how to handle the truth.

My eldest sister was the only one who supported me. My mother was the only one who responded, which in time came in the form of tirades against psychotherapists, who she claimed put such terrible ideas into people's heads, as she continued to deny that anything bad ever happened to me. Yet, her ongoing advise was to forget the past, without explaining why I had to forget it if everything was so good.

LATE 1989

In the early years of therapy from 1986-1989, when the memories first started to come back in tiny puzzle pieces and disconnected flashes, I didn't have the inner strength to bring any of this up to my family. I couldn't face arguing with them or losing them, while my marriage was crumbling. I knew that much earlier, my sister had confronted my parents with childhood abuse, without even suggesting that what had happened to her was done by our father, and she was ostracized from the family for a decade.

In late 1989, before I left for China, I had gone over to my parents' house to visit. My mother asked me how I was doing, and unlike my usual response, which was that I was doing fine, I stopped myself in mid sentence and told my mother that I was not doing fine. I was still deeply conflicted about ending my marriage of 23 years, and my psychotherapy appointments were exceedingly difficult as more and more of my childhood memories were leaking out through the cracks of my life-time defense. After saying this, but without accusing my father, I did, finally, tell my mother that I had been raped as a child. It was as if I had dropped an atom bomb in the room. She adamantly denied that anything bad had ever happened to me and told me with sharp intensity that if it had happened, she would have known. For over an hour, she attacked me with what felt like venom of a snake for daring to say such vicious lies, and for turning against Jesus—I never quiet figured out how she concluded that my saying bad things happened was a rejection of the religious training I had as a child.

When she was finished with her attack, she sat in stiff coldness and asked what I wanted from her. I remember taking in a deep breath, and saying, "*If I had a little girl who came to me and told me she had been raped, I would have held her in my arms and asked her to tell me everything that happened. And, if I had a 45 year old daughter who told me she had been raped as a child, I would have held her in my arms and asked her to tell me everything that happened.*"

She sat in her chair for some time, just staring at me without looking into my eyes, and then got up, walked to the other side of the table, and put her arms around me. They felt as cold and unloving as the arms that wrapped around me when I was on a cot, breathing in the cold air of the Alaska night, when I was 8. I asked her if she could say something to me, but nothing came from her. I waited and then asked again; that next time, she said, "*Honey, It had already happened. If I had known I couldn't have done anything anyway. Wouldn't it be better to just forget the past?*" I was stunned by her response that felt empty of compassion and I was unable to say anything to her. Then she began to cry. Sounding more like a little girl than a woman, she told me she knew I would go to China and would probably never come back. She said she would lose me forever and her cries turned into sobbing. She kept saying that I would never speak to her again and she would never feel loved again.

In that moment, I became the mother to a little girl and assured her that I was not going forever, and that I would always love her. We never spoke of this again.

EARLY 1989

Sometime before I left the US for China, but before I had the conversation with my mother, I talked with my father, explaining that I was dealing with difficult memories from childhood around seeing people die, as well as other really bad things that happened. I didn't directly accuse him of anything and asked if he would be willing to meet with my sister and me to talk about our childhood. He agreed, and to my surprise he showed up at the appointed time at my sister's home. The first question we asked was if there was a possibility that we had witnessed a murder. He pursed his lips, tipped his head down as if looking at the table, and after an uncomfortable moment of silence, he lifted his head back up and simply said, "Yes." Without looking at either of us, he then suggested that the shock of seeing a murder might well be the cause of why we believed all sorts of other things happened to us, things that never really happened. He didn't explain how we might have seen someone murdered or anything about his response. At one point, I told him that I didn't feel loved at home, and he responded with the explanation that our mother wasn't a person who could hug or get all warm and soft, likely, because there were so many of us. He didn't say anything about himself.

I don't recall much more of the conversation, but I was aware of how it seemed he tried to lighten things up by redirecting attention from our concerns about our childhood to other topics about himself and some events that were remembered from the preferred memories. He left with what must have felt to him like a persuasive answer to our questions…that the murder we saw created images of all the other bad things we thought happened, but didn't.

As more difficult childhood events were coming into my awareness in therapy it became impossible for me to remain silent. I wrote my father a letter with events spelled out, again, with no accusations directed toward him. He agreed to talk and made three appointments to come to my apartment, but canceled the first and then the second at the last minute. I was surprised when he actually showed up for that last appointment. He came in to my apartment without taking off his coat and was holding my letter in his hand.

He sat down on my couch, and sounding more like my mother than my father, as he told me that my therapist was filling my head with things that just were not true. I remained grounded in my knowledge that what I was remembering was coming from me, not fed to me by anyone; his response was to become angry and defensive. At one point he exploded, and in a state of rage, he told me that I was too young to remember what I had remembered. I was completed taken back by his words, and looking directly into his angry eyes, I asked with strength that I didn't know I had, *"Too young to know what, Daddy?"* My response sent him into another raging torrent of words, and attacks against therapists…and again he said that I was too young to know…and I said even more emphatically, *"Too Young To Know What?"*

His anger became even more explosive and agitated. He stood up and walked toward my front door, when, again, his self-incriminating worlds slipped out…that I was too young to know what had happened back then. When I reflected his own words back to him, from a place of even greater power and strength…no longer saying it as a question, but more a demand for an answer, **"TOO YOUNG TO KNOW WHAT, DADDY!"** he stormed out of my apartment, saying as he left, that he would write a letter addressing every point I had made to prove to me how wrong I was.

I never received the letter, and we never spoke of it again. From that time on, until I left for China in early 1990, and after I returned in late '91, and for the next 5 years he was alive, he avoided me. Whenever I called to say that I was coming over, he left and would be gone until after I departed. When I was invited for a holiday meal, he remained in the kitchen preparing the dishes, serving, and making sure that empty bowls were refilled with potatoes, gravy, vegetables, or whatever…and while we ate, he cleaned the pots, pans, and dishes, not sitting down with the family. Following the meal, he disappeared into the basement for the rest of the time I was there. And no one acknowledged his absence, no one encouraged him to join us, and no one invited him to stay upstairs after dinner. My father and I never spoke to each other again, other than the formal comments that could not be avoided in public, with the exception of one crazy conversation about his tax plan I had with him in a hospital cafeteria when we all believed that my mother was dying in the mid 1990s.

***

For the majority of my time in therapy, I sought verification outside of myself for what my body and parts of myself revealed to me. It seemed if I could get someone else to acknowledge what I was seeing inside was true, then, I could convince the doubting parts and myself, as well, to accept the truth. For six years, I hoped my father or my mother would finally be able to acknowledge what they had done, and what they allowed to happen to me. I had been telling them that I loved them even when they refused to hear it, hoping that through love they would trust enough to face the truth. At the time, I didn't know that this was manipulative, because I was sending an inauthentic love hoping to get something back from them. It took much more work to understand the kind of love that could exist for my parents despite their ability or inability to verify what I believed I needed from them.

1987

In the spring of 1987, I had been in psychotherapy treatment for just a little over a year, but in that short amount of time, so much was emerging for the deepest places inside. Memories that were too overpowering for me to face alone caused me to call my oldest sister to help me handle what seemed too impossible to deal with by myself. I called to ask her if she believed there was any possibility that we could have seen a murder in Alaska when we were children. At first, my question was met with silence, and then, she asked me why I would ask her that. Not really knowing how to trust anyone, but knowing that I had to tell her what was going on with me, I explained about these horrible flash images that were invading my head causing me to believe that I had seen a murder and that I must be crazy to believe such a thing.

My sister asked me to meet her right away. Still afraid of the people who had committed such terrifying abuse, she was afraid someone might find out that she was sharing with me things she believed should never be spoken, so she arranged to meet me in a place where we could park our cars and not be seen or heard by anyone. She got into my car, turned up the radio, just in case, and we began to speak. After I told her of the pieces of memories, like little shards of glass that made no sense to me, she asked me to follow her home. She wanted to be sure I knew that after we talked with each other she would not go home and draw images that matched what I had just told her. So I followed her to her home. She pulled out a box, and then files with notes and drawings... and I was astounded that she had drawn some of the images from the memories that I wanted to believe were the product of my insane mind instead of something that really happened.

There was one image that caught my attention most profoundly. It was a drawing of a room in the basement of the Jesse Lee Home, a children's orphanage on the outskirts of our town. She had drawn the support pillars in the room that had an uneven floor. And she had drawn boxes piled up and I knew exactly where I had been in that room when I was about four years old, but I had no memory of her being there. She knew where she stood and didn't remember me being there, either, but we both knew there were other people with us. The room she had drawn was exactly the same as I remembered it. One part of her drawing was not finished, and I was able to explain what was missing. It would have been something I saw from my vantage point, but she couldn't have seen from hers. What was so devastating for us is we both had flashes of a memory of someone being murdered right there in that room where we stood with other people, and we both had a very strong impression that our father was somehow involved in the murder. The murder took place next to a long box that had words printed on the side, in black. In that moment, I knew we had to go back to our hometown to see if the Jesse Lee Home was still there, and if we could find the room where so much had happened.

***

Not long after that meeting with my sister, we decided to take a trip to Seward to attempt to find something, anything that might give us answers about our early years, and what happened that shattered us so greatly. I had so few memories of where I had spent the first 9 years of my life, and she, her first 12 years, though for a period of time we moved around Alaska to various towns while our father worked for the government, and for a time was a territorial representative in the legislature. In those many moves, we lived in rented houses, apartments, and a rooming house where all of us slept with my mother in one bed, and we lived in a basement hole in the ground, that had no house on the top. In that basement house the entry was a trap door on the ceiling and a ladder that led from the outdoors to the underground. The space had no windows, no light, and no stairs. My mother had to purchase lumber, saw the long boards to hold treads, and construct the wooden stairs to let us get in and out. But the majority of the time in

Alaska, we spent in Seward. It was there that both my sister and I knew most of the horrible things happened.

***

I made plane reservations for my sister and me, and at the end of March of 1987, we headed back to the frozen north where our lives had begun. We rented a car at the Anchorage airport and started out on the 120-mile drive to Seward; but the sunny spring weather turned into a blizzard. I had insisted upon driving because my sister had told me of a dream she had before we left. In the dream, she was driving a car that skidded off the road and over a cliff. The dream bothered me because the road we were on was exceedingly dangerous with sharp curves and cliffs, sometimes on both sides of the road. I, also, knew that a year didn't go by that there wasn't someone, or more likely many people, killed on that highway in just that way. I drove until the snow accumulated beyond my capacity to feel safe, and my fear of the sixteen-wheelers that were speeding past us going 60 or 70 miles per hour in the ice and snow coupled with my inexperience with driving in that kind of weather overcame my fear of her dream and I relinquished the wheel to my oldest sister.

In spite of the 1964 earthquake that devastated Alaska and the tidal wave that had destroyed the dock area, most of Seward seemed unchanged. It looked as if the little town had been frozen in time, like a lot of old towns look, buried somewhere in the 1920's or 30s with only small pieces of evidence that decades had come and gone. Some of the streets had been paved, where they had been hard packed mud streets when we were children. The wooden sidewalks from the 50s, which overflowed with slush and muck during the run-off season in the spring, had been replaced with cement sidewalks. The buildings looked pretty much the same, mostly of wood construction, single or two storied, and the tallest building was the condemned hotel that was boarded up and appeared to be in some stage of renovation.

There were the familiar churches: the church where the children from the Jesse Lee Home attended each Sunday so many years before, the Lutheran church where my father was lay minister for a short time between real ministers and the Presbyterian church where my parents

163

were married. The bars and taverns abounded in the late 1980s, as they did in the 1950s. Someone jokingly said that there are more taverns than churches in most Alaskan towns, something I am sure was true.

After dropping our luggage at the Seward Hotel, my sister and I drove past the small white two-story house where most of our first years of life were spent. The house, still tin sided, whitewashed, and topped with a tin, barn shaped roof, looked very much the same. The back yard was stark and mud-dirty. I had forgotten how much of Seward was mud-packed earth with debris scattered amongst weeds. There were no lawns and no spring flowers growing in the yard, no flowers anywhere.

We parked the car, got out, and walked along the street in order to get a better sense of the town as we experienced it when we were children. When we walked down the street where we lived, I tried to remember the 1950's, a time that seemed to be a-hundred-lifetimes ago. I tried to remember the warehouse down the street that had outside steps to the upper floor where a man lived. I knew that the inside of that place made me both terrified and sad when I was a child, though the little dissociated child-self that I was didn't know why, back then. I remember the fire that destroyed that building when I was maybe 5 years old or so. They said children set it on fire, but no one ever found out for sure who had done it. I recall flames shooting out of the shattered windows and men running into the building to save what they could of fishing nets. There was such intensity in the air, among the onlookers and the men pulling out the ropes and nets, but I simply watched in detached disinterest. Much later in therapy, I discovered that I was with the children who started the fire. That warehouse was where some of the horrible childhood events had taken place and, perhaps, children who were hurt there believed that if the place could be destroyed, the hurt would stop; but it didn't.

The big Oak tree on the corner was still there, and for some reason, that made me very happy.

We knocked on the door of what had been our house so long ago, and asked the owner if there would be any chance we could see what it looked like inside. There had been lots of changes, but the one place that stood out so profoundly, was the basement, accessed by a narrow set of cement stairs. The space had a musty evil feel to it, and on the far end of the room was an opening that went into a dark room with only a cot and a lantern that looked as if it had not been entered for decades. The woman who was showing us the house told us that she had only seen that space once, and had never gone down there again. She wanted her husband to seal it up because it felt evil to her. When I saw the space, I knew wickedness had happened there. As I look back on that experience now, I can see how that horrible basement area looked like a more rustic version of the dungeon built by Fritzl.

After our initial reconnection with our hometown, my sister and I separated for a time and wandered the streets of Seward to touch our own realities in whatever ways we needed. I came upon a log cabin gift shop and entered to browse through the carvings and trinkets available to whatever tourists might find their way into the isolated little fishing town. Our visit was before the Alaska cruise lines made Seward a popular point of interest for thousands of tourists each year.

The woman who managed the store was my sister's age. She had come to Alaska with her family just after our family left. I decided to trust her with questions about her memories regarding the town 30 years before. In our discussion, I told her that my sister and I had come back to try to find our lost childhood, something that seemed to interest her. She mentioned she had twin brothers much younger than she, who, also, came back to Seward as adults a few years earlier to do the same thing my sister and I were doing. One had only limited memories of his life in that Alaskan town, but the other had absolutely no memory of childhood and felt a powerful need to discover what or who had stolen it from him; he hoped that seeing the town again, walking the streets, and looking into buildings might help him remember, but apparently neither were able to find what they hoped would open for them.

My sister and I met with the woman in the shop later that evening and she continued her tales about the town that was our place of origin. She said that some of the people that "ruled" the town back in those days where still in charge. When her family first arrived in Seward in the mid 1950s, young men overran the town and broke the law without any constraints; they destroyed property, stole, and raped, but no one did anything about it. There was one notorious "boss" who apparently was the only one who seemed to have control over the young men; when he spoke, they obeyed. From what we could tell, there was little difference in our town after we had left.

This woman had gotten pregnant when she was still in high school, decided to keep her child, and moved into an apartment above one of the downtown stores. Her neighbor, the "boss" she spoke of earlier, had taken her and the baby under his wing, treating her as if she was his daughter. One night a group of the "boys" decided to take over her apartment for a party. She begged them to leave, but fearing for her safety, and the safety of her infant if she angered them, she barricaded herself in her bedroom while *the boys* tore her place apart in drunken brawls.

When the boss came home later in the evening and found the gang having their destructive party in the girl's apartment, he entered her place in what she called his "Mafia style" and ordered the young men to, "...*leave and never disturb the girl again.*" They seemed to respect his threat that he better not hear they ever touched a hair on her head, because they never bothered her again. She said she hadn't thought about those horrible years for a long time, but acknowledged that that same man who ran the town, ruled the unruly, and protected her back in the really wild days, was still in a prominent position. Without actually identifying him as the same person, she insinuated that he had become the director of town's mental institution and it was common knowledge that he was sexually abusing people who were confined there. Everyone was too afraid to accuse or challenge him. She was too afraid, or maybe too loyal, to give us his name.

The next day we wandered through the town and got up the courage to go to the police station to ask carefully worded questions about the early days, but no one had been there during the time when we were children. Instead they told us about a museum that had old photographs of Seward and offered to open it up for us. There, among the pictures of the old docks, the fishing boats, and railroad tracks that had all been destroyed by the earthquake and tidal wave, was a picture of the Jesse Lee Home with army camouflage paint, exactly the way we remembered it. Other photos showed there had been an addition built onto the home sometime in the late 1950's, after our family had left. Both of us became fixated on that older image of the ugly square shaped building with trees and leaves painted on it that we knew were in various shades of green and tan, though the photo was in black and white. We both thought how ridiculous it was to have painted a building in camouflage green, making it even more obvious against the white of the winter's snow.

It was getting late and we had not yet gone to the Jesse Lee Home, which was one of the main reasons we wanted to return to Seward. We decided to get directions and drive out to what we were told was, now, an abandoned and boarded up building. My heart was pounding in near terror as the car rounded the corner and there on a grassy hill stood the building that had haunted both of us for so long, looking ghastly and ghostly in its empty, darkened state. All of the windows had heavy chicken wire over them and the doors were sealed with plywood sheets nailed and wired, as well. We drove past the entrance, but both of us knew it was not how we entered the building when the awful things happened. We parked the car in what was the back of the original building and began to circumvent it on foot looking for any possible entrance.

We were nearly half way around and approaching the newer section when I noticed a side entrance where the chicken wire had been cut and pried back enough to allow a person to crawl through. I told my sister that I would go in and she decided to follow. We crawled on our hands and knees being careful not to catch our clothing on the sharp wire and made it to the other side, which provided the passageway into the building.

The interior was completely gutted, only studs and raw boards remained where walls used to be. We cautiously walked through the corridor that connected the new building to the old part, listening for any noises that might suggest someone was checking on intruders. We could hear the tapping of our footsteps on the old, somewhat rotting wood floor and continued until the walkway opened into the old building. To our right was an entrance to a basement. It didn't match what I remembered, but I decided to descend anyway. I looked around for a moment and commented that this was not the place, and we continued our search. A little farther ahead was another opening and another set of steps. Again, I descended and had no sense of ever having been there before.

Then, we turned into what had been the kitchen of the original building. We both knew it instantly, not that it even looked like a kitchen in its gutted state, but we knew. The phone that had been on the wall to the left was gone. The floor had been covered with a yellow vinyl when I was there as a child, but the yellow was gone. On that first horrible occasion that I had remembered being in that place, a number of people were in the room, as well. And there, in front of us, just where they were supposed to be, was the narrow stairway; the steps, now broken, caved-in, and filled with decades of silt and dirt led to the basement, which held the horror that lived in my body nearly my whole life. This was, the place of that murder, but also, it was the place where the *worst of the worst* happened, something that took me much more time in therapy to work through.

Before descending the steps, my sister looked down a hall into a main living area. She commented that it looked so much like the place, but there should have been a front door that didn't seem to be there. She remembered that some of the people came down that hall into the kitchen from the front door. We walked down the hall, and there to our right was a 4'x8' sheet of plywood covering what had been the front door.

We returned to the kitchen, where the ominous looking stairs seemed to be calling us. I decided to go down into the basement, stepping carefully on each tread to avoid falling through the rotted, collapsing boards. It was difficult for my eyes to adjust to the darkness, but before I could see clearly, my body began to shake uncontrollably. I shouted up to my sister that I was feeling strange body sensations. I was not afraid of the place, although my body was shaking from the inside out. The massive all-encompassing trembling, over which I had absolutely no control, increased as I worked my way toward the far wall where I knew I had stood that horrible day the man was murdered not quite four decades before. Despite my felt sense of calmness in my mind, every cell in my body continued to respond with spasmodic trembling, as if I were in shock from being back in this place. It was as if my head was in 1987, and my body was back in the late 1940s.

The floor was uneven and filthy. There was an old boot cast in the center of the room. I made a 360-degree turn to look into the shadows of the room and I could clearly see the large space with support beams, pillars, and cement walls around me. I called out to my sister for her to come down, but she was hesitant. From where I was standing, I could see the narrow staircase, though now decrepit with age, exactly as I had seen it in flashbacks and as my sister had drawn it years before. In front of me was a square door that opened into another room, maybe a storage room of some kind.

By this time, my sister had come down and began to study the room, as well. She stopped where her memory told her she had stood so long before. She pointed out where the box had been, where the people were, and where the man lay dead on the floor beside the wooden box with large black letters and numbers printed on its side. I stood there taking all of this in and began studying the wall far in front of me. Despite all the body responses and felt-verifications that this was the place, something just wasn't right. I said to my sister,

"Something is wrong. Maybe we want to believe this is it so badly that we are making everything up. Maybe that's what is making my body shake. Everything seems right, but there is not an arch doorway. I remember there was an arch doorway at the end of the room and I am very sure that it led to the outside."

It was getting darker and we decided to end our excursion into the past and return the next day when it was lighter and we could see more since the dusk had taken control of the afternoon and made seeing difficult. I felt a sense of confusion from the inconsistency between what felt so right in my body, and the awareness in my mind that what should have been there, wasn't. The powerful reaction still pulsed through my body like earthquake after-shocks, but there was no arch door at the end of the room, and I was confused. From what I could tell, it seemed obvious that such a door had never been there.

We retraced our steps through the now shadow-covered hallways and corridors and found our way back to the entrance with the hole in the wire mesh. We crawled back out and scanned the area for anyone who might have seen us enter, but assured ourselves that there were no curious onlookers and hurried to our rental car to return to the hotel.

Morning came, and we went to the newspaper office to see if there were any collections of old papers reporting events from that terrible time in our lives. We hoped they might help us find out if there had been any reports of murders or strange events from the late 40s and early 50s. We were greatly disappointed when we were told that the newspaper office had burned twice in two separate fire incidents and there were no old records from that time. The man behind the desk recommended that we go to the Seward Library to see if they might have anything that could help us. We were directed to the "archives," which consisted of a couple of rooms in the library basement with a few shelves that contained old books, photo albums donated by estates of "sourdough" Alaskans, and a microfilm collection of the Seward Newspaper.

My sister and I found nothing from 1944-1954, as if those years had been erased. Nothing was there, at all. And then, I noticed a fairly new looking cardboard box filled with photos and old family records, and I asked the librarian about it. She told me that someone had recently died and the family brought the box, but no one at the library had had the time, yet, to go through it to catalog anything. She said it would be fine for us to browse through it if we liked.

I began to "unpack" the contents and found, buried in the bottom, a stack of random newspapers from 1944–1960. We discovered articles that appeared to corroborate our personal memories that the town was, in fact, a treacherous place, crime ridden, and out of control, not so unlike the late 1950s town described by the woman from the gift shop. There was a 1948 newspaper editorial warning parents to never permit their children to wander in the streets by themselves and for men to be sure their wives and children were never out after dark— for Alaska, that meant all but a short time in the middle of the day during the winter. The writer of that editorial lamented the violence of the vigilante groups that had taken over the town, perhaps being as much of a threat to safety of townspeople as the criminals they were attempting to destroy.

We found other articles about corpses found floating in the bay and missing persons presumed dead. There were articles about attacks and rapes of women in the town, including some wives of prominent town citizens. A picture of an out-of-control town began to form that seemed to fit the insane puzzle pieces that had so devastatingly shattered the beginning years of our lives.

My sister ran the photocopy machine making copies of many articles to be sure that we would have some tangible proof if something happened to the newspapers we found. After returning to Seattle we contacted both Juneau and Anchorage and found no newspaper records from that period of time in Seward available from these sources, either.

After getting all we could from the library, the two of us collected our cameras and headed back to the Jesse Lee Home. The sun was bright and reflected against the whiteness of the snow that had fallen during the night making the countryside look postcard pretty as we drove to the outskirts of town and turned onto the dirt road that led to the abandoned orphanage. We parked the rental car, walked to the same opening, crawled through the hole in the fence, and walked down the now familiar corridors. With much less fear, we descended the stairs to the basement. I entered first, camera in hand, and walked slowly from the entrance to the posts and then to the far side of the room where I had stood when I was a child. I looked at the walls, the floor, and the discarded boot as my sister was coming down the stairs. But then, I cried out for my sister to look at the wall in front of me.

From where I was standing, I was able to see through the existing rectangular frame opening, into the adjacent room and to the back wall of that other room. The tall church-like window that rose above ground level to illuminate this back storeroom, provided entry for a stream of light to shine in and cast sunlight against the back wall in the shape of an arch. The sun shown so brightly against the wall that it looked as if the arch was a doorway that led to the outside.

I cried out in palpable relief, in great joy, and deep grieving sadness. I was relieved that I was not crazy, joyful that I had really seen an arch when I was a child, so many years before, and sad that what I had allowed myself to think might have been something my mind had just made up, was, in fact, true. As much as I had wanted proof, I hoped that none of what I had remembered about that orphanage was true. My sister and I had been in that basement long ago; our bodies knew it, and had communicated to us what had happened when we were in that basement as little children. And now, the most skeptical parts of my mind had to acknowledge a truth that was most difficult to want to accept. There were many times to come when I dreaded, as well as hoped to find this kind of substantiation of memories, because it meant that I was not crazy, but also, I could no longer live in the safety of denial.

The part of me that so strongly resisted any unacceptable information from coming forward about my childhood and my family stepped aside and, for the most part, let go of resistance to the discovery of the truth. But always, there was at least a miniscule amount of doubt.

1952

School was out for the summer of my eighth year, and I was relatively free until September and fourth grade would start. My father had business to conduct somewhere on the Kenai Peninsula and all of us went along for a camping trip that would include staying at a cabin on Lake Kenai while he did whatever it was that he did. Before we were to head out for our family vacation, my oldest sister and I went to the schoolyard to play on the playground equipment. We were having a great time on the merry-go-round when we noticed our father walking toward us with the walk that communicated trouble. He demanded that my sister go home, and then, for some unknown reason, began to push the bars of the merry-go-round faster and faster until I begged him to stop. He began to curse me for disobeying him, though I was not sure what I had done to be punished like that. I started to get dizzy and begged him to stop, but he kept pushing until I was completely disoriented. He pulled me from the merry-go-round and dragged me into a wooded area and sodomized me with a viciousness that engraved itself in my bones. The pain was so fierce that I literally tried to separate from the pain by attempting to wrench my upper body from my lower body. If I could have ripped myself in half and remained in my upper body, I wouldn't have to feel the horror of what was happening below.

It was then that I decided that I didn't want to be in the world anymore. It seemed as if the brutality would never stop.

Two events came together that helped me find what seemed like a very good way out of living this horror. The first was that one of my sisters, had discovered the "funny feelings" she got from breathing in the exhaust fumes from a car left running in front of our neighbor's house. When my nine-year-old sister came staggering into the house, and my mother found out what she had done, she told her with great intensity in her voice to never, ever breathe in fumes like that again. She said, *"If you do that again, you might go to sleep and never wake up!"* The second event had to do with the cigarette lighter and holder that were supposed to be in the back seat car door but had somehow become missing. As a result, it was not unusual for exhaust fumes to leak into the car when we were driving. As a precaution against asphyxiation, we drove with the back window down and an army blanket across the legs of the 4 back-seat girls to protect us from the cold. Being cold was better than being dead.

On that trip, following the most horrifically painful attack by my father, I decided that if I put my head under the army blanket, I could breathe in the fumes, go to sleep and never wake up, just like my mother said would happen. So I put my head under the blanket and went to sleep. Sometime later, I woke up lying beside the Seward highway with the army blanket under my body. My siblings were watching over me, wondering if I was going to die. I recall a car stopping to ask if there was any trouble, and my father waved them on, telling them that I was carsick.

Years later, my father told me after what seemed like an eternity of not breathing and being unresponsive to any effort to revive me, I leaned over and threw up a very long stool, something he said he would never forget. I imagine that I had been so damaged by his raping of me near the playground, that my anus had completely closed off. When people are near death, it is not uncommon for them to lose control of their bowels and bladder, something my body was unable to do, so what was in my intestines went upward into my stomach instead of down. When consciousness returned I vomited up what should never have been in my stomach.

My mother tried to make me walk around before we got back in the car, but my legs were incapable of supporting me. I was promoted to the front seat where I lay across my mother's lap with my head out the window to breathe in as much fresh air as possible. We arrived at the cabin and a cot was prepared for me out on the screened in porch where I was to sleep for a couple of nights. I remember trying to get up to play with the other kids, but had to go back to the cot until my legs could become stronger. My mother lay on the cot with me that first night holding me in her arms; I remember her words, as clearly as if she had spoken them last night, *"I don't know what I would have done if I had lost you."* And her words meant nothing to me.

1948

Two little girls stand in a basement room, beneath the kitchen in the Jesse Lee Orphanage. They are with a group of Caucasian men and one Eskimo man. It is daytime. One child looks around the room and sees the staircase that brought her to the basement, a stack of boxes and barrels, a box with black letters and numbers on it and an arch doorway, opposite where she is standing, that leads outside into the sunshine of the day. She wonders if there is some way she can sneak away from where she is standing, escape through that door, and into the world outside where this terrible feeling is not happening inside her. But she is frozen in place. The Eskimo man is standing in the center of the basement room, and in a moment of explosive anger coming from the group, the man in the middle of the room is attacked by one of the men with a shiny object that looks like a knife. The Eskimo is on the floor; he is dead.

The child is in total shock; terror has caused her to shatter into many pieces that hide inside in deeply buried places; some of the places look like the other side of the arch doorway where there is only light and some places look like the corners in a darkened basement.

As they are taken home, the children forget the Jesse Lee Home, the basement, the group of men, the Eskimo, and the murder. Later, the children's parents seem to have a new threat that works wonders in controlling the behavior of the children in the perfect family and that is if the children are not good, they will be left at the Jesse Lee Home when the rest of the family leaves Seward. The children are very, very good. If her mother says no to little Sandy and shakes her head, the child stops whatever she is doing that displeases her mother. And whenever trips out of town take the family past the Orphanage, the two girls look through the car window and little Sandy quietly whispers to the rest of her siblings with sadness in her voice, *"There is the Jesse Lee Home,"* causing her siblings to look at the building with army green and tan camouflage trees painted on its sides to feel the sadness of their sister, or, it is possible that some of the others have experienced their own versions of terrible events in that basement room.

BACK TO THE PRESENT

Though I have been in that basement a thousand times in my mind and have rescued my little child-self more times than I can count, in this moment, I realize that there is something that I have not yet done. I have not freed the child of the guilt she has been carrying for decades. The guilty child-self has remained stuck in that basement unable to escape for all these years because she believes what happened was her fault.

When I was 4 years old and raped by my father in the woods outside my house, I believed I deserved to be hurt because I had not gone home when I was supposed to go. Everything in my body hurt when I walked along the path that I had made earlier in the forest. I walked across the dirt road and climbed up the cement stairs and opened the front door of our house. I'm not sure how I had the strength to walk with such pain between my legs and in my heart, but I did.

Even though I believed that I must have deserved to be punished, there was something so incredibly mean about the punishment that I just couldn't understand. How could my daddy want to hurt me so, very badly? There was no answer. I walked into the kitchen to see if there was some way I could wash myself better than the leaves in the woods had cleaned me. My mother found me in the kitchen looking dazed and terrified. When she asked me what happened, I told her that daddy had hurt me, followed by the rest of what I explained earlier. Before being buried in the box, my mother demanded that I tell her the truth. I told her that an Eskimo man was the one who hurt me.

In retrospect, I believe it is possible that someone in my family, perhaps my mother, told someone from the vigilante group what an Eskimo had done to little Sandy, and vigilantes must have gone out in search of the man and brought him to the Jesse Lee Home, which seemed to be a meeting place for such things. I was brought down the stairs and stood with a group of people and was asked if this Eskimo was the one who hurt me in the woods. I knew that he was not the one, but I had already said it was an Eskimo. I knew they wanted me to say he was the man, and I was too scared to say the truth. So I said, yes.

Someone near me leapt toward the Eskimo and attacked him with something that looked like a knife. There was blood, and the man was dead. They put him in the box with black letters on the side. I only saw the back of the man who attacked and killed the Eskimo, but I remember that my thought was, *"Daddy why did you do that when you know it wasn't him?"*

The child believed that she caused that man to die and has believed she was so bad and that would never change. She did something that could never be taken back. How could anything ever be good again when she was so, so bad?

***

Though the part of me that forgot what happened that horrible day grew up, the little girl who blamed herself for what happened that day, has remained in that basement all these years, trying to figure out how to undo what she had done. Her thoughts about herself are what made my adult self always feel like I was a very bad person, even though I had no idea why I thought that. As I write this, I know it is, finally, time to go into that basement room and free the child from her self-imposed prison by telling her the truth.

***

As I approach her, she is in total shock, frozen in her place, frozen in that time so long ago, feeling the horror of that moment as if it is still happening…but I find the entire room is frozen in time. Everything is as it was then; nothing has changed. I am the only one moving. I walk in front of my child-self and kneel down, eye level with her. I

176

tell her that I have come for her. She begins to quiver. Everything in her is shaking from the inside out. She seems to have no control over the massive all-encompassing trembling. Every cell in her body is shaking with spasmodic trembling. The shaking energy breaks the spell of the freeze. I can see she is terrified and frantic. She throws her arms around my neck and begins to cry hysterically. Her sobbing is so deep she is having a difficult time breathing. Wailing sounds come out between the choking and sobbing, forming the words that she made a very, very bad thing happen. She clings to my neck and presses herself against me as if she is trying to escape all that is there. She seems so tiny to be filled with such intense pain, fear, and guilt. I hold her tightly in my arms and reassure her that I am here for her. I tell her I know everything and that she is not bad. I tell her that I love her and will never leave her.

The words seem to calm her down a little and I ask her to look directly into my eyes so she will know I am telling her the truth. I tell her, *"No matter what you would have said, the same thing would have happened. These people were ready to kill the Eskimo man. They had made a box for him even before you arrived. I know, although I don't know how I know, that their intention was to kill him. You were their excuse. But they would have done it no matter what."* She could see in my eyes that I was telling the truth and her hysteria turned into quiet releasing sobs for all she experienced.

My child-self already knew what her daddy could do when he was angry and she was terrified to say what he didn't want her to say, like when she told her mother that he had hurt her. He was using her fear to make her say, yes, when she was asked about the Eskimo. She was too little and too scared to say anything else. She knew that all the others in the room wanted her to say, yes, too. She was not grown up enough to have the power to counter everyone in the room. They knew it. She was just a little girl.

***

As I write this, for some reason images of April 1968, when Martin Luther King was assassinated, are coming into my mind. Over the years, I have learned that when images like this come into my thoughts,

177

seemingly intruding into something that I am thinking or when I am writing, it is important to follow them and not to put them aside.

I was in Seattle, scheduled to fly into the eye of the storm the very next day after King was shot to spend a week with my young husband at Fort Campbell in Kentucky. He had been given a week's leave to spend with me during spring break, but was ordered back onto the base the day I arrived. Jake's captain allowed me to come on base and stay in his home so at least Jake and I would be able to spend our nights together. I recall that the entire base was on red alert. An extremely long convoy of troop-filled personnel carriers, manned machine gunners, tanks, and everything else military was readied to move out into what the top brass thought would be riots in the streets. All through the day and night, for the whole time I was there, the blocks-long caravan was primed and ready to move into whatever city would be their focus to take over if martial law was declared. The vehicles were continuously manned and war energy was palpable. It was clear the uniformed men who sat behind the wheels, and in the trucks were ready to take full charge and kill if they had to; that's what they were trained to do.

Now that I have remembered the images of 1968, I can see energy among the vigilantes in that basement room of the Jesse Lee home was so very much the same as the energy of the troops waiting in the long caravan line for orders to roll out. The significant difference was that the military was ruled by law, while the vigilantes were not.

When the orders to stand down were finally given on the Fort Campbell base, the trucks and carriers were all driven back to the motor pool and all the men who were ready for battle were dismissed and went home. It is possible that some of the men, who, for days, had been revved for domestic war, might well have gone home and beaten their wives and children, or gone to bars to find a way to get into fights to let out that pent up energy that had primed them to fight and kill, but most of them likely would have found a way to release the pent up feelings, maybe by going to the gym, by running, or doing some other intensely physical exercise, released the energy, and moved on with their lives. Most of the soldiers may have been relieved that they didn't have to experience a domestic uprising that would require turning against angry American citizens.

The vigilantes, on the other hand, didn't have anyone telling them to lay down their arms and stand down. Even if the little girl would have said that this wasn't the man, they were primed to kill and would have found a way to override the child's statement to hear what they wanted to hear. She believed her yes killed him; her mind linked her word to his death. Thought it looked like the truth, that linkage was not true.

As I communicated these thoughts to my child-self, she knew I was telling her the truth. I asked her if she needed to say or do anything before we left this terrible basement room. She asked me to walk with her over to the Eskimo who lay on the floor. She squatted down and placed her hand on his forehead and told him she was sorry that this happened to him. In that moment, and I have no idea how I know this, I realized that the other people in the room had accused him of molesting and raping other children, as well. Apparently he had done some of the things for which he was being accused; my sense of it is that he did those things after he had been drinking. And others had identified him as the man. Those people gathered there would have killed him, no matter what little Sandy had said, but I believe that my father wanted to be sure that this man, not he, himself, was found guilty of what he had done to me.

My, oh, my! It is still so very hard for me to write those words about my father. Just putting this accusation in this place where other people will read and will know, is causing my throat to tighten. Both my child-self and I are crying at this moment. Neither of us ever really and truly wanted to know this.

Little Sandy needed to tell the other men, also frozen in time, that she knew that some of them had done the very things they accused this man of doing. Like my father, some had molested and raped their little girls. Somehow, she knew what each of them had done that caused them to use the cover of the vigilante group to distract from their own wickedness. I don't know how she knew about these people, but she did. One by one, she walked in front of each of the men, frozen in time, and told them what she knew. She walked back to the dead man and asked him to forgive her for telling a lie. She heard his soul say that he had already forgiven her and that he was okay. He told her that he had learned a lot from that life and forgave her for being so scared that she couldn't say the truth. He said good-bye and was gone. She was finally ready to leave the basement and all the darkly dense energies it represented, and come with me to live in 2009 and beyond.

I realized there was one more thing I needed to do before taking the child into my present. I sent a message through time to all the men that participated in this incident. Some felt justified in executing people they judged as evil and others were using the planned killing as a distraction from their own evil. I opened the images of patterns of killing and being killed, so they could see that what they had done to this man would be done to them. They were living a pattern where they played parts, switched roles, and repeated the energies from lifetime to lifetime. This would go on and on until someone decides to stop. I shared the story of the kicking pattern and let them know they could choose to stop the executing and being executed pattern and live free of the energies lived over and over again. I, also, let them know that they could free themselves from the basement and return to the light if they chose. It was up to them. Little Sandy and I left the basement and she came with me to the present. We released the pattern of the fear of saying the truth and recognized we were not responsible for the choices of other people.

She is here with me now, resting in the heart of my heart, forever safe and loved. As I look back on that trip to Alaska and everything else connected to that incident, I have no doubt that the feelings I experienced when I stood in that basement room of the Jesse Lee home in 1987, were the same feelings that my child-self felt when my 2009-self re-entered 1948 to free her from being frozen in the horror of that time. I know this can be a lot to wrap a mind around. Let me say it another way. In 1987, I felt the tremors in my body when I walked down those rotting stairs and entered that crime scene. My body was shaking uncontrollably, but my mind was not in the fear, at all. In that 1987 moment, I believe I was literally experiencing three separate times, past, present, and future. I was experiencing what the little girl felt in 1948 a microsecond after seeing the man murdered. The shock froze her in time until I came for her, just moments ago, in 2009. My 1987 self was emotionally disconnected from both her child-self and her future self when the internal quaking registered in her body, which was connected to the child of the past who saw the man murdered and to the future adult, who traveled back to 1948 to bring healing to the child. We have been so schooled in the belief that past, present, and future are irreversibly separate, but my experience has taught me that this separation is not true. Attempts to grasp what I have written can be a major challenge to traditional thinking.

I am feeling exhausted from this excursion into the past and trust that I will sleep very well tonight.

Reflections

Often we are told to stop looking back, to forget the past and move forward in our lives, but if parts of us remain stuck in the past, there comes a time when too much of us is stuck along the way of past wounding, and there is not enough of us to move forward.

A very powerful way of understanding what you hold deep inside you that remains in the past is to begin with what you are experiencing in the present that limits you in body, mind, heart, or spirit. Feel what happens in your body when you are experiencing whatever is disturbing you. Notice the thoughts you hold in connection with the limitations. If you feel disturbed, disarmed, distraught, disconnected, disoriented or disempowered from some experience in which you were hurt, even if it was long, long ago, let the feeling grow inside instead of forcing it to go away as is a more common response. Ask the feeling to take you back through time, back to the original cause of this feeling, the first time your body ever felt it. By going back, you can find the source of the hurt, and often, you will see glimpses of similar hurts along the way from the present to the past. Bring love and truth to those hurts and let the parts of you that have been stuck in the past join you in the present with present day awareness instead of remaining with limited awareness of the past. By going into the past, you can finally free yourself to fully enter into the present and move forward into the future.

Chapter Eleven
BACK AT THE BEGINNING

Our beginnings contain many of the themes and the protective patterns present in our lives that no longer serve us but will revisit us all of our lives until we bring love, truth, and healing into those themes and patterns if only we would allow our selves to take the time to look deeply at our beginnings.

Very much like the lawless American West of the mid to late 1800s or the dangerous inner cities anywhere in the world in the present, Alaska of the 1940s and 50s was a territory ruled by the unruly. Conflicts abounded among power groups all struggling to gain control of the wealth of the land. Gold and the new gold—which was the burgeoning oil business—as well as the position of Alaska as a gateway to the Orient, represented untold riches that attracted the entrepreneurs and the scoundrels, alike. At times it was difficult to tell which was which.

I was born in the middle of the struggle among the railroad interests, the shipping interests, the oil interests, the military, and the criminals, all seeking to gain control of the lucrative land and its resources that surrounded my hometown. With the war still being waged in Europe and in Asia, the territory of Alaska was seen as a significant defense buffer against a possible invasion from Japan, and Seward became a logistics center for everything military that was to protect the lower 48 states from an expected Japanese onslaught.

Like camp followers, far too many shady characters seeking to take economic advantage of the military, collected in and around this little port town. During the war, there was not enough military personnel to handle the unloading of military equipment and supplies, so in their infinite wisdom, the government gave early outs to prisoners in the lower 48 states if they would "volunteer" their services on the docks. So added to the population that lived more unconventional lives and didn't mix well with civilization, were incoming thieves, murderers, and rapists who took advantage of their ticket to freedom by going north to Alaska.

Largely a population of men for most of its history, the town of Seward maintained a red light district where the dark side thrived abundantly, and for the most part, the town tolerated its existence. Recently written historical reviews of the city of Seward and the red light district, more *affectionately* referred to by the locals as *The Line*, have painted a picture of necessity and near-respectability for prostitution in our town, not unlike what was depicted by Dodge City's Miss Kitty, on the radio and TV series, *Gunsmoke*. Kitty was the Tavern owner, with subtle hints that she was, also, the town madam, made respectable by her relationship with sheriff Matt Dillon.

Like the fictional Dodge City of television, Seward had, at times, a 4 to 1 ratio of men to women. I suspect that those who wrote about the phenomenon of socially acceptable prostitution in my hometown weren't taken into the red light district when they were children and subjected to the cruelties that occurred behind closed doors. Though we were warned about not going to the Line to sell our newspapers or to play on Alley B, between 2nd and 3rd avenues when we were wandering around our town in the day, I knew, too well, what that place was like at night.

The little shacks where the women of the night stayed were tiny, and some of the hovels smelled badly. My father talked about the "pissing contests" that patrons got into to see who could project their urine the farthest; but nobody asked him how he knew such things. When I was verifying my memories about Seward, and did an Internet search, I found Rachel Mason's article titled, *The Red Light Ethnohistory in Seward, Alaska,* I was amazed to see her description of the elaborate red velvet brocade furniture in the ornately decorated abode of one of the well known madams, as it seemed to match the forklift dream I had that included a room with the Victorian décor with red brocade patterns everywhere including the wall coverings. In that dream, the angry masculine energy in me tore it all apart with his forklift. I am sure that a child-part hated that place, which was made to look elegant but under the plush velvet it was pure ugliness.

Apparently politicians and police, like many men in town visited the Line often. According to Mason's research, while numerous immoral and technically illegal activities were thought to take place on the Line, its central function was prostitution. Because the "activities" were seen as a necessary evil in a town overrun with men, what went on there was not monitored and the rest of the more civilized towns-people tolerated its presence as long as trouble remained there.

Eventually, vigilante groups organized in the community to protect the more civilized residents from the violent outbursts of fighting men, but this seemed to be more about other issues, rather than prostitution, and whatever else might have been connected with the seedy underbelly of the town on picturesque Resurrection Bay. Like the struggle between cattle ranchers and farmers in the old west, dockworkers, truckers, and railroad men fought for control of the jobs, while their bosses struggled in much larger arenas for control of the business and wealth of this far northern territory.

***

My life began in the crosshairs of all of this, born to a father who did not want children and both lusted after and hated women, and to a mother who wanted only boys, and felt deeply disappointed when she had a series of girls. Shortly after the first sexual assault when I was four years old, I was taken to the red-light district and sold to men who had a propensity for children. By the time I was six, I was used in child pornography films in the early years of that industry and I watched as other children and adults became the victims of pornography, and on one horrible occasion, a snuff film.

I have snippets of memories of psychological testing performed by men who appeared to be doctors and military officers. I have no way of knowing if they were acting out roles in some heinous film or if they were professionals who participated in the abuse. These people administered electric shock treatments and injected drugs into me, perhaps as a way to erase memories of abuse that had been inflicted, though I don't know that for sure. It was this abuse that came back to me when I was having an operation for cancer in March of 2008 and my last conscious memory was being strapped down to the operating table, so similar to the straps that held me down when I was a child. It took me months to work through the trauma of the past to which the hospital experience connected. But, as a small child, by the grace of God and the gift of dissociation, I was spared having to deal with the memories when I was too young to know what to do with them.

Except for those few newspapers that my sister and I found in that box in the basement of the town library in the mid 1980s, that corroborated the vigilante groups, the murders, and the dangers of living in my town, I have no verifiable proof of any of my memories of what happened to me. Though my sister's drawings certainly added to the veracity of what I had remembered, they were not proof.

Something happened between 1953 and 1954 that caused many of the prominent families to leave Seward, including my own family, and in 1954, the Line, where prostitution had reigned for decades, also, was closed down, with no explanation found for either exodus.

For almost two years after leaving Seward, we lived in a distant suburb of Anchorage. Much of what we owned remained in Seward so we bought many new things after we arrived at our new home. And it seemed that most of the bad, bad things were left behind, as well. There were no more waking events in the middle of the night when I was taken from my bed to go to the terrible places. There were no more boats or church basements, no more electric shocks, and no more Jesse Lee Home visits. Anchorage seemed to be a place where I could notice new buds on trees that appeared in springtime and there was financial abundance, at least for the first year we were there. The new house, new car, new clothes and new everything made life seem really fresh and good.

My mother found another job at an Anchorage hospital to replace the one she had in Seward, and as before, she worked nights so she could be home with the kids in the daytime. When she could, she brought home little gifts for us, and one morning, she brought home a 33-RPM record player along with several brightly colored plastic records that I came to love. I especially liked the Johnny Appleseed record accompanied by a storybook, about a man who planted apple seeds as he wandered from east to the west during the pioneer days of our country. The song that touched my heart so deeply, repeated throughout the story, told the listeners to *get on the wagons, roll out west... out to the great unknown...*get on the wagons to head out west, or you would be left alone.

Johnny was a seed planter, wandering from town to town bringing the gift of apple trees to whoever wanted them, and something about that felt so, so very right. He went into a town, planted seeds and later returned when the apples grew...and then he moved on with a new satchel of seeds from the apple trees that had grown to find the next settlement, the next town, or village where what he had to offer was received. He was a wanderer, traveling through the Western territory from the time he was young until he became very old. Much later, I found out that Johnny was a real man, not just an imaginary character in a child's story.

I felt great empathy for the old man Johnny, when at the end of the fable, the angels came to take him to heaven, but he told them that he just couldn't go, because he *had crops to harvest and seeds to sow*. But the angels said God needed him in Heaven to fill the hills there with apple trees. My child-self wanted to reason with God and the angels to give old Johnny a little bit more time, but the record ended the same all the time, with the refrain to get on the wagons to roll out west, out to the great unknown. And Johnny accepted a ride with the angels and went with them to the great unknown after having spent his life planting apple seeds.

It is not a surprise that beside the Johnny Appleseed song, two of my childhood favorites were *The Happy Wanderer*, and *Far Away Places*, but as much as I loved those songs about people spending their lives on the road, moving from place to place, expanding horizons, and discovering the wonders of the world, these songs, also, made me sad. As far back as I can remember, sadness always seemed to be a part of my wish to move forward in my life and that ongoing resistance I've felt most of my life to letting go of what I was leaving and moving forward. So, Johnny Appleseed represented moving into the unknown for me.

***

The many experiences I had that first year in *Turnagain-by-the-Sea*, a distant suburb of Anchorage where my family lived after leaving Seward, contained so many of the good memories from my childhood: ice skating, singing, snow angles, discovery of islands, happy valley, and of course, Johnny Appleseed. But after our first year in Anchorage, life began to change. For reasons I will never know, my father became extremely depressed and for a time, thought he was going blind. He spent a great amount of the time in my parents' bedroom with the curtains pulled tight to shut out all the light, and we had to be very quiet to not disturb him. There were times we ran out of food and couldn't pay bills because what my mother earned was not enough to support a family of seven. Back then, there were no food pantries and there was no store that would let us buy food on credit, as there had been in Seward, and later as happened in Seattle. In the middle of the tough times, my father developed a strangulated hiatal hernia that required an operation, which began the next chapter in the life of our family.

When we departed from Anchorage in 1955, we left without knowing that we would not be returning; all of our belongings were left behind, but what was most painful was that we left our two dogs, as well. Though the worst abuses of my childhood ended, more normal family dysfunction continued.

***

As I mentioned earlier, my mother attempted suicide two times that first year in Seattle, and my father threatened suicide nearly on a daily basis. He numbed himself with two to three packs of unfiltered cigarettes a day, and he distracted himself with his *dirty underwear type women*. On occasion, he, also, numbed himself with drinking, which is something adamantly denied by most members of my family.

My mother numbed herself with bible reading, burying her heart and mind in daily devotionals for hours a day, underlining and writing notes in her red cloth covered bible, all allowing her to avoid seeing what was going on around her. She diligently prayed for everyone in her family and tried to save anyone who didn't hold the same religious views she held.

The rest of the time I lived in my parents' house, until I was 21 and left to get married, were tension-filled years. We all knew there were major problems between our parents and in our family but none of us dared talk about them. My father's girlfriend gave birth to a child, and he tried to figure out how to live two separate lives, without either family knowing of the existence of the other, and much later, we discovered that he actually had a third family.

My mother struggled trying to keep her family, her marriage, and her finances together, and failed at all three of them because her husband was not interested in those goals. She flipped between being quiet and passive, a gentle Christian woman trusting that Jesus would come again to make her life good, to being an insane woman, exploding in raging fits, and when the shifts would happen was fully unpredictable. While the outer shell of her personal life was being held together by crazy glue, she went to work every night to bring babies into the world as an obstetrics nurse, rarely missing her shift, even when the glue could no longer hold.

While a part of her carried out her mothering from a distance, unable to hold or hug her girls—she never seemed to have a problem expressing her affection for her boy—and incapable of showing compassion or tenderness most of my growing up years, another part of her mourned not being able to have ever really experienced being a mother. The whole time her children were growing up, she was the major bread winner, working nights year after year and sleeping her days away, very disconnected from the hearts of her children, something that made her heart suffer. I recall one day when I was in my mid teen years, several of us kids were seeing how long we could stand on our heads while leaning against a wall. My mother came out of the front bedroom and decided to join us in our play. She attempted a headstand, slipped, and injured her neck. I assisted her in getting back to bed and brought ice

189

to help the pulled muscle feel better. As I was tending to her, she began to cry, telling me that all her life she had wanted to be a mother, but her kids were nearly all grown and she never had the chance. I didn't know how to comfort her in her sorrow except to tell her that I loved her.

Years later, she told me that she relished the suffering of her life because it was proof that she was living the way Christ wanted her to live. He suffered and she believed his followers had to bare the crosses that were assigned to them, as Christ bore his. The suffering made her one with Jesus, and she claimed she wouldn't have chosen any other way. She had found the way to make her sorrow and her suffering something good.

I wish there could have been a way to tell her then what I have come to understand, now, that human suffering is not a pleasure to the creator of the universe. If one believes in suffering, then suffering is reflected as a loving gift of the universe to help the suffering person become conscious of what is believed. Once known, the person can make a choice to release or to continue to hold on to those beliefs. Suffering is not something that proves our worthiness; it is our mirror. It took many years of healing from a house of suffering for me to understand this truth, something I couldn't have known back then, but do know now.

***

Perhaps, like Johnny Appleseed, I know I have seeds to plant. My seeds contain the idea that our beliefs create our reality, a seed that was planted in me many years ago; it has grown, and is in the process of maturing within my own heart. This is a seed I want to offer to the hearts of others in the settlements and towns, the cities and the nations, wherever the message can be received. *We are the ones who are creating the lives we experience, whether we want to believe it or not, and we are the ones who can transform our experience by bringing healing to our beliefs.*

If some of us begin to really get this idea, and live based on an deep understanding of its truth, we can transform the world into one that reflects back to us the prayer of St. Francis of Assisi, when he wanted to be an instrument of peace instead of war, love instead of hate, pardon instead of injury, hope instead of despair, light instead of darkness and joy instead of sadness. Part of the reason I am writing this trilogy is to add to the growing number of people who are planting this seed, too. And another part of the reason for my writing is so that I will be able to embrace this truth, not just in my mind, but also in every cell of my body, as well. And I suspect that this is a lifetime project.

***

I've been aware that people who experienced extreme abuse early in their lives, often, must choose between healing and dying. If they choose healing, their inner search often leads them into deeply buried pain that has a way of cracking open the protective shields that, over time, turned into dungeon prisons most of us have built around the magnificent essence within. However, people with less damage might find fairly effective ways to live acceptable or even abundant lives without having to go into the painful digging until the midlife crisis or the later years when despair often arises, which might cause them to become self-reflective. If they continue to resist that inner search, they live out those lives feeling something is not quite right, that there is a place inside that feels empty or disconnected, as if they missed something in life's journey. Without knowing it, they missed the fulfillment of their connection to that amazing essence within.

Whether abuse was extreme or mild, until healed, we experience the internal constrictions and contractions or the push to extend until we can't extend anymore. Living from either contraction or extension without relief leads to an eventual collapse. And like steel cables, our bodies begin to pull us back into the fetal position, returning us to our ending as we began. In the process of not seeking healing and reconnection with our essence, the loss of internal balance and harmony are reflected to us in our illnesses, in disturbances in our relationships and in our lives, and disharmony within ourselves.

As I look at the world our species has created in these beginning years of this 21st century, I believe we are now experiencing the collective reflection of all our beliefs about pain, separation, conflict, lack, suffering, and so much more. Once we make a choice, both individually and collectively, to bring healing to false beliefs, as well as to the problems that those false beliefs generate, transformations can take place allowing us to live the lives we came here to experience instead of being distracted by and entangled in fear and pain.

Reflections

There is value in writing down your beginnings. They often provide a great source for revealing the patterns and themes in your life. Even if your beginnings are vague or information is consciously non-existent, you can begin with your first recollections. It is not unusual for the first memory you have to contain your life themes and reveal your protective patterns. Reflect upon your place in the world in that first memory. How were you interacting with your world? Were you fighting it, trying to understand it, disappearing in it? How was your world interacting with you? Was it welcoming? Critical? Supportive? Attacking? And what did you interpret about your world and about yourself in that first memory? Were you passive? Were you active? Was there conflict? And, if so, what was the substance of the conflict? What were the feeling tones? What could you see, and what could you not see as you reflect on that memory? Did you feel safe? Loved? Cared for? Wanted? Valued? Notice as much as possible and ask as many questions as you can. Then let yourself move through the passage of time to the present, looking for the major events of your life. Notice what themes and patterns come forward. Were they similar to what you saw in your beginnings or your first memory?

Was your first memory positive? If so, was there anything that happened that challenged that first positive memory? What did you lose? What did you accept as true after the challenge? Study your answers to see the truths and the lies in the themes and patterns.

If you are to heal, the lies must be transformed into truth. If you do not know the truth, ask your higher self, ask God and the angels, your spirit guides, your wise self, or whatever you choose to call that which is greater than you, to help you to see the truth and to bring that truth to whatever lies you hold. Then, notice how your life transforms.

Chapter Twelve
A HOLE IN THE SIDE OF MY FACE

Thoughts, like physical matter, at their core are formed by energy patterns. Thoughts are as real as matter. Just because we cannot see them in physical form does not mean that thoughts are not real and do not impact us. When we take on painful or negative energies of others, including thoughts, feelings, or experiences, they can affect us as powerfully as anything that can be seen in the world of matter, and they can influence the form our physical world takes.

For many years, when I was under a great deal of stress, it was not uncommon for me to be oppressed with a headache on the right side of my face, so intense that I often lost vision in my right eye. I have no specific memories of this headache before ninth grade, but it was there at least from age 13 and stayed with me until I worked with it in therapy, decades later. I recall telling my therapist that it felt like there was a hole in the side of my head where my right eye should be and no matter how hard I rubbed it, I could not make the pain go away. When I closed my eyes and saw myself from the inside, I saw my skull with no right side. For decades, I had no clue why I experienced this effect and didn't know what it meant.

***

Almost from the beginning of doing inner work, a cameo image would float into my mind of a little blond girl with shoulder length hair and a narrow face with eyes that were close together. She was not very pretty though she seemed to be very well groomed. I saw her sitting on a large bed in a shadowed room with a single window covered by old lace curtains that were lightly blowing in the wind. I presume it must have been in the summer, because the window was open and there was evening light coming in. The girl's hand grasped a carved bedpost. Every time I saw her face in my mind, I felt apprehension and my stomach became sick. She slipped into my mind often, but I didn't know why. With all the other things going on, I just noticed her; I didn't place a priority on trying to figure out why she kept appearing in my mind.

The body therapist I worked with for almost three years, Michael from Bellingham, Washington, was a gifted Rolfer, and sometime early on into the process of realigning my body, he started to focus on the bones of my head that were badly out of alignment. I experienced an intense physiological response unlike any I ever had before or since in a therapy session when he pressed against the orbital bones around my right eye. My entire body began to shake uncontrollably from the inside out as if all my cells were quivering with surges of electric shock, vibrating, overloading, and exploding all at once. I had no control over what was happening.

While this was occurring, a strange thought passed through my mind that convulsing like this is what a body does when it has died in shock. I had no idea where that thought came from because to my knowledge at the time, I had never seen a person die. Though, later in my work, I was to discover that, in fact, I had seen shocking deaths occur on more than one occasion.

Much later, while in a hypnosis session with my psychotherapist, I saw the same little girl again in that room with the lace curtains, but this time she wasn't just sitting there, she began looking back and forth, seeming to be very frightened. I knew my child-self was in the room and when I looked for her, I saw little Sandy curled up on the floor, pressing her body up against the walls of the far corner as hard as possible.

In a microsecond, I shifted from being an observer of what was happening to being my child-self, experiencing what was happening. We heard the door open and both of us looked at the person who came in to get us. The man walked toward the bed and took the little girl's hand and left the room with her without coming for me. I was so greatly relieved I was not the one taken into the next room. Though I don't know how I knew, I had no doubt that what was about to happen would be very bad.

Though nearly all of me wanted to stop seeing what was happening, I asked the therapist if I should let myself see what was in the next room, and he said I could if I wanted to. Back in that past incident, I had already crawled from the corner over to the doorway to look through a small crack of the door and saw a bed with a white and red sheet. The wall was painted red to match the color in the sheet. That was all I saw. It didn't mean anything. The therapist asked me to look again, to see what happened before what I was seeing. And I saw the little girl sitting on the bed wearing only white panties. Then I saw her with the same blue dress with puffy lace trimmed sleeves that she was wearing when she was in the bedroom with me. Nothing made sense. But I knew something was terribly wrong. I saw the bright lights, the wires, people standing on the edges of the room and one man was carrying a stick. In an instant, all of the segmented pictures came together. Before the merging of the images that day in my therapist's office, I had been seeing the events in reverse order and, then I saw the sequenced events that made me scream out in horrified pain for what had happened.

Back at the time this event was taking place, right after the man and little girl left, though terrified, I had crawled from the corner over to the door to see what they would do to the little blond girl because I was sure that whatever was about to happen to her would happen to me next. Hiding as much of me as possible, only the right side of my face was exposed, and the door covered most of the rest of me.

The child had been told to stand near the bed while bright lights were shining on her. A man came beside her, lifted her up and sat her on the bed, with her feet hanging over the edge, as she was not nearly tall enough for her feet to touch the floor. He sat down beside her and unbuttoned her dress and pulled it over her shoulders leaving her naked except for a pair of cotton panties. The man stood up and left the girl who appeared to be terrified. Two other people came into the room and seemed to be arguing. Their arms were thrashing about as they screamed at each other.

As I was peering into the next room, I shifted my position just a little and in doing so, bumped into the door, making a tiny noise, which attracted the little girl's attention, and she turned her head toward the partially open door leading to the bedroom. For just a moment, her terrified eyes looked directly into my one exposed eye, and both of us knew the other was terrified for what was taking place. That image of her head turned slightly toward me was very similar to the look she gave me when she was sitting on the bed, and I was in the corner. It was the cameo image that had been slipping into my mind for months. Then, there was a cracking sound so loud that everything became silent in my ears, and I saw the child's left face and eye blow out of her head exploding red across the bed and against the wall. I felt the pellets fly into my head and take out my right eye and a portion of my brain, and I wailed in silence as the child lay quivering in her own blood while the lights continued to flood the room and a camera purred its recording of a death scene. The stick I thought I saw was not a stick. I described it to my therapist and he told me what I had seen was a sawed off shotgun.

My face had taken on the energy shock of the little girl whose eyes were looking directly into my right eye when she was shot, and that horrible shock exploded into mournful guilt that crashed into me like a tidal wave of bullets. I hated myself for being relieved when they came to get her and not me, and without knowing what I was doing, I tried to make it me, so that somehow she might live. But all I could do was carry her shocked pain and my guilt in the right side of my face and eye.

As the memories such as this one, were in the process of being exhumed, so often I cried out to God to make the memories stop and let me die. The guilt of the little children parts of me who were forced to observe or participate in ugly events had no image of themselves except one of total self-repulsion, and they had no feeling within themselves except for the feelings of the victim at the moment of death. Because, before this event, I was relieved that I had not been the one selected to go into the next room, I believed what happened to her was my fault.

Those parts of me who carried the shattering pain of the event had to endure the life-crushing pain all over again as I was remembering it. They were convinced that reconnecting to feeling the horrors of that whole experience would kill them...would kill me, would kill all of us. As a child, the shock, if felt in full force, would have very likely killed me. What my therapist and I had to do was to convince the children, who lived frozen, disconnected existences within me, each carrying but one piece of the event, that I was, now, strong enough to take in the totality and live. The truth is, there were times I was not really sure if I really was strong enough. But the only way I could know for sure was to open and "take the leap" into fully knowing what took place so long ago.

It was not just this horrible information that I had to acknowledge, feel, and release, but also, I had to contend with the parts of myself that my inner system created to hear nothing, see nothing, and feel nothing. They were the ones who were formed following whatever terrible thing happened, and their purpose was to have no memories of the events so I could move forward in my growing up. They existed to deny that anything bad ever happened. Without them, I am very sure I could not have lived through my childhood; yet, they wreaked havoc with my sanity all during the healing process. At times, the denying parts turned against the parts for which they were created to protect.

There seemed to be two groups of denying parts. One group really didn't know what happened because they were created after the events occurred, and these parts concluded that I was fully insane to believe that anything bad had ever happened to me. Then, there were denying parts that apparently did know, but didn't trust I was capable of knowing the truth. They were so effective that they decided it would be better for me to die than for the truth to be known. There were a number of occasions that other parts that wanted to live had to save me from those that would choose death over knowing.

After significantly intense therapy sessions, where information came forward, but without enough time to find understanding, forgiveness, and release, it was not uncommon for me to sit in my car for an hour or two in the parking lot, unable to drive. Later I might find myself driving in extremely dangerous patterns, more than one time with my eyes closed, or in some altered state, completely unaware of lanes, road signs, or other cars. These parts were responsible for internal messages that made going to sleep and never waking up sound like a viable alternative for the pain that seemed to increase beyond my capacity to handle it. And there were times these parts would imagine how much better things would be if I just drove my car into a cement buttress on the freeway. Aspects of my self that wanted to live and my essence, or what some call the Inner Self Helper (ISH), or Higher Self, helped me move through difficult times such as these.

***

In the mid 80s—the beginning years of the therapeutic response to people who experienced such extreme abuse as I had—there were no protocols for therapists to handle what was coming up for their clients. Up until that time, people with a great amount of psychic damage were either hospitalized, sometimes for the rest of their lives, or were drugged to keep them from harming themselves or others.

After Freud introduced psychoanalysis over 100 years ago, for those who could afford the extended, often 5-day a week treatment, the wounded person could enter analysis, but the accepted view was bad things such as molestation or rape didn't happen; the assumption was the child had sexual fantasies about the parent and that is what created the inner conflicts. It was easier to call somebody insane than to entertain the possibility that the person's symptoms were a very normal response to extremely bad experiences.

After federal funding for state-run mental hospitals ended and many long-term facilities were closed during the Reagan years, there were few places disturbed people could go. Those who didn't die or end up on the streets could turn to psychologists, mental health counselors, or other mental health professionals. However, therapists were generally left on their own to figure out what was the best thing to do for patients who experienced extreme symptoms.

By the 1980s, professionals who dealt with clients presenting with extreme trauma and abuse had come to believe that the recall of information that had been dissociated, along with the expression of whatever emotions were related to it, was enough to bring healing, and many continue to work with this model. However, my own work with myself, and with hundreds of clients over the years, has shown me that not only is recall and emotional release important, but also, discovering and releasing debilitating beliefs and meanings that were attached to the incident is critical to dissolving thought, behavior, and life patterns formed from the beliefs. And the final piece is to allow the dissociated part of the client to release the event, along with the time the event occurred and to enter the present of the adult self.

As I write this, now, all these years after that memory of the little girl in the blue dress entered my conscious awareness, I realize I had only done a partial process to free my child-self from that horrible event. There was no doubt that my body released a huge amount of stored energy that I had taken in from that horrific incident of my seeing the child shot and killed. After the memory came back, I no longer suffered the headache on the right side, nor did I have periods of blindness in my right eye when under stress. But, what remained behind my mask was the immense self-judgment for feeling relieved that the man had taken the other little girl, not me.

A side effect of that self-judgment and guilt was that I never liked competitions in which one wins and one looses, because should I win, I could not be happy for myself when my heart felt deep sadness for the one who lost. I have always rooted for the underdog, and felt immense sadness when the underdog remained in that position. But then, if the one who was not the underdog lost, I would feel so very sad for that one. There was no joy possible in victory. I have no doubt all of this is related to that incident so long ago. At this moment, I must take time from writing to be able to find my way through this…

***

An amazing thing happened as I typed the last statement about needing to work through the guilt and shame for feeling relieved that I was not the one taken into the next room and murdered. I looked up at my computer clock and noticed it was time for an East Coast client to call for a session. He was someone with whom I had been working, on and off, for the past couple of years. On top of struggling with cancer, he recently had a mild heart attack and was concerned with how the anxiety he was feeling around whether or not he would be accepted into an experimental drug trial for cancer might impact his heart.

As we worked with the anxiety, he was surprised that as much as he wanted to be selected for the trial, he felt badly that his being selected would mean that someone else would not have the chance that such a trial might offer. If he won, someone else would lose, and that felt so unfair to him. He couldn't find the way to defend his being selected over another person.

As he was talking, I saw an image of a person running in a race and winning. And then I noticed all the other runners; I shared with the client what I was seeing. The rules of competition tell us that there is only one winner, and essentially, all the others are losers. But this designation may be very far from the truth. Many of the runners may have never finished a race before and just finishing was winning for them. Others might have believed that they were nothing if they could not win. The pain of losing had the potential of breaking them open enough to find the place inside that held the lie that the only way they could be worthy would be if they won. Once cracked open, there would be a chance for them to discover the silliness of the lie that connected worth, value, and identity to winning. Those willing to see the truth can gain winning out of losing. And there may be many runners who simply enjoy the competition, the exertion, the experience of being in a race and being there is winning. Even though there would be just one person who finished first, there could be many who were able to win.

This man had spent his life being a caretaker of other people. He did all he knew how to make his parents happy, and failed because they were both committed to unhappiness. His biggest concern about his dying from cancer or another heart attack was that his wife would be unable to handle the loss and his sons might not be able to handle the stresses of their lives without him. He carried anxiety because one of his sons was getting a nasty divorce. He was concerned that the son might not be able to get through it all, alone. Another son had lost a job and felt so broken by the experience that he had not been able to enter the market to search for another job. He saw this son as fragile, vulnerable, and likely unable to make it through by himself.

Life struggles had made this man feel as if he was responsible to take care of everyone, which was a belief that traced back to his child-self who had concluded that the only way he could find happiness was to figure out how to make his family happy. I asked him to look beyond the struggles of everyone, both past and present, and to notice that within each of these persons was light, in which a beautiful, powerful, strong being existed. He was able to see the light underneath all the conflicts and struggles of everyone, including himself.

The story of the butterfly came to mind, so I told him about a child who watched the movements of a cocoon and knew from his science class that a butterfly was about to emerge. He saw how hard the tiny creature was struggling, and carefully pulled the cocoon apart to set the butterfly free. The beautiful creature fell out of the cocoon onto the child's hand but was unable to fly. What the child didn't realize was that the exertion to free itself is what gave strength to the wings so this little being could fly out into the world. If we are disconnected from our true selves, all the work we go through can help us find out who we really are, so we can learn how to fly in our own lives, too. One son has the opportunity to learn he is not a divorced man, or any of the identifiers this condition could cause him to believe about himself. And the other son has the chance to know he is not an unemployed man, along with all the meanings attached to that condition. Both sons are amazing beings learning about themselves and in the process are experiencing struggles that hold the potential to teach them so much if they are willing to learn.

His gift to them would be for him to learn that he is not his heart attack or his cancer, that he is not one who is responsible for the struggles of everyone else. He could learn that inside him is the amazing, unique light of his essence. From that place there is no struggle, but only his being. Once he experiences who he is, he can look past the troubles of those around him and see who they are deep inside them. His ability to see who they really are can give them the opportunity to see who they, themselves, really are, too.

I reminded him that he is a man who is experiencing cancer and a heart problem and through the experience he can open to being more and more of his true self. His anxiety about whether or not he would

201

be accepted into the trial and if accepted, his anxiety that he took the place of someone else was the result of belief in a lie. If he is selected, there is something his soul can learn from the experience, and for those not selected, there is something their souls can learn…and all is good. If he is not selected, he will be able to learn something that the universe has made possible for him to learn from this experience. From this view, there are no winners and losers. Everyone is moving along a path of self-actualization, self-knowing, and connection to essence, however they choose to do this.

When he first spoke of his son, who was involved in a very difficult divorce, my client told me that he had been feeling a great amount of anxiety about it all, and he just hoped the young man would get through it. His concern about the other son was that he might not be able to get it together because he was so fragile. His concern for those not selected for the trial was that they wouldn't make it, and he was afraid that if he died, his wife wouldn't make it. Near the end of the session, I asked him to notice that when we are drawn into others' struggles, we no longer see their amazing essences, but only see the struggle and are drawn in to believe an untruth. We enter their struggle because it matches our own. In fact, he was concerned that he wouldn't make it, that he was fragile and might not be able to get it together…and that if he was not selected that would mean that he would lose.

I asked if he would be willing to take his focus off the struggles, the worries, the anxieties, and the fears of what might happen to him and to the others, and experience his true essence and notice that when he is in that space, his body is able to relax. And the amazing gift of relaxation is healing energies are promoted when the body is free of tension. Anxiety produces the very thing that inhibits healing. By focusing on what he fears, he produces the anxiety that creates what he fears because fear energy creates contraction and tension, which blocks an environment of healing. If he would be willing to embrace what he is experiencing in the moment as a gift from his soul to know his true essence, whatever the outcome of his illnesses would be healing.

In a matter of one hour, a man who had been living with such intense anxiety stated that he felt so relieved, not just about his family, but also, about the trial, as well. He could see that selection or non-selection could be winning for all persons involved, if everyone, including himself, allowed it to be. He could also see that he was only responsible for his own response, and all the others were responsible for themselves. The ultimate truth is he could not create what they needed to heal. Only they could create their own deep relaxation.

***

In working with the client, I discovered my answer for the child who still held the profound guilt for having not been chosen where *not being chosen* was interpreted as winning. It was *not* my child-self's wish that the other child be selected or that the she die. It was my wish that I not be selected, which is a very different thing. If my truest wish had been fulfilled, neither she nor I would have been taken into the other room and she would not have died. My wish for both of us was to live. I was not responsible for what the perverted people, who decided to create the horror, had done. And I have no idea what the soul of that other little girl was working through in that very short lifetime.

My child-self let me know that she had something she needed to say to the soul of the murdered child. I felt her move from the bedroom, through the doorway and into the room where the child lay on the bed. She touched the empty side of the child's face and told the little girl that those mean people didn't have the power to blow away part of her. She explained that even when a leaf has had one of its sides cut off, the energy pattern of the leaf remains whole and special cameras that take pictures of the energy of objects show the leaf as still being whole. I had learned this in one of my courses related to fractals in graduate school, and my child self was sharing this information with the other child. The truth is that the little girl is still whole and she can take her focus off what happened in three-dimensional reality and can feel her wholeness wherever she is in the universe. She will always be able to see out of both eyes…they couldn't steal that away from her if she allowed herself to focus on her energy body instead of the shotgun blast.

My child-self took a journey with the little blond girl and taught her so many things she had learned about non-local consciousness, other realities, energy, healing, eternal life, and much more. She explained that what we focus on is what we create…so if the little girl focuses on having an eye missing, she will likely create whatever meanings she attached to that experience in future lifetimes until she decides to focus on who she is instead of what happened to her.

My child-self returned to me, having released the guilt she carried, that I carried, nearly my entire life for having lived while the other little girl died. I know that so many people who survive awful events feel that same kind of guilt when others didn't survive. People who are capable of thriving in their lives might, also, feel guilt for thriving, for experiencing good lives when so many others are suffering, and unconsciously prevent themselves from fully living in the abundance of joy, beauty, wonder, and flow in all the levels of their being.

Behind our masks might be guilt for things we did for which we had responsibility but have not, yet, taken it; however, there, also, is a likelihood that behind our masks is guilt for the things that we did not create and were not our responsibility, but we believed were ours.

***

I reflected back on what I had written on page 199 from the point where I had to take a break to consider the guilt that I had carried most of my life…but what I didn't realize until I read back over what I had written about supporting the underdog was that my heart broke for the ones who I interpreted as having lost, because I was still heart broken, not just for others, such as the little girl, but also for what I believed I had lost. I realize that I am still grieving for having lost so much of my childhood. Like the metaphor of the ice cream cone, much of my life had fallen on the ground and melted, only I never got to taste it…And maybe even worse, I never got to know what I really did miss, I just know that I did. In this moment I am feeling extremely deep sadness, and tears are streaming down my cheeks. I am feeling that what I lost, I can never, ever get back…it is gone forever.

***

A few hours ago, a dear friend called and we were talking about what was happening in each other's lives. She said she thought she was 95% happy and I responded by saying that I knew that was not at all true for me. I felt content most of the time, but not happy. The hummingbirds had returned two days earlier, and I commented that I was aware how happy that had made me feel. And I recalled the late summer and fall of 2006, when I drove across the country from the Southeast to the Northwest with Jenny, how many times I was filled with such happiness with the great beauty in nature that abounded around us. So often, I pulled the car over to look at some magnificent scene and exclaimed to my little dog how lucky we were to be able to be alive to see all this. During that trip, going off somewhere without knowing where that somewhere would be, driving and experiencing what was in front of us, I was so filled with happiness and joy.

Not until this very moment did I realize how much of that joy I have not accessed. And, there are so many wonderful experiences that could touch the joy inside me, if I would just open to let myself feel the pleasure they offer. I know that I am the one who has chosen not to open to joy. In this very moment I realize I have believed in *everything has been lost* and lived it.

Now, I need to do for myself what I suggested that the loving parent could do for the little child whose ice cream fell on the ground and melted. I am feeling so much like that little child right now…looking at the strawberry mess and not seeing anything else but what was taken away from me.

***

At first, my thinking-self reasoned with my-broken-hearted-self trying to convince her to look at today and all the future days to let them be happy and let go of wasting any more time in sadness for what I lost, but that didn't work. It was coming from my head, and was not connected to the feelings where this part of me now is experiencing life. That is a thinking response, and *thinking cannot help feeling to feel better.* I was actually sounding like my mother when she encouraged me to forget the past and look to the future, and that never worked, either.

Then I heard the wise and powerful voice of my dear friend, Oregon David. Years ago, he and I began writing a book together on the process of releasing, but both of us had so much that we, ourselves, hadn't released that we didn't finish the book. But despite the fact that it has not, yet, been finished, the conversations we had around it were meaningful. David's words came back to me, reminding me that if we don't like the universe we are in, the only way we can move beyond what we don't like is to accept where we are and embrace it. Otherwise some part of us is denying the truth of where we are, which, also, denies the part of us that lives in the place we have denied. We cannot take a part of ourselves that we deny somewhere else. That part remains in what exists in the present universe, while we, also, remain stuck there, longing to be in another universe. Based on the many hours we discussed this topic, I knew I needed to begin by acknowledging the loss that happened because of the childhood I experienced.

***

I connected with the Sandy who experienced her life as one of loss. When I allowed myself to open to her, my heart began to feel the loss, and tears I had been unable to access for decades began to flow. Through the sobbing and the tears, I acknowledged that I did lose so very much. I lost knowing my connection with my body and feeling the joy of being in it. I lost a lifetime of trusting feeling loved. I lost having parents to protect me and having a family I could turn to when I was afraid or not sure what to do. I lost knowing that I would always have a place where I could feel safe if the world felt unsafe. I lost the joy of my sexuality and the excitement of my first time. I lost feeling strong and confident in myself and lost knowing my own mind. I lost having a marriage filled with love and sharing each others lives into old age, and I lost having children and grandchildren who would come home and throw their arms around me and let me know I am loved forever. My arms never held my infants and they grieved the loss. My breasts never suckled any tiny baby, and I never got to hear my child's first words, or watch those first steps.

And what the traumas of my childhood did not take from me, I took from myself because I lost the ability to trust life. All of this fell to the ground and melted at my feet, and from the time I was so very little until now, I had no power to take back or transform what I lost.

I have been living in a world of loss and grieving that loss without even knowing that has been what I've done. Every loss, every line I have written about loss is opening my heart to a deeply buried grief… and I can't stop the tears. I am not just my child-self, I am the one that is writing in this moment and I am filled with grief for all the irretrievable losses.

As my heart is mourning, I feel the arms of future Sandy embracing me and simply providing space for me to cry. I am curled up in her arms, crying like a little child clinging to her mother…grieving for what can never be hers.

I let myself cry for a long time, as the little child, but I knew I was my adult-self, crying for the many years that were wasted from loss. I don't recall every crying like this before…it was pure mourning, maybe like Jesus cried when he sat outside the grave of his dear friend Lazarus because he had not been there to do anything when his friend went through his death alone. I grieved because no matter what I visualized and no matter how much healing I could create, I couldn't give myself a happy childhood, or bring me back to being 21 in a loving marriage; I couldn't give myself motherhood, holding my infant in my arms and I couldn't give myself a partner that grew from youth to middle age to being old with me. I could never give to my love the card I bought for him when I was 22, that said *grow old with me, the best is yet to be*. There was no reason to take the card out any more, like I did each year to look at it and put it away hoping that the next year might be the year he would understand it. That young woman's wish is forever gone. My strawberry ice cream had fallen in the dirt and I could never get it back.

***

Something unexplainable just happened! While in the center of the agonizingly painful grieving all that I had lost, I looked outside my window and saw the branches of the mountain pine trees ride the waves of a gust of wind, and it looked as if the wind and the branches were dancing with each other. Then several hummingbirds hovered above the feeders and landed with such elegance that my heart opened to feel the silent music of all that was playing out in front of me.

My attention shifted from the grieving to the beauty of the world outside my window, not because I became distracted from my broken heart, but because my heart had completed its grieving for the losses in my life and opened to what is in my life in this moment. I looked around at the golden pine walls of my tiny carriage house that provide a cozy space for me, and felt the embrace of this place that I found "by accident" when I drove from Florida without knowing where I was going. I took in the aroma of soup I had begun to make earlier and felt the nurturing that my morning self was giving to my afternoon self. I could feel my heart smile.

For the first time since I started writing this trilogy, I feel deeply happy about sharing what I have learned with others, with you, in whatever ways open for me. Leaving the mountain no longer seems like such a risky thought. I know there is a whole world out there that is filled with *"Jenny and Sandy moments"* when we can take in the beauty of wherever we are and I can tell my little dog how lucky we are to be alive. In this moment I invite little Sandy who was metaphorically represented by the boy whose ice cream fell to the ground, to release her focus on what she has lost and join me in seeing what we have found together on this beautiful day that I grieved and the wind danced with the tree branches. My child-self is able to see the silver lining instead of being swallowed up by the darkness. She is able to see that her delight is not in the things that she has lost, just as the little boy's delight was not in the ice cream cone, but in his own inner feelings. The "lost things" were only objects, and they stimulated thoughts about those objects in the three-dimensional world upon which the little girl and the little boy focused when they first opened to delight. In fact, the delight is and always has been inside them.

When I was working with the energies around the child who had been shot, my child-self told the little girl that she could experience her wholeness if she would focus on who she really is instead of what happened to her, but I still had that lesson to learn, myself. What I had to do was open to the feelings of the loss instead of trying to repress them—because repression requires constant focus on what we want to avoid—and then allow the natural process to take place that allows the feelings to move through and be released instead of being trapped inside, eating away at our experience of life.

I know something very important is in process. It will be interesting to see where all this leads.

Writing this chapter has opened my eyes to something I knew in my head, and needed to embrace in my heart: it is okay for me to win, and it is okay for me to express grieving. Writing about grief helped me better understand the reason I had such a difficult time in Yoga. My body not only held the pain of the wounding from my childhood, it held the grieving for the losses that grew out of the wounding, as well. I discovered that when I stopped resisting the grief that was in me and embraced it, I could finally bring healing to it, which, in turn, allowed me to embrace all the goodness I have in my life.

***

When I completed writing the previous section, another image came into my mind of the furniture that I "sold" when I left Florida. Though my head had made the decision to let the furniture go my heart had not been included. Now I can see what my heart felt, not only grieving for the loss of the furniture, but anger for feeling as if my mind completely dismissed what my heart held as important. This was a parallel to my mind trying to tell my heart to stop wasting any more of my life and just look at the future and all I could have in it, without recognizing the need to meet my heart where it was, honoring what it was feeling before trying to lead it to all I could experience in the present and future. My heart had an important story to tell about the meaning of the loss of that furniture, and the story had to be expressed.

***

When Jake and I got married, I had absolutely no money of my own. I had just graduated from college with student loans, and had nothing in the bank. He rented us an apartment on Capitol Hill in the city. It was in a new building and was the most beautiful place I could have imagined. My family was much lower on the economic ladder than his, and I felt as if I was the lowly Cinderella who had married her prince and was taken off to live in a castle. For a couple of weeks before we were married, each day I gathered up the wedding presents that came to my parents house, and carried them via city bus to the apartment, and carefully put everything away in their proper places. All of the lovely gifts we had received completely supplied our home with everything for the bathroom, bedroom, and kitchen, so we would want for nothing.

We had not lived together before we were married, and our wedding night was going to be the first time we were really together; our coming together to make love for the very first time would be in our new home with everything brand new. However, after the ceremony, when we went to the apartment, I found that he and his friends had had a bachelor party the night before and had trashed what was supposed to be our place. The sink was filled with dirty dishes, which were our wedding gifts, and the bed I had so carefully prepared for our first night together was slept in and left unmade. The guys must have showered because they left towels on the bathroom floor. The towels were, also, brand new wedding presents, now no longer new. And the living room had take-out and pizza cartons scattered around that I had to clean up before our guests arrived. Whatever I had visualized in my mind about a place of our own was lost. It was as if all the first times were stolen from me. I held in the pain and said nothing.

Jake made the decisions about where we would live from that time on, and he chose the furnishings. It wasn't that he negated what I wanted; I never voiced an opinion. All that was accumulated in our marriage, I believed was his. Even in our 3600 square foot house, that we owned much later, there was not a single room that was mine. When I separated from Jake in 1987 and began looking for a place to live, the only places I believed I could afford were tiny studio apartments in the parts of town that I would never be able to feel safe. I didn't believe I had the right to ask for anything that was his. In the end, the only way I was able to move into a comfortable one-bedroom apartment in a good suburban neighborhood was that my husband agreed to pay my rent and he purchased my furnishings. They were beautiful, but I didn't feel they were really mine, despite the fact that I picked them out.

In late 1989, I sold almost everything and moved to China in early 1990, where I lived for nearly two years in a tiny space in a cement building with minimal furnishings supplied by the university where I taught. There was no real shower, and the air conditioner/heater couldn't be on without blowing the power for the entire 6-story building. The living space was better than most of my Chinese peers and many times better than the students who lived on campus, eight to a room, which was much smaller than my 3 room place. But compared to American standards, my living conditions were very, very low. And nothing in my living space was mine.

When I returned to the states and moved to Florida, I rented a room and bought furniture from a second hand store, and later, I moved into a single bedroom apartment, sparsely filled with the cheapest possible furniture for my living room and bedroom.

Finally, as the 21st century was opening, my practice had flourished and I had earned enough money to buy a household of truly fine furniture for a beautiful new apartment with cathedral ceilings and huge windows that overlooked a beautiful lagoon pond surrounded by mangrove forests and wildlife. I loved how I felt in my place. It was decorated in a way that reflected me. Even though it was an apartment, it felt like it was truly mine, a feeling I had for the first time in my life.

For the many years I lived in Florida, I knew that I would be leaving for some unknown destination, but I didn't know when or where. And then, one morning in the spring of 2006 I woke with an intuitive knowing that this was the time to leave though I had no idea where I was to go. So I began preparing to leave what had become my home, including getting rid of my beautiful furniture.

As I look back on that time, I now see that my heart had not let go of the furniture because of the meanings I had attached to it. I had a king sized bed that was all mine with a wonderful firm mattress, so wonderfully comfortable, unlike any I had ever owned. The bed was part of a matching bedroom suite, something I had never owned before, either. It was a beautiful ivory colored marble with gold accessories that looked so elegant. The living room furniture was overstuffed ivory colored leather. The balcony off the living room looked over the lagoon, as did the bedroom and den. I had a huge desk system made of natural wood, surrounded by bookshelves for my many hundreds of volumes. In that beautiful den, I had everything I needed to study and write and still look out the window to watch wildlife around the lagoon.

For the first time in my life, I had a home where I knew I belonged filled with furnishings that reflected me, and my heart was happy. I attached my feelings of happiness, my newfound financial stability and freedom, my sense of safety, my personal choice and expression of myself to that furniture, and there was an underlying belief that if I let it go, I would never be able to have anything so very beautiful that represented all those feelings again. Deep inside me, I believed you only get one chance at anything, and if you lose whatever that was, you will never have a second chance.

While my head was looking at the economics of keeping or selling the furniture, my heart was feeling a loss of everything that furniture had come to mean to me. My heart was grieving the loss of so much that mattered to me and was very angry at my mind for so callously making a money decision that demeaned my heart's sense of value. There was no amount of money the purchaser could have offered that would have made my heart feel comforted, unless it could have been the full amount I had spent on it, to let me know that I could buy replacements later. But even then, because styles change, I could never buy exactly what I had to give up. And $600 wouldn't even begin to come close to buying even one piece of what my heart had lost. The war between my heart and head resulted in an imbalanced body that was unable to work together in guiding the flatbed cart down the hallway of the storage unit. My muscles contracted in rage for what had been "stolen" from me, and ripped apart in pain when I jerked the cart back, a pain I felt for the next 33 months.

Now, as I am writing these words, I can let my heart know that the meanings I had placed on the furniture were not in the furniture, they were in me. I can always recreate an outer representation of those inner meanings of my financial stability, my freedom, safety, choice, and expression. I can thank the furniture that I used to have for being a part of all that I opened to feel during those years it was in my life. And in thanking it for its contribution to my environment, I can release the furniture to find its way to someone else's home to reflect whatever they need. I can find new furniture someday in the future when I am ready to send roots down someplace in this world. I am as capable, now as I was then, in creating what I want and even more.

As I write this, I am aware that there are still little places inside that do not trust that I can do all that most of me knows that I can. When the right time comes, I will work with those energies, and healing can come to the parts of me that still have not learned to trust…all in its time.

***

There is something almost mystical about how this chapter has unfolded. It wrote itself and I simply followed along. When I was finally ready to face the guilt I had carried since I was a small child, I was able to grieve the losses I experienced in my life that were formed because of my belief in loss. And once released, I was finally free to open to the goodness that surrounds and embraces me. I know that experiences and meanings related to what I wish for in the world are in me; I cannot lose them. And when I am ready, I will feel the truth of what I write in my body, as well.

Reflections

Fear coupled with guilt or shame can cause you to become vulnerable and can open you up to take on energy and beliefs that are not your own. But, also, shock, sadness, empathy, genuine caring, and love can cause you to take what is not yours to take, as well. When you take on other's beliefs or energies, your own body, mind, heart, and spirit can be affected in ways that you may not even fathom. If you realize that all participants in an event drew the event to them, you can discover how to be responsible only for what you created, and release any responsibility for what you did not create. You can empathize and care with love, without taking on the pain-filled energy.

If someone you love suffers, it is not unusual to try to take on their suffering to make it easier for your loved one, but what happens by taking what is not yours, you deplete your own energy and are in less a position to be able to support them in dealing with what they are experiencing. And, your taking on the suffering does not make suffering go away from the one you love. This might be a good time to allow yourself to look through your life to see what you may have taken on that does not belong to you and release what needs to be released, or give back what needs to be returned.

Let yourself experience whatever dark or negative emotions you feel. Be with those emotions and honor the expression of them. Allow yourself to discover what new worlds can open up for you when you let go of denying where you are, acknowledge what it feels like to be where you are, and let the expression of your feelings take you to a fulfilling life wherever you would prefer to be.

Chapter Thirteen
THE BOAT

When we take responsibility for what is not ours, we disconnect from three significant responsibilities that do belong to us. One is caretaking of ourselves with love; the second is taking responsibility for what we have created, and the third is releasing responsibility for what we did not create.

Back in the mid 90s, I had accepted an invitation from a time-share company to get a rental car, drive from Clearwater to Miami, and catch a cruise ship that would take a friend and me to the Bahamas for a 3-day vacation, which included looking at a presentation about time-shares. But the day I arrived, at the Miami hotel, and began unloading the rental car, the trunk hood collapsed on my head, knocked me to the ground, and gave me a concussion. The headache from the impact lasted the entire trip and ruined my vacation, as well as cost me a couple thousand dollars in medical bills to determine the extent of the damage to my head, but the car rental company didn't want to pay for anything. I checked with a couple of local attorneys who basically told me that no one would be interested in representing me for such a small claim, so I called an attorney in Miami where the travel agency and car rental company had their home offices.

I was supposed to drive to Miami, again, but this time to meet with another attorney regarding the possibility of him taking on this mild head injury case. But I was extremely tired and was not looking forward to the 5-6-hour trip at night since the appointment was first thing in the morning. At the time, I didn't want to pay for a hotel bill after having paid the medical bills. I was sure I would get the same response from this new attorney as the others had given me.

As the departure time drew closer, I began to experience the feeling of silent, mournful cries choking my throat, and my head began to pound on the very top center with a very different pain than the one that came from the concussion. Both body-responses—the pounding headache and the choking feeling in my throat—were signals that something from childhood was about to emerge again.

I took my dog, Sara, for a walk the night before I was supposed to leave for Miami, to let her relieve herself, as well as to help me relieve the pounding headache, and during the walk, I knew I would cancel the appointment. As my feet rhythmically hit the pavement sending out soft tapping sounds into the silence of the night, I felt myself become six years old and my child-self turned the Clearwater street into a street in Seward. But instead of holding on to the leash, as my Lhasa tugged at me to walk faster, the tug on my hand was coming from a big hand, not a little dog.

My six-year-old-self was being forced to walk somewhere and my throat wanted to cry out that I didn't want to go where I was being taken. But I had long since learned that such expression was pointless and resulted in worse treatment.

When I was a child, it was not uncommon for me to be wakened in the night and taken to places where I had to do things or where things were done to me—unspeakable things that had to be hidden away because they were…well, unspeakable. To make the things go away from my conscious awareness, I hid them in the sound of a footstep or in the feel of moistness of the damp air of shadowed nights. I could hide the bad things in the movement of tired little legs forced to walk in the middle of the night or in the wallpaper or ceiling lights in the places I was taken. The similarities of that Florida night seemed to tell me that I had walked another street, so much like this one, long before.

For no apparent reason, a certain combination of sensations would send me back to another time and place and I would remember what had been hidden away decades before. It was not uncommon for one memory to be hidden in the same place as others. A number of memories were connected to my feet walking on the mud packed streets in the night, because so many bad things happened at night, and I was about to discover another one of those hiding places.

***

On that night in Clearwater, moist air, the sound of my footsteps, and the tugging at the leash connected to walking home after I had spent part of the night on a boat. Perhaps the memory was coming forward because I was about to take a trip to Miami that I didn't want to take to protect me from something that happened, which wasn't my fault, to try to get somebody to take responsibility for what was their fault. But I was sure they wouldn't, and all of that connected a boat in the present to one in and past.

I didn't know why I remembered the walk home, but not the walk to wherever I had been, or why that walk was a hiding place, but it simply was. The information coming forward from childhood was not particularly new. I had remembered the walk home some years before, which was connected to something terrible that happened on a boat, but the actual boat memory and what happened there had been hidden in the sound of engines and slapping waves that unexpectedly came back in the mid 1980's while on a boat trip with Jake.

***

My husband had been raised in the Northwest where water sports were a prominent part of his life. With the pride of a little boy excited about his new toy, Jake took me for a trip in the new sailboat he had purchased. But instead of feeling the excitement of sharing this magnificent experience with him, I found myself having to repress a growing panic that I could not explain. After that initial excursion, the inner turmoil made it harder and harder to remain calm with each trip. Over time, the sailboat was traded for a small cruiser and then for a large one. A more complete picture of what made being on the boat so difficult took several years and many more boat trips to come into focus.

In 1989, Jake and I were on the last cruise we were to take before our divorce. I was feeling the headache that always accompanied a period of confusion and dissociation when a past event was near the surface, but not, yet, fully remembered. I decided to go below deck to the master bedroom of our 42-foot cruiser to see if I could make the headache go away. I curled up on the king sized bed with a large soft pillow to try to push the feelings back down inside me. The feelings seemed to be powerful enough to make my head explode if I could not find a way to keep them repressed. I closed out the daylight and tried to turn off the throbbing sound of the engines that seemed to intensify with the increasing swells of the waters surrounding the San Juan Islands of the Pacific Northwest.

The pain in my head became unbearable and I felt a constriction in my throat, which seemed to be a part of an internal process to hold back the scream that lived in my throat. While my husband navigated the open seas of Puget Sound and Straits of Juan De Fuca that lead out to the Pacific Ocean, the rising and falling of the boat moving through the waves in the present put me into a deeper trance, and I slipped into the dark numbness of no feeling, no motion, and no sound. I had become my child-self on another boat in another time. My body was that of a small child in some past event, and I lost connection with Sandy of 1989.

It was so very dark, and I could feel the sound of engines throbbing in my bones. There was a horrible smell, a musty dead smell. I tried to figure out where I was. My little-child-self's hands began to search the floor around me in the darkness for some clue to explain this unexplainable blackness. I touched a piece of cloth that felt thick and fuzzy, and my hand continued to move, sculpting the shapes into my thoughts when I jerked back in terror; my hand touched the large cold fingers of someone. I wailed a silent cry into the darkness, curled myself up into a tiny ball, and pressed myself into the vibrations of the engines that hummed their pulses through the wall and into me.

The sounds of the engine kept me from hearing the sound of the trap door being opened, but a feeling of movement disturbed the air. I opened my eyes to see what made the air move. The light from the open hatch illuminated a portion of the floor near me and I saw the man whose hand I had touched earlier. He was very large, unshaven, and was wearing a plaid wool jacket and wrinkled brown wool pants. His stomach was large. I closed my eyes in terror. When I opened them again, he was gone and I was in the master suite of my husband's new boat.

It was much later during a therapy session that I remembered the men who climbed down the stepladder and dragged the large dead man across the floor of the old fishing boat hold, with great difficulty hauled him up the ladder, and disappeared into the darkness above. The hatch closed; the engine started up again and the next thing I was able to remember was walking home on the mud packed street. The smell of dead fish, the feel of a cold dead hand, the image of light beams cast on a wooden floor, were all locked into the vibration of the engines, and the sound of my feet walking home on the hard mud packed road. And my feet remembered while my throat choked back the howling cries of those parts of me who had experienced that horrible night and went into hiding behind my mask.

There was another dock memory that was hidden in the sounds of waves splashing against pilings the time I saw a dark skinned man hanging from a meat hook in the cabin of a wooden fishing boat. This memory was connected to another, which was hidden in a dim light bulb that swung back and forth on a frayed wire attached to the ceiling of the fishing boat cabin. It was in this horrible place that I was sold for sexual purposes to a fisherman who put me on his bunk and raped me while I lost myself by gazing into the filament of a dust covered light bulb.

After he was finished, he led me to a junk-filled table, cleared a spot, and sat me down on a rough wooden chair while he heated a can of tomato soup in what looked like a pan that would be used on a camp out. I watched him as he stirred the contents on a single burner stove and then served it to me as if I were his little child. I felt comforted as I ate the soup, spoonful by spoonful. Sometime later, my father came and got me. He walked me home, holding my hand, in the coolness of the shadowed night while my footsteps tapped a rhythm on the mud packed street, which led from the docks to my house on Sixth Avenue.

Much later, I deducted from pieces of other information, that I couldn't remember walking to the fishing boat because my father had carried me there. Based on how I was feeling, I must have been given some kind of a sedative and was beginning to come out of the sedated state, as I was being carried across a narrow wooden dock. I remember that incident from the dizzy, fuzzy images that came back to me of being carried aboard a boat. I was aware of the sounds of waves splashing against the pilings and could see the wooden slats and the black water reflecting lights from the boat, but everything seemed to be swirling and unclear. Once on the boat, my eyes came in and out of focus, but most of the time they were closed. I had been placed on a coil of ropes and was seeing everything fuzzy in those moments my eyes could open.

A shaft of light, coming from a pole, lit a portion of the boat deck, and I was aware that there were several men standing together. They turned to face another man who was walking backward toward the boat rail. I felt very sick in my stomach and wanted to run, but my legs wouldn't work; even if I could run, there was no place to go. There was scuffling and fighting and one of the men from the group took out a curved knife and slashed the throat of the man that was facing me. I could feel the pain of the blade in my throat as I watched in shock. And then the group of men dumped the man, whose throat had been cut, over the edge. I heard the splash. Panic filled me as I imagined the man struggling in the water; I wanted to jump in and save him, but I was too terrified. I was frozen in fear and when the men turned toward the ropes, I pretended to be asleep.

My father left me there, and after a while one of the men took me to the cabin where I went into the dusty light bulb and afterward ate tomato soup.

It wasn't until all of the puzzle pieces came together that I realized how getting hit on the head with the trunk lid created the dizzy feelings similar to those I felt when I was being carried onto the boat. And in the mid 90s, after my head received the blow, I was about to go onto a cruise ship that connected to the experiences on the boat when I was little. In my adult-life experience in Miami, I knew the car rental company was to blame for what happened to me, and did all it could to keep from taking responsibility. But I was unable to access my anger to demand they pay for my losses due to their faulty car, because someplace inside me, I thought it was my fault for having accepted their invitation for the "vacation package." I realized that deep inside me, my little-girl self believed she was responsible for the death of the man who was thrown overboard because she was too terrified to run to the rail and jump over to save him. The truth is that she was incapable of running, much less jumping over the rail, and even if she could have run and jumped into the water, she could not have saved a man from drowning, much less one whose throat was slit. And as the adult, I couldn't have known that the spring in the trunk was faulty causing the lid to crash onto my head, but I felt like somehow, it was my fault.

From the time I was a small child I have been taking responsibility for what was not my responsibility and it was time to stop! As I got older, I became so concerned when my parents fought; I tried to do whatever I could to say the right things to make them stop fighting. A belief that had been deeply embedded in me was that if people fight, someone will lose control and another person will die, so I had to make people stop fighting with each other by becoming the family peace-maker. I often failed to create peace.

***

When I was in my early teens, two of my sisters had gotten entangled in a nasty verbal fight. It was too painful to stay and felt too dangerous to try to intervene so I left the upstairs and went down to the living room. My mother asked me what was going on, and I told her that my sisters were fighting because the younger of the two had taken my older sister's posters off the wall while cleaning their mutually shared room. My mother got that look on her face, which, over the years, I had learned to know meant terrible things were about to happen. She stormed upstairs and I followed, perhaps to see if I could intervene and make everything go back to being peaceful.

But when my mother entered the bedroom that my sisters shared, she must not have liked the reason the younger one gave her for what she had done. My mother pulled off her belt and began whipping

221

with a fierceness that looked like she was going to kill my sister, who after the first few slashes, had ended up on the floor in the corner of the room trying to protect her torso and face with her bare arms and legs. The belt continued to burn welts into my sister's flesh until my father entered the room, overpowered my mother, and took the belt away, and then, the beating stopped. My sister lay silently on the floor covered in angry looking welts. I had been standing in a frozen position near the doorway, and then I began to sob uncontrollably. I believed it was my fault that my sister had been beaten, and my fault that I hadn't stopped my mother. It was my fault, I believed, because I was the one who answered my mother's question that sent her into the rage. On a subtle level, I knew I had "tattled" because I was upset with the fighting and wanted someone to stop it, but I didn't want it stopped with such viciousness.

***

In retrospect, it is clear to me that I was not to blame for the insanity that filled our house that day. Whatever made my mother go off like that was inside her; I didn't cause it. No matter what or how I had answered her question, my mother was primed to attack my sister. This sibling was the only one who challenged my parents' rules and followed her own mind from the time she was a tiny child; early on, she saw our parents as fallible and trusted her own decisions over theirs.

By the time she got to high school, this independent sister decided to wear makeup despite my parents' order that she not wear it, applying makeup in the girls' restroom before school and washing it off before going home. But they knew she continually disobeyed them. Though my mother was a redhead and my sister was blond, both had fair skin, white eyelashes and white brows. As I mentioned earlier, my mother believed she, herself, was ugly and was devastated by that comment her father made to her when she was a teen, getting ready to go out with friends. My grandfather told my mother that she would do well to put on makeup to make herself look as good as possible, considering what she had to work with. He insinuated that without it she just was not attractive. My mother was so filled with pain and rage she swore she would never wear makeup. And apparently that defiant decision to not wear makeup filtered down to her daughters as a rule that had to be obeyed.

Despite her light facial hair, my sister was stunningly beautiful. She had white porcelain skin, golden blond hair, and the figure of a movie star that attracted most all the boys in school. Because my sister was flirty and enjoyed the attention she received, my parents believed she was sexually active though she was not. With my mother's deeply negative attitude about makeup and sex, and her knowing, without choosing to know, that my father was sexually abusing her daughters, I would not be the least bit surprised if she blamed my sister, as she had blamed me, for whatever my father was doing because this independent daughter wore makeup and her body was beautiful.

There are myriad possibilities of what was going on in my mother's head when she pulled out the belt and began the vicious whipping of my sister, all of which had nothing to do with me, or for that matter, had nothing to do with my sister. I would not be surprised if the part of my mother who pulled out the belt and began whipping, was the little girl whose ringlet curls had been steamed out of her hair and because of that was whipped by her father. The rage she must have felt while sitting on that piano bench at her recital likely contributed to the whipping energy that inflicted pain on my sister. My response was another example of my pattern of taking responsibility for something that I had not caused, and it was one more proof my child-self held of how getting angry is dangerous, because it can lead to vicious beatings, or worse.

***

From the experience on the boat, when the group of angry men slashed the throat of the other man, and other experiences I have shared previously and will share later, I had taken into my internal world, the belief that getting angry was dangerous because it could lead to someone dying, and that it was my responsibility to stop fighting as the way to prevent someone's death. I can now see that this combination of fear in the face of anger and taking responsibility for what was not mine to take was the cause of my not taking responsibility for myself by defending me early on in dating and in my marriage when Jake's disrespectful behaviors first started, and much later, by not demanding that a car company take responsibility for their mal-functioning car to be rented out to customers where it could hurt them.

In all of our years together, my husband and I never got into an angry argument or fight, not because we didn't have differences or reasons to argue, because of this deep unconscious pattern. My unwillingness to defend myself against Jake's unkind treatment contributed to the waning of love I felt for him. On some level, not taking responsibility for my own wellbeing, and not defending myself was one of the many factors that actually caused our marriage to die. Fighting, especially if it could have been fair fighting, might have allowed our marriage to live and grow into something much better.

As difficult as it is for me to admit this, I can accept the possibility that if given the right combination of circumstances, I might have done my version of pulling out a belt and whipping somebody just as my mother did. Repressed anger, not expressed about what is really happening can explode in uncontrollable attacks on an undeserving person, like my mother whipping my sister. As much as I was committed to non-anger, I was capable of attacking, even if the attacking was energetic, and the "somebody" I could have attacked was my own self. Certainly, the *hoodie* parts of me that attacked the cells in my vulva creating cancer are examples of myself attacking me. Because they held my feminine-self responsible for my having been raped when I was a child, these cells felt justified in the attack. And, the angry masculine part of me, who hated my father, and turned that anger on me, resulted in anal bleeding. This was visible when that part of me metaphorically rammed everything in sight with the forklift prong spurred on by deeply angry energy in me and rooted in energy patterns similar to my mother's attack on my sister, the rapes from my father, and the vicious killings I saw when I was a child.

***

Over the years, I have worked with many clients who told me they were so filled with anger they could have killed their husbands, their wives, their children or someone else if they had had a weapon in their hands at the time. Rage has a way of reconnecting us with *out of control tantrum energy*, which is age appropriate for a two-year-old child who lacks language and communication skills. However, this kind of rage is dangerous when expressed in an adult with a fully-grown body capable of maiming or killing. And, unfortunately, too many people express this *out of control energy* by attacking others…or themselves.

When parents who were abusive or non-nurturing to their children grow old, it is not uncommon for the adult to turn on their parents. Children who suffered years of abuse in their childhoods, too afraid to challenge their parents long before, and now are in the position of power, might feel justified in giving back some of what they received. My felt sense is that just as child abuse is not uncommon, so, too, elder abuse is not uncommon, though we prefer to believe that both are rare. Children neglected may become neglectful of the needs of the old person they have come to hate for a lifetime of unspoken hurts or angers. Even if they deny that they are angry or deny they neglect the elderly person's needs, the care they give to the older people can be done with obligation and disconnection instead of love.

Like pedophiles being attracted to jobs where there are children, I believe raging adults, who repressed anger toward their parents when they were children, can be attracted to jobs where they can reign over parents, even if they are someone else's parents in nursing homes. This may account for the generally known but unaddressed elder-abuse in elder care facilities. Certainly, this is not a statement that all, or even most people in these types of jobs abuse; it suggests that the jobs represent a potential opportunity for abuse. Our responsibility is to become conscious of anything that we are doing that is abusive, or of anything that is being done to us, as well as those around us, and stop the abuse by communicating what is happening and not accept such treatment being meted out on yourself or others.

If there is something that causes us to be angry with another, it is our responsibility to express our feelings in a healthy, productive way and to release taking responsibility for what we have not created. Once we verbalize what is going on inside us, we can discern what is and what is not our responsibility. We can choose to offer support and love to others in a way that is loving and supportive of ourselves. This is so different from taking responsibility for something that is not ours by disconnecting from self-responsibility.

When I did past-life work that helped me trace the energies that were connected to what happened to me in my childhood, I was not saying I was responsible for what happened to my child-self. The abusers who chose to kick, rape, terrify, and do all manner of evil to little Sandy are responsible for what they did to her, which was neither her fault, nor my fault. Even elder citizens who were abusive to their children decades earlier are not responsible for the abuse they receive at the hands of those children when they are old. Those parents are responsible for what they did, and the grown children are responsible for they do. There is not an acceptable link between the two abuses that exonerates the actions of adult children who abuse. And what I may have done in some past life does not exonerate those who abused my little girl-self in this life. Retribution is destructive to the soul of those who seek it and is never justifiable.

My responsibility regarding my past life self's abusive behavior is to recognize and release the energy patterns that created the behavior, to forgive myself, and ask for forgiveness for past lifetime actions that may have stimulated the abusers to enact retribution in this lifetime. But their decision to carry on the abuse was their responsibility. If there were a court that had jurisdiction to imprison us for crimes committed, not just in this life but through all our incarnations, for actual physical abuses, as well as for energy crimes committed through negative thoughts against the energy bodies of others, there would be no one to guard the prisoners because we would all be incarcerated. Retribution does not heal, nor does it stop the patterns that create the harm. Harm can end when the patterns are released.

What I finally was able to see through this process was that I had taken on a belief pattern that I was powerless to stop the terrible things happening around me, but was still responsible for what had happened. I, also, believed when things got too difficult, I could just go away, and when I came back, the bad things would no longer be there and I didn't have to figure out what to do with them. This dissociative behavior, though it allowed me to survive my childhood, is what caused me to avoid dealing with problems that I was too afraid to confront so many times in my adult life. By the time I was forced to deal with them, they were usually too far along the road to destruction to salvage what might have been saved had I dealt with those problems earlier. And, another important lesson I have learned is that I couldn't have confronted and dealt with the problems in an effective way when I was a child or even later in my relationship with Jake because I hadn't, yet, had the experiences created by the patterns that finally cracked me open, which allowed me learn to deal with confrontation in a healthy way. Fortunately, life is a learning process.

Reflections

Whenever you take responsibility for something that is not yours to take, you diminish not only yourself, but the other, as well. The message within this act is that you are more powerful and the other is less powerful, and that's not true. When you don't take responsibility for what you have created, you prevent yourself from learning from your actions and the likelihood is you will continue to experience whatever it is that you neglected to own. The result of taking what is not yours or not taking what is yours is the diminishing of yourself and of the other, which constitutes the creation of the codependent triangle as a pattern in your relationships. And, codependency does not foster love; it fosters control.

Let yourself look at your relationships to see how much you need to control the thoughts, actions, and feelings of the other, or how much the other tries to control yours. Remember that control is never about love, even when you try to exert control to try to make things better. If you've taken responsibility for what is not yours to take, release it. If you have not taken responsibility for something you've created, accept your responsibility. Ask forgiveness of yourself if you took what didn't belong to you and ask for forgiveness from others if you did not take responsibility for what was yours to take. And then, stop the behaviors.

Though what happened on a number of boats in my childhood, and what happened to the little girl that I wrote about in chapter twelve, as well as the murder of the Eskimo were really horrible experiences with life-altering aftereffects, they were not the *worst of the worst*. Getting myself to write about that experience was very much a part of that pattern of dissociation that hopes everything that is difficult or seems unsolvable would be gone when I open my eyes. Notice if you find ways to avoid facing difficult situations, as well. If you do, ask yourself why you do this, and listen for the answer.

Chapter Fourteen
THE THREE LEVELS OF ABUSE

There is so much that many of us want to know about ourselves, about what is true, and what is real. And also, there is so much we are afraid to know about these things, especially when finding out requires us to change what we thought we knew about truth, reality, and us.

Once I finally was able to start writing this second book of the trilogy, the first thirteen chapters seemed to flow easily, only held up by processing what I was writing, and how fast my fingers could type the words that were already in my head, ready to appear on virtual paper. But, then, it all stopped, and I experienced a blockage, something that made no sense at the time.

I spent weeks going back through the chapters, adding sentences, deleting paragraphs, rewriting sections and making corrections that were needed to clarify a thought, but I just couldn't move forward. Something I could not identify was holding me back. But I had no idea what it was. And then one Monday morning after a weekend of non-stop snow in the Colorado Rockies, I woke to rays of sunshine streaming into the windows of my carriage house, with a realization that fell together, not unlike the coming together of memories when enough of the pieces were known.

In that waking moment, I saw among other things hidden within us, are three levels of abuse that live in the shadows, behind the mask, and though I had been able to write about the first and second levels, I had resisted including the third level. And that is why I was blocked.

I didn't know how to approach the *worst of the worst*, which was first mentioned in chapter one and alluded to in other chapters along the way, without going into level three that seemed too difficult for me to write about, and I was sure would be far too difficult for other people to read. And then I remembered a shamanic journey I had taken that seemed important, though I had no idea how it would help me with my blockage. I have come to trust what happens in my process, when what seems totally unrelated emerges in my awareness, much like the 1968 images of my experiences around the assassination of Martin Luther King coming into my thoughts when I was working through the murder of the Eskimo in the Jesse Lee Home. The images came because I needed to see how the two incidents were similar, and even more, what made them different. So, in dealing with the causes of blockage, I needed to reconnect with that journey.

***

Years ago, I had been working with a particularly dark memory that had come back into my conscious awareness. After recovering from the shock, I sensed that it was necessary to understand the original source of being totally engulfed in fear, so I asked my spirit guide to take me back to the origin of that fear. Instead of going back to a place in my childhood, or even to some terrifying event in a past life, I seemed to have gone back to some primordial time, even before the existence of forms, back to the very first impulse of life's consciousness in matter.

That journey taught me something that is so much more powerful than words. My sense is that we all carry in our DNA, not just our personal coding of our physical bodies—hair color, eyes, height potential, blood type, body type, innate intelligence—but also, our parents DNA; the combination of theirs resulted in ours. We know that our parents' DNA had to have carried their parents, and their parents carried our great grandparents' DNA…and this goes back and back and back to the very beginning. Each of us carries the entire history and memory of our branch of our species. And however we choose to interpret the meaning of us being made out of the dust of the earth, actually or metaphorically, we carry the history of the Earth in us, too, because, one way or another, we came from and remain intricately interconnected with the Earth.

Somehow, in my going so very deep in this journey in search of the origin of my fear, I accessed something very profound related to my inner being, and I have come to believe all of us hold deep in our DNA coding the experience of the first time consciousness separated from essence.

I wrote a two-fold relaxation process based on that amazing journey to provide an experiential explanation of the understanding I gained when I went back to find what frightened me enough to separate me from essence. The wording of the process is intended to provide a passageway to go deeply within to reconnect with the wonder of being, and then to discover what might have caused a belief in separation from the wonder of essence, followed by a feeling of separation from other beings.

Since we cannot reconnect with something we have forgotten exists, my intention was to create a process that could remind me, remind anyone, of the wonder that exists in each of us and then to bring into our mutual consciousness what it must have felt like the first time we separated from that amazing and unique mystery in us, that *is* us. Remembering what happened holds the potential to redirect our attention from the external back to the internal, from observing life to experiencing it, from closing down to opening back up, and from being afraid of life to being able to embrace life.

When you read the script below, you may find the experience to be more powerful if you read it word-by-word without speed-reading through the section. If you are willing to open to this experience, let yourself feel the words and let them take you deep inside yourself. It might be helpful to allow yourself to read this when you are in a place where you can focus without having to be interrupted so you can feel the "vibration" of the words, even if you don't know what that means. Give yourself permission to hear the words as you read them as if you were listening to a CD.

For those who have never gone deeply inside, or might find such an experience to be too overwhelming, you might want to be sure there is someone with whom you can connect afterward in case difficult feelings arise. If you do not want to experience what I have described as a major, and perhaps shocking change in consciousness from connection to disconnection, skip the next few pages and begin reading where there are five ***** asterisk marks, knowing when you feel ready or have the necessary support you can always come back to this page.

***

Take in a really deep breath…and slowly let it out. Avoid the impulse to move on to the next line until you have taken in that breath and slowly let it out………take in another really deep breath……and slowly let it out………and take in a third really deep breath…and hold it…………………and then let it out, and notice your breath can now be normal, deep, relaxed. Notice how much more relaxed you are now than when you first were directed to take in a breathe and slowly let it out. If you are not more relaxed, try closing your eyes and doing the deep breathing and releasing, just focusing on your breathing…until you do feel your body letting go and relaxing. You might need to repeat this exercise several times before you finally get to feel the relaxation. You are worth it to close your eyes and focus on your breath until you feel yourself let go.

And then, thoughtfully read the next sentence…paragraph…page.

Continue to be aware of your breathing and feel your muscles letting go…with each breath you take, you can find yourself becoming more and more relaxed.

And, now….notice how easy it is to allow yourself to imagine that you are resting so very comfortably, perhaps, if you like, on an air mattress, floating easily on a calm and very safe body of crystal clear water, like the water in the healing pond in alternate reality, feeling a gentle *rising and falling* in the water…..as if your breathing is matching the *rising and the falling* that is taking place in the water, that is somehow you *rising and falling* ………*rising and falling*………..*rising and falling*………Let yourself feel the rising and falling in your body as you read the words and let yourself hear the words that you are reading. And the *rising and falling,* ….*rising and falling,* …..*rising and falling*….. gives you a feeling that takes you deeper and deeper into relaxation………sensing the reflection of sunlight shimmering off the surface of the water, becoming flickering light and shadows softly touching your skin.........and you find yourself dropping more deeply into that in-between place, between waking and sleeping ......finally feeling something deep on the inside let go.

All the cares and concerns of the day seem to be floating away....... drifting away with each of the gentle waves that are rising and falling. For this moment, you are simply being you, deeply relaxed.

Now so deeply relaxed that you drift into a place where it is hard for you to tell the difference between you and the water ....You are aware of the hypnotic rocking, *the ebb and flow* as if you are feeling the water breathing, you breathing.........the water breathing through you.........*lifting you up and letting you drop down so softly*.........again and again.........Until, in some unexplainable way, you float on the water, no longer needing an air mattress to float. You are safe and secure, calm and relaxed as the mat has melted away and what is inside you has become crystal clear water floating on the crystal clear water, so deeply relaxed.........

Even when the water upon which you float begins very gently to move, you move with the water as one, with only your skin as a separation between the water within you and the outer water, so much at peace, so relaxed that it is not possible to tell that the water is moving......... And you are in the water, and you are the water..............*rising and falling*..........*rising and falling* ....aha! Let yourself be in this moment for as long as you would like. Give yourself this time to simply be...to be relaxed and nothing more.

...So hard to tell the difference between you and the water...no difference between you and the water.

Take time, even if you would like to close your eyes for a minute...or two....or more....to feel the profound goodness of being in the water, being the water...no difference. And when you are ready you can begin reading again...knowing that you can come back to this deeply peaceful state any time you choose.

Be aware of what you are feeling in your body, this very moment. You might close your eyes for just a few moments to notice how it feels to be you being relaxed.

And now take in another breath and feel how deeply relaxed you are, and notice how easily you can reconnect with the *rising and the falling....* *the rising and the falling...*So good to let your entire body relax, your entire mind relax, being only here, now, with no concerns about yesterday or tomorrow.

Breathe in the relaxation....Ahhhhhhhhhh

Imagine as you float on the crystal clear water...in a microsecond, you feel a swift and unexpected movement in the water that does not seem to match your gentle movement and in that same microsecond you can feel the crystal clear water ***split*** in half and part of it becomes profoundly jet-black, while the other half is filled with pure white light.

.........And in the next breath you take in... you can feel the split in the crystal clear water ***move through your body*** as it moves through the water feeling as if it is splitting you in two, one half pure white light, one half ink black. And everything has changed! Close your eyes after you have finished reading this sentence and notice what you feel...and when you know your feelings, open your eyes and continue to read.

What are you experiencing in your body now? What is happening in your mind...Take all the time you need. What are you feeling?

What is your response to the movement? .... What is your response to the split in the water? ....What is your response to the split in yourself? ....Where is your awareness in all of this? What are you looking at? What are you feeling? ....Take time.........notice... be aware. Take a moment to write what you experienced, perhaps in the space below so your experience won't disappear from awareness. You might want to write it now while you feel it. Use the space below and on the following page if you would like.

***

Did you allow yourself to experience the floating? If yes, what did it feel like to be drawn into the words and into the feelings? Did you stay with the feelings formed from the imagery? If your answer is no, can you ask yourself why not? Can you allow yourself to feel your answer? What does it mean to you to allow the feeling in the words to take you someplace? If you didn't allow yourself to be in the experience, are willing to reconsider? If you would like to reconsider, you can go back to the words and allow the words to take you into the experience before moving on.........Notice your response.

Then let yourself remember how you responded to the last difficult experience you went through in your life. Compare your experience to the imagery in the previous words to your response to life or crisis. What have you discovered?

*****

While doing the inner work that spontaneously took me first to *experiencing being* water floating in water and then *feeling* the split from crystal clear to black and white that caused me to feel separate from the water—as if I were a stream in an ocean—I felt resistance and fear. When we resist anything, our bodies experience shock, and shock is interpreted as pain, which produces fear and a need to separate from the source of the shock and pain. This microsecond sequence of experiences and interpretations began a history of responses I carry in my DNA and I believe in my soul's equivalent to DNA, which linked fear to many life experiences. I felt anxiety about potential change even if the change could have held the possibility of being something better; I found myself holding on to what I have had in my life, even if it did not feel good, and most of my life I felt mournful sadness in the losing of what used to be, even if it was not good. Change produced a sense of hopelessness because I believed change meant being forever alone, separated, disconnected with no way back. I am sure that lots of others have this inside them, as well, whether these negative responses to change are predominant or if the responses exist in them only subtly.

Something in me, however, had determination to overcome the fear and discover if there may have been other meanings of the shift from clear to black and white besides the original fear response. I have been relentless in my focus to discover how to feel reconnection to my own essence and the essence of the Great Mystery in every cell of my body in the healing process while releasing resistance and fear related to the split.

***

Because we operate in a world with others, our own responses and behaviors are not independent of other people who have their own internal responses and behaviors. If you are open to it, I would like to continue the experiential imagery as a way to explain what I discovered in the process of what I have called heuristic self-search inquiry where you begin to feel the essence that flows inside you and recognize your own responses in a way you may never have felt them before. If you would prefer not to feel deeply into this experience at this time, skip down and move to the next section that begins with five ***** asterisks. If you choose to skip this, know that you can always come back any time to experience some of the feelings that you hold inside. Join me?

***

We have the ability to adapt to changes, and in this imagery you are about to experience, let yourself notice you have adapted to the light and dark in the water and in you. What had been a swift and unexpected change is normal now. Reconnect to the pattern of your breathing, and as before, allow yourself to become connected to the words by reading them slowly and breathing gently as you read.

Take in a long and comfortable breath…. And slowly let it out…..and take in another long and comfortable breath……..and… slowly let it out… And then, take in a third breath…and…hold it………….and let it out. As you let out the third breath, allow your breathing to be natural and deep.

Let your body take you back to that state of being deeply relaxed and floating on the mat floating on water…safe…floating…relaxed.

237

Imagine now, that you are back in the experience of self as water in the water, and you have adapted to the split, the light and dark, and the movement........but now, because of the shift you notice that there is a difference between you as water and the outside water.

Perhaps you now notice that you have become a stream of water in an ocean.........Rivers and streams in the ocean have a different path and a different flow pattern than the ocean, even though they are a part of the ocean. Just like the sky above us that moves one way can have jet streams of air that flow differently, so too, does the ocean have streams in it that move differently. This internal vision of you as a stream in the ocean is no different from the ocean in the outer world or the sky above you.

Feel your stream-like movement in the ocean...flowing....gliding ... feeling your watery stream-self flowing in the ocean, noticing the difference between you and the ocean. You can take time, anytime you want to become aware of the sensations. What are you feeling? Are you moving quickly? Do you feel as if you are moving more slowly than the ocean? Are you warmer than the ocean or cooler? Or are you the same temperature as the ocean. Let yourself feel the answers to these questions.

Then imagine you become aware of other streams in the ocean .... some flow near you and some not so near as they flow and glide in the ocean.........allow yourself to feel these other streams.

What are you feeling? How are you responding to other streams above you........below you? Do they seem too close? Too far away?

And notice that some streams seem to flow near and join your streaming self, forming a river in the ocean. What are you feeling? Are you feeling invaded, or feeling connected...or something else?

Some streams move faster than you, some slower. Other streams are flowing in the opposite direction. Be in the moment, and let yourself feel whatever is in the moment. What are you feeling?

Take time...all the time you need, perhaps by closing your eyes at the end of this paragraph to allow yourself to become aware of the ocean space around you and all the rivers and streams that flow near or far from you or flow into your stream or cut through you. How are you feeling about being in this ocean filled with other rivers and streams?

*****

If you allowed yourself to feel what was going on inside during this ocean-stream-river process, compare your feelings in the process to how you respond in relationships to others in the world around you in normal waking life. If you give yourself time with this process, even going back to it now and then when you find yourself having particular responses to people who cross your path, you can discover the workings of your inner world in relationship to your outer world in your life, and you can notice how you change in time.

Allow the image of someone you know to come into your thoughts as another stream in the ocean and feel your stream-self responding to them. How does it respond to this person? If the feeling is positive, ask what about the other's energy feels good to you, and if negative, let yourself notice what is it in that person's energy that does not feel good. Practice this exercise as many times as you wish. When you meet a stranger, notice how your inner stream-self feels in his or her presence.

***

In my own internal work with energy movement, I found I was able to direct how I responded to external energy. I noticed that I could move faster, or slower, toward other streams or away; and by opening the flow of my watery-self, I could allow streams to flow through my flowing or I could close to prevent them from flowing through by putting up an energy shield, which caused them to flow around me, or I could move around them by moving in another direction, thus preventing cross currents. But while I was doing this, other streams were making responses, as well. Some seemed to respond mutually... if I wanted to feel close, they came close, if I wanted to avoid them, they avoided me, and others did not respond mutually. While some drew near when I wanted distance, others wanted distance when I wanted to feel near. I was able to feel the responses in my inner-stream awareness, and I could see how I placed meaning on various responses that fit with my original shock and fear response when the shift led to the split between light and dark. I could see that these responses also fit with my child-self's interpretation of the world and others in it.

Whatever I resisted, I experienced as being painful. When I was out of sync and felt other stream energies moving toward me when I wanted distance, I interpreted that as aggression or when I wanted to move toward other streams but they avoided my stream, I interpreted that as abandonment. I found that emotions sprang from sensations and interpretations corresponding to being in sync or out of sync with other movement, and from those emotions, behaviors sprang. Movement from other "streams" that felt disregarding, disrespectful, damaging, or dangerous I interpreted as abusive. And what was abusive I felt as painful. In my own processing, I found pain, which was unexpressed, created blocks to experiencing the flow of my life stream in myriad dimensions.

***

A thought that rose was how close the energy vibration of fear is to excitement. The two might be identical, except for the meanings attached and the behaviors that follow. From a place of fear, the vibration in the shift creates the fight-flight pattern that seems to be related to separating from what is feared. But from a place of excitement, the vibration of the split is sought and there is an energetic opening toward embracing the vibration.

There can be many after-effect behavior patterns that grow out of fear and excitement that become the templates from which we live our lives. Because either response comes from the same vibration—with two interpretations—we have the potential to live from one or the other interpretation or move between both. If we allow ourselves to look deep enough into our life's behavioral patterns we can see whether or not we mostly withdraw from what we interpret as external or if we seek it.

Another thought entered my mind; there could be other responses, besides fear and excitement. One response might be to simply experience the vibrations and the changes without contracting in fear or running toward the experience in excitement. Another response some might have would be to long for a return to how things were before the split and the change. Like the experience of being the river, some people feel threatened by other rivers, some want to connect with those other rivers, while others long to go back to no rivers, no streams, and just being alone in the ocean. I know this is important to what each of us carries deep inside us, and how we respond to the world.

My sense of all of this is that the fear I held, embedded in lifetimes of beliefs, thoughts, emotions, and behaviors brought me to this life in which much of my energy has been directed toward changing the impact of the original shock I felt and supporting those who are open to redefine change for themselves, as well. Responses that block the flow of life, such as what happened for me when I could not move forward in my writing have a way of creating crises, which contain the opportunity to reinterpret the original meaning given to change. Because we are complex human beings, there is likelihood that we have all of the above responses going on simultaneous inside us in various levels of our being.

I am very sure that my original and most immediate fear-response was not unique. Perhaps many others, maybe even most of us if not all of us, have experienced something very similar at the core of our DNA, and if so, that deep place within all of us that is our unique essence may be calling us to transform original responses, and resultant patterns that do not serve us, into new ways of interpreting ourselves and the world in which we live.

***

Finally, I was able to see why I remembered this process. By re-experiencing the inner feelings, I was able to apply what I had learned to the writing process that had become blocked. When my writing had come to a halt at the end of the previous chapter, I accessed my internal feelings about writing *the worst of the worst*; it was very clear my sense of internal flow was gone. No matter how I approached it, I found no entry point into writing, which would lead to exposing what I didn't want to include. I seriously considered going back through all the chapters to eliminate any reference to *the worst of the worst*, as well as any references to the levels of abuse, thus, ending the struggle with the blockage by making it a moot point.

Then it struck me that I had rejected the credibility of my experience of level three and had judged myself for participating in it. Since part of me had not accepted what I had experienced, I believed you would not accept it, either, and judge me for lying, but if, by chance you did accept what I wrote as another part of me had done, you would judge me as guilty for having the capacity for committing unforgivable, level-three abuse as I had judged myself.

I felt as if I had re-entered the pain of being unable to know what to say when someone demanded that I tell what happened, when telling the truth meant life-threatening punishment for what was judged as lying. My writing had been blocked because of my fear that putting my experience into words would cause others to reject or judge me as my mother had done and as I had done to myself. The result of that childhood experience connected me to the horror of being left in the box, under the ground, lost and forever alone, which linked to the fear of the split that happened in the crystal clear water, still buried and unhealed in my DNA.

I suspect that almost everyone has experienced times when making decisions was a struggle and going forward was nearly impossible, and couldn't figure out why. Once the fear can be identified, the chance opens for moving forward. And the same was true for me.

***

Being able to see the three levels of abuse provided a way to re-enter the writing by revealing what I saw and explaining why I was so afraid to write what would take us fully into level three. In that vision, I was able to see why most of us reject that level three is as common as it is and that it exists in all of us, not just in a few truly evil people.

The first thing that waking vision brought into my awareness was that all abuse, given or received, no matter which level it is on is the result of the experience of absence of love. *Notice, I said experience of absence of love, which is not the same thing as absence of love.* And, I saw that each of the three levels of abuse rests on a continuum from mild to extreme abuse. I was aware that the designation of the level is based, not on the pain inflicted, but on the *intentions* of the abuser, whether those intensions are self-defensive as in level one, retaliation or retribution-based as in level two, or destructive as in level three. Self-defensive abuse is intended to protect the self against whatever is interpreted as doing harm to the self, specifically to stop the harm. Retaliation is directed toward harming the source of the pain even if the pain is no longer being experienced in order to control the behaviors of someone else to make sure the unwanted behavior won't happen again; and destructive intention is focused on inflicting harm, not on stopping a behavior or controlling future behavior. That harm is usually beyond the physical, and it could be inflicted on anyone whether or not the one targeted is the cause of some original pain.

Because we are complex beings anything we do, which comes from anyplace but love, is also complex. It is likely that any single abusive act can have more than one intention and can incorporate more than one position on the continuum from mild to extreme. As a result, observation may not provide accurate designations of categories.

In this explanation of the levels, my intention was not the creation of scientifically based categories; rather, I wanted guideposts to help me understand what caused my resistance to moving forward in my writing, which was a metaphor for my not moving on in my life. Seeing these categories helped me understand why there has been a more universal resistance to acknowledging some forms of abuse as being real in the world today than other forms. Although, with the recent increase in heinous crimes, it might be that people are more willing to acknowledge the presence of what we call evil that rests on the far end of all three levels. Before explaining the details of these categories, or specific facts of the levels of abuse, it might be useful to understand more about the essence within us, beyond the experiential process provided earlier in this chapter, because it is this essence from which we separated when we first experienced pain and began the patterns that have ruled most of our lives from one or more of the three levels of abuse.

ESSENCE AND SEPARATING FROM ESSENCE

Essence is neither a thing that can be pointed to, nor an object that can be described or defined, nor is it a set of components that can be listed. It is magical, mystical, and ineffable, and is known through experience not by observation or through any of the other physical senses. Essence is what gives life to the physical, 3-dimensional world and gives pulse to life. *Essence gives us the ability to experience essence.*

When the first traumatic experience occurs in an infant's or child's life, even if for just a moment—like the experience of the split in the crystal clear water—the focus shifts from experiencing the self in relation to the external world to observation of the external world. The shift occurs as a way to regain what is believed to have been lost. An example of this would be when an infant wakes and notices that parents are not there, momentarily, it experiences disconnection from parents, separates from its own internal experience of the love that is always within essence, and cries out to get the attention from the outer world. If there is a loving response, and reassurance is given, the infant may be able to feel safe enough to return to experiencing essence.

For those infants fortunate enough to have loving parents who are connected to their own essences, at least most of the time, the infant's experience of essence might continue into early childhood, until some trauma is not resolved. In that case, instead of restoration to *being in essence experiencing self in the world*, the child could begin a life-long pattern of living life disconnected from its true self, *observing the external world* with fear or longing, or both most of the time.

Long periods of separation from essence can result, not only in the loss of connection to the essence that flows like the stream within the self in the Universal ocean, but also, in a loss of knowledge of the very existence of essence inside the self and in the Universe. And when the knowledge is lost, deep in the unconscious, there is a feeling that indicates something is missing that cannot be found, a feeling of emptiness that cannot be filled, and an existential loneliness that cannot be quenched. Sometimes, in the teen years during the period when youth seek identity or much later in life, usually during that infamous period of mid-life crisis, the need arises to search for that long-forgotten something. Perhaps this is the draw so many feel to search for the symbolic *Holy Grail* or the compulsion to take outer vision quests or inner journeys to fill emptiness, extinguish loneliness, and find the "something" that feels missing.

Though these beliefs that something is missing, that emptiness and loneliness are real, and that something unknown is lost are not true, they can *feel* true, and, certainly, they can feel real. Unfortunately, from this *perceived reality* about our world and ourselves, we build our self-constructs reflecting who we believe we are and our worldviews, which explain our world to us and gives "everything out there" the meaning we attach to it.

I believe what happened to me as a child, what happened to all who have ever been neglected and abused, what is happening globally with current world problems, as well as what is happening in the multitude of human crises impacting us today on every level of our being, all originated from a generalized perception of separation in our species. Our reaction to the meanings we attach to separation and our need to protect ourselves from it lead to both inflicting and receiving abuse. This condition is not just causing so many of us to live separated from the experience of our essence, but also, to lose awareness of the very existence of our essence. And most of us don't even know we have lost it.

When people experience the results of having lost the awareness of their own essence, they can easily become terrified of or angry at the presence of other *streams in the ocean.* They interpret others as being threatening, and feel terrified of or angry from feeling threatened or rejected. Because others are experienced as the enemy, people who do not experience connection can become defensive, protective, aggressive and violent, which can lead them to seek retribution, or destruction of others. People, who feel disconnected from their own essence, can also, feel the need to connect with someone else to try to find safety, security, and love. They can become needy, clingy, or dependent on another or many others hoping that someone else will fill the emptiness. From these patterns, people experience abuse or inflict abuse as an attempt to create safety in an ocean that no longer feels safe.

When we live as if we are separated from our essence, our lives are impacted by abuse that affects us on three levels that I saw in the sunny Monday morning vision.

LEVEL ONE ABUSE

I saw a bubble, and in it were millions upon millions of clippings from films of people's lives. Each clipping contained an incident in a person's life in which that person felt the need be protected from whatever felt abusive, and in that protection, the person became abusive. I saw a young mother, exhausted from too many nights of not enough sleep, entering the room of her crying infant in an energy field of frustration covering over anger that prevented the mother from accessing love as she tried to find the source of the disturbance to stop the crying. I saw a young man pull out a knife to protect him self from an angry store owner who believed he was being robbed. I saw people from all walks of life through all the ages breaking all the social and religious taboos, committing myriad crimes, rooted in fear or anger regarding some perceived threat.

It was very clear to me the first level of abuse contains self-defensive responses when we experience being hurt by another by what they did or didn't do, by what they said or didn't say, or simply how we interpreted something about them. As many scenes from the pile of film clippings played in my mind, I could see that level one abuse occurs when we believe someone else is responsible for providing us with feelings of love, peace, safety, security, happiness, wellbeing, or any other condition, but our experience is the person has failed to provide what we need. This happens, all too often, for most of us on a daily basis, as the most common way we experience relationships.

When our intention is to protect ourselves from the source of what we interpret as having hurt us, among many possible responses are abusive actions intended to stop experiences we don't want or to generate what we do want. And nearly all of us participate from this level by inflicting abuse on others including those we believe we love or receiving this kind of abuse from others. As mentioned in an earlier chapter, this kind of abuse comes from a need to control the other, and creates the drama that is characteristic of codependency.

In the codependent-drama triangle, we operate from this level when we take on the role of being the victim and want someone to rescue us, and when we take on the role of rescuer, believing that if we sacrifice for someone else, they will fill us up with what seems missing in us. And if either the victim or the rescuer does not do what the other one needs, either can turn on the other by taking on the role of the persecutor to force the wanted behavior. Any one can experience themselves in any of the three roles and will abuse the other to get what is wanted, even if participants would not identify what was being done as abuse. Codependency by its very nature is abusive because people are seen as filling roles and holes in our lives instead of as the sparks of God that they are, and others are seen as objects to use for the benefit of the self. Our behaviors operate out of a need to control them instead of out of love…and this kind of control of others is abusive.

An infant, by its very nature is dependent, which is very different from codependent. If an infant's first experience of separation from essence occurs as a part of the first level trauma in a mild form—a baby wakes with hunger pangs and mother wants to respond immediately but cannot feed her infant exactly that moment—it is likely that the child will experience separation until feeding happens and can more easily return to its essence, at least for meaningful periods of time because the feeding experience is one of mutually shared love. Mother is not covering a feeling that rejects the child's need. Reassured of safety, the infant is able to reconnect with its essence. If mother is exasperated by the infant's needs and when she finally addresses the baby's hunger pangs without love, the infant is not able to return to the safety of its essence, because the outside world feels threatening.

We send out first level abuse when we slam drawers or clang dishes in the sink as a non-verbal communication of anger that something we wanted didn't happen or something we didn't want to happen, did, and we want the other to take notice and change. This could be an adult version of a temper tantrum. First level abuse can occur when we say something sarcastic as a way to stop another's behavior, or say something mean with an intention of defending ourselves against others. Neglect or lack of caring can be a part of first level abuse and so, too, is the withholding of love, becoming distant or unapproachable as a way to get what is wanted or to protect the self from anticipated hurt. The list of first level abusive behaviors can be as long as there are people in all their ways of acting unkindly toward each other.

The purpose of first level abuse is to make someone else responsible for that which we do not want to assume for ourselves or believe we can't assume. When an irritated parent inflicts unloving energy on an infant, the underlying message is that the baby should learn to not cry for attention when the parent needs to sleep or not throw a tantrum when the parent has something else that must get done; thus, making the child responsible for the parent's needs. It is not unusual for little children to read these silent messages, causing the child to become caretakers of parents by sublimating their own needs to keep the parent happy.

In my practice, I found one of the more common underlying causes of people seeking therapy later in life originated from conditions in their childhoods that resulted in them becoming the caretakers of their parents. When children become the parent of their parents early in their lives, it is not unusual for them become unwitting, and later, unwilling caretakers of everyone else, and they just can't do it any more. Their response to this untenable situation might be to become first-level abusers, themselves, defending themselves against what feels like abuse coming from the ones for which they have spent their lives caretaking.

Abusing at this level does not have as its intention to bring another person pain, though pain is almost always the result. The intention is to put an end to feeling pain.

First level abuse usually grows from an unconscious belief that says, *"I am the center of the universe and everyone else exists for my benefit."* Most of us would never admit this is our belief or even recognize this as true, especially if we have lived as servants to everyone else all our lives. But for most humans, it is one of the beliefs hidden behind the mask. The intention, whether conscious or unconscious, of the behaviors of one who believes he or she is the center of the universe is to be in control of that universe by controlling all others who populate it, even if we do this by serving all those in our world. However, there is something about this kind of service that feels *sticky*.

A corollary to seeing self as the center of the world in first level abuse is the lack of awareness of the personhood of another. This often results in doing or saying things without noticing the impact on the other. All those years my mother told me on my birthday how disappointed she was that my birth spoiled my sister's first birthday, she was inflicting first level abuse on me, and indirectly on my sister, who felt badly that I was continually reminded of how much hurt I brought into our family. I don't believe my mother was trying to cause pain for either of us, although for many years, it did. She was expressing a wound in her that obviously had never been healed, which painfully revisited her every year. She didn't know how to make her pain go away, except to express disappointment; but it didn't bring healing to her original hurt because she didn't deal with what was happening deep inside her in her unconscious mind/body.

This first-level abuse she inflicted on me was minor compared to the life altering extreme first-level abuse of her attempted suicides even though she was not intending to abuse her children at that time, either. In both cases, the abuse to my siblings and me arose because she wanted something different to happen in her life and didn't know how else to create it. She was operating out of self-defense. However her suicide attempts, when applied to herself, could have had aspects of all three levels of abuse in them.

Like in the other levels, there is a full spectrum of pain that can result from first-level abuse. While the mildest form of first level abuse can result in momentary pain and temporary loss of connection to essence, the most extreme first level abuses can create a lifetime of disconnection or could possibly end in death.

When abuses accumulate, over time, the child can lose trust in every person, not just the abuser. Without healing, the effects of level-one abuse can impact every aspect of a person's life for the rest of his or her life.

LEVEL TWO ABUSE

The second level of abuse, like the first level, is caused by, and leads to experiencing life separated from essence within the self, which means feeling separated from the essence that flows within and in the Universe, as well, since the essence, which is in us and that which is in the universe are intricately and eternally connected. Although second level abuse originates from not getting what *is* wanted or getting what *is not* wanted, as in first-level abuse, what is different is the focus and *intention* of second level abuse is to inflict pain on the one seen as causing the hurt. The abuser wants to "get even" by making the other suffer—whether emotionally or physically, or in both ways—even if the inflicting pain might cause the one getting even to experience pain in the process of inflicting pain.

When I was given that morning vision, I saw a bubble filled with millions upon billions of events in what looked like film clips from myriad lives, just as I had seen for level one abuse. I saw the images of people hurting and being hurt, kicking and being kicked, killing and being killed, and I saw tribes of people invading and massacring each other decade after decade, century after century, millennia after millennia, and nations declaring war against nations, generation after generation, with each century, each millennium becoming more and more violent.

I saw parents screaming at, spanking, beating, whipping, maiming, and raping their children, drivers exhibiting road rage, people finding ways to harm the reputations of others to get even with other people.

Like level one, level two is relational, in that it has to do with how one person or group interacts with another. It was clear to me that level-two abuse is not focused on stopping the harmful or hurtful behavior of another, but rather, it is focused on inflicting painful retribution, to teach a lesson or regain a superior position. The one doing the abusive act is focused on the one receiving the retribution. While in level one, the focus is on self-defense.

This focus on the one being abused makes second level of abuse, even in a milder form, feel more threatened than most first level abuses because the *intention* of the abuser is to bring pain to the other. The one being abused must *focus outside self and on the abuser*, and eventually, that becomes generalized to the whole outside world, which the abused person sees as source for the supply of all needs. With this external focus, there is a loss of connection to the essence within the self. Before traumatized persons can allow themselves to know what they want, they first must find out what the abuser wants to be sure to provide it. Without first taking care of the the demands of the abuser, it is impossible for the victim to feel safe enough to have his or her own wants satisfied. On the global level, this may well explain why nations that cannot feed their own people will develop powerful militaries to defeat their enemies.

In time, abused persons disconnect from their own wants and wishes as they focus on the wants and wishes of the abusing other. Eventually, all they know is what others want, need, or expect from them. They often become people pleasers, and may come to identify themselves as truly liking to please others, but as much as that might be called love, it is not real love. The difference between authentic love that chooses to please others, and fear-based people pleasing is the presence of authentic loving kindness toward the self, considered as important as being kind to another, and ones own wants and needs are honored and known, not just the other's. People pleasers often don't know what is good for them or what they want.

Relationship styles formed in childhood to recreate safety in an unsafe world, to create connection in a world filled with separation, to create something that feels like love in an unloving world, or to manifest any need by controlling others—otherwise known as personality or behavior disorders—become templates people use in their adult relationships even if these patterns are painful and do not provide what the patterns promise. These kinds of patterns include people pleasing, self-deprecating, quiet suffering, self-sacrificing for others, throwing temper tantrums, bullying, lying, manipulating, lying, dissociating, distancing, being vulnerable to those who do not deserve vulnerability, and more.

According to Josef Fritzl, his mother abused him when he was a child with painful treatment related to his masculinity and his sexuality. He grew up into a man who intended to inflict pain on his mother in her old age, as retribution, and later, on his daughter to aggressively get even with all women who he blamed for his pain. His intention and focus was to inflict pain—second level abuse—not to stop pain from happening to him, which is first-level abuse, though whatever satisfaction he received from his horrific acts that made him feel better might have arisen from level one abuse.

My father, like Fritzl, hated his mother and wanted to inflict pain on her, but was unable to do so. Instead, he projected his pain onto his daughters, whom he saw as females like his mother, and in his worldview, all females deserved pain. When my father saw me as being the one who could disrupt his world if I ever told anyone about what he had done to me, he purposely hurt me as painfully as he could, short of killing me, to make sure I could be controlled. Like with Fritzl, what my father did was one of those more complex behaviors that contained both level one and level two abuses. Later, it may be very clear that level-three abuse was, also, connected to both my father and Fritzl's cruelties.

Because second-level abuse, even in milder forms, can feel deeply threatening to the one receiving it, an unconscious interpretation of the abuse experience is that focus must remain on the external world, almost exclusively, because someone out there is intent on bringing harm. The objective of this focus is to discover how to find safety, security, and love in the world that seems no longer capable of providing those conditions. The ability to surrender to essence and to one's own being is lost because to open to the self is to release external focus and embrace internal experience, which would be far too dangerous to allow.

This second level of abuse is what so many of the TV programs and movies have as themes these days, and this second level is what fills the news most nights. At the mild end of the continuum of level-two abuse is the bully stealing lunch money and shoving the weaker kids in lockers to make them terrified. It includes hazing of incoming college students and crimes fueled by greed, hatred, jealousy, and revenge, that revels in the suffering of the focus of their anger. On the extreme end, this level can be seen in the father who kills his children to make his estranged wife suffer. The deaths of his children are incidental collateral damage in the fulfillment of his intention, which is to cause his wife to suffer. Again, because humans and their actions are complex, there may be more than one level going on in a crime such as this one.

Second-level abuse can also include socially approved punishment intended to create suffering rather than rehabilitation for abusers who have been caught and found guilty of committing heinous crimes. When the State of Florida was preparing to execute serial killer Ted Bundy back in the 90s for the murders he committed, there were "Fry Ted Bundy Parties" all over the state, and likely in other states, as well. I remember seeing a news story that showed a group of revelers who partied outside the prison waiting for the zero hour that indicated the electrocution had happened; the people were like those waiting for the ball to drop in Times Square on New Years. They wanted him to suffer, and enjoyed the thought of him "frying" in the electric chair. Without knowing it, they were exhibiting the same level-two abuse toward Bundy that he had exhibited toward his victims. It is amazing how that works. Though there are aspects of level three in this display, the major focus is on wishing for suffering, as in frying parties, which makes this level two.

Second level abuse has built into it a desire for revenge against someone or a group deemed responsible for the abuser's pain, and in this sense, street gangs, arsonists, some vigilante groups, and people who threaten to kill, or actually do kill their families can perpetrate second level abuse. This is the level that is referred to as the underbelly of a culture, the seamy side of humanity. It is the level where the things that take place in it, are what *the shadow knows.*

This second level includes terrorist actions, torture, and genocide. Nations, groups, and individuals can live from this second level of abuse, as well. But also, it includes a parent's delight in denying a child what the child wants as punishment for something the child did in order to make the child suffer; this moves into level two, as well, because the focus is not on teaching the child, but on making the child suffer. Like level one, there is a wide range of abuses on the second level, from mild to extreme. And like in the first level, giving or receiving such

253

abuse, causes and is caused by separation from the love that emanates from the personal and Universal essence.

***

If the abuse we experience early in our lives comes from extremes in any of the levels, it is likely that not only will we feel emptiness, loneliness, fearfulness, and all else that comes from disconnection from our essence, we will feel the agony of experiencing ourselves as disconnected from all that exists, as well.

When painful experiences are ongoing or come from extreme abuse from any of the levels, it can be much harder, if not impossible, to find the way back to essence without determined intention, even after the pain ceases. For the person who has been traumatized by extreme forms of abuse, life becomes a struggle to find safety in what is seen as an unsafe universe, a longing to find love from what is experienced as an unloving world, a wish to experience acceptance when there is no hope for being accepted, and an aching for connection when connection feels threatening, even connection within.

If any level of the first painful abusive event is extreme in its nature, and then, the first is followed by many other events of extreme abuse while the child is forming personality patterns, which usually solidify somewhere between age 4 to age 7, the splitting of the self from essence can be accompanied by splintering of the personality, as well.

***

I continue to be amazed how many people whose lives are falling apart—reflecting an inner world that is falling apart—start their work with me saying they came from a loving, non-abusive family and for the most part everything was quite good in their growing up years with no trauma and no significant pain. But, when they begin to move below the surface, behind the mask, they discover that things were not as good as they wanted to believe. There is something about the process of digging down into the deeper places inside us, behind our masks, that opens our eyes to see those things that we hoped would remain hidden our whole lives.

My work with many clients over the years supports the idea that our current lives are rooted in the patterns of the past, and bringing healing to the past transforms the patterns, which in turn transforms the experience of our present lives. But we have to acknowledge the patterns and release them at their root level if we are to find deepest level healing. I have come to believe that many people don't want to go behind the mask to look into the first and second level abuses, trauma, and pain that were committed against them, as well as the abuses they inflicted on others because deep within, they know that this digging around can lead into level three, which feels too frightening to enter. This is why I believe there has been such a great deal of resistance to look beneath the surface and behind the mask, and why there seems to be a collective denial that the *worst of the worst* exists, even in me.

Reflections

Until we are willing to know what is true, we will not be able to know who we are or what is real. Though we often resist knowing the truth, there is something deep inside us that keeps calling us to know. Ask yourself what you have resisted knowing? When you know something is true, but deny your knowing, you prevent healing from happening to whatever hurt you. You will remain stuck in patterns that grew out of that hurt if you don't acknowledge the hurt and bring healing. As much as you try to make what is not real feel real, you live in an unreal world disconnected from everything including yourself, and nothing feels real or true.

Be patient with yourself as you take your steps on your quest toward truth, reality, and knowing. This is not an easy journey to take, and there are so many reasons to deny what is true and end your inner search. Whatever you buried behind your mask, you did so because you believed that having it exposed would hurt you deeply or even kill you. So facing what you have hidden may cause you to believe you might die. And thought that is always a possibility, it is not a probability; but living without truth, without what is real and without knowing who you truly are may well be worse than death.

Chapter Fifteen
THE LONG-AVOIDED PASSAGEWAY
TO THE WORSE OF THE WORST

Human life is about making choices. Good and evil, light and dark, truth and lies, yes and no, right and left, masculine and feminine exist in pairs in this three-dimensional world to provide us with one aspect of choice. Choices formed from fear create patterns intended to keep us safe, but seldom do so because they diminish our ability to choose. Choosing to release protective patterns that don't protect us awakens consciousness. When consciousness is awakened we are able to create what we prefer from a place of power, a place of knowing, and a place of love for ourselves and everyone else. Choice can then shift from opposites to preference. If consciousness remains asleep, when we are hurt, we will return to protective patterns, which create more hurt, and the effects of hurt can go on and on until we make a choice to awaken.

AVOIDANCE

Without consciously being aware of it, I was avoiding writing about the third level of abuse, not only when I wrote the first 13 chapters of *Behind the Mask*, but also, while I was writing chapter 14, which I had intended would include level three. I was unconsciously resisting writing about a level that I know many people refuse to acknowledge exists; but, if they do accept that it is real, they want to believe it is very rare, and certainly, not something in them. I feared if I talked about what happened to me when level-three abuse invaded my childhood, readers would believe I had made it up in my mind for whatever reason I would make up such things. Also, I was sure that my suggesting we all hold the capacity for level-three abuse in us as something we could potentially inflict on others would be fully rejected. However, as much work as I have done on myself, I know that my presumptions about others rejection or resistance to accepting level three is more about me than about you.

You might wonder why I would say I resisted writing about level three when I had already written about being raped when I was four, buried in a box, and watched as a man was murdered in the Jesse Lee Home. I had also written about the murder of the little girl and the man in the boat. But as horrible as these experiences were, they were not level-three abuse. Though there may have been aspects of the third level, they were predominantly levels one and two. When my father raped me in the forest, he was angry with me and wanted to hurt me, which is a very extreme form of level two. When he buried me in the box, he was operating from level one because his intention was to frighten me into never telling on him again…it was an act of self-protection, though it was on the very far end of the continuum, and may well have, also, had level two in his actions, as well.

The porno film that ended in the child being murdered, which was so viciously cold was, in my estimation, level one. The child shot in the face was collateral damage for people who wanted to create and sell a shocking film to earn money. She died as a result of a level one action that came from people who saw themselves as the center of the universe and used the child's death as a way to get what they wanted. Their intention was for personal gain, and the child suffering and dying was a side effect. Earning money at the cost of others comes from a place of fear that there is not enough, or that they will not get what they need. As perverse and twisted as that was, trying to get enough is self-protection. This act belongs on the very far end of the first level of abuse continuum.

I have no idea why the big man in the hold of the boat was dead, but if it was a part of economic wars, it may have been level one or level two, as was likely the case for the man whose throat was slit. Most of the murders we read about related to other criminal actions are mixed level one and level two. As I mentioned in the last chapter, level three is more sinister.

Because, ultimately, we are all connected and because we all hold what is potential in being human, I believe that not only first and second levels of abuse are present in all of us, so too is level three—something I will explain later—not just those few who move into this level of sadistic cruelty on a regular basis. This third level holds an intention to bring not just pain to physical bodies, or fear to the minds of another in retribution, but is focused on attempting to murder the souls of their victims. This is the level that incorporates torture that revels in the suffering for the sake of suffering. Despite its presence in us, most of us will likely never choose to live from this level, though without knowing it, we can touch into it in its milder forms, more often than we might be aware.

I come and go with the acceptance of the fact that in my childhood I was subjected to extreme third-level abuse in its most cruel forms, but my deepest knowing reminds me that until I embrace this truth, the same as I embrace my essence, knowing that both are true, I will not be free of the fear of what is behind my mask. I had written chapter fourteen as an entrée to finally write about what had been so difficult and found myself not writing about it in that chapter. I continued the avoidance when I first began this fifteenth chapter by making it more of a treatise on evil, rather than going deeply into my experience of level three, and I deleted what I had written.

Finally, I pulled up on my computer the manuscript I had written in 1992 titled, *Melting the Chains*. I had included in it some of the details of the extreme abuse inflicted on me in my childhood, but did almost nothing to get the manuscript published. I did a document search to find the chapter that contained what I had avoided for all these years. To my surprise, I found the information was in chapter 15, exactly the same as this chapter in *Behind the Mask*, perhaps significant for anyone who studies the meaning of numbers. I, also, had included references to level-three abuse in the original manuscript that became my 2004 book, *E Pluribus Unum: Out of Many...One,* but deleted it for fear that the publisher and readers would reject my work if I had kept it in. And again, I was struggling in 2009 with how to write, not just this chapter, but whether or not I should consider revamping the entire book to erase all references, not just to the *worst of the worst,* but also, the references to the three levels of abuse that would have had to include the pure destructive evil that was connected to level three.

Some of the very few who knew about this aspect of abuse in my childhood suggested that I write a novel to avoid any rejections or attacks that might come my way by writing in autobiographical format. But saying something is fiction when it is true, seemed to be as unethical as saying something is true when it is fiction, especially when the motivation for such a disguise is fear. If I continued to hide what had been buried behind my mask for decades, I felt as if I would be re-abusing the parts of myself that experienced what was intended to be *soul murdering* level three abuse events at the extreme end of the continuum.

For 17 years, I struggled to find the courage to speak the truth of what little Sandy experienced. Maybe it was coming to the backbone of the US, in the Colorado Rockies that allowed me to tap into the energy of the mountains that finally gave me the courage to write what I had avoided knowing for most of my life, and once I knew of it, avoided including it in anything I had written...until now.

When I read the first words that introduced that nearly two-decades old 15th chapter in *Melting the Chains,* I knew it was time to release the fears and include in this book what happened in my childhood, which was so painfully connected to level three. Nearly all of the next eight pages contain what I had written in that unpublished chapter fifteen, back in 1992. I know it is time to release avoiding all of this!

RELEASING AVOIDANCE: RECONNECTING WITH MELTING THE CHAINS

The focus of my therapeutic work from 1986–1988 was largely on the crumbling of my marriage and the complications around the relationships that assisted in breaking it apart. Though I had made contact with my internal life and the parts of myself that lived in alternate realities and were trapped in events of my childhood, I didn't really start working with them until the trip to Alaska in 1987. Finding the basement room and outside light that formed the image of the arched doorway convinced me that there was truth to what I had been seeing in the puzzle-piece flash-backs that were sprinkled here and there in the therapy process of the previous year.

In 1988, I began to see images of abuses that were worse than the sexual abuse that first demanded my attention. This more atrocious level of abuse was responsible for splintering of my personality into so many parts of parts... eventually numbering over 250. To not include these memories, some of which took more than a year to put bring together, would be a perpetration against the truth.

Four years of intense therapy had taken me to the depths of darkness and through some of the most soul murdering memories. My first therapist had spent three of those years with me as the foundations of my life had shattered in spite of my resistance to allowing the shattering. He called it "falling apart" in order that I might come back together in a form that matched my spirit. My second therapist had begun working with me after the first one had moved out of state. Building on the foundation I had constructed while working with my first therapist, the second one was with me as I journeyed into the most deeply hidden memories from the first years of my life, made more accessible because I had become strong enough to handle what was coming forward, both emotionally and psychologically. The needed strength grew out of my sometimes faltering, shaky, and usually unsure ability to confront and deal with the shattering confusions of my 1980's life.

***

One by one, I wrote about the memories that had been locked in the darkest of hidden back rooms and dungeon cells as the puzzle pieces came together clearly enough for me to make sense of them. It was not unusual for me to begin writing in the past tense and then switch over to present tense as I left 1992 and entered the events from 4 decades before.

THE SILVER CUP

We were in a room. I think I was five, or maybe six. That is my best guess. There were several other children in the room. I don't know how many, I can just sense their presence; little heads in rows in front of me, are silhouetted against the brightness of the stage filled with flood lights that are very bright in front. It is dark where we sit on little benches. I see the shape of my sister's hair and the dark profile of her face against the bright lights. There are adults, several of them who are like classroom monitors. We are supposed to watch what is happening in complete silence. We are tapped with a stick if we turn away or close our eyes. We must watch. If we don't...

There is a man on the stage. He is strapped onto a tilting board. He does not move very much. His mouth hangs open and his eyes are open, but they do not seem to see. I remember being aware he must have been feeling like I felt when they put the needles in my arm many times before to make me be quiet. You can't feel anything but you really can—you just try to think you can't. It is like every thing is slowed down and fuzzy. The people come out in black robes and hoods. One is holding a silver cup, like a wine glass, not really shinny, not all of it is shinny. There is a big bowl that makes funny sounds like something cooking. The liquid in the bowl makes sounds and a very bad smelling smoke comes out of it.

The man in the black hood robe fills the cup and now the cup crackles. He carries the cup to the man on the slanted table. The man with the cup pours the liquid onto the strapped man's arm. There is a crackle sound and smoke. It smells very, very bad and burns my nose. No one is supposed to make a sound when the man moves his head and screams out a sound that groans from his belly. I cannot cry. I cannot make a sound. A child in the row in front of me and to the left makes a sound. One of the adults moves towards her and hands her the cup. She made a sound. She should not have made a sound. It is her fault. She has to hold on to the cup. She has to pour what is in it on the man. He makes a horrible sound that almost makes the sound of the crackle go away.

My throat is tight. I cannot make a sound. I cannot make a sound. I cannot make a sound. Everything is quiet. I feel far away and everything turns dark. It is hard to see. I am so afraid. I cannot make a sound. The pain in my chest moves to my throat. I hold so tight. I cannot make a sound. The man with the cup comes in front of me. He touches me. *"I didn't. Please, please I didn't. I didn't make any noise. I held it in my throat."* His arm drops, and the cup is now in my hand. I have to take the cup. It crackles. *"Please don't make me take the cup. I didn't mean to make a sound."* My mouth opens...A silent scream fills the room. It feels like my thoughts are screaming, *"I didn't make a sound. I didn't mean to."* I know that I have to take the cup. I cannot take the cup. I cannot take the cup and pour it on the man; but I am holding the cup. I feel his screams. Everything is gone. I am gone. Everything is black.

That memory came back, like the others, in pieces while in therapy. As I regained the memory of my arm reaching up and my hand taking the cup, holding onto the stem and smelling the atrocious fumes coming from it, I went into shock. The horrible electric shock waves passed through my body, leaving me as devastated as the first time I remembered in the first therapist's office when my therapist took me back to talk with the little girl in the playroom. I asked her to open the door, but instead, she pulled back the curtain that sent shock waves through me so powerfully it stopped my heart from beating for a moment and my therapist had to do some kind of energy healing to bring me back to life.

I was with my second therapist when this silver cup memory came together. I had been handed the cup because I had made a crying sound. There had been some kind of sick rule made by the people in the long black robes that we children had to watch the atrocity that was being committed against the drugged and bound man, saying that we had to watch without making any sound. Anyone who made a sound had to participate in the ritual that required pouring some kind of sizzling chemical onto the man. The chemical ate away his clothes, skin, and muscle. The smell was debilitating.

I have no idea why the man was being so horribly punished. Because I had made a sound, it was my turn to take the cup. I went into shock and experienced a splitting of myself. One of the parts left and another who knew nothing of the previous few minutes came out to take the cup as an adult led her to the stage-front where the partially decomposed man lay in agony from whatever was in that cup. The shock of seeing and smelling the man caused that part to go away and another part of me came out. That next part stayed there until the moment the cup had to be tipped and another split occurred. I had to pour the liquid on the left side of the strapped man. It singed his clothing, making his shirt foam and bubble and ate away skin and

263

muscle exposing tendons and bones. I do not remember blood. I am aware of a horrible smell, though I am not sure what it was. There were dozens of parts of me that were formed during that most ugly mind-splintering event.

Writing this has left me very weak. The pain in my arms has turned into a heaviness that feels as if I cannot lift them from the keyboard. The choking in my throat is gone; all that seems left is a whimper, a quiet powerless cry with no tears. The bottoms of my feet hurt very badly. I don't know if I have the energy to let my mind think about all of this right now. I am extremely exhausted.

THE TINY INFANT

I am not sure how old I was; my sense is that I was five or maybe six. I was brought to a place where there were people with black robes. There was screaming in a back room, screaming of a woman. A very tiny naked baby was carried from the back room and brought to a tall table in the front of the room. There were candles on the tall table. Two people in black robes brought the woman into the main room. She was naked; there was blood running down her legs. She had dark hair that was pulled back in a knot on the top of her head but some of her hair was hanging down in strings. Her face was wet from her tears and she was still crying, though not as loud as before. Her body was wet and bloody; her eyes looked shinny.

The two men were holding her up under her arms and made her walk into the big room from the back room. She was looking at the tall table. I was sitting on a man's lap. At first I didn't realize that I was not dressed, then I realized I was naked because I could feel the man's skin under me. I was not permitted to make a sound. I could feel what seemed like a rock under me. But I was not permitted to make a sound. If I made a sound, the baby would not be allowed to make sounds any more. The tiny baby was crying. I could feel the rock growing under my legs, even though rocks are not supposed to grow, and there was pain. I felt a terrible, horrible pain. It felt as if the inside of my body was being torn apart by the rock. I tried not to but I must have screamed. It was my fault. I made the sound, so now the sound must be taken away from the baby.

I was taken to the tall table with the candles and the baby. A man in a black robe with a hood that covered his face handed me a knife. It was big and had silver carvings on the handle, a dragon I think, or maybe a snake. My hand was placed on the handle of the knife, but it was too big for my hand to hold. The man with the hood put his hand over mine and put the knife in the baby's side. It was my fault. I made a noise. There was a pain in my side, a pain that made me feel like I was dying. The pain in me matched the place where the knife went into the baby. I tried as hard as I could to make the knife not hurt him...if I could take away the pain maybe my hand on the knife would not hurt him, but I took the sound away from him. The baby stopped crying. Oh, the little baby stopped crying! I could not make a sound, but a horrible wailing cry grew into my chest anyway and buried itself above my heart...and the pain in my side grew to match the silent scream in my chest.

There was a box with soft insides on another table. I was placed in the box and the baby was put in the box with me. I was told that this was the baby Jesus and it was my job to make him come back to life. The lid was lowered and everything became dark. I can feel the baby lying against my left arm and chest. He is so tiny, so quiet, and I feel him grow cold. I send my thoughts into the baby Jesus and with everything in me I tried to find where he was hurt so I could fix him with my thoughts.

I tried and I tried, but I couldn't find the way to make him alive again. I searched everywhere for his life, but it was not there. I have no idea how long I was in there, a few minutes, ...a few hours...a day...no idea at all. But they took the top off the soft lined box and tried to take the baby from my arms. I held on to him and begged them to give me more time, *"You didn't give me enough time. Please, Please, if you can give me more time, just a little more time, I can do it."* This is the cry that has been screaming within me all my life. If you can give me a little more time, I can find the way to make everything okay

Writing this has been very hard for me. It took over three years for all of these memories to come back and connect one to another until I was able to see the picture of what happened to me when I was about five or six. Breathing is difficult at this moment. My chest feels caved in and the tears are hiding behind a headache that has re-erupted, full force. I feel nauseous and ready to throw up. The first tiny picture that was a part of this memory came back the very first time when my therapist brought me back through hypnosis to what was behind the curtain and I went into shock in his office September of 1986, just before my grandma died. The last of it came back in my second therapist's office, November of 1989, shortly before I left for

China. I have seen the pieces and knew the connections but have never put it all together at one time and put words on it until this moment in 1992. It is an extremely painful thing to do, even now, and my inner self wants to cry out...No! No! No! Extremely painful!

***

After returning from China, I was aware of painful memories that were emerging making moving ahead difficult. While working with two physical therapists in Florida who had teamed up to assist in relieving some of those difficulties, I felt my body go into a fixed spasm. I knew there was a scream that had to come out of the center of me but it could not find the way out. The physical therapist had been working on my head when I began to see the pictures again. The pictures were of the baby with the knife in its side and the wound in its chest. I began to see more pictures, some new ones, but I saw a knife in my hand and I knew what I had been expected to do.

Tears of agony mixed with the pool of perspiration that drenched the paper sheet protecting the massage table from my perspiration. The physical therapist asked me what I was seeing. I opened my mouth but no words would come out at first. Then, I could hear my voice. Each word came out with a struggle in tiny sounds...T h e y   m a d e   us c.c.c.c. T h e y   m a d e us c.c.c.c.c. I could not let the word be formed in my mouth. They made us c.c.c.c.u.u.u.u.u... but finally the sounds filled my throat and exploded into the room. *They made us cut the baby.* Saying the words tore at my insides. Putting words on a picture always seemed to make true what I tried so hard to make not true. All of my life I had tried to *unmake* things by not saying them, but somehow in my heart I knew...I knew....I knew.

There were several of us children. We had to dismember the baby. The knives were placed at appropriate places in the joints by big hands; with them guiding our hands, we had to cut, to separate the baby from itself. My hand was forced to separate the left arm from the tiny baby. The horror was too devastating to even describe in this writing. There were a number of major personality splits with this event. Again, as before, with all the Sadistic Ritual Abuse, we children were not permitted to make any sound.

I have no memory of events immediately after the dismemberment, but I know, later, the bones had been placed on pieces of soft red cloth and each child was given a place in front of one of the red cloths. A polishing cloth was placed in the hands of each of the children scattered about the room; and a bone was placed in the hands of shattered children, scattered and shattered by an insane ritual that makes my hands shake and my head spin in dizzy sickness as I recall it, again, and as I write it here. Each of us had to polish the bone we were given. I remember that we were at a table where we had to eat raw meat and drink from a glass of what I told myself was thick salty tomato juice. And I hear dreadful crying on the inside.

THIS COULDN'T BE JESUS

I have only one memory that ties a time of year to an event. I was with my sister and several other children. We saw a small baby placed on a table. When the adults left for a moment, my sister removed the baby from the table and we hid under the stairs with it. We wanted to protect it from what was to happen. I recall looking at the baby in her arms and questioning with a statement, *"That couldn't be Jesus because it is June."* In my child-knowledge, I knew that Jesus was born at Christmas, in December. And this newborn baby couldn't be Jesus because it was June and he wouldn't be that tiny in June.

From what I have learned since that memory came back, it is not unusual for such rituals to be done opposite of Christian rituals. A baby is sacrificed instead of a man. Instead of December, the baby that is used in the ritual was born in June. Ceremonies that mock Christian ceremonies are practiced where the members drink the blood of the sacrificed baby and eat his flesh to gain the life energy of the baby. This is a parallel to the Christian ritual of drinking the blood of Christ, and eating his flesh in communion, something I could never wrap my head around when I studied church doctrine to be confirmed in the church. Part of the graduation ceremony was to participate in communion, something I just couldn't bring myself to do long before the memories of this childhood abuse came back to me, so the church didn't allow me to be confirmed. In the twisted rituals, the most innocent are made guilty. Bones of sacrificed babies are used in ceremonies as icons and worn in necklaces and other jewelry. I have chosen, at this point in my life, not to become more aware of what SR abusers do because it hurts too much, still.

THE PERFECT DANCE

Braided between the most atrocious events that included people who wore black robes were the incidents that involved filming. Because they contained so many of the same experiences, most of them blend together and it is impossible, at least at this time in my life, to be able to separate them out and describe them from beginning to end. In some, several of us children were used to dance and play as precursor to some other event that involved adults. One in particular stands out because I really felt pretty that day, I loved my frilly dress and shiny black Patton leather tap shoes and my hair was in ringlets. I began to do the routine I had learned, when a clown jumped out and another part of the filming began. I had believed that I was to be the "star" like Shirley Temple, but in a most painful moment, I knew that I had been used and no one cared how good I had been. My daddy didn't even care that I had done the dance perfectly. I became overpowered with the deepest shame for believing in myself when it was very clear that no one else even cared about me, or my performance. One part of me ridiculed another part of me for not seeing the wires and the camera, but had not figured out what was really happening. The critical part believed my child-self was very stupid, and condemned my self-assurance that I could dance the most perfect dance. And the part of me that had felt so good about her dancing, felt such deep shame for her stupidity. I have never let myself be proud of my accomplishments since.

THE WAREHOUSE

Another time I was in a warehouse and it was very cold. My daddy pulled my dress off and I stood with only underpants as protection. I cried in hysterical protest to not have to have my dress taken away because my spine was shaking from the cold. Instead, I was held down and one of the adults put a needle in my arm to make me stop crying. I don't remember what happened next, but I imagine that was the tipping point that resulted in that warehouse at the end of our block being burned to the ground.

THE ELECTRIC CHAIR AND ALL ITS CONNECTIONS

I have never been able to figure out why I was put in what looked like a child-sized hand made wooden chair with straps on the arm rests and legs and other straps on the back of the chair. There were wires running to the straps. I must have been put in that chair more than once, because when the memory came back to me on the way to a therapy session, I realized that my child-self knew what was going to happen and fought very hard to avoid being strapped down. That particular evening, while driving to my appointment, Largo experienced its very worst lightening storm in Tampa Bay history. There were lightening strikes everywhere, flashing and cracking around me, and when I finally got to my therapist's office, I was trembling in shock. I walked into the office in tears with thunder and lightning still exploding around us, and immediately began to tell him about the chair, the shocks, and the struggle.

After being strapped into the chair, electric shocks were administered to my legs just above my ankles and then to my arms just above my wrists. The pain was excruciating. When I tried to pull my body away from the shocks, electrical charges snapped at me in the places to which I tried to move for relief. The most painful shocks went into my spine, which felt as if they splintered my own flow of energy in my spinal column and made it impossible for me to know what was my energy and what was the foreign energy that was splitting me into many pieces. There were also shocks that went into my head from a headband that fit too tightly. Shocks were administered through my temples and then down into my spine. It felt so painfully hot that I thought the vertebrae in my spine had fused together. While all this was going on, there was a big tape recorder that seemed to be saying something in a very low, slow voice, as if you took a recording and slowed it down until words were impossible to understand.

When my therapist asked me what I did with the words that were being spoken in slow motion, I told him that they did not match any thing inside me, so I stored them in boxes on shelves in an inner room in my brain. He asked what I wanted to do with them, and as soon as he said that, I saw parts of me dumping the boxes into a wheelbarrow and the contents were dumped into a huge bond fire that felt as if it was burning everything up that didn't belong and heat poured out of me, from the inside out. I never had an explanation that felt clear enough to understand what exactly happened, but I have no question that I easily released whatever was intended to be in me because it had not been assimilated.

***

These were the events I recorded in *Melting the Chains* in 1992, but was too terrified to make public at that time. They made their way in the drawings that were included in my first book, *E Pluribus Unum: Out of Many…One,* in 2004, but the actual words explaining the events were deleted. Not only was it difficult to acknowledge what had occurred in those most horrific events, I was aware that what I had included up to this point was not everything. Before I could move into what was still not included, there were residues in other arenas of my life that needed to be addressed.

Reflections

Over a lifetime, we can come to believe many things about ourselves that are just not true. Anything that suggests you are less than a most amazing and wonderful spark of God is a lie, even if you have done many things that do not match the truth of who you are.

Take this truth into the depths of yourself and approach with love any part of you that believes the lie, and allow the truth to set you free of all that has prevented you from living the life you were born to live.

You are not what happened to you. When you let go of needing to judge yourself for what happened, you will discover that judgment from any other person will have no power over you. Acknowledge what happened and release the meanings you attached to the events in your life. This will give you the courage to face whatever seemed too painful to face.

Chapter Sixteen
DEALING WITH THE RESIDUES OF 2009

If we avoid looking at the shadow because we fear what might be hidden there, we give the shadow far more power than it really has. The shadow's power is derived from our fear, and when we face the fear, its power melts away, replaced by the strength that has always been ours.

Apparently, I released the stored information that was sent into me in that electrical shock experience in the earlier work in therapy, but the energy in my arms and legs stayed in me for many more years, which was somehow related to my being held back in 2009. I needed to find out what was going on.

The burning pain in my arms and legs that I was very sure came from that horrible electric chair experience when I was six, coupled with a constellation of pain in my neck, shoulder, and back, which somehow seemed related, as well, led me to Greg, a clinical hypnotherapist in Denver, Colorado who had the same training in the Alchemical Hypnotherapy process that I had had years before, beginning in Florida and completed in New Zealand in the early 1990s.

While feeling stress over the discomfort in my body, I was also distressed about getting this book finished and published with the *worst of the worst* in it, writing the last book in the trilogy, *Under the Mask,* and becoming my own version of Johnny Appleseed, traveling and planting the idea seeds I spoke of earlier. I knew I would be addressing the issues we hold individually as well as the world problems, the crumbling of our institutions, the wars and disasters and the links between the collective problems and the ones we experience individually.

After explaining all of the above to Greg, I felt a need to explain one more concern that I had not voiced to anyone up to that time. I told him that for some reason, while all this stress was going on in my body, I had been hearing many references to December 21, 2012, something that caused additional stress. Many of those who focus on this date, when the Mayan calendar ends, believe that the end of the world will come on that day. Recently, there have been a number of movies and TV programs based on various interpretations as to that date in human history. Some believe that this is when Jesus will return to set up his 1000 year reign of peace, but not before huge natural catastrophes and human disasters occur; others believe that this will be the day that aliens of superior intelligence and far more advanced technology will descend on the Earth to forcefully prevent us from doing major damage not just to the Earth, but to our Solar System and to our galaxy, which then would impact the rest of the Universe. Though I doubt either of these views are mainstream, I sensed that they hold underlying influences on many. And those who don't hold any particular ideas about 12-21-12 are being marinated in fear from the media presentations regarding the demise of our world.

As much as I've looked at these projections and interpretations of the dark future of humanity, I've been unable to see any significant differences in thinking about what has been called the *end of days*, between those who believe Jesus will be coming and those who believe aliens will come to overpower humanity. The two major groups seem to be looking for something from the outside to save us from ourselves. My understanding is that the conditions that confound us have been produced by millennia of people believing in separation, and the ultimate solution to what is happening to us is for each of us to heal ourselves by embracing the truth. Each of us must reconnect with the light within, the essence from which we have separated. Once reconnected, we will be able to create a world so very different from the one we are experiencing at the beginning of the 21st century. I was filled with such deep sadness because I could not find a way to communicate what I know to those so committed to their beliefs about the end times, anymore than I could find the way to connect with whatever was blocking me from writing about *the worst of the worst.*

I believed that the message everyone needed to hear about deep internal healing of the separation that has plagued the human species from the beginning would go unheard, and whatever I knew would be considered useless to those who are terrified of 2012, those who have no concept of 2012 being anything but another year, those who are not interested in masks, much less what lies behind masks and what exists under the mask, and those committed to holding together the world structures, no matter the cost. As I spoke to Greg, the pain in my shoulder and back intensified, as well as the burning feeling in my arms and legs. I told him that it literally felt like something had attached itself to my back and was doing everything possible to hold me back from moving forward with this book and the next. It's intention seemed to be to prevent me from going out into the world to plant my idea seeds about each of us being responsible to transform ourselves by reconnecting with the essence within.

When I focused my attention on my back and asked if what had attached itself to my back was a part of me, I got a very strong message to the contrary. What had attached to me was a man I knew from a past lifetime. I asked who he was, and he told me his name was Jeff. Immediately, I found myself on a journey to sometime in the mid 1800s. I was at a barn dance in the old West and was a teenager enjoying flirting with a young man who seemed attracted to me, as well. It seemed that we had known each other for a little while, as he was a hired worker on my father's ranch. After dancing for a while, he walked me to a private place behind a stack of hay and kissed me. My heart opened. I thought that Jeff might well be the one that would take me away from my difficult family life.

I could see how I had hoped for the same kind of rescuing in that past life as those other groups in the 21st century are hoping for external rescuing now, and how that same pattern exists, not just in those who focus on 2012, but so many who focus on their personal lives, believing that some other person will save them from unhappy or lonely lives. This seems to be a common human pattern of looking to something external to solve what can only be addressed inside us.

In that 1800s life, I was the only girl and youngest child of a family with many older brothers. Our mother passed away a long time before, and I had been the substitute mother since my childhood. My job was cleaning up after my brothers and father, cooking, and maintaining our household. It was a hard and thankless job.

In the moment of the kiss that felt so beautiful, so welcomed, several of my older brothers in that lifetime physically accosted the young man to frighten him away. I was devastated by their actions, but was afraid to say anything. They collected around him with aggressive intimidation, and his fear caused him to pull out a knife in self-defense, but instead, his action caused them to attack him. He slashed out to keep the attackers away, and he killed one of my brothers who had lunged at him. Another brother stabbed Jeff in the back, and continued attacking until the young man was dead. The shock of this murder caused my heart to snap shut with a feeling that my own body had been stabbed.

Jeff was a gentle sweet boy and never deserved to be murdered for a kiss. If my brothers had not terrified him, he would not have needed to defend himself and the one brother would not have died, which would have meant that he would not have been executed by the other brother, either. I took on the belief that my flirtation, which caused him to be attracted to me, was what caused him to kiss me and then die. I was sure that my brothers accosted him because they didn't want their little sister to leave their family and serve a stranger instead of them. They assumed the young girl I was in that life was *their* servant, not anyone else's. After that horrible incident, I withdrew from the outside, never allowing my eyes to meet the eyes of anyone again, and remained the family servant for the rest of that life.

My awareness shifted to a later life of that young man. Jeff and the brother that had killed him in the 1800s, each incarnated a few decades later in the early 1900s, and conflict arose between the two again. I have no sense that I was connected to either of them in that lifetime. The man in the mid 1900s, who had been Jeff in the 1800's and died, was found guilty of a murder of a transient in a bar in the mid 1900s and sent to the electric chair. The transient in the 1900s life had been my brother in the previous life in the 1800s.

My feeling is that his electrocution happened in the early 1950s, very close to, if not the same time that my little child-self was strapped in the wired chair and given excruciatingly horrible electric shocks while tape recordings were played. I sensed that Jeff, who had been attracted to the flirtatious teen in the 1860s, became attached to her instead of returning to the light. The connection the girl that I was then and Jeff seemed to have in common was our mutual belief that he was supposed to be my protector. He believed he failed to adequately protect me from my brothers, and my belief was my wanting him to fill the protector role for me got him killed. After my brother murdered him, he attached to me to become the protector in death that he couldn't be when he was alive. He took on the job of holding me back from doing anything that could result in my getting hurt. I opened to the attachment because my soul felt responsible for Jeff's death.

When I worked with this past life memory in the session with Greg, I sensed that my energy became fused with Jeff's when I took in the stabbing of the knife in his back—much like I took the shotgun blast that had gone into the little girl's face in this life—and I also took in his fear about going out into the world because it "gets you killed." His venturing away from his home to get a job on my father's ranch led to his death, causing him to link going away from home to getting killed. I had taken on that belief when I withdrew from any thoughts of venturing out or allowing someone to take me away back in the 1800s life.

***

The body feelings associated with the stabbing returned in the late summer of 2006, when I was preparing to leave Florida. It was then that I felt a contraction that began in the middle of my back, where several vertebrae felt as if they were fused together, creating stricture of movement and burning pain. The muscles from this place in my spine attached to my shoulders and neck, as well as into the muscles in my groin, which felt as if they turned into steel cables being drawn tighter and tighter, pulling my body into the fetal position. Now, as I write this, I see that the painful places I felt in my body were the places in Jeff's body that received the knife wounds, and the pulling into the fetal position was the protective position his body took before he died.

I took his dying energy into me, and it resurfaced in this lifetime when I was going to leave "my home" without knowing where I was going.

When I previously wrote, *"All of this was related to painful burning in my forearms and lower legs, a burning that went deep down into my bones and once it began, there was nothing I could do to make the burning stop,"* I believe I was describing what Jeff experienced when he was being stabbed to death by my 1800s brother and again in his next lifetime after he killed the transient and was put to death in the electric chair.

When I was strapped to the chair with electric charges as a child, his life force being burnt out of his body somewhere in the country reconnected with my energy field in Alaska, not only because of our previous attachment, but because we were experiencing something very similar. He died and reattached himself to me in this life, and I lived, but with his energy field attached to my back, literally holding me back any time I considered going out in the world. It was clear to me that every time in my life I have ever made a decision to "go out into the world" there was always an inner struggle where part of me wanted to go, and part of me fought against going—between the part of me following the inner *Johnny Appleseed* call and the part of me that feared going out because if you do, you can get killed or someone you love might die.

When I saw all of this, I turned my focus to Jeff, and explained to him that I didn't need his protection from the world. I explained that I have learned enough to recognize that I created what I needed to finally discover the truth that my life experiences are my creation, including my relationship with him. I explained to him that he was not responsible for me, and I was not responsible for him. I told him I still see him as a sweet boy, not a murderer. I thanked him for being a bright light in that life we shared a kiss. I talked to him about the light and then released him from his attachment to me to go to the light if he was ready to go. In releasing him, I released the knife energy I had taken into my back that matched the knife in his back, an energy that was literally holding me back in this life. I felt his energy leave me; for the first time in 33 months, the pain in my shoulder and neck that was reactivated at the end of summer in 2006, finally released. The burning sensation in my arms and legs released, as well.

276

I believe his thoughts of letting go to die, both in his life as Jeff and the life that ended in the electric chair, entered my mind as I sat in the metal chair by the fire pit a few months before and considered letting go and dying because the pain was so bad. I attached his thoughts to my body pain, believing it would never stop until death. I was very close to giving up on life because of the overpowering belief that the pain would never stop. In releasing Jeff, I also released the thoughts of dying as the only way to escape pain, and I felt myself embrace life.

CONSIDERING PAST LIVES

As a side note, I am well aware that readers who do not believe in the concept of past lives might find what I have written to be totally absurd, if not just fanciful imagination. For most of my life, I thought the same thing until my inner journeys to find the source of a current life issue took me back to experiences that could not have been in this life. At first, I thought I might be tapping into genetic memory, stored in my DNA, but that didn't make sense when some of the memories were of lives as ancient African tribesmen, Indians, Chinese, slaves and servants that were not Caucasian, as is my genetic heritage. The two lives I wrote about in *The Mask*, both of which ended when I was not, yet, 5-years-old—the life in China ending in 1937, and the one in a Nazi concentration camp ending in 1943— could not be explained through genetics.

It is, also, possible that I could have been tapping into the collective unconscious, retrieving information about human experience, but I have noticed three factors that are not answered from the collective unconscious theory. The first is that when I tap into someone else's experiences (Jeff, the subordinate that I kicked, the Nazi soldier who turned my family in to the authorities, and so many more over the years) I do not feel an emotional charge of deep cell level identity like I do when I open to an experience that my consciousness tells me was myself in a past life. Secondly, there is a visceral response in my body and in my emotions that feels the same as when I recall some powerful event in my childhood. These are somatic responses that cannot be created or duplicated by imagining. The third factor is that when I understand the event in that past life and bring truth into the experience, like I do with child parts of me trapped in some trauma in my childhood, healing happens and my life experience transforms. This is a transformation of how I am in the world that goes much deeper than a realization in my thoughts. All of these feelings have caused me to conclude that I have lived lives before this one and will likely live more lives in the future. And, who knows...I may be living parallel lives, as well.

HEALING REBECCA

In this moment as I am writing, I realize in the work I did with Greg, I released Jeff's attachment and his energy field, but I didn't work with the teenage girl that I was in that lifetime, an aspect of whom still seems stuck in a belief in servitude and suffering. I need to take a break from my writing and do that now...

***

For one and a half hours, I did an inner journey to find and free the girl from that past life in the 1800s. I lay down on my bed, went into a relaxed state and asked to be taken to the young woman who had experienced the trauma of Jeff's death. At first my mind began to fill with images of all sorts, bouncing around from one possible scenario to the next like I was a playwright considering alternate plots for a play. It was very clear that all this was going on in my head and wasn't connected to what was true for the teenager. I requested that my head stop whatever it was doing and allow the journey to lead me to the young woman. As soon as I said that, I found myself sitting beside the girl on some kind of a wooden bench along side a road in a country area. I asked her what her name was and she replied that it was Rebecca.

I drifted into a very deep state of consciousness and saw the girl's life at its beginning. Her mother died in childbirth with this seventh child after having six healthy boys; the youngest of the brothers seemed to be a number of years older. Rebecca had been a late-in-life pregnancy. Her father had little to do with the child, blaming her for the death of his wife, and the brothers felt little affection for an infant who was responsible for the loss of their mother. The baby was taken care of by a relative until she grew old enough to do household chores and was returned to her family, where she served them all.

The girl believed she was to blame for her mother's death, as that was the thought-field in which she had been marinated her entire life. So before I could free her from her attachment to that lifetime, she had to be freed of this heavy burden of responsibility she was carrying. When I saw this situation, I could understand where Rebecca would have believed she had caused not just her mother's death but her brother's death, and Jeff's death, too. A side effect of her feeling this burden and not being fully freed from the beliefs of that life, was that I brought this thought field into my life and continued to take on responsibility for the lives of everyone around me.

In the many years of working with parts of myself trapped in some untenable trauma, I found value in taking those parts to a higher place to gain a better perspective. I don't know exactly where the higher place is on the physical plane, because I sense it really isn't a place, as we know the concept of place in three-dimensional reality, but it is where patterns and truths can be seen, which normally are not available to us when we are in the middle of something. So I took Rebecca where she could see what really happened.

Rebecca's mother had been married off very young to an older man whose first wife had died from what they called fever. Her parents were suffering economically and could not afford to keep her at home, so she became the child-bride of this older man. Life for her was hard, having to care not only for her husband, but also, over time, for her six boys. There was very little joy in her life. I could see how much she suffered, and then how much Rebecca suffered, as well, as she took over the responsibilities left by her dead mother. As far back as I could see it was very clear that so many women believed life is suffering. I decided to take Rebecca out of the *thought field* that believed in suffering as being a descriptor of life, but it was very hard finding any place in the world where such a belief was not there prominently or subtly. I found myself dropping into a deeper state and something important happened, though I don't know what it was.

After our journey to the higher place, Rebecca and I could see that her mother was too overwhelmed with the responsibilities of life and simply did not want to keep going in a life where there was little love and no joy. She left her body while her seventh child was coming into the world. If the child were to be a boy, he would be the seventh son of a seventh son, and her belief was that the child could either be a great force for good or for evil, and she didn't believe she was strong enough to direct him toward good when she was so oppressed by her own life. After seeing this, Rebecca was willing to let go of her guilt for her mother's death. Mother had chosen to let go of life when she was presented with a choice point.

In that deeper journey, I believe we may have traveled through the rest of Rebecca's life following the death of Jeff. I believe that while my soul moved on beyond that life when I was Rebecca, I eventually reincarnated into the life in China where I died as a small child in the 1937 Japanese invasion of Nanking, and then shortly thereafter in Hitler's Germany, only to die as a small child in Auschwitz in 1943. Not long after that death, I came back in this life in pre-statehood Alaska. But in those incarnations, a part of me remained attached to the life in which I experienced the death of Jeff. After seeing all she was shown from that higher place, Rebecca was finally ready to release that life, as well as the beliefs she carried, and join with the rest of me in 2009. She was prepared to see life in a very different way, which meant that, I, too, would be living in a transformed way.

***

As a sidelight to the belief in suffering, when I, as Rebecca, was standing between my brothers and Jeff, before the knife attack, I wanted to communicate with all of them, but I knew none would listen to me. My sense of all this was that the current life beliefs about the groups related to 2012, created the same sadness about something bad that was going to happen because no one would listen. The bad that I was afraid of in 2009, was that if I did speak, people would not listen and the results would be catastrophic, and if I did not speak, the results would be catastrophic, as well. I feared people would not seek inner healing, and instead, they would create the meltdown and destruction of our world on the global level, predicted by those who follow the

Mayan calendar, and those who interpret scripture's reference to the end times of *Armageddon* being fulfilled, now. I could see how I had taken on the responsibility of the world in this life, as I had in that past life when I took on the responsibility for Jeff and my brother's deaths, which was rooted in my taking responsibility for my mother's death followed by taking on the responsibility of my brothers and father when I lived as Rebecca.

***

I believe my soul's delight has always been to go to the far away places, to open to other cultures' perspectives, and to share my perspective of the world with any who might be open to consider it. However, Jeff's attachment from the time I was about six, strapped to the electric chair, made the thought of such travel, though delightful, something that made me very sad...after all, I had taken Jeff's sadness for the loss of his life when he ventured away from his home and I had my own sadness from my venturing beyond my 1800s family, an action that seemed to have caused the death of someone I cared for. I believe that was why I was so drawn to songs in my childhood like *The Happy Wanderer* and *Far Away Places*, and to Dolly Parton's *Wildflower* song that a dear friend gave to me just before I left for China in 1990. All these songs opened my heart to expanding into the world, but at the same time made me feel so very sad about leaving what had become home.

The closer I came to completing this book, and seeing in my mind's eye book number three finished, the more I was sure I'd be receiving the message to begin to move out in the world like I received just three years before when I was in Florida and woke with the awareness that this was the time to leave. I believe that is what caused the familiar old body-pain patterns to return in early 2007, and again in 2009.

It was clear to me that Rebecca, didn't cause either of the deaths—my brothers and Jeff's—or, for that matter, I hadn't caused my mother's death in that lifetime or my mother's attempted suicides in this life. These men were connected to some pattern and I, as Rebecca, was the excuse they used to recreate a conflict that continued past that lifetime into the next for them. My pattern of my taking the responsibility for other people's patterns was replicated when I took responsibility for the actions of the vigilantes who used little Sandy as an excuse to recreate whatever patterns they were executing in the basement of the Jesse Lee Home. I did it again when I believed I was responsible for my sister being belt-whipped by my mother and for the events of my childhood that were inflicted on me.

COMPLETING THE RELEASES

Greg suggested that I call together the two families—the one made up of the brothers from the 1800s and my current family—and the two groups of people who I was afraid would attack me for my idea that healing of our selves, our family systems, and our world had to come from inside us as individuals, not from some external force that would swoop in and transform us. None of them would be able to hear my interpretations of truth unless I spoke up and told them, and then it was up to them to listen, if they chose to do so.

First, I spoke to the family of brothers from the 1800s. I told them they had no right to act as if they owned me and from now on, I am choosing to take ownership of my own life and responsibility for myself. I announced that I would follow what delights my heart and would no longer serve them. Then I spoke to my family from this lifetime. I told them that I hold a different understanding of the world and my place in it than they do and I would no longer hold myself back from speaking what I see as my truth in the world. I explained that I have no need to invade their space with my beliefs, but I no longer am willing to let my fear of their response to my speaking my truth hold me back. Speaking these things to both of the families felt very empowering.

Then I addressed the hordes of people that represented the opposing ideas about 2012. I told both groups that I would no longer keep silent for fear of antagonizing either group. Bottom line...I will speak my truth even if I am the only person in the Universe that believes to heal our world and to heal our lives, we must deal with the universe we hold inside ourselves. I told them I believe we will continue to have wars in the outer world as long as we still have wars inside, and the wars inside won't end until we release our belief that we are separate from the essence within and separate from the Great Mystery that is in all.

Saying this seemed to open something inside me and I felt a strength flowing through my spine and my body that was profound.

Greg asked if there was anything more I needed to say to anyone in my family. As soon as he spoke those words, I saw the sister who had been whipped by my mother and I saw how my teenage self had felt responsible for what had happened her. My heart had broken back then because I didn't know how to protect or defend her from what was such a cruel, vicious, and totally uncalled-for whipping. Seeing her image connected me to an incident when we were in our middle teens.

Not long after the whipping, the sister that I loved with all my heart—the one who shared with me 3 days of being the same age, the one whose class room I snuck into when I was in the first grade because I missed her and wanted to have lunch with her instead of being with strangers in my class room, the one who climbed the tallest trees and taught me to have the courage to follow her up as high as possible—was talking on the telephone to a man she had recently met. She sounded like a person in her 30s, a woman of the world, with an air about her that was not my sister. Even her face no longer looked like my sister. I suspect that this is the first time I really understood about wearing masks, though I wouldn't have known what to call it, back then. I remembered looking at her and realized that if she continued to pretend to be who she was not, she would forget who she really was and I would lose my dear, sweet sister forever. I wanted to tell her how broken hearted I was because, somehow, in that moment, I knew I would lose her. Seeing her take on another personality, right there in front of me, felt as if I had lost her already.

While in that session with Greg, I saw how so many of the hateful events in our family had caused the sister that I loved so deeply to drift away, not just from me, but it felt like she had drifted away from herself, as well, and my heart ached for the loss. As she drifted further and further away, with tears streaming down my cheeks, I told my sister that I loved her...that I would always love her.

When Greg asked me to step into her to understand what she was experiencing, I sensed that she felt such deep pain and anger for our parents for not seeing her, and for judging her to be someone she was not. Because my parents did not know how to see her, she was determined that she would make others notice her, but they saw only her mask, since her authentic self, her essence, was locked deep inside for protection. My heart ached.

Greg suggested that an angel of love could be called in, and as soon as this magnificent angel appeared, my sister fell into his arms and she knew, maybe for the first time since she was a small child when the two of us could see each other, that she was really seen. As I saw this, I knew that these were my own feelings, as well. The angel took my sister into his heart; she seemed to be deeply happy. I experienced my own version of being seen. I released my parents from having to see me, and I told my sister that I would always see her, and in saying that I was telling myself I would see me, too, even if frightened, angry people couldn't see either of us. My heart opened to the love I have always felt for my sister who was not quite a year older than me, and I was so grateful she was in my life.

Then I saw an image of my little brother, being punished for telling the truth about my father. When my brother was barely a teenager, he was very sure our father had been lying to us about where he was going at night when he supposedly left for work. My brother had checked the mileage on the car, for several days and found the numbers did not match what they should have been if my father had gone where he said he had gone. So one day, my brother hid his bicycle outside and when it was time for my father to leave for work, my brother followed him. He discovered that my dad was having an affair with the mother of one of my brother's classmates.

With amazing courage, my little brother confronted my father with the truth and demanded that he end the affair or my brother would tell my mother. My father, using all the fear tactics he had used on us over the years, threatened my brother telling him he had better not repeat the accusation to anyone, but my brother told my mother anyway. My mother's response to my brother, which I believe he may never have gotten over, was that he should remember she loved my father first. She then demanded that my brother apologize to our father for telling lies. When my brother refused, his punishment for being disrespectful to my father was that he had to dig up the huge front lawn, shovelful by shovelful to prepare the soil for new seed. The ground was extremely solid; it was filled with rocks and deeply entangled with weeds. That soil never before or since has fostered a healthy looking lawn.

From the living room window, I watched my little brother as he was carrying out the totally unjust punishment, digging up the entire yard all by him self, stabbing the shovel into the earth with what looked like loathing hatred and pain on his face as he carried out his punishment for telling the truth. My heart ached because I was too afraid to stand up for him. Buried deep inside my internal dungeons, was the memory of what happened to me when I told the truth at age four, followed by telling a lie. In my family, punishment happened whether you were truthful or lied.

In that 2009 session with Greg, I explained to my brother's soul that I was so sorry for how much he suffered and how sad I was for being too young and too scared to help him. I told him that someday I would grow into a woman who would develop a backbone and not be afraid of our parents and I would learn to speak my truth. I told him that I would always love him.

Without realizing it, I projected my childhood fears of my parents and abusers, onto groups of people today who have interpretations of the world and "salvation," that I believe could be dangerous to the world, fears that caused me to believe nobody was interested in what I had to say about the power of transformational healing from within. Again, as in childhood, I believed I would be punished and silenced; the fear, itself, was silencing me.

I had to see how this entangled set of patterns grew out of the abuses that connected the lifetime with Jeff and brothers who silenced me, my own childhood that silenced me, and my fears of anyone in the world who might be powerful enough to silence me. Only when I saw the very complicated set of patterns could I free myself from the snare of these fear-based patterns that made me feel responsible for everyone else, while at the same time, believed none would listen to what I truly believe they would need to survive what may well be ahead.

It was never my job to save Jeff from his pattern of being killed for protecting himself. It was never my job to save my parents from the lives they lived, or my siblings for the unjustified suffering at the hands of my parents. My choosing to wish for life did not mean that I was wishing for someone else to die. I could ask forgiveness for being so terrified that I didn't know how to speak the truth, as a little girl in the basement of the Jesse Lee Home, as a teenager when my siblings were so cruelly treated, and as the adult who wrote *Melting the Chains* but was too afraid to get it published and later resisted including *the worst of the worst* in this book.

***

I speculate that most children do not survive growing up when they are exposed to extreme abuse, such as what was inflicted on me in my childhood. Fortunately, I had found a way to split off and not remember what happened, without going totally insane. I had learned how to dissociate by going into the rock when, at four-years-old, I was raped in the forest. That ability allowed me to split from the later horrors and forget until I had become strong enough and learned enough to go back in time and rescue the little child parts of me that had been so brutally tortured in my early years. The strengthening that grew in me as an adult by facing the events of my childhood, also, provided the pathway to past life trauma that needed healing, and opened to the even deeper level of human trauma that I believe all of us hold in our DNA. When I worked with what I believe may well have been the original trauma of spiritual incarnation into three-dimensional awareness, I asked the dark to notice that it carried the light and the light to notice it carried the dark. Because each carried the other, neither had to be afraid of the other. I will share more about this in book three, *Under the Mask*.

I suspect those children who were as painfully abused as I, but were not able to find a way to split it off and separate the memories from the rest of their lives, did not survive into adulthood, or if they did, they may have had to erase the memories with alcohol, drugs, or other self-abuses. Others may have separated so much from their feelings that they became sociopaths committing the same kinds of torturous abuses on others like the abuses that were inflicted on them, acting out what happened to them because they couldn't allow themselves to feel what happened.

A child who slipped and told a friend about the abuse might have become one who others had to watch being sacrificed. That might have been what happened to the little girl, perhaps a year or two older than I, who had the side of her face blown off. This was the fear that held me back from discussing any of this with anyone for most of my life. It kept me from opening to anyone except my therapist until I tried to write about it in 1992. But still, I did nothing to allow the manuscript to become a book. It took 17 more years to strengthen my backbone enough to know that I could release the protective patterns that held me back from speaking my truth and prevented me from living connected to the love that resides in my essence. These protective patterns that controlled my responses to life for so long had prevented my mind, body, heart, and spirit from experiencing the flow of harmonious balance, which creates freedom to experience personal power, authenticity, and spontaneity.

CONSIDERING SILENCE ONE LAST TIME

It was not just this horrible information from my childhood that I had to acknowledge, feel, and release. I had to contend with the parts of myself I spoke about earlier that my internal system created to hear nothing, see nothing, and feel nothing. They were the ones who were created to have no memories of the events, and their designated purpose for existence was to deny anything bad had ever happened. Without them, I could not have lived through childhood; yet, these denying parts created blocks in the progress of the healing process, and kept me from fully embracing life.

***

Even now, 17 years after I first wrote what I included in this chapter, and 20 years from the first time that the memories came back in therapy—memories that I was *too young to remember*, according to my father—I still feel the sadness and oppression of what happened to me when I was so little, and what was happening to other people, other children, other infants. I am aware that in this very moment of this current writing in 2009, my head is pounding with a headache and breathing is difficult.

I can hear my own voice, as well as voices of others telling me maybe it would be better to leave all of this in the past. Maybe the forgetting was the best thing I could have done. And, certainly, there are places inside that believe this is true. But it is the forgetting what I know and the fear of letting myself know that have created the patterns of being silent, the patterns that tell me it is not safe to be in the world, and how much better to remain isolated. Fear is what causes me to hold myself back from speaking what I hold in my heart that I know I have been called to communicate.

If I am going to create for myself a world that no longer needs to reflect back to me all that has been hidden behind my mask, I need to transform the fear into strength and embrace the courage to speak.

OWNING THE EXISTENCE OF LEVEL THREE

I believe until we own the existence of level three in our world and in ourselves, we will not heal from its effects. And as much as I have wanted to reject the idea that I hold level-three abuse potential in me, I can understand you, as a reader, rejecting the idea that it exists in you. Years of working with all the levels of abuse in my life and in the lives of many clients, I have come to believe that we all experience times when we turn against our essence and in doing so turn against the essence of other persons without being a part of the truly dark energies. This turning against our essence is what identifies level-three abuse.

Turning against our essence does not have to look as unfathomably cruel as it did in the hands of those very depraved people who inflicted such horror on me and on others in my childhood as I described that existed along the path to the *worst of the worst*. Turning against our essence can be expressed in much milder forms like when we go into depression or consider thoughts of suicide, or perhaps thoughts of just not wanting to be here any longer. Level-three abuse can show up when we are deciding on a career, and our soul wants to do something that all reason would say is not financially wise. So instead of listening to the music of our soul, we choose a profession that makes us seem important, one that would please our parents, or promise to give us money instead of purpose. In making choices against our essence we are committing level-three self-abuse.

AN EXAMPLE OF LEVEL-THREE ABUSE

In early 1987, I had separated from my then husband, Jake, and for almost three years, he and I made a number of attempts to see if we could salvage our crumbled relationship. In the late summer of 1989, he asked me if I would go on a cruise with him for a month in the San Juan Islands between Canada and the US to see if we could recreate a foundation for rebuilding a life together.

Part way into the trip, a storm started to brew and we needed to anchor down. He told me he would take care of the front anchor and directed me to row the dinghy toward shore and tie down the back of the 42 foot cruiser to a tree that was growing sideways out over the water. I was trying to maintain course while struggling with the ores in the choppy water and took my eyes off the tie-down rope that was unwinding with every forward movement. But as I approached closer to the shore, the rope unwound and flipped out of the dinghy. I struggled to get back toward the rope, when Jake saw that I had lost the tie down. He pulled it back onto the boat from his end and ordered me back to the cruiser. Obviously angry that I had failed to do the job correctly, he told me to get out, and then angrily told me if he had wanted the job done right, he should have done it himself.

He offered me no help in getting back onto the cruiser, took over the task, and began rowing toward the shore, fuming with rage at my ineptitude. But as he approached the tie-up tree that hung out over the water and rocks along the shore, he stood up to catch the tree and began to lose his footing. As I watched him struggle to keep his balance, I wished he would fall into the choppy water. I didn't want him to hurt himself, or die; I wanted him to be embarrassed in front of me. I knew if he fell in he would feel shame, and for him, humiliation would have been excruciating, even if only for a minute, maybe even worse than dying.

In that moment, a flood of awareness washed through me. I knew that when we returned from our trip, I would complete the divorce. I realized that if I continued to be with him, I would turn into a hateful woman wishing harm on my husband, and I couldn't do that to myself or to him; despite his sometimes cruel treatment of me, I loved him. That moment that I wanted him to suffer deep in his soul, I had entered level-three abuse in my mind. And because thoughts are energy, I sent that energy in his direction completely disconnected from love. The pain I felt from his attack of me, caused me to separate from my essence, and then I turned on him, and wanted something to happen that would separate him from his essence in shame and cause him to feel crushed. This feeling of wanting him to feel something that had the potential to destroy his spirit was beyond level two, though there was level two in it, as well.

Situation comedies made up with segments like this between wives and husbands fill the airwaves nightly and we laugh at level-three abuse because we identify with the feelings, without knowing under the laughter is energy that wishes destruction of the essence of another, even if only for a brief moment. And certainly much of the reality TV involving destructive energies directed toward competitors can tap into our own destructive energies as we watch. Though we engage in level-three abuses in mild forms far more often than we might imagine, most of us would never move into the extreme, as did the adults in my childhood, but…if pushed hard enough to experience rage, we could be capable of moving beyond the very mild expressions along the continuum of the third level of abuse to do something we could never imagine doing.

LEVEL THREE ALL AROUND US

The third level of abuse is not just a product of separating from the essence within as in levels one and two because of an external focus, but it is formed when there is an intention to destroy the essence of anyone who becomes the target of abuse. On a subtle, unconscious level, when anyone wants to crush the essence in another, that person turns against the essence within, as well. This level moves beyond the viciousness and cruelty that can characterize the extreme end of level two that wants to hurt another because of what they did; it moves into the arena of the sinister, and often this kind of viciousness can be turned against someone or many others who never hurt them.

Far too often now, we hear stories of kids who were pushed too far by bullying students, made into targets of the abuse, and made to feel completely rejected, not just by the bullies, but also by everyone, because no one defended them. The ones whose hearts were broken so deeply that they turned cold inside might become ones who return to their schools with guns, terrifying and killing those who had been heartless or had not stepped in to protected them from the heartless ones. Husbands and x-husbands return to the houses that used to be their homes, and they kill wives and children but then continue their killing spree to include others not connected to their pain, killing for the sake of killing. People who believe they were jilted by significant others, by institutions, or peers, come back to make those people feel the same way they felt, which is totally disconnected from their essence. As I write these words, the news has broadcast a report of a man who walked into a gym and killed three women, and then him self because he felt rage at 30 million women who did not find him attractive. Level three is all around us, and even if we don't want to acknowledge it, we have it in us, as well. While level two grows out of rage and wants to inflict pain or suffering to feel vindicated, level three delights or feels a sense of satisfaction inside or release in watching another suffer, with the abuse done for the enjoyment of the feeling of suffering, rather than retribution for having been hurt.

The stories we have been hearing all too often lately about crazed people going into malls, stores, churches, and schools to kill as many people as possible, and then turn their weapons on themselves, are examples of this third level of abuse. This level includes sociopaths and serial killers like Ted Bundy who is believed to have killed at least 100 women on a killing spree from Washington State to Florida, and the Columbine assassins, Harris and Klebold, who killed 12 of their fellow students, a teacher, and then themselves.

Some of the more recent youthful killers can be linked to murderous video games that seemed to tap into the minds of these damaged people who had a history of abuse in their homes or abusive rejection from their peers.

Every now and then, stories are told of unfathomable wickedness, torture and cruelty that seem impossible to understand like the one of Jeffrey Dahmer, who, from 1978-1991, murdered and cannibalized 17 male victims. But before killing some of them, he anesthetized them, drilled holes in their heads, and poured acid in the holes like he did to animals when he was a child. The men and boys survived for hours up to days, acting like zombies, according to his testimony. After killing them, he salvaged their larger muscles and froze them for later eating, and saved skulls of others as souvenirs of his conquests. The remains were dissolved with acid and washed down his bathroom drain. Horrors like those committed by Dahmer sound too close to my childhood to discount what happened to me as impossible. I wouldn't be surprised if Dahmer had experienced something similar to what I experienced when he was a child. But instead of holding it all in, splitting apart, remaining silent, and becoming so depressed that thoughts of suicide were always near the surface as was my experience, he turned the destructive level-three energies outward into the world. This turning took the form of the torture and murder of animals when he was a child and humans when he not only dismembered the victims, but also, tried to separate them from their essence by turning them into zombies. Whatever happened to him in his childhood or in a past life must have made him feel as if he were a zombie inside.

***

For most of my life, I believed that the vast majority of people would have been repulsed by reading of such horror in real life and have preferred to believe that something like the Dahmer story was made up in the deranged mind of some writer of fiction. But instead, it has become clear that many people are drawn to this kind of horror. Walter Mosley, in an article in the August 9, 2009 issue of *Newsweek* pointed out that we are obsessed with crime because we are trying to figure out how to live in a world that could crush us and not even notice what it had done, and also, because we ourselves need forgiveness and need someone else to blame because everybody is guilty of something. So we focus on the darkest of the dark, which from my perspective, reveals the third level of abuse where we seek to understand, and perhaps, control what we fear that is inside us.

The success of the film, *The Silence of the Lambs*, a fictional story about a cannibalistic murderer not unlike Dahmer in the real world, indicated that I was wrong in my original conclusion about people turning away from knowing about the worst that is in us. In fact, the serial killer Hannibal Lecter, from the 1991 film was voted by The American Film Institute to be the most memorable villain in film history.

According to the critics from Best-Horror-Movies.com, *Silence of the Lambs is shocking, no matter how many times you watch it, as the events unfold leading to the conclusion. Silence of the Lambs truly deserves all the praise and popularity it has received over the years.* This film began a genre of crime related movies and television programs that depict images of horrific mutilations and destruction of human beings that seems to have drawn the interest, not just of millions of viewers, but sponsors, too. I think it is no accident that our culture has drawn these most horrific examples of human torture and mutilation because it reflects the condition that exists inside too many people living with the otherwise unexpressed level-three abusive thoughts. The obsessions around 2012 and Armageddon images, from my perspective, are also reflections of what we hold inside us, but don't want to own.

***

All of us have cancer cells in our bodies, but most of us have immune systems that locate them and rid us of the danger before these potentially life-threatening cells become embedded, spread, and harm us. We all have bacteria in us that if allowed to grow in number, can cause infection in our bodies. No matter how obsessive we might become about cleaning ourselves or how hard we scrub the outside of our bodies or cleanse the inside of our bodies, we will always have germs, viruses, bacteria, and parasites on us and in us, but like the cancer cells, most of us will not be overtaken by them. This is the same for level-three abuse. We all carry third level, abuse-inflicting potential, no matter how much we want to deny that we do. And its presence within us may frighten us more than anything else could. Like little children, afraid of what might be hiding in the shadowed corners of their rooms at night who bury their faces under the covers hoping for sleep to take away the fears, many of us hide from level three, not noticing that what we are afraid of out there is really what is in us that we have projected into the corners and into the shadows behind the mask.

LEVEL THREE IN HISTORY

Human history is peppered with level-three abuse horrors. Most of us are aware of World War Two Nazi concentration camps where millions were identified as being sub-human and experimented upon in ways none of us want to think people could do to others, and after the grotesquely inhuman treatment, the victims were led to their deaths in ways intended to go far beyond body torture into torturing of the soul. And if we went through traditional education that included world history, most of us know of vile atrocities committed against thousands, if not hundreds of thousands of women declared to be witches in the middle ages.

Tribal wars, which resulted in entire tribes being massacred, continue today in some parts of the world and are reflected in gang fights in urban areas of modern societies. Empire building where those who were defeated became slaves to the winners, under the dictum that claims, *"To the victor goes the spoils"* can be seen, not just in the past, but in the present with drug wars that are taking the lives of thousands of people, resulting in profits, as well as enemies lives' taken by the winners.

When reports of vicious murder or raping of little children become known, it is not uncommon for many people to wish for the same kind of cruelty to be meted against the perpetrator. When there is a wish for retribution that causes the abuser to suffer as he or she made the victim suffer, and the thought of this suffering brings deep satisfaction to those contemplating this, level three has been entered. But with righteous indignation, it is possible to be convinced that the abuser deserves such treatment. None-the-less, the world of level-three abuse has been opened. Even aggressive behaviors behind a wheel that are called road rage that can begin as level two directed at someone to make them stop driving in a way that disturbs the raging driver can turn into level three abuse when the intention turns to murderous thoughts and out of control violence becomes directed not just toward that other driver, but also, anyone else that might be on the road.

***

What I included in this chapter and the previous one was the passageway through which I had to go before I could take you to the dungeon that held the *worst of the worst,* mentioned in the first chapter and in a number of other places throughout the other chapters. Finally, I have garnered the courage to include that horrible event that has caused me to hold myself back on so many levels throughout my life. So now, it is time to tell you what happened on another most wicked day in the Jesse Lee Home.

Reflections

Abuse cannot be ended unless we acknowledge that abuse is real. After Freud's paper disclosing childhood sexual abuse in the lives of his clients was rejected, first by his colleagues and then by himself, the continuation of the cover up allowed sexual abuse to continue, nearly unchecked for the next century.

If we are going to decrease abuse of humanity by humanity, we must be willing to acknowledge its existence. We need to allow ourselves to be aware of our patterns of abusing others, as well as our patterns of accepting being abused, even if it is subtle and unconscious. All levels of abuse, whether given or received, have the potential to inflict life long damage.

Notice what you do when you want something and don't get it. Be aware of how you treat other people when you are disappointed, when you are tired, or don't want to be distracted or interrupted. Be conscious of times you become upset enough to want to hurt some one else or when you want to make them suffer. Notice if you allow others to treat you unkindly, disrespectfully, cruelly or in any other painful way. What do you do with the feelings? What do you keep yourself from knowing or doing?

Become aware of how your body responds when you are confronted with something that angers or distresses you or breaks your heart. You might convince yourself that you are good at controlling your emotions and acting calmly, but notice if you are shaking on the inside, getting high blood pressure or developing illnesses such as Parkinson's disease, cancer, rashes, allergies, and more that indicate your body is taking on what you are not expressing. Healing does not come by way of exploding the emotions outward to do damage to the cause of your distress, but rather to become aware of the part of you that is distressed, angry, or broken hearted, and bring love and understanding to that part. From a place of love, you can decide what you need to do to protect yourself from the source of damage.

If you want to contribute to the awakening of yourself and humanity, take time to examine yourself. One by one, we can make a difference if we hold an intention of releasing the patterns of all three levels of abuse.

Chapter Seventeen
THE REST OF THE STORY
Overcoming the Worst of the Worst

It is not unusual for us to assume we know everything when we reflect back over our lives, but all too often significant pieces are left out. To understand who and how we are today, we may have to look deeper into yesterday to finally know the rest of the story.

For 70 years, the clearly recognizable voice of recently departed Paul Harvey would tell a news story on the radio providing the details and facts in such a way that created the illusion that the listener knew what happened, but he would pause for a commercial with a promise when he returned he would tell *the rest of the story*. In a way, I have told important aspects of the story of my early life in the first fifteen chapters, but now, it is time to tell you the rest of the story.

Back in 2004, I woke very early one morning with a dream. In the dream I was calculating the cost of five books…and I hated the job I was given. The books were extremely expensive. As I was adding up the figures, a pain in my leg began to intensify to the point that I could not concentrate on the task, which caused me to become very angry…I threw the pen down and began to shout that I hated doing this calculating of costs. I couldn't find a way to relieve the pain so I found a wheelchair, sat down and elevated my leg, but even getting off my leg didn't help it feel better. I woke in the middle of the anger, the shouting, and the pain.

I knew the pain from the dream, which was also very real in my waking life was related to the part of Sandy with whom I could not connect the day before I had that dream, the one who was being dragged to some horrible experience down the steps and into a most dreaded room in the basement of the Jesse Lee Home…something I had been avoiding knowing for my whole life. For nearly two hours after waking from that most disturbing dream, I processed it, by dropping into a deep state, seeing images from the distant past when I was probably about six, as well as images from my first days in therapy in the mid 80s, images from the day before the 2004 dream and the previous night.

As I had done time after time, in the weeks, or more likely months, from the time the pain in my left leg had gotten increasingly worse, I had gone into the pain and asked it to show me what was causing it. The image was always the same…and it was the image that I had not wanted to accept, because I didn't want to believe it was real. The Sandy who I kept seeing every time I attempted to get to the source of the pain was resisting whatever was about to happen; she was struggling with someone I couldn't see. Her arms were extended in front of her with her wrists locked together, as if some adult had a hold of them and was pulling her forward. She was pulling against the forward motion as hard as she could, with every muscle in her hips and legs locked into rigid resistance, and her little butt pulled back and dropped down in a vain attempt to become dead weight so she could not be forced to go to whatever was about to happen.

Finally, I told the child that I could see her…but I couldn't see the person who had a hold of her wrists. I asked her to forgive me for not seeing and for not believing that anything had happened to her when it was clear she had been trying to reach me through the pain in my leg for quite a long time. As I connected with the child, the pain in my left knee intensified beyond what it was when I'd wakened, something I hadn't believed was possible until that moment.

The child didn't seem to notice that I was there…she was as blind to me as I had been blind to her circumstance. But I knew that she was in me, causing pain in my leg…maybe so intense that it could result in my becoming crippled, like in the dream, if I couldn't find the source. I had to get to her, but I didn't know how because, as much as I tried to make myself believe it, I didn't believe what happened to her was real…I didn't want to believe it.

It's not like I hadn't done myriad interventions like this for people, or even for myself, in the past, but for some reason, I was disconnected from my knowledge of how to reach this unknown part of myself who was living with such profound knee pain that it found its way through the decades and into my knee in 2004. And then...the words my therapist was demonstrating for me from so long before came into my thoughts...when he said that I should teach the little girl to get angry...enough to yell at her parents and demand that they not treat her badly or that they stop giving excuses for their bad parenting. He used the words *bull crap* to describe excuses they had given for her bad treatment, and then, as if *he* were talking to little Sandy's parents, he said, *"Hey you stupid a-- ----s...get you're a---s back here and pick up this scared little girl."* His words jumped out at me when I heard them the first time because they were not words I used or expected him to use. But his words were in my thoughts when I began to use a version of them on the invisible person pulling my child-self toward whatever unknown event was about to happen.

In this 2004 experience, I assumed I was yelling at my father for dragging my child-self to that unknown place after the burial when little Sandy thought she was being left in the ground to die, but as I continued to focus on my child-self, I began to see another event as if it was buried underneath the image of my father's vicious act. This time I saw the image of a woman dragging little Sandy to a basement room, an image that I had dismissed as insane the first time I saw it nearly a quarter of a century ago, and then buried it myself.

I began to yell at the woman who was in this image from decades ago, and then at all of the people involved in this most horrific event, but they didn't seem the least bit affected by my screaming. I felt myself become the child and allowed myself to grow exceedingly big, so big that the woman couldn't drag me anymore, but that wasn't enough to stop her or the whole group of people from doing what they were doing. I asked the biggest, toughest *justice angel* to come into my body and his energy exploded at them...He sliced through all of them to make them stop. He rescued this little girl from the worst day of her life, though I was still unsure of what had happened to her, even though a part of me had remembered this whole event, years before.

But again the denying parts of me had buried and forgotten that I had remembered, as was a pattern in the process of retrieving memories. After the rescue, I held the child in my arms, as she began to howl cry, so deeply grieving some unknown something. For the first time in decades she didn't feel pulled anymore. I felt my hips begin to straiten and the pain in my left knee began to subside. Something important was going on as the child surrendered to me.

And then, like some mystical command was given, all the pieces fell into place…things I hadn't thought of for decades came together. The pieces didn't come in a time sequence order that I can remember right now…but as each piece dropped into place, the whole event finally became clear.

***

Back in 1986, a short time after I had begun therapy in Seattle, I was sitting in the recliner chair in my therapist's office. This gifted doctor had begun an induction, one of the first hypnosis sessions in our work together to talk with a child part who might be ready to talk with him. As was my practice after therapy sessions, I wrote about what happened during the hour in my journal and later included it in *Melting the Chains*:

As I look back on the summer of '86 I recall that my therapist had encouraged me to more actively pursue making contact with little Sandy. I have no memory of the words he was saying or the issue we were dealing with when I made the first contact. I recall feeling a strange sensation that caused me to believe my body was not mine. I was unaware that my consciousness had shifted and I was thinking and seeing from my child-self's perspective, as if I had become a child, but I was in an adult body. I could not understand why my body was so big, and I was in a room I did not recognize. There was a man with a gentle, low voice sitting beside me in a chair talking to me, and I had no idea who he was.

And then, the child that I had become felt normal; my arms felt like mine, and my legs were the right length for my six-year-old self. My feet were long enough just to hang out in the air beyond the seat of this very large, comfortable chair. I could see my thin legs and knees not quite covered by a cotton dress. Then, I felt tightness in my chest: tears would not come out and a silent scream filled my throat but not my ears. My right hand began to lift off the armrest, and I felt my arm rise up with no volition on my part. It was moving upward on its own. It frightened me. It seemed to be moving as if in slow motion and I could not control what it was doing. When my arm was nearly straight up, my hand closed into a fist as if it were holding something, a stick maybe, a small stick; more than anything, I wanted to believe it was just a stick. My arm rose up above my head and stopped. The stick felt like a knife as my wrist turned downward and my arm followed by coming back down, again...all in very slow motion.

My entire body went into shock. The small child whose feet barely extended beyond the seat in my therapist's office vanished and I was back feeling myself in my adult form, terrified at what had just happened. In that same instant of returning to the 1986 adult, I screamed out "She is trying to show us what she saw" I don't remember if I cried or not, but I kept repeating: "She is trying to show us what she saw...She is trying to show us what she saw."

*I was dreadfully upset by the session and tried to put it out of my mind. And I was pleased that my therapist did not have enough time to push me for any explanations that I probably couldn't have given anyway. However, I knew as I was saying those words over and over again, that the truth was **it was not what my child-self saw** that she was demonstrating, but **what she did**. However, I could not accept what I knew, and my terrified words, **"She is trying to show us what she saw,"** became my reality.*

***

Two years after that terrifying event in my therapist's office, I read an announcement in the newspaper that a well-known psychiatrist, author, and radio and television personality from Los Angeles, Dr. David Viscott, was coming to Seattle to do a weekend workshop on relationships. Because I was still struggling with whether or not I should complete my divorce, I thought this might be good for Jake and me to attend. Perhaps, an hour or so later, I saw a local television program where Viscott was speaking about his workshop, and a few hours after that, I had gone to my husband's and my boat on Lake Union for an afternoon break. As I stepped out onto the dock, a group of people exited the other boat that was moored next to ours. One of the men was Dr. Viscott. I was totally surprised by this unusual contact, three connections all in the same day of a person I had not heard of until that morning. In that moment of seeing him, I knew it was a message from the Universe about the importance of my attending Viscott's workshop the next day.

***

Most of the people who were at the workshop were couples, but Jake wouldn't go, so I went by myself. David invited anyone with an issue to come forward to work on it; after a few others went forward and worked with their concerns, I left my seat and went to the front of the group. I told Dr. Viscott that I was ambivalent about leaving my husband. I told him about the dream I had a week before Jake and I were married, where I dreamed there were two Jakes and I didn't know which was real, the one who was crying or the one who was going over plans and giving me orders…and I woke feeling very upset about getting married because I didn't know which one was the right one. David asked me a few questions about the dream and about my life and then told me that I didn't like either Jake…the withdrawn and sad little boy or the controlling man and that I should get on with my life and divorce him.

I left that day feeling very upset, shocked by his recommendation, and did not intend to follow his advice. But I returned the next day, despite my negative experience. As the workshop began, Viscott invited people to come up for help, and this time he looked directly at me as he said, *"I can't help you if you don't come forward, so come up and get the help you need."* Since there was a large crowd and only a few people had the chance to work with David the day before, I hesitated…but then, decided to interpret his words and his direct eye contact with me as an invitation.

No one else moved, so I walked to the front and sat down next to Viscott, as I had previously done. I began by explaining my hesitancy to take another chance to work with him since I had the opportunity the day before…and then explained that I couldn't divorce my husband like he suggested. I told him that what was wrong wasn't my husband's fault. The problem was my fault because I just couldn't get angry. And then, I began to give all the reasons why Jake didn't deserve such bad treatment. Every sentence I gave in defense of Jake and why I couldn't be angry with him, David responded with, *"Bull Shit!"* I was in shock each time and defended my position harder and harder, while David kept saying, *"Bull Shit!"* louder and louder to every sentence I spoke. It was as if I had hit a wall that would not budge. No one had ever spoken to me so harshly with such stinging words, all the while looking directly in my eyes in a way that seemed to require me to look into his eyes. Something happened, and I cracked!

I completely lost it! I began to scream out...I can't get angry...I can't get angry...I can't get angry because... And the words that came out of my mouth next shocked me as much as they must have shocked the audience. But in that moment, I was completely unaware of the audience. I only saw David Viscott sitting there, looking into my eyes... as I cried out, *"I killed a man..."*

I felt like a small child, sobbing and sobbing. I was no longer adult Sandy in a workshop who had come to defend her marriage; I was a little child who had a knife in her hand and could no longer allow herself to get out of control, ever again. David asked me how old I was, and I told him I was six. He sat quietly beside me for a moment and then asked me if I could see the man, and in the same child-like voice, I said, *"Yes."* Then he asked if I could touch the man...and I reached out my hand.

Tears flowed down my cheeks...and I told David that the man was cold. In that moment, a most profoundly mind-altering realization flooded through me that the man that I stabbed was already dead.

Before the stabbing, I had been dragged to the basement by a woman who held my wrists and pulled against all my efforts to resist. When I was in the basement, I was told I was going to be killed. I had seen enough murders in my few years of life to believe what I was told. There were lots of buildups of seeing terrible things happening to other people, and there, in front of me, I saw my mother. She was given a knife and a look came over her face that absolutely made my heart stop beating. She went into a crazed frenzy and began to wildly stab the man until she was totally exhausted from the ordeal.

I don't know how I knew this, but I understood that I was supposed to take the knife and stab the man, as well, and if I did not do it, my mother would attack me with the knife as she had done to the man. I was filled with unspeakable terror; something in me knew that she was capable of killing me. One of the adults placed the knife in my hand, and I felt my arm lift up in the air, moving on its own. It frightened me. It seemed to be moving as if in slow motion and I could not control what it was doing. My hand was closed into a fist. My arm rose above my head and stopped. My wrist turned downward and my arm followed by coming back down, too...all in very slow motion. And then I completely lost it! It was like I had gone totally crazy, just as my mother had done previously. My mind no longer belonged to me. I was the knife, I was the stabbing motion...I began stabbing wildly. I felt the knife go into the body many times. And I continued the wild stabbing until everything went black. All my life, this deeply buried secret made me believe I was so evil; I could never be good. And now, the secret was out.

***

After that life-altering session with David Viscott, I knew in my gut, that the man I stabbed was already dead...but what I found impossible to integrate was the fact that when I had been whipped up into such a frenzy of fear and anger that I wildly stabbed the dead body, defending myself against being killed, I felt an adrenalin rush that was nearly intoxicating. Like the other memories that were too horrible to hold, this one was buried until that day in my therapist's office when I only saw one very small puzzle piece of the event and then with David Viscott, perhaps two years later when I saw the whole event, when I discovered that I had not killed the man... and then I buried all I had remembered, again, for a very long time.

With great heart-wrenching sadness and deep empathy, I have always understood soldiers or police, or even criminals who began to shoot and then went crazy shooting...I understood that feeling of relief in the completion of killing in a moment when *to not kill is to be killed* acts as an intoxicant and activates some kind of adrenalin or a natural opiate rush inside. I had long forgotten about all of this. And though in 1994 a most profound integration process was completed that I wrote about in *E Pluribus Unum: Out of Many...One*, this was one of the pieces that remained outside the circle of integration; too horrible to bring in. It remained hidden behind my mask.

In retrospect, I also wonder if my mother's illness that caused her to not be able to walk and caused her to fight for breath, looking as if she might be dying, which I wrote about in the first chapter of this book, was somehow related to the horror of the insane stabbing event that occurred when I was six, which was about the same time she became ill. If she had dissociated or suppressed the memory back then, as I had, it may have expressed itself in the psychosomatic illness that looked as if she were dying.

As I worked with everything related to this perverse experience, I realized that I was terrified of ever feeling anything like that again. I couldn't allow myself to feel anger that might re-stimulate that rush, fearing that if I did, I would go out of control, become the anger, as I had become the stabbing and could kill. Anger at being dragged into this horror preceded the fear of being killed and the horror of going crazy came before the rush. In order to be sure I would never go crazy again, I had to be sure I would never get angry. All my life, I disconnected from my feelings before anger could even register. My terrified child-self really believed that her anger could kill, because she believed that it already had.

It wasn't until I began to work with this little Sandy more deeply that I understood another very important piece of the puzzle. When I was 19 or 20 years old, at the University of Washington, Jake and I often studied together in the Science Reading Room, a very quiet place in the basement of the main campus library. One evening when no one was there but the two of us, Jake began to kiss me and touch me. Although we remained dressed, he pressed his body against me in such a way that I had become greatly aroused. I had my first and last complete orgasm, without nakedness, without penetration.

While working with these issues around anger and loss of control, I realized that the full release after the total intensity of a sexual orgasm was almost identical to the release I felt when everything went black after the stabbing. It was a feeling of total collapse, a total release of all muscle tension, maybe some kind of surrender. Without ever knowing that I had done it, my unconscious mind blocked my body from ever feeling that again, because to feel any kind of an adrenaline rush followed by the total collapse of my body could connect to memories of what happened when I was a child and became the knife, became the stabbing, and I could not allow that to happen. In retrospect, I can see that I have always had a reservation about me, never allowing myself to become fully involved in anything I was doing with other people so much that I lost myself and became what I was doing. The only things that I have ever fully embraced and embodied has been my writing and photography and that does not hold the same energy because there is no other person involved and there is no rush, just intense focus and absorption into a non-agitated process. As I am writing this now, I realize that my photography has always focused on nature, on landscapes, on horizons, and I have not wanted to have anything human-related show up in the vast majority of the pictures I have taken.

Though there have been many contributing factors to my weight gain over the years, I now believe that one of the most significant ones has been to stop me from feeling any form of sexual rush. When I am fat, I don't feel sexually attractive so I block myself from directing that energy outward toward a man to whom I may feel attracted. My internal defense mechanisms could not allow me to ever surrender to anyone or anything ever again. I have been aware of this blockage in the past, but I never knew why until this writing.

When this whole terrifying experience fell into place, the pain in my left leg dissolved. I carefully put my feet on the floor as I got out of bed and I was able to walk without shooting pain crippling me. I had, finally, been able to remember everything about this heinous event in my life…but I had not accessed the feelings of anger related to it, not until the forklift dream and past life journey into the kicking energy.

***

I saw another synchronous event that had been connected to this childhood nightmarish experience when a dear friend asked me to write a book with him. His request came shortly after those puzzle pieces of the *worst of the worst* fell together, and he asked if I would take on the chapter about releasing anger. I became horribly stuck. When I tried to access anger, all I could see was the little Sandy who experienced the most horrific day in her life, when she believed she killed someone, and could no longer allow herself to get angry. As an added protection against feeling anger, even after I remembered what happened, she made sure I disconnected from her, and if anything would come close to reminding me of what happened, she made sure I would not believe she existed. So even after having remembered, I continued to forget or went into doubting what I remembered. I couldn't write about what I hadn't been able to do, myself.

***

In the middle of being stuck writing the chapter on releasing anger back in 2004, I had intended to go to a movie, but was so depressed that I stayed home and turned on Oprah. As synchronicity would have it, her program was on the worst day of several women's lives. Two of the women had children who were killed by their x-husbands. The first woman who spoke was still living in the home where her former husband shot and killed her 4 children. The murderous event happened two years before, in 2002, and she was still living in shock, unable to access her anger. She was still not sure if she wanted to live. The second woman had allowed herself to rage at her husband for murdering their three sons, and eventually moved on with her life, remarried, and at the time of the show, had given birth to two other children with her new husband. Both murdering husbands wanted the women to suffer by killing the kids, and then killing themselves, assuring that their former wives would live with the pain.

The third mother, Ronnie, had five children. She had four of them in the family van with her after school and was on her way to some activity when she decided to stop by her house for just a moment to drop off a bird one of the boys had taken to school for show and tell. She ran into the house and was gone for 2 minutes…but in that brief time, one of the little kids picked up a lighter and caught paper on fire. In moments, the entire van burst into flames. All of the children were badly burned, but the baby literally melted. He had 90% of his body on fire, yet survived. The accident had been a couple of years before, and the 5 children came out to be introduced to the audience. When I saw the baby, about 2-years-old at the time, my entire body howled a mournful cry. The child appeared to be completely made of solid scar tissue. He had only holes for eyes, nose, and mouth, and one of his arms had been burned off. I listened to the mother and to her children. And for the first time, I understood my mother. After watching the show, I wrote a letter.

Dear Oprah:

I have lived with my Mother's many worst days of her life, as my Father tortured his family. My mother did what Ronnie talked about today, but in a totally different context. Ronnie said: *"When a mom sees her child hurt she can't take it, and she pushes it away...They were in so much pain I had to shut it out to live."*

To live with the pain that went on and on at the hands of my father, my mom pushed it away, too; she shut it out. And to live with her and our father in that home, we all pushed it away, as well. We all tried to live as if nothing was happening…but we were all scarred by what we went through, as horrifically as Ronnie's little baby was scarred, only our scars were on the inside and couldn't be seen, making them too easy to deny.

I have been in great pain lately, living with buried anger, anger that was so not safe to express in a household of horror. And my legs began to scream at being dragged to the unbearable places, making walking very difficult, lately. I have been able to touch the pain, the sadness, the fear, but have been unable to touch the anger…though I have worked on this for decades! Last week I made a commitment to work on accessing the anger, but instead, I went into a dark depression and began to deny to myself the childhood that crippled me in many areas of my life, and now is threatening to become a physical malady. And today on your show, I heard Shelley, whose three sons were murdered by their father, say, *"If I don't go on, he wins, and I will not let that happen."*

I have decided to not let my father win. I have held myself back in too many ways, crippling myself by not being who I came to this planet to be; I have not spoken the truth and I have shut it out, just as my mother had done…but my body aches from the wounds inflicted by the hand of an angry, vicious, evil father. Thank you for your show today. It is exactly what I needed to hear to stop my own denial that, until now, has inflicted debilitating pain on my inner child and me.

Dr. Sandy Sela-Smith

***

I went to bed that night promising to work with anger and woke remembering the dream that began this chapter in which I was angry and in pain.

It was just now, writing this to you that I realized that the dream had begun with my calculating the cost of 5 books and feeling frustrated and angry that I couldn't do it. I see the 5 books as my four siblings and me. And my dream was telling me that the pain of focusing on the costs was crippling me, something that wasn't just a metaphor.

So, little Sandy is angry—adult Sandy is angry—and I acknowledge that though I did not kill a man when I was a child…I was terrified enough that I could have. And though I have never killed anyone at any time in my life…I cannot pretend that I do not hold within me a murderess, a part of me who is capable of killing. I believe every one of us holds this potential; however, the difference is that I know it is there, and many people have no idea they hold such a part inside them, as well; maybe even you, reading these words right now, don't know you have that potential…but you do.

***

One Sunday afternoon, while visiting my mother, I was sharing thoughts about my morning breakfast at a fast-food restaurant filled with fathers and their children. My sense that many of the men were divorced fathers having their day with the kids seemed to be a social commentary that made me feel sad. My mother's immediate and angry response was fathers had no business taking care of children. She was obviously disturbed by the thought that children would be with fathers when mothers were not there.

She then told me that she hated it when men who were not the husbands of pregnant women about to give birth wanted to go into the delivery room. That familiar fire in her eyes reminded me of so many times she would be out of control with anger when I was a child, and with clenched teeth, she told me that when she was an obstetrics nurse, she would never let such men into the delivery room. She, then, focused her rage on the mothers who dared have babies without being married. She said it made her so angry she wished she could have a knife and stab, both the women and their illegitimate babies, who she believed didn't have a right to come into this world. She seemed to have transformed into that terrified, angry mother of long ago, mimicking the stabbing motion that I saw when I was a child in the basement of the Jesse Lee Home. But on that Sunday afternoon, she was repeatedly thrusting an imaginary knife, not a real one, into the imaginary pregnant belly of an unmarried woman, instead of the body of an already dead a man. With teeth clenched just as they were decades earlier, and fire in her eyes, she kept repeating that she would just STAB and STAB and STAB, with each thrust coinciding with that wicked word. After that frightening display, she took in a deep breath and changed the subject to something completely different. Like so much of what happened in my family, once something was over, it was over! It was never discussed again.

What I had seen, as demonstrated in front of my adult self, is what my terrified child-self had seen, not as a demonstration, but as a reality. It all made sense to me—the fear of getting angry, the fear of being all-consumed by anything, the fear of allowing myself to surrender, the inability to get close to anyone for fear they would find out who I really was, and the belief that I was so bad that I could never be good again.

I understood the constellation of pain in my right shoulder that was revived in my adult life with an inner war between two parts of me, that connected that horrible event when I was a child, the terrifying event of the stabbing in the past life with Jeff and the experience of being *stabbed in the back* when a part of me wanted to hold on to the furniture that made my heart happy—not unlike the young man who wanted to defend his right to have the flirtatious girl at the barn dance—and the part of me that made an economic decision to sell the furniture. The inner war in the summer of 2006 matched the outer war in that past lifetime. I understood the connection to knives and stabbings, from past lives and this one. The pain that had been stuck in my shoulder along with the words, "*I did it!*" when I "*lost it*" and went crazy in the stabbing of the dead man that must have connected to Jeff's stabbing of my brother in the lifetime where he was executed for murder. These were all energy patterns that exist even if we don't understand or don't accept into our world-view the idea that much of our lives are controlled by unconscious energy patterns.

The energy pattern of defending myself with a knife was in my field of choices, just as kicking and being kicked was in my field. The childhood experiences, first in the little house on the Line when I was viciously kicked between my legs, and then in the basement of the Jesse Lee home caused such shock to my system that I chose to never allow a kicking energy pattern and later the stabbing pattern, or anything related to them to be activated again.

Knife stabbing patterns were in my family system, as well, since both my mother and father participated in stabbings in which defense and offense were difficult to separate. And knife-stabbing patterns had to do with observations and forced participation in my childhood, as well.

Other patterns in my family system included mothers' abandonment of their children, mothers' attacks on their children, and fathers' abuse of children with mother doing nothing to intervene. These patterns are not unique to my family; they are present in many family systems, and likely, are a part of species energy-field patterns.

***

While I was writing *The Mask*, a distant cousin contacted me about our family tree, wanting to fill in missing information, and in further correspondence, I found that one branch of my family, generation after generation, had many people who were in mental institutions for depression and suicide attempts, with at least two successful suicides. It is no surprise that my father threatened to kill himself, my mother attempted suicide twice, and I attempted it once when I was eight, and planned a second when my life was spiraling out of control in my mid forties. That pattern was in the energy field of my family system as a

311

choice for a child who believed that a treacherous life would not get any better. And it is not a surprise that the thought of suicide is what caused me to seek the help of a therapist in 1986.

Without knowing I was doing it, I was choosing to begin a harrowing process of looking at energy patterns and releasing those protective patterns that were not at all protective, but, in fact, were destructive.

***

Details of events that happen in our lives are of little importance when compared to the effects those events can have on our lives. When something happens that shatters us so deeply, it profoundly impacts our view of the world and of ourselves in it; and certainly, the day I experienced *the worst of the worst* everything in my world changed, including my sense of myself. All the other events had caused me to be terrified of the world, but this worst event, also, caused me to be terrified of myself.

I came to believe that I was different from everyone else. I believed that it was not safe for me to allow anyone to get to know me; if they did, they might discover who I was, making them become terrified of me, and leave me forever alone. I believed it was not safe for other people to be around me because I could hurt them if I ever got angry. I believed that I had become so bad that *I could never be good again*, and that belief was buried in my right shoulder and arm—the part of my body that I believed committed the terrible act—the place that talked to me with tears when I was in the Yoga class, and then exploded into a howling volcano that engaged all the pain in every bone, muscle and fiber of my body. So along with all the other losses that I had grieved when I finally allowed those emotions to be expressed, there was the painful loss of my innocent self.

All of my life, I carried the belief that I was so bad, there was nothing I could ever do to make myself good enough to be able to go to heaven. As I would translate this today, for most all of my life, a significant part of my unconscious self hidden behind the mask had experienced herself so separated from her essence that she believed she could never find her way back. And even if by some miracle, she could find her way, she believed pure essence would not allow this very bad part of me entrance, and she would be left alone forever. My adult-self had learned the lie of this conclusion, but this little child-part of me had not fully understood the truth.

Just in case this little girl didn't clearly understand, I told her that I know all that happened to her; I know what she had felt and what she had done, and I love her, still. I invited her to come to me, and for the first time, she trusted to let go of her need to remain separate. She let me hold her in my arms because she didn't have to hide anything anymore, including her very self; I knew, and I will always love her. Like the frightened children in Golding's *Lord of the Flies*, who fell into their rescuers arms ending the torturous hell in which they had been living for far too long, little Sandy collapsed into my arms and finally knew she was safe. Finally, after decades of hiding, she discovered she could be both seen and loved.

I explained that though she felt like she was separate and hidden, both were impossible because she was a part of me and would always be. I let her know that she would never be alone, and I would always be with her. I could say that because I know my essence is eternal. Even though the experience was unfathomably horrible, it allowed her—it allowed me—to have a much deeper understanding of the power fear can have if we believe we are separated from true power that resides in us and is eternally connected to the Great Mystery that is in, around, and through everything that exists, always.

As I held the child, I thanked her for being willing to experience what she did so that I could learn what I learned. On some mystical level, I know my higher self, my future self, my essence opened to that childhood experience so I could learn many deep truths when I was developed enough to learn them. Through these experiences I was able to embrace truths that I may not have been able to learn any other way. Instead of hating what happened to me, for the first time I embraced it, not as a mistake, but as important to my growth.

The work I did to release the *worst of the worst* allowed me to release the beliefs that had formed my life, and the patterns that had imprisoned me, likely for centuries if not millennia, all of which was pushed behind the mask I wore in this life, as well as in others. The war was finally over inside me. The denial was over. I had nothing to fear, not even of exposing the *worst of the worst* in a book that was very near being ready for publishing. And deep inside me, I knew that I was never separated from the creator of the Universe. I carry the Great Mystery within me.

Reflections

There may be experiences you had in your life that made you believe you are flawed and the flaw has turned you into someone you've judged as separate and unacceptable. Allow yourself to see what you have learned from those experiences. Forgive yourself and embrace yourself for having the courage to seek healing.

Even if your worst is worse than my *worst of the worst*, you can still bring healing and connection to whatever parts of you feel estranged and unloved. If you need to ask forgiveness of another, even if they have long since died, or if you need to make amends for what you did, you can do that. You can discover the underlying, hidden beliefs that caused you to do whatever it was that you did, whether great or small, and you can make the decision to release the patterns that were a part of the behavior, and come to peace.

Allow yourself to turn toward the light that is in you, the light that resides in your essence and is eternally connected to the Love filled light of the Universe that surrounds everything, exists in everything, and is connected to all there is. Love has been waiting for you to turn and see it, to let go of the debilitating patterns that have caused you to feel separate. Embrace that Love, and experience your oneness with all that is.

Listen to whatever is going on in your head right now; feel what is going on in your heart. Continue to ask for clarity as you discover what is true, what is real, and who you are.

Chapter Eighteen
THE REST OF THE SECOND STORY
Caring for the Causes of Cancer

We are far more powerful than we think we are. We are powerful enough to have created all those things we have experienced out of the patterns formed from the beliefs hidden behind our masks. Consider what we could create once we set ourselves free to live more from our essence than from the patterns behind the mask.

Back in chapter six, I mentioned I had received the devastating news that the edges were not clear from the March 2008 operation to remove the vulva cancer, something that needed to be watched, and that current symptoms strongly indicated I had uterine cancer. The results of my November 08 checkup meant a second surgery that would be far more extensive than the first. While I was still trying to adjust to the news that I had to have another operation, my elder sister called to tell me that she wanted me to go home for Thanksgiving because all indications were that my mother was failing very quickly and was losing her ability to remember things. My sister suggested if I wanted to see her before our mother would be unable to recognize me, this might be the best time. I had another feeling that my family was afraid I would die from this cancer, and they wanted to see me before that happened.

When I explained that I wasn't in a position to buy tickets, especially so near the holiday when prices would be high and so much of my income had been spent on medical bills, she offered to buy my ticket. So 3 days after returning from Florida and the news that I would be having another operation, I boarded the plane to Seattle, arriving

315

Thanksgiving evening. I thought I might be able to talk to my siblings about *The Mask* while I was there, especially because I assumed the book would be out in the world in the next month or so, I still hoped by speaking the truth, we could develop authentic relationships, but there was no chance to talk about what no one really would have been comfortable discussing. Everything was hectic, as usual, and there was no private time with anyone.

I know that we all created that mutual experience of not talking about our childhoods, and as much as I hoped to be able to speak, there was a part of me that was afraid of the consequences of speaking the truth I presumed no one wanted to hear. Despite my best intentions, I was experiencing an inner war between the parts of me that wanted to speak and the parts that wanted to remain silent.

One thing that touched such deep anger in me while on that very short visit to Seattle was a comment made by my mother when my sister was taking pictures the day after Thanksgiving. My oldest sister had taken several photos of the sister who is not quite a year older than me and wanted to get a shot of the two of us together, but they weren't turning out because of the distance between us. My elder sister was in a low riding high-back chair and I was in a wooden dining chair, so I scooted my chair over to get closer to her and leaned against her shoulder. My mother literally ordered me to stop getting so close. She looked directly at me and said, *"That is your sister not your lover,"* spoken with a tone that sounded to me like disgusted judgment.

A rush of rage pumped through me. In that moment, I realized how much little Sandy was denied the expression of love for my siblings, and probably for everyone and everything. My mother must have seen any sign of affection as "evil" and I am sure she viciously judged my child-self's loving spirit. I could see how that must have slashed at my very soul.

I turned to my sister and put my arms around her as an act of defiance, but I wasn't feeling the loving feelings...I was just feeling anger. No one else said anything, either. And, all my oldest sister could say afterward, was that my smile didn't look natural. Later, I remembered a similar mean spirited comment made by my mother two decades before.

Sometime in the late 80s, I came upon a beautiful German shepherd along the side of the road. He had been hit by a car and was dying. The boy that hit him couldn't fit him in his car to take him to a vet, and he didn't know what to do. After doing energy work with the dog to calm him down, I stayed with him for a long time, visualizing healing energy pouring into his body. I asked a few men who had stopped to see if they could help, to assist me in putting the big animal into my truck, and then I took the dog to the emergency vet and sat with him for a long time that night. After an examination, the vet informed me that the dog would likely die during the night, but everything in me wouldn't accept that, because I knew that he would be fine.

The next morning, I drove the dog to the regular vet who told me that if the dog survived, he would never walk again because of the severity of the damage done to his spine...but I wouldn't accept that either, because deep inside, I really did know he would be fine. While he was in "intensive care" at the vet hospital, I visited him at least a couple of times each day, sang to him, and did energy healing for the beautiful dog. The way it seems to work is that my hands interact with the wounded body, and my hands and the body apparently communicate with each other. My hands are directed where to focus energy, which supports the flow of the body's own healing energy to repair whatever was wounded. Not only did this amazing animal live, but he walked after a few days and by the end of two weeks, he was chasing Frisbees. After his complete recovery, I searched the neighborhoods around the accident and was unable to find the owner, so kept the dog in my one bedroom apartment, along with my other dog, Sara, and my cat, Fred. It was crowded, but we were happy.

Not yet able to find a home for my new friend I named Pal after my childhood dog, I had to leave Seattle for a several weeks, and my mother agreed to take care Pal and Sara, while my estranged husband took Fred. When I returned from my trip and went to my mother's house, Pal came bounding to the front door and jumped up, putting his paws on my shoulders. He gave my face many sloppy licks. He was so full of love and so happy to see me. He was more welcoming than any human had ever been in my life, and that brought lots of smiles and laughter to my heart. My mother became upset and told me, *"That dog is treating you like he is your husband!"* I remember being so shocked at her response, for her to think that a dog loving someone was disgusting. I hadn't thought about that incident until her picture taking comments about the expression of love for my sister after Thanksgiving reminded me of it.

With such critical judgment toward any sign of affection in my childhood, I know I withdrew much of the radiance of my love and hid it in my heart, behind my mask for almost all of my life. I think part of my rage was that I locked it up, too, even after I left home. I know that most people who have known me would identify me as a loving person, but there was sadness for how much I had withheld in my expression of love, and certainly, how much I blocked feeling love coming in from others, fearing judgment and rejection. And along with my loving self, my angry self was locked away in an inner dungeon, as well.

The parts of us that are hidden behind our masks are not just the negative aspects of ourselves, but also, we can hide the most wonderful aspects of ourselves when those around us reject them. Families that only allow their sons to express themselves in sports can have sons with little musicians, poets, dancers, mathematicians, actors and myriad other parts of self hidden in the shadows behind their masks. Little girls can have their strong, determined parts locked away, as well as angry parts, and their little climbers, adventurers, and independent parts might not ever be given permission to see the light of day. Children growing up in tough neighborhoods, where gangs rule, can have bright, studious parts of themselves hidden behind their masks. What a loss to the world, that so much of our very best of who we are can be hidden away as if there is something shameful and unacceptable about exposing them.

***

Later during the Thanksgiving visit, when I was sitting next to her, my mother picked up my hand and told me how beautiful my skin was. She said hers was so wrinkled and mine was smooth...and then she said that she wished she could find a way to peel off my skin and put it on her hand and give me her skin. On some level, she did that already when she skinned me of the safety of expressing the love that was in my heart. Of course, everyone took her comments as a joke, and laughed, and I did, too, but I was, also, very aware of the dark side of her comment. There was some part of her that had no qualms about taking what was mine and giving me what she didn't want that was hers, which is what she did, not so metaphorically, my whole life.

I didn't feel well those couple of days in Seattle, and wasn't looking forward to another trip to Florida less than a week after returning to Denver. Saturday evening, I began to bleed quite heavily. My body was in a great amount of pain; the pressure of a distressed abdomen pushed against the arteries in my legs, which made walking nearly impossible. My mind began to think that maybe my body was collapsing and I would have to wait until my next life to complete the learning and live the dreams I had, including sharing the messages in the trilogy, *The Meaning of Three.*

I felt a giving up happening inside me, almost an acceptance that cancer had overtaken me. I felt really sad that what I know about the power of doing inner work, which I've taught and written about for years, would fall on deaf ears, should I die from a cancer because I could not heal it in myself. Yet, I know how important healing is...even if dying happens. But, I could see where people would choose to use numbing addictions to push away consciousness of what they have buried inside and refuse to open up the wounds if after opening to the pain they believed that death happens, anyway. I believed if I couldn't find a way to heal my body, other people wouldn't have trust in what I was teaching. I really felt sad for what seemed like my failure to create what I know is true. When I was feeling all this, I didn't notice that I had taken on responsibility for others instead of just being who I am.

When I began writing about Pal, I realized how much I believed in healing, and this was a dog whose backbone was broken and spine nearly completely severed. I committed myself to the healing process with him, something he joined in, as well, and I realized I hadn't done the same for me. Though I did that work with my friend Bill in Atlanta, around the hoodies and kicking energies, as well as the angry man with the forklift and his killing energies, I also recognized that I had not really made that deep commitment to me like I did with Pal and his healing process. The work with Bill was important, but I was sure it is not complete.

Because of the impending second operation, I canceled my trip to Connecticut to spend Christmas with my dear friends who are part of my family of choice, and scheduled a flight to Florida.

When I was on the plane headed to Tampa and the operation, I went inside to talk with my bleeding uterus, and was surprised to find there were five petrified fetuses still hanging from umbilical cords inside me. It was as if the energy bodies of the five miscarried babies were still there. So instead of holding that image, I visualized my whole vaginal area as a lovely garden and at the end of the garden was a nursery with a beautiful crib...representing the place that holds my creativity. I was holding this new image in my mind, as I walked into the examination room to see the doctor.

When the doctor attempted to insert the instruments that would allow her to see inside my cervix and into my uterus, not only did my muscles close tightly when she began the probe, but also, when she pushed to force an entry, the uterine muscles actually pushed back against her. She was quite surprised at the strength of the repulsion of the instruments. Though she wasn't able to get a full inspection of my interior, all the indications were that there was cancer and she recommended that everything be removed. After the visit, the doctor scheduled surgery. I felt devastated because I know the power of visualization and of healing. I've seen it so many times, and the fact that it didn't work with me made me feel even more like a failure when the doctor said she was 99% sure I had uterine cancer based on what she was able to see.

I called my friend, Bill, to tell him what had happened and shared with him the visualization about the petrified fetuses. He asked me to talk with my uterus...and when I connected with it, I felt a mournful sadness. My uterus told me that it would not let anyone come in and take the babies, and then, it said, *"No one can come in here and see anything,"* as if a part of me was standing guard at the entrance to protect against unwelcomed visitors peering in. It was as if a manic mother was protecting her dead children from harm. There was, also, self-protection going on, guarding against judgment that the uterus had not done enough to protect the fetuses and was unable to keep them alive. My uterus felt such shame that instead of being a life-generating place, it was a place that killed five little beings.

When Bill asked my uterus why it resisted being helped, I heard the message that it would not let anyone in who disrespected me. I had felt disrespected by the system that passed me from doctor to doctor with each visit, and that didn't let me see the surgeon except for the very first visit. When the resident came in to conduct the exam, she was wearing blue plastic gloves, which meant she probably had turned the knob on the door that must have been filled with all kinds of germs. She used the gloved hands to move the monitor closer to her, as well as to swirl around her seat, to make it taller. She touched the underside of the chair to adjust it to her height with her gloves, and then, she used those same gloved-hands to start to look into me. I was upset, but didn't say anything. I know that is a pattern of mine, to see something that is not good for me, but say nothing. I didn't take care of myself.

The penetration process was extremely painful, so I asked if someone could hold my hand. An intern stepped up and took my hand, but a nurse removed it and put two round squeeze-balls in my hands, instead. What I really wanted was human contact, so my body would know I was okay, despite the pain, but after that abrupt disconnection, I didn't ask any more. The nurse, also, slapped at my bottom and told me to let go of the muscles. I wasn't holding on to those muscles on purpose, at least not consciously. My body was terrified at what was happening, and I felt so disrespected but, again, didn't speak up.

Since I was going to be operated on by several of the people working with me during the exam, I was afraid to antagonize the very people who would be participating in the operation. Even if their conscious minds would not intend to "get even" for any criticism I might have given, it would be their unconscious mind that would be in charge of the operation, even if they didn't know it...so like far too many times in my past, I didn't say anything to protect myself because to speak up in self-protection seemed to not be protective.

Bill asked about the pain caused by instruments that were inserted, and I explained that insertions always hurt...like sex always hurt, and he asked if I had ever told a doctor about the pain. And again, the answer was, no. I didn't think a doctor could do anything about my body's resistance to being poked, probed, and penetrated. Bill told me that there were doctors out there who could be so caring and gentle that it would not hurt to have insertion procedures done, and there were men out there who could make a sexual experience beautiful and not painful. I felt myself recoil, as if I could not accept his words.

He told me that my description of my vagina sounded very baron to him. He told me that he saw the vagina as a beautiful Iris, with soft, inviting petals. And as he described his experience, I realized all of my life I had seen my vagina from the perspective of the how the abusers must have seen it, and when I tried to visualize it another way, my image was more a picture to cover over the horrible war-torn waste-land image I had always seen when I visualized it in the past, rather than seeing it something like Bill described. He suggested that if I could let go of seeing my body and vagina with the hate and disgust from those men, as well as from what I am sure was my mother's image of my pelvic area, that I could draw better energy from not just men, but from my doctors, as well.

I knew that my fear of being helpless and subject to the invasion of disrespectful people could actually draw that energy to me; I would create it if I believed in it. I wanted to trust that no one has power over me because I am the one that creates what I believe. When my intention is to create my highest good, then I can go about trusting that whatever happens, even in that operating room, is for my highest good. I felt a very significant energy shift. The bottom line truth is that my higher self is in charge, not them. But when I am in fear, it can feel as if they are in charge. I needed to trust that my higher self, my unique mystery, not doctors or nurses were in charge of what was going to happen to me.

Bill asked me if I would be willing to consider the possibility I might have been mistaken about my interpretation that I had a "killing" uterus because I had five miscarriages. My response to him was I knew energetically my uterus was the center of my creativity, and I was very creative in my life—even though I didn't have children— but, he asked if I was open to hear something very different. When I agreed to listen, he said that my uterus was very successful at creating a place for 5 fetuses that chose to come into this world and live for a very short period of time without coming to full term and birth. My taking complete responsibility for what they created was disrespectful of them and their souls participation in the decision.

The belief I wasn't a good mother, that I was a killing mother, faded away, and instead, I felt like I needed to connect with their souls. In the moment that I sent out the message of intention of wanting to communicate with the five fetuses, they appeared as light beings, and they all expressed that there was no need for them to forgive me, because I didn't do anything wrong. They had been working with false ideas about living and because I, too, was working with similar ideas, they were drawn to me.

The light beings told me they allowed the dead fetus energy to remain in the mummified form until I could be free of those ideas about who I was in this world and release them. My childhood experience with the dead man had taught me to believe that I was a killer, and the five miscarriages caused me to believe that my uterus was a killing uterus. Neither belief about my being a killer was true. Though anyone put in the "right" position could kill, killing does not make a killer. Like these five light beings, I am a radiant light, a spark of God; that is my only true identity.

Another important shift happened, and I felt waves of gratitude wash through me for the presence of these light beings in my life. I could see that carrying the mummified fetuses, even in the invisible energetic form, was not healthy for my body. As I observed this inner vision, I knew if I allowed air to touch them, the mummy forms would disintegrate like dust...so I visualized air coming in and what had been dead energy forms attached inside began to blow away.

It seemed that the five beings were waiting for me to recognize them. They wanted to say thank you to me for holding a place for them until they learned what they needed to learn about life and about themselves, as well. After all these decades, I, their mother saw the light in my five babies and reflected it back to them, which allowed them to see the magnificent light in themselves. That was what they were waiting to experience and we all were healed. The truth was, I would not have been able to see the light in them if I had birthed them, and because of their own previous life wounding they would not have been able to see their own light, as well. I thanked them for staying until I could know my mother-self and experience the babies I though I had lost. And they thanked me for working with my beliefs and patterns until I could finally see them, something that a healed mother connected to her essence does for her newborn children. They were waiting, not just for me, but to be able to experience being seen and having their essence reflected back to them. We experienced that profound mother-child recognition, and in that moment the light from those five magnificent beings lifted and moved on.

***

Not long after that significant conversation, I was seated in the hospital's admitting area, ready to have my name called to go to the pre-op area to be readied for my second operation for cancer in less than a year. I still had no idea what the extent of the surgery was going to be, whether it would end up being an in and out procedure for day surgery or if the initial search would lead to the radical surgery the doctor expected, which would include removing most every part of my whole genital area, both internal and external. I had asked if a rectal exam could be conducted at the same time, but the system didn't allow it. I would not be able to find out the cause of the rectal bleeding, not this time.

Before being called, I spoke to my body and assured it that whatever was in my highest good would happen. Whatever needed to be removed would no longer experience its existence within me, and I would accept whatever that was. I told my body that I surrendered all of this to the Great Mystery, that amazing Spirit in union with my unique spirit, and this united essence in me would be communicating with the surgeon and the assistants to do what was in my highest and best. It felt as if my entire body breathed a sigh of relief, trusting that I would be fine no matter what happened.

When the anesthesiologist came into the pre-op space, I told him that I had a special request that might sound really crazy to him, but I needed to ask it anyway. I told him about the previous surgery when I saw my left arm being strapped down and how that impacted me for weeks afterward. I told him that I had a history of sexual abuse and parts of me would remain alert in the operating room even if the rest of me looked very much unconscious.

I asked if before the surgery began, he would send a mental message to any part of me that might be alert, even if she didn't show up on his monitor, that he would make sure I was safe. He reassured me that he understood exactly what I was talking about, and he didn't think I was crazy; he said before he trained in this field, he was a psychologist and did understand the multi-dimensions of our human condition. I could feel that every part of me knew that I had finally developed the backbone to speak up for myself and for all the little Sandy parts of me who had never had anyone speak up for them before. This was so very important. It was the reason I had gone to the Colorado Mountains, to absorb powerful backbone energy from the backbone of our country. It seemed to have worked!

The resident doctor approached me when I woke up in the recovery room. She told me that the surgery went well. Investigation of my uterus revealed two cysts, both were benign, but only one was removed. My ovaries were healthy, my cervix was just fine, and the vulva area was clear and clean with no cancer cells. The only other thing that was removed was a tiny scraping for a PAP test, which came back negative a few days later. All reflected full and total health.

My heart was filled with gratitude, and I smiled! Somehow, I felt the smiles of five light beings, who, also, expressed gratitude for what they had learned from their very short attachment, but eternal connection with me. I had taken the lesson that I create my own reality to a much deeper level. I had learned to speak up for myself instead of living in fear that to speak was to destroy any chance of protection or connection.

***

When I was a little child in that first year in Anchorage, listening to the Johnny Appleseed song, I knew that I would be wandering, not

325

unlike the seed planter. The first time I ever heard the *Happy Wanderer* song, another song about being a person not tied to any particular place, my heart rejoiced in its openness and in 2005, while I was preparing all the legal papers around wills and death, I rewrote some of the words to the wanderer song to reflect my feelings about being a person who was open and free, a song I planned to record sometime later to have played some distant time in the future at my funeral:

> The Reformed Happy Wanderer
>
> I loved to go a-wandering along the mountain track. And as I walked I loved to sing, companions at my back.
>
> I loved to wander by the stream that danced well with the sun. So joyously it called to me, come join our happy song.
>
> I waved my hand to all I'd meet, and they waved back at me. Lovely birds called loud and clear, from every tall pine tree.
>
> Overhead the magpies winged, they'd never rest at home. But just like, me they liked to sing, as through the world we'd roam.
>
> I wished to go a-wandering until the day I'd die and wished to always laugh and sing beneath God's clear blue sky.
>
> The *me* that lived this gift of life continues on and on, in mountain stream and dancing sun, I sing with you this song.

When I look back at the song that drew me in when I was a child and that I reworded in 2005, almost two years before I found the mountain cabin beside the stream that danced well with the sun, where I came to write, and to find my backbone, I am amazed that I had actually created my heart-song from my childhood into this three-dimensional world. My little place in the mountains, with the stream that flows outside my window is rich with birds of all kinds singing and dancing between the water and the sun. It was in this beautiful mountain place that the trilogy was writing itself and in doing so opened my heart and taught me what is really true so that I could offer this message to anyone else who is open to hear.

When I first heard the actual words to that song, and the one about far away places with strange sounding names, I must have known I would be a wanderer...I knew that I wanted to be a wanderer, and I always felt sad because I attached being alone to a wandering life.

Now, I can see that I can create what will make my heart smile, and if traveling by myself, which is not the same as being alone, would make me happy, I can do that. If traveling with companions will make my heart happy, I can create that, too. And now that I know separation is a belief, which exists behind the mask, one that isn't true, I can embrace another thought. Wandering can be something that allows expansion in my experience of connection to the people in my life who will always have permanent places in my heart. Just thinking of this makes my heart feel very happy.

Reflections

Look inside yourself with open eyes to allow you to see the themes that have been running your life. Ask if they serve you. If your beliefs are holding you back from experiencing what truly makes your heart smile, ask to be shown the source of those beliefs so you can bring healing there and set yourself free.

It doesn't matter how old you are or how sick you might be; you can heal even if a cure is not part of your path. It doesn't matter what you have done in the past or what you should have done that you didn't do, for which you carry shame and guilt; you can still heal.

All the Universe asks of you is to be honest with yourself when you search for the beliefs that caused you to create what you created. If your tendency is to blame someone else, remember that you drew that person into your life to reflect back to you what you hadn't let yourself see. What you create will always come back to you. When you take responsibility for what you created, you can decide if you want to keep creating whatever that is. If you want to change what is your reality, you need to look at what is true, and be willing to change your perception of who you thought you were.

Chapter Nineteen
THE REST OF THE THIRD STORY:
Owning My Place In The Universe

Look around you. Everything that exists has a purpose; everything belongs or it would not be here. You belong. I belong. We belong. Even our flaws and vulnerabilities belong. We can create experiences to make belonging a thing of joy. When each of us comes to the last day in this life, we can look back and see what a wonderfully worthwhile experience it was, even if what made it wonderfully worthwhile is that we finally learned we belong.

Perhaps, one of the most painful lies people can believe is that they do not belong because they spend their lives trying to figure out how to belong instead of just being themselves. So many see themselves as being on the outside looking in, feeling disconnected from family, friends, fun, life, love, purpose, direction, and all that comes from belonging. This *outside-looking-in* experience is the ultimate result of the belief in separation, which is a lie, though it may well not feel like a lie. Whatever was your experience of the first shock, that first trauma, or first abuse that caused you to lose trust in the Universe, very likely resulted in your loss of knowing the ultimate truth that you belong.

***

On May 13, 2009, eighteen chapters were finished. I looked over what I had written and believed I had finished book two. Three months had come and gone since I began writing with even more intensity than the first book, *The Mask*, which had taken me 9 months to write. In writing *Behind the Mask,* it was not unusual for me to be at the computer from very early morning to late at night, and it was not uncommon for me to wake around 2 in the morning and write for an hour or two. Even when I got stuck in moving forward, I spent the time writing and re-writing the chapters that were already done.

When I reviewed the chapters, I noticed, like in the first book that contained three themes, in this book there, also, were three themes, one of which I had not even noticed before the review. The first theme began in chapter one; it had to do with the impact of the *worst of the worst*. I knew I needed to confront this in me if I expected to write anything that would be valuable to any other person seeking to heal what felt as if it were too difficult to face. If I couldn't find the way to bring this out from behind my mask and heal it, I would leave you with nothing of value to support you as you confront your own worst experience. And it took writing 16 chapters to do this. The underlying message of this theme is that *we are not what happened to us.*

The second theme was introduced on page 2, though it began in chapter 23 of the first book. This theme had to do with my struggles with *the meaning of cancer*. That theme revealed the connections between what happens to us physically and what we have not resolved emotionally or psychologically, and it took 17 chapters to work my way through this theme. The underlying message of this theme is that *we are not what erupts from us*, in our body's attempt to communicate what happened to us.

It wasn't until I looked over everything I had written that a third theme drew my attention, and I knew I needed to write one more chapter. It was subtler than the first two, and might have easily been missed, had I not gone back through the manuscript, chapter-by-chapter, even though the theme had been there the whole time. The theme that almost went unnoticed had to do with *claiming my place in the Universe*. I find it interesting that my inability to know that I had a place in the Universe showed up as my inability to notice the theme of finding my place in the Universe. What an amazing metaphor!

When I wrote the other chapters, my practice was to wait until the chapter was complete to get the pulse of what had been included before I would write the introductory statement. However, I felt compelled to write, not only the statement, but also, the first paragraph that talked about feeling disconnected from belonging and how this is the result of the belief in separation and loss of trust in the Universe. As soon as that first paragraph was completed, I felt exhausted and went to bed early…well, relatively early.

***

From the time of my return to Colorado from Florida the last day of January 2009 following the operation for cancer that was no longer there, I had felt exhausted. I attributed it to the stress around the operation and the long hours of writing, but underneath, I felt it had something to do with my heart. I had two previous heart attacks, and both had come after extremely intense times in my life; however, despite the intensity and the heart concerns, I noticed differences that caused me to dismiss what I was feeling.

I attributed the shortness of breath to having been at sea level for nearly two months, and my body was adjusting to the mountains. And, because of the extreme cold, the snow, and the intense writing that followed, I had not gotten much exercise. Though I had begun Yoga about the same time I began writing *Behind the Mask*, after working through the issues of being in my body, coupled with a series of snow storms and sweat lodges scheduled on Saturday, I had not gone to Yoga for many weeks. So it made sense that not only would I be experiencing shortness of breath, but that any exertion would bring exhaustion.

For the first two weeks of May 2009, I felt like I had the beginnings of flu, but it never developed into flu. I had chills a couple of days, and some of those other telltale signs, like aching muscles and weakness, as well as that general, mild flu kind of feeling, that could be credited to those conclusions, mentioned earlier, as well.

Tuesday May 12th, two days before I began to write this new last chapter, I needed to take a break from the intensity of reviewing and editing the earlier chapters, so I turned on the Oprah show. She was having a tribute to Dr. Oz, for his last day as an official part of her program. A number of people who attributed their lives being saved because of something the doctor mentioned on previous shows were featured. One woman thanked him for talking about symptoms of heart attacks for women often being different than for men. She talked about the flu like symptoms that preceded having the attack, which caught my attention, but also, said she had jaw pain, something I didn't have. So I dismissed that, as well.

Then, just before turning out the light that night, I watched the Late Show, and Letterman's guest, was Robin Williams. The topic of the night was the experiences the two men had with open-heart surgery. Both talked about shortness of breath and weakness as precursors to the diagnosis and immediate surgery that they credited with saving their lives. For many years, I have been aware of the power of synchronous experiences that provide me with information that helps me know what I need to do, and I turned off the TV moments later, very aware of the pressure in my chest and the shortness of breath.

I didn't want to focus on the whole medical worldview of operations and heart attacks, but that seemed to be present, and I had to decide what I was going to do with it.

***

Less than a week earlier, on May 9th, the day before Mother's Day, I received a call from Luke, a most wonderful leader of the Lakota mountain sweat lodge, 3000 feet above the mile high city of Denver, inviting me to do a sweat lodge ceremony later that afternoon. Of course, I said yes, knowing it would be powerful, though I had no idea what would emerge for me during that time. Something inside let me know that despite my heart concerns, I needed to participate. Very early in the wee hours of the night following the experience at the sweat lodge, I wrote an email to my dear friend, Oregon David sharing with him what happened on that Saturday:

Hi David...It is early morning May 10, Mother's Day. A few hours ago, I was at another sweat lodge. Luke, the one who leads the lodge ceremonies, called yesterday and asked if I wanted to come to the lodge around 3 PM. A group of his Indian friends and family had arrived from South Dakota and they decided to have a special lodge ceremony that afternoon. I had made this huge pot of soup Friday, and when I saw how much it turned out to be, I wondered why I had made so very much. I really didn't have any place to store it, and there was no way I could eat it all before it would go bad. Then the next day, I got the call from Luke, telling me about the sweat ceremony later in the afternoon and I knew that's why I had made so very much.

Since the invitation was such short notice, I assumed there would be a small group, but when I arrived, the parking area was filled with cars, far more than I had ever seen before. The lodge holds up to about 20 people, and it looked like there were more people than that, based on the number of cars.

Despite the synchronicity of the soup and the call, I thought it might have been a mistake to come because even with 20 people, there is no place to stretch out, or lie down. And when the lodge gets very, very hot, which it has gotten the last few times, finding a place to stretch out on the ground is essential for me.

Based on the Lakota tradition, rocks are the oldest of grandfathers that connect with those of us who are living through the heat. Large rocks are heated in a fire all day long and prayed over by the one who tends the fire. After all the people enter and before the first round begins, 16 boulder sized red-hot rocks are dragged into the lodge and placed in the center of the fire pit, and then water is doused on them to produce great amounts of steam. Before each of the following three rounds of the ceremony, more red-hot rocks are brought into the lodge and placed in the fire pit, with more water poured over the smoldering rocks. This creates an environment hotter than any sauna I have ever been in and the full ceremony lasts much longer than time spent in a sauna in such heat. There have been times it has gotten so hot that participants have had to leave before the end of the ceremony, some of which have lasted four hours or more.

When I arrived at the ceremonial area on the top of the mountain and saw the number of cars, I thought I might drop off my post-lodge potluck contribution, and then drive back home because I hadn't been feeling well. I had to park some distance from the house, and the pot was very heavy. About half way between the house and the lodge, I had to stop. There was no way

I could take another step. To take the soup to the house, I would have to climb a higher than usual flight of steps, and that seemed untenable. At that moment, a man came walking down the hill from the lodge looking like he was headed toward the house, so I asked if he could take the large pot to the kitchen for me, which he was happy to do. I don't think I could have carried it any further; I was nearly out of breath and the pressure on my chest was quite uncomfortable. Even at this point, I thought that it might be better for me to turn around, go back to my car, and head for home, but I continued ahead. Everyone had already gathered at the lodge and most had already been smudged with sage smoke. Some had begun to enter.

If I had arrived earlier I would have asked to enter first, because the first person crawls in and around the fire pit clockwise, which would have allowed me to sit at the entrance, making an easy exit should I need to get out during the ceremony, and it would allow the cool air to ease the power of the heat in between the rounds when the entrance flap is opened to bring in more rocks.

I was the last woman to crawl in. There were 13 women followed by 13 men, which meant that I was directly opposite the door and in the back row, the hottest place in the lodge, except for Luke's position, which was directly in front of me. We were packed in like sardines with each person having just enough room to sit cross-legged with no space to stretch and most were curled up in a sitting fetal position.

The sixteen rocks were dragged in and placed in the pit, and the door flap was closed. When the water was poured over the rocks, the steam felt unbearable. Luke, who usually leads the ceremonies, didn't take that role this time. Instead, a powerful Lakota Indian led the ceremony, speaking both in English and in his language, which his sister translated for the rest of us. After the first round of prayer, song, and calling in the grandfathers and grandmothers, and the healing spirits, more rocks were brought in and the second round began, during which each person was to pray for him or her self to present a pure heart when praying during the next rounds. But for some reason, instead of noticing that there were 26 of us and normal length prayers would make the first round very long, prayers seemed to last twice as long as normal. The steam and heat was beginning to become more and more difficult for me to take. I actually thought of leaving during the second round, but stayed.

When it was my turn to pray, my request was simple. I wanted the courage to complete what I was writing in a way that would allow the message of the Great Mystery to be expressed, and then to open to the writing that was ahead in book three: *Under the Mask*, which is going to be about the union of the Great Mystery with the unique mystery in each individual.

In the writing of both this book and the previous one, I have been aware that each book had written me. I was living what I was writing, and this time it really seemed to be taking its toll on me. Lately, my heart has been giving me more trouble. When I was out walking Jenny in the field behind the house on Friday, the day before the sweat Lodge, I wasn't sure I could make it back home. The effort my heart needed to take me even a few feet made me wonder if this might be it for me. I can't say I was scared, but I was feeling disappointed that I might not complete book two, and never get to book three. Maybe I was feeling what Johnny Appleseed was expressing in that record from my childhood when he said, "*Dagnabbit, Angel, I just can't go...I got crops to harvest and seeds to sew.*" It just didn't seem right to leave this life with only one book of a trilogy completed, a second nearly completed, and a third not, yet, begun.

My belief is that the messages in these three books will be very important in offering insight into transformation in consciousness, not just for readers, but also, for myself. And even though there has been no evidence from the sales of the first book that any more than a handful of people would ever read what I've written, I have an inner knowing that it won't stay that way. Though I didn't want to die before the books were finished, I didn't feel the sadness that I felt as a child about Johnny, and I didn't find myself trying to reason with God to influence a decision one way or the other.

Actually, since the day that I allowed myself to grieve the loss of so many experiences in my life and then had that shift in me, I felt like something important changed in my willingness to allow the flow to happen with regard to my books and my life. I believe that on some level, my own blockages were preventing the energy of the book to take itself out into the world. So my lodge prayer was that the way be opened for me to complete the books and to teach the messages in them by releasing my own blockage of this from happening.

Between the second and third round, more red-hot rocks were dragged into the lodge, and the heat became nearly torturous; I thought I should send the message that I needed to leave the lodge when the person next to me asked to leave, and there was just enough room for me to stretch out a little. By the end of the round, I began to feel the pressure on the left side of my chest, again. It felt as if my heart was about to explode, and I was just about to mention to Luke who was seated right in front of me that I might need to leave, as well, when another person in the back row asked to leave, making enough space for me to stretch out. Luke noticed my distress and encouraged me lean into the heat instead of resisting it. I hadn't told anyone that my heart didn't seem to be doing well, but I decided to stay longer if I could.

As the heat intensified, I began to silently cry, and then as round three was completed and more very large, very hot rocks were added to the fire pit, I spoke up and asked the group to pray for my heart, that it open to the inward flow. When I looked into my heart, it seemed like the arteries and veins were only allowing a very small amount of blood to come in. I told the group that my prayer was for both my physical heart, but also, for my emotional and spiritual heart, as well. I could no longer stop the tears, so I just allowed them to flow without holding anything back.

During the time between round three and round four, a man offered a prayer for mothers since the next day was Mother's Day, but when he spoke that prayer, my heart nearly exploded with pain. I began to cry; I prayed that my heart discover how to open to receive my mother's love. Instead of being my adult self, I felt I was my 8-year-old-self the night I was recuperating from my attempt to *go to sleep and never wake up* by breathing in the exhaust fumes from our car. My mother made up a cot for me on the screened in porch so I could get more oxygen, and she held me that night in the spoon position, with me in front, but I could not take in her love. I felt her to be a stranger to me and I had no sense of connection to her or to her words, when she told me that she wouldn't know what she would have done if she lost me.

For decades, I wondered why I felt nothing that night. Then the memories of those first 8 years of my life began to tell the story. How could I open my heart to a woman who didn't want a girl when I was born and who raised me without warmth and tender love and turned me over to my father to punish me for lying when both she and my father knew I had told the truth that it was my father who had raped me. She had not been able to protect me or express love to me all the years I lived at home...but the one night that she was in touch with her mother love, I was unable to feel it.

Just a couple of days before the sweat lodge ceremony, I was working with a client to help her see the essence inside herself and then inside those people in her life, with whom she had felt so estranged. I suggested that when she looks at what is behind the mask instead of what is under it, it is too easy to get caught up in the struggles, the tornadoes, and wars that cover the essence and loose contacting what is real. If she would let herself see beyond the layers that cover over the true self of those in her life, she would discover she could love them for who they are, not for who they seem to be. The suggestion I made to her came back to me in the lodge, and I allowed myself to see the essence of my mother deep inside under the mask and beyond what was the non-mother energies behind her mask.

For the first time in my life, I was able to see who she is under all her pain and anger...under all the darkness of what has been behind her mask...and I saw her pure essence. Eight-year-old Sandy looked into the heart of my mother... and for the first time I allowed her love to come into my heart. In the middle of the total darkness of the lodge, filled wall-to-wall with people, and pulsing with the sounds of the rattle, drums, and chanting, little Sandy began to cry as my heart opened and received the in-flow of love. I felt myself turn toward my mother, instead of having my back to her. I felt myself in her arms and received her love for the very first time in my life. My entire body was deeply moved, even transformed by this experience.

I wasn't sure I could make it into round four, but I stayed. The woman next to me had placed her hand on my back over my heart, and I felt something profound happening deep inside. Luke poured water on me to keep me breathing, and at one point pouring water on my wrists to cool me. Near the end of the ceremony, the Lakota Indian told me to take a trip soon to see my mother. And another suggested that I take something of hers, put it in a bundle with sage, cedar, and sweet grass, and take it to the ocean and release it. I had planned a trip in July for her birthday, and this seemed to be a statement supporting that idea. The Lakota man indicated that she might be passing soon. I had had a similar thought that kept coming to me over these last few months. When the fourth round was finally over, everyone cleared

337

the way and allowed me to crawl out ahead of most of the others. I entered the cool evening air, totally soaked and feeling as if I had been fully cooked from the inside out. The intense heat coming from my body caused me to be extremely lightheaded and I was only able to crawl over to a sitting-log where I sat for some time until most all the others had gone back down the trail to the main house. I shared with a few of the people sitting around me what had happened, and my heart felt so very full.

When I returned to my little mountain home a few hours later, I was totally exhausted. My breathing eased somewhat and the pressure in my chest was nearly gone. I visualized my arteries opening, and all the material I used to close down the flow to my heart began melting away.

I know our bodies reflect our emotions, and over time, my body found the way to stop the flow of nutrients into my heart, matching the stopping that I did when I was eight, and the stopping of the flow of love that I have done with nearly everyone, my entire life. I have been able to send love out, but have had a very difficult time allowing love to flow in. The kind of imbalance takes its toll on bodies, and certainly I have been imbalanced in this area. I think I have only a few more passages to complete in book two; I am so, so curious about what book three will hold and how writing it will transform my life. I think it is already beginning to happen.

I send so much love to you... I know that you are sending love to me as you read this...and my heart is opening and receiving it. Thank you...Love, Sandy

***

After writing that message to David, in the very early hours of Mother's day, I went back to bed to get what sleep might be there for me. The next morning, my body was still generating huge amounts of heat; but, as soon as I began to move around, the constriction in my chest returned and breathing became difficult again. Even taking long deep breaths didn't seem to ease the feeling that my lungs weren't getting enough air. I thought there would be some difference because of all the work that happened for me in the sweat lodge, and the fact that there was little if any physical change the next morning was discouraging. I continued writing and editing and took a break to watch Oprah on the 12th and later, the next night Letterman on the 13th, after which I went to bed wondering what I should do about my heart, which takes us back to where I was when I started this chapter.

***

After a few hours of sleep, I woke and looked at the clock; it was 4:04, the morning of the 14th of May. The thought came to me that this was a very fine heart number—in the Eastern tradition, the number 4 is the heart number—but I couldn't connect with writing, so instead I stayed in bed. For the next hour or so, I became immersed in an inner journey to bring healing to my heart. I lay there in the darkest part of the night sending love to my heart, asking it to receive love, when I began to cry. The sound was so deeply sad, so mournful, and then I saw myself standing in that beautiful temple made of unusual shimmering white golden marble tile that was not tile…and a healing pool with water that was not wet. The water contained the vibration of billions of microscopically tiny healing angels, when brought together, looked and acted like living water.

But the pool was filled with people. All those people who had kicked and had been kicked were still there, swimming and splashing— generally having a very good playful time—and that was just not the energy I had come to find for myself. I needed peace and quiet; I needed to find a place where I could be alone. An angel came and led me through what seemed like a lush tropical mountain area to another pool. It was smaller, but had people there, too. They were far more quiet, more contemplative, but still there were people, more than I felt like I could handle.

So the angel took my hand and brought me to another place, smaller yet, but I was not alone. I felt I could not heal whatever was going on in my heart if I was distracted by the presence of other people. I began to cry, a most powerful cry…with a belief held in the vibration of the sound that felt as if *I would never be able to heal this pain inside me*. The sound of my cry and the words that were connected to the sound transported me back in time.

In an instant, I was my 2-year-old self, sitting on a kitchen counter in a stranger's house. I was inconsolably crying. My mother was headed to the hospital to give birth to her fourth child, and was leaving me there by myself with people I didn't know. She went out the door without giving me a reassuring hug or saying good-bye to me. I felt totally abandoned. I have worked with this incident many times in the past, but, apparently, there was something lingering on in my heart.

My adult-self approached the child and I held the little one in my arms. I told the 2-year-old that her mother didn't know how to be with her, but I promised to be with her forever. Though her crying lessened, she still remained in the center of her heart pain. As I held her in my arms, I realized how lost she had felt in her first two years. She was the girl child to parents who wanted a boy in a family that didn't have time for her. She was just one of the crowd. She was "you kids" or "the girls" not Sandy, and now another child was coming. She knew that there would be even less room for her and the thought of that left her feeling so deeply and mournfully alone.

Just saying what was hurting her made her begin to cry even more. So, I brought her to Jesus, someone she had made connection with early in her life. She buried her face in his chest and clung to his ivory colored robe, almost whimpering now, having nearly exhausted herself from the crying earlier. She told him that she wanted to be special and she knew there were so many other children in the world and she could never really feel like it was just herself in his arms, just like there was no room for her in her mother's arms. She longed to feel as if she mattered, not because she was one of the millions and billions of people, but because she was herself.

***

In that moment, I saw an image from a shamanic experience from long ago that I hadn't remembered for years since it happened. I had taken a journey into the stars in search of my amazing little dog Sara, who passed away. My heart had never felt so broken as the day she died. Little Sandy needed to *feel* the story of Sara, my first Lhasa, the only being my child-self ever felt really loved her the way she needed to be loved.

***

Though others might not have agreed with my assessment, Sara was a magical being. I had wanted a puppy of my own for years, and had searched dog books for the breed I would get, if I could. The one I knew would be mine was a Lhasa Apso, the kind of dog the ancient Tibetan Monks trained as temple sentinels. Jake wanted what he called a real dog, like a German shepherd or Doberman.

One of the first things I did after I separated from my husband was to go in search of my dog. I opened the Seattle Times and looked in the pet section and found one Lhasa. I called and was told that the pup was coming in from Portland on the Greyhound bus and a man from Alaska was coming in to look at her, but whoever got there first would have first choice. I drove to downtown Seattle as quickly as I could and very soon thereafter, the tiny golden blond Lhasa was on her way home with me.

I didn't name my puppy; she named herself. When I brought this tiny Lhasa pup into her new home, I sat her down on a towel on the floor and walked to the end of the hall. I told her I wanted to know what her name was and began to say names alphabetically, as this lovely little bundle of puppy just sat and looked at me. When I got to the Ss, I said Sara, and she came running down the hall from the still position and leapt into my arms. I put her back on the towel at the end of the hall, and spoke a few more names and said Sara again, and when I said it, she ran to me, as before. I did this one more time—it seems like I have always done things in threes—and only when I said Sara, did she jump up and run to me. So I held her in my arms, and said, *"Well, little one, I guess your name is Sara."*

This very tiny puppy, much smaller than most Lhasa Apsos, was the runt of the litter; but to me, that made her even more precious. She came into my life the week that I left my husband and she became my family. It was clear from the very beginning that I didn't own Sara. I was her caretaker; yet, there were many times she was the one who took care of me. There was no doubt we were connected at the heart.

She was as heartbroken as I was when I left for China and lived there for two years, but when I returned, she had fully forgiven me and our love grew deeper than I had ever felt from any human. She was my heart's delight. We went everywhere together and when I was going through the lowest times in my life, she was beside me. The times I felt I could not go on in this life another day, she looked into my eyes with such concern; I knew I couldn't leave her again. She sat beside me for hours or curled up at my feet as I sat at my computer studying and writing when I began graduate school. She cherished our late night walks and loved searching the brush for armadillos or other interesting critters in Florida. I couldn't imagine being without Sara.

I had a heart attack in early 1997 while on a Shamanic journey to release my unhealthy attachments to my former husband, and not long afterward, my sweet Sara was diagnosed with congestive heart failure. I recovered, but my precious dog did not. I went into a grieving that felt worse than death. The only being to whom I had ever fully surrendered my heart was gone. I felt as if I had taken my mother's heart pain from my father's death and Sara had taken my pain from the release of Jake. I wasn't sure I could survive the grief.

For two months following Sara's Death, I worked with the most painful feelings around my loss of her, with unresolved childhood issues, and past life issues that I carried into this lifetime, as well as old belief systems that were ready to be released that were all connected to heart pain. I was amazed at all I had learned. But in spite of the learning, my heart still grieved for missing Sara. Little things would reduce me to tears. One morning while taking a bath, I reached for the shampoo and picked up Sara's shampoo that I had not removed from the rack...I cried through the whole bath time. Seeing her chain hanging on the wall or her dog dish in the cupboard sent waves of pain through me. Despite the pain, I couldn't take these reminders of her away.

One afternoon, I began straightening up the office room where I spent so many hours with Sara at my feet or close by my side. She had a special place on the back of the couch where she could see out the window while I worked on papers for graduate school courses. I had placed a towel on a board that went from the back of the couch to the window so she could watch what was going on outside while I worked for hours at a time. She loved being the princess, reigning over her world from her second story perch. In cleaning up, I decided to take the board down when a pain shot through my heart that felt like I would die. The towel I had wrapped around the board to make it softer was marked with her smell and the dirt from her last walk in the rain. I didn't want to take it down. My thoughts were far from rational, but my heart cried out not to change the room in case Sara ever wanted to come back.

I felt as if I had tapped into a deep pain from lifetimes ago when I experienced a similar aching for someone I loved who had gone away. I didn't want to leave for fear he would come back and find me gone. I felt there were other times I had my own pain of returning and finding ones I loved not in the place where I left them. A fear that became embedded in my soul was that I would search for the rest of a life but never find the one I loved. It came out as fear in this lifetime that if Sara's spirit were to want to come back to me, she might not recognize my place if I changed anything in it. She would be lost in the Universe, forever searching for me, and I couldn't bear to have her suffer like that.

I am sure that the other part of not wanting to change anything, to remove what she had touched, what had touched her and held her scent or the mud from her paws, was that I thought I would lose her.

I knew that the deeper truth is Sara would always recognize the only thing that really matters; she will recognize the love in my heart. She could find it no matter where she is in the Universe, no matter where I am in the Universe. But while I was in such deep grieving for her loss, it had been so easy to forget what I knew and, instead, drop into this horrible pain.

I had been thinking about the love Sara taught me. We didn't have to work at it or struggle to love each other. Love was just there. We had to work out differences. Sometimes I didn't play enough for her needs or take her for long enough walks. There were times she wouldn't cooperate when I took her out for walks and then she'd come in and soil the carpet when we returned. She was finicky about what she would eat. But I never, ever, was angry at her soul. I never wanted to change who she was or how she expressed who she was. I do believe that Sara was my soul twin, who had come to teach me what love meant.

She taught me how to open my heart to receive love from that most vulnerable tender place where Sara lived.

On one of those days filled with such intense grieving that my heart was feeling painfully compromised, I had an appointment with the body-therapist I called Clearwater David. I mentioned to him that I had a dream the night before that felt very important but could only remember one image.

In the dream that had much more to it than I could remember, I saw a most beautiful waterfall. David began to do energy work with me, and asked me to go over to the waterfall and to see myself standing in the water, and then he suggested that I take my heart out of my chest and wash it in the cascading water until it was clean. I did that and watched it become crystal clear. Then I leaned back and allowed cascading water to wash through my whole chest. David asked me to put my heart back inside and, then, to invite all those I ever loved to come into my heart. I began seeing images of those loving beings that have made my life full, and of course, Sara was most prominent. One by one, I began inviting them in.

Then I saw images of other people I loved, but I felt they had not yet learned enough for me to trust them on the inside of my heart. I decided to move to a future time when they had learned enough, and when I had learned enough, as well, to invite them in. I began to see hundreds, thousands, millions...even billions of souls flow into my heart. It was the most beautiful vision I had ever seen. The entire inside of my crystal clear heart was shimmering with the lights of billions of souls. It looked as if every soul who had ever lived was inside my heart, and I, too, was one of those billions inside my heart looking up into my own heart as if it were a sky filled with brilliant soul-stars.

To my amazement, I noticed that the beautiful stars that filled the Universe in my heart took on the form of a most radiant woman dancing through space. She was a dazzling princess, outlined in lights, sort of like in a connect-the-dots drawing in children's books, but she was three-dimensional and was filled with such radiant joy as she moved throughout the Universe with amazing grace.

I became aware of a most awesome, powerful being, also made of stars and galaxies, who was watching the star woman, enthralled with her beauty. He exclaimed with profound love that she was beautiful. She seemed to feel the love flowing in his words and those words attached to the exact position she was in when the vibration of his words touched her.

As I watched the princess dance, I began to feel my own body as if it were dancing. I experienced the moment and the vibration that the love-filled words contained as they touched her body, which I felt in my body and then, to my surprise, I felt what seemed like slow-motion distortion of my face like I was responding to some awful horror movie. As I felt and watched the distortion on the princess's face, I felt an excruciating pain flow through me, as it was flowing through her. I was feeling the pain of the star princess in my own body there on the therapy table.

I could sense everything in her. I knew that because she was moving at the moment she received the loving words that she was beautiful, she went into shock because she was unable to hold on to the exact position that held his loving words. With horror and pain, she believed that anything different from the exact position she was in when he spoke the words was not beautiful. She believed that any other position was a distortion from the perfection he named beautiful. She turned away from the very one her heart wanted to embrace, the one who called her beautiful, so he would not see how ugly she had become. She withdrew from him in agony and tried to return to the exact position she was in when he called her beautiful, so she could be worthy of his love but could not find it. She agonized for no longer being beautiful; she believed she had become flawed.

And then in this vision, my attention was drawn to the one who had called her beautiful. He watched her withdraw from him and felt such sadness that his words had resulted in her withdrawal. The more he reached, the more she withdrew. His words created the opposite of what he had intended. He cried out to her that when he called her beautiful, he was not placing those words on the exact position she was in, but on her essence and the expression of that essence in her dance.

345

She stopped and fell to her knees in mournful sadness for all the eons of time she had wasted withdrawing from him and his love, and all the eons of time she had attempted to find the exact place that he had once called beautiful. She hated herself for all she had lost because of her misunderstanding. He held out his arms to her and told her that none of her movement was wasted. He told her that everything she did was all a part of her dance, even the withdrawal. Everything she was and is, and all she had done, as an expression of who she is, was always and will forever be beautiful.

She turned around, looked into his loving eyes, and ran to the open arms of her eternal partner. The two danced, and sang, and loved. As I watched this miraculous reunion and dance, my heart whispered: "How precious!" Feeling my whisper, the precious princess turned her head in my direction and I recognized her. I thought my heart would leap out of my chest as she came running towards me. She was the essence of my sweet Sara, not in the same form she had been in when she was my dear princess, but my heart knew who she was.

Not long after that amazing journey, I looked up Sara's name in the book of baby names, and my heart smiled when I saw that her name means princess.

***

I had written this piece about Sara, my losing her, and my finding her in the Universe of my heart, and in the process finding a deeper truth about love that expands beyond my heart, to the entire Universe on Labor Day weekend 1997. Hours later, on that same weekend the world mourned the death of another Princess, grieving that was experienced around the world, as the *Princess of the People* died attempting to escape the invasion of camera eyes of unconscious paparazzi. The chase was not a desire to make connection, but a drive to invade, snatch, and expose. Diana, whose name means Goddess of the hunt, was considered by many to be the ideal feminine of our age. In the moment of shock of her death, the vast majority of people on the Earth became one in their grief.

Thirty-three years, earlier the Prince of Camelot was assassinated. John Kennedy was considered by many to be the symbol of the ideal masculine, the father-defender for a world that went into shock from his loss. In that moment when this twentieth-century version of the shot that rang out, and was heard *round the world*, much of the Earth became one as it mourned for the loss of its mythic prince.

In the death's of these two human beings who privately were just ordinary people seeking to understand their purpose, discover their place in the world, experience their power or lack of it, and live their lives, and who publicly became representations of twentieth-century mythology, all of us had the opportunity to become aware of our connection.

Lord Jeoffry Arthur of England stated that Diana was the brightest star in the cosmology, suggesting that in spite of her imperfections and mistakes, she won the hearts of the world in her vulnerability, touchability, and the dignity with which she experienced heartbreak and loneliness. Listening to his words brought into my mind, the image of the star princess I watched take form out of the millions and billions of people I invited into my heart, just hours before the announcement of Diana's death. That Labor Day weekend, people from all over the world experienced the same feelings as the young woman who wanted to be queen of people's hearts was being memorialized. In the deaths of both Diana, Princess of Wales, and John Kennedy, Prince of Camelot, each person who opened their hearts to feel the experience, had connected to a much grander consciousness, perhaps Jung's collective unconscious or what I call the Great Mystery that connects all of us into one. For a couple of moments in time, the vast majority of people on this planet were one, reflective of the words spoken by world renowned dream interpreter, the late Dr. Montague Ullman when he said,

"Just as our bodies are made up of billions of tightly compacted single cell organisms, all attempting to act as a unified system, so too, is human kind, but we are a highly fragmented species, splintered and scattered in billions of ways. Unless we can learn how to connect,

share empathy, and love, we will not survive as a species any more than a fragmented body could survive."

Years later, Bruce Lipton, a cell biologist, professor of biology, and internationally recognized authority on bridging science and spirit has reflected the same thought as Ullman presented, but with biological perspectives instead of in psychological terms, that each of us is not a single being as we think, but a community of 50 trillion cells that *have* learned how to live in harmony inside us, and now, our job is to discover how they have accomplished such a cooperative union so we can replicate it among the billions of people in mutually beneficial cooperation with each other, with the entire ecosphere, as well as the Universe.

My sense of our bodies is that while the cells have learned how to be in general harmony, there remains much in disharmony due to the experience of and belief in separation. When we learn to overcome the disharmony by bringing healing to that belief, our experience will change and harmony will not only be true within us, but in our world, as well.

***

Labor day, from a feminine perspective, is a day of giving birth. It is a day of connection and separation that can lead, again, to a new awareness of connection that knows whole and part, as well as a part and apart. It is a day of dying to an old way, and being born into new awareness. An infant is separated from its mother and in the separation discovers both separation and connection in a new way.

On that Labor Day weekend, over a decade ago, the world had been given the opportunity to discover itself as a unified system, learning how to connect, share empathy, and love, as each of us individually and collectively mourned the death of one of us, the Princess of the People. On some level, almost all of us came together, even if it was because of a tragedy. This new way of coming together to find oneness is not so different from what an infant is being called to do following the mutual labor shared by mother and child, when each looks into the other's eyes and reflects the light that is inside, back to the other.

On that day, the world was collectively doing what I had been doing individually for several months in mourning the death of my princess. In that very painful year of 1997, I learned that each moment a heart allows love to enter, there is no separation from the one loved. I know in my heart that as I learn to love, the radiant sky princess of my visualization will stop being fragmented, scattered, torn apart by the opposite needs of running away in fear and longing to be embraced in vulnerability, and she and her lover will be one. This is true for all.

***

After my recalling of that profound shamanic journey years ago, my awareness returned to my two-year-old child-self who had been crying so deeply because she had been afraid that she would never belong, that she would never matter. After seeing that amazing vision of the sky princess, I knew she held all that is love, and my child-self, who had been trapped in that lost place for decades, felt herself become the star princess and her essence, not child, not adult, just her own special light being, surrendered to the Universe and became one with it. She knew, I knew, that I do belong. I am here because I was meant to be here. This Universe is my home, forever.

I felt myself breathe a deep sign of relief, of connection, of love as I sent that love into my heart, into my arteries, and gave permission for them to allow the flow of love and nurturing to enter my heart. I saw thousands of water-angel beings join together to form what looked like a spinning whirlwind taking on the form of a router instrument that entered my body and continued the process of expanding my arteries and veins to allow the flow of blood from my heart to my lungs and into the rest of my body, and from lungs to my heart.

My child-self was able to release having to have her mother, father, and siblings provide her with the sense of belonging. She no longer needed to have their home be hers, because she had a home in my heart and my heart belonged in the Universe, which in a magical, mystical way were both the same. For the first time this little 2-year-old Sandy knew that she is unique, not just one of the girls, and, yet, in a most magical way, she is one of the girls, one of the millions and billions of beings, and one with the One reflected in all the millions and billions of unique beings.

***

I drifted off into a deep sleep. A couple of hours later, I woke into the morning, but after I rose and began to do the normal morning chores, the pressure in my chest returned and breathing became very difficult again. I had not written any more of this chapter besides the introduction message and the first paragraph that I had written the night before.

The thought returned to me that maybe I really was going to die, which caused a wave of disappointment that maybe I wouldn't be able to finish writing this last chapter with all I had learned about hearts and love and opening, or book three, after all. As the thought passed through my awareness, I surrendered to my essence, even more completely than when I thought I might die out in the field a few days before. I surrendered to my eternal unique mystery in union with the Great Mystery, to the magnificence of the princess that I visualized just a few hours before. I knew that should I be called to return to the One, I would not protest like I did on Johnny Appleseed's behalf when I was a child. I had learned so much that was important and even if the learning was just for me it had value. I was important. I mattered. I knew that when I released expectations for a trilogy, about speaking engagements and everything else that could potentially be ahead in this life, if this really was the time I was being called to a new experience beyond this three-dimensional life, a new journey on the other side would be something worthy of being embraced.

It felt to me like all the work I had done to take off the mask and look for what was behind it had been wonderfully healing, which made a failing heart seem misplaced. I went inside to ask my heart if it was healthy, and it told me it was. I looked at my arteries, and I saw that they had shifted, allowing a greater amount of blood to flow, but I was still having difficulty breathing.

In that moment, I thought I should schedule an appointment with an excellent chiropractor whose office is just 15-minutes from my place.

As much as I might have needed an adjustment earlier, I hadn't gone to him since I returned from Florida because of all the bills from the surgery. I didn't think I could afford to go. But now, it felt like I couldn't afford not to go. I was pleased to find out that he had time for me.

He worked with my body, releasing locked up muscles and bones that seemed to be pinching nerves, that in turn were not allowing the easy flow of blood into my heart and lungs. The intensity of nearly non-stop writing for three months had taken more of a toll than I imagined. As Dr. Doug worked with my back, I felt relief from the pressure in my chest and my breathing that had been labored for three months eased. His wife had 30 minutes before her next appointment and offered to give me a half-session, so I moved from his office to hers. She placed hot stones on my back that allowed the muscles to relax for the first time in months. I asked if she could talk to my heart and ask it what it needed. She indicated that it told her it needed my support.

My intuitive sense was that if I had not gone to have my muscles released and bones adjusted, the constriction might have actually led to some kind of heart problem, brought on by physical depletion of blood supply and the stress of wondering if I was dying. I believe some hearts can fail from cutting back on body movement, as a way to avoid the pain buried in the tissues, and the pain in the tissues is brought on by unresolved emotional trauma. We avoid the pain by not moving, when moving is the very thing we need to do to access and release what has been stuck inside us, perhaps for decades, which in turn, brings health back to the body.

People have come to believe that they get old and their bodies age because their muscles stop moving like they used to, but I believe that when there is something unresolved in their lives, people stop using their muscles and they age. When they don't heal a broken heart, when they don't allow a hardened heart to melt or, release heart rage, their hearts fail. I also believe that dying can result from falling into fear that death is coming. When I sat out on the chair by the fire pit a few months earlier, feeling every part of my body in agony and I wondered if I wanted to continue to fight for life, I was very close to saying maybe this struggle was not worth it anymore. I believe that when we tell ourselves that it is not worth it, even if just a little more effort could allow us to break free and really live, our decision to stop the struggle is what can cause us to die.

An hour after I had surrendered and accepted the possibility that I could die without finishing this book, but at the same time embraced the fact that I wanted to find healing and complete the writing, the breaths into my lungs became deep and sustaining. That sense of not getting enough air was gone. I knew I was going to be okay in that moment, and that was all that really mattered.

When I returned home, I went outside to breathe in the air and took Jenny for a very long walk. After returning, I decided not to go back inside to my computer for another stint at writing. Instead, I went out to the pile of wood and began loading pieces of chopped wood into the wheelbarrow and stacked them in rows that my neighbor had begun earlier. I felt muscles that I had forgotten I had…and the wood stack grew with the deepening of my breath.

The sun was shining, the wind was blowing, and Jenny was by my side as hummingbirds darted everywhere, trying to decide if my red t-shirt was a nectar-bearing flower. The stream that runs beside my carriage house was exceedingly full from the abundance of snow and rain that fell in the mountains the past winter and spring. Growing to almost a river, the stream tumbled its way over the rocks past the place where I was standing beside the woodpile. The flowing stream continued down the mountain to join the South Platte River, which flows on into the Missouri that joins the Mississippi and empties out into the Gulf of Mexico. And the Gulf is just the name identifying a division of the Atlantic Ocean that really doesn't exist except on maps, and the Atlantic Ocean is just a name for a division of the Great Ocean that really is not separated into the five oceans of the world. All of it—the streams, the rivers, the Gulf, the ocean—is really just one living, flowing connected body of water.

I looked up into the walls of the canyon covered by tall Colorado Pine trees that rise above my mountain place and gazed beyond to the clouds that were dancing across the most radiantly beautiful blue sky. Those pure white clouds were formed somewhere over the ocean that washed against the gulf, which received the waters of the rivers that were fed by many little streams including the stream so near where I was standing…and the clouds moved over the land and the mountains, dropping rain and snow on the trees that stand so majestically reaching toward that beautiful blue sky. Those trees provide not only nest space for the hummingbirds darting all around me, but the tree bark, leaves, and branches are food for deer, who together with all the other creatures drink out of the stream that runs by my carriage house. And the roots of those trees stretch down into the earth holding the soil together, drawing water into themselves and keeping a balance that allows water to drain through the soil without washing it all away downstream. Without the balancing of all the parts, and the holding, all the water and soil would mix into a grand mud pie covering the face of the earth, with no land for us to walk on, no streams, no rivers, no oceans, and no flow to feed the trees and no trees to feed the animals, and no food sources for humans. And the mud pie would dry out and become dust blown around by the wind. The amazing interconnection of each part of creation allows each aspect to remain its own unique expression, while retaining connection to everything else in oneness.

Everything I saw as I stood beside that woodpile has its own energy that contains its own unique pulse, which vibrates into this amazing connection of all that is. And it is here, in a little space connected to everything in the world, that I came to write…and to let my writing write me.

Like so many other people's experiences in life have taught them, my life taught me to believe in separation when the truth is that connection is what is real. It couldn't be anything else. Separation is an illusion, a static-like disturbance that prevents hearing the truth that caused me to miss the third theme hidden behind the mask. And when I missed the third theme that had to do with my struggle to overcome the belief I did not belong, my writing called me back to look again. I needed to access a higher frequency that required very careful tuning in to the message of the universe, not unlike the tuning of that radio of my childhood to reduce the static when we listened to what the shadow knew. The higher frequency allowed me to receive what I had missed before, which was the message that it is impossible for me not to belong because I am a part of everything; I am a light being in a universe of light. I am a star that is part of the princess, and I am the princess who dances through the Universe. I am the prince, and I am the understanding in the prince who beholds and loves the divine beauty of the princess, whether she is made of the stars scattered across the Universe, or if she is in the form of my Sara or my Jenny or myself...or you. Life is Good!

So, the first theme carried the message that I am not what happened to me, and the message in the second theme is that I am not what erupts from my body as it attempts to communicate what happened to me so I could heal it. The third theme told me who I am...I am an intricate part of a great mystery and I belong because I am. And to think, I almost missed that message, except for the fact that what has been writing this book in me, did not want me to miss this significant message.

Reflections

The Universe, your true home and the expression of the Great Mystery, which is the essence of the Universe, continually sends you messages. Do you make any special time to tune in and listen to the messages, and do you pay attention to the synchronicities that hold information and direction for you? Ask for awareness when these synchronous things happen, because they happen all the time; we usually just don't notice.

Do you experience any anger, any fear, any depression, any anxiety, any pain, any conflict, any frustration, any sadness, any jealousy any guilt, or any shame? Do you feel as if you are not good enough, or that what you do will never be good enough? Do you ever feel like you don't fit in or there is not a place for you? Do you feel like you are on the outside looking in? Do you notice that you want to inflict pain on those who have hurt you? Do you think about dying or killing? Do you wish you didn't have to be here or do you believe that life dealt you a bad hand? Do you feel unsafe in the world or around other people? Do you feel like you have to prove yourself or get other people's approval to be okay? If you answered yes to any of these questions, you or a part of you still believes in separation. Ask inside to discover what caused you to believe in separation, and bring truth and healing to whatever aspect of yourself became trapped in that belief. The ultimate truth is there is no separation even when it feels real.

Just because there are five names for oceans does not mean there are five oceans. Categories and separations are not true, and because they are not true, the answers we get based on separation are not accurate. If you want to experience authentic healing of the deepest wounds within you, there is a way this can be done; it may not be easy, but the results are profoundly transformational within you, as well as in the life you live. To experience this, allow yourself to go deeply inside to reconnect with what you have resisted for years or even decades. When you bring love, truth, and forgiveness to your own self for what you have kept hidden for so long behind the mask, you can find healing. If you choose not to do this, the likelihood is that you will continue to live with the painful effects of the deep wounds.

EPILOGUE
A Deeper Understanding

From the time I came into this world until that day in May of 2009, when I finally released my life to Spirit as to whether I would live or die, I had lived in fear of total surrender and in fear of being vulnerable in reaching out. It isn't that I had never experienced times of opening and trusting or times of knowing that Spirit was present and creating amazing synchronicities in my life. I believe that my mind, for the most part, had accepted the magnificence of the Great Mystery operating in my life for many years, at least, from the time that I began my healing journey in 1986. And, certainly, my heart was closely connected to Spirit and listening to the *Still Small Voice* that had been leading me most of my life.

But despite what I had learned and came to believe as my truth in all the years of self-healing, I still struggled with fears related to myriad beliefs behind my mask that were deeply buried in my body. For the vast majority of my life, I wore the mask of the good daughter, the good girlfriend, the good wife, the good teacher, the good therapist, and even the good writer. Most anyone who knew me would have called me one of the good guys. It wasn't that I was not good; it was that the goodness I presented to the world, as well as to myself, was a mask I wore to cover what deep inside me, below my conscious radar and behind my mask, I believed was the real me: the murderess, the adulteress, the liar, the hatemonger, the letch, the bad girl, the sinner condemned to hell, the unwanted, the unloved, the one without value, the one who does not belong, and more. And I feared that despite appearances, others wore masks that hid their ability to commit murder, tell lies, feel hate, contain lechery, and live in wicked sin. Reaching out to others and surrendering to them not only caused me great fear that they would discover what was hidden in me, but in my unconscious mind, I feared what I would find if I reached out to them.

From the time I was in my teens and became aware that others wore masks, I had no idea that I wore a mask, as well and no idea that there was this darkness behind a mask that I didn't even know I was wearing.

Every now and then, there were little hints, letting me know that there was more inside me than I realized. And occasionally I did things that didn't match the mask I wore, especially as my marriage was crumbling, but I had no idea why. It wasn't until the false life I had been leading began to fall apart that I felt driven to find out what was true.

When we become committed to finding the truth, the truth has a way of finding us, and letting us discover what is and is not real, and who we are and are not. The struggle comes when we have to move through who we wanted to be as represented by our mask, to find who we believed we were behind the mask, after which we may, finally, discover who we truly are. And one of the characteristics of the energy behind the mask is its dedication to not letting us see who we believe we are, because that energy believes that what it covers is who we are.

The deeply buried places inside that held the parts of me, which had been most damaged, were, also, the hiding places for the parts of me that were most angry and most afraid, as well as the parts that carried guilt and shame for my being who I thought I was. Because of the unresolved physical, emotional, and psychological pain that I thought defined me, on the unconscious level, I believed I needed to cover it all if I were to have any hope of finding love, safety, and connection with others. But I had no way of knowing that the ones from whom I sought safety, connection, and love, were themselves hiding, unable to be a safe haven for me or offer authentic connection and love.

My unconscious need to cover up and put on a mask to conceal what I had come to believe was my unacceptable self had warred against my need to experience what was authentic in me and in others. The inner war literally produced the illnesses that impacted my body. I can see that cancer of the vulva, vagina, and uterus were shouting the story of invasion to uncover what was not just terrifying to have experienced, but also, was terrifying to reveal because of what I believed it meant about me.

When I look back on my life, it is so easy to see that the stress from the struggle to hide what was behind my mask or to reveal it, led not just to *cancer*, but also, to *heart problems* that were integrally related to my feeling that *I did not belong in this Universe*. And these were the three themes that weaved themselves into the patterns throughout this book and in my life, though I didn't know it until the book was nearly finished.

Our individual desperation to cover what we believe would not be accepted about us is mirrored by the collective need to cover what is not supposed to be known. Only when we are willing to go down into the dungeons to find what has been hidden, bring healing to what is there, and release both who we tried to be and who we believed we were, will we have the chance to experience our true identity. As each individual uncovers what has been hidden, the collective slowly follows, and opens the way for all of us to heal as a species. But we can't know something needs healing until we are able and willing to see the wound. The extent of the wounding forced me to look very deeply into what was hidden in order to learn enough to understand what I've been able to write in this book and the others in this trilogy.

***

In retrospect, I recognize that I didn't have what would be called a normal life. Certainly, it was extremely difficult, although, as I was living it, I didn't know it was not normal or that it was difficult. I found a way to push it all behind my mask. As I look back through the years, I can see how the things that happened in my childhood and my response to them prevented me from having what most people expect from life. I was so guarded that I didn't know how to fall in love, and I was so physically damaged that my body could not provide a place for the development of babies. No matter how much I accomplished, I was unable to connect with my successes enough to feel the enjoyment or the bliss that others might have been able to feel from their accomplishments and successes. I have suffered with a lifetime struggle with weight, had a couple of heart attacks, and bouts with cancer. But for many of my years, even with all of these clues, I didn't know I was wounded, so I didn't know that I needed to heal.

When suffering from the wounds becomes great enough, we can be pressed into service of the soul, which is calling us to go in search of the cause of the suffering to bring healing.

I believe that my evolving soul made a decision to bring healing to many lifetimes of suffering by drawing me to a mother who believed in suffering and a father who believed in causing suffering, which meant that they both suffered and both caused suffering to the other, to their children, and to themselves. A corollary to believing in suffering is inflicting suffering on self or on others…or both.

On the highest level, I can honor my parents for playing their roles so well that I was given a very clear choice between releasing the belief in suffering by healing or continuing to hold on to the belief in suffering. When I chose healing, the Universe conspired with my soul to fully support me, just as it supports all of us in whatever choices we make. The Great Mystery has never abandoned the unique mystery within any one of us, and continues to bring to us what we believe so we can become conscious of those beliefs and, therefore, what we create. This allows us to make new choices when we become ready to do so.

Though I am sure there will be continued healing experiences in my life, more opening, and unmasking of what remains hidden, I know it is time to publicly and personally announce that **I boldly release the belief in suffering**. This is my intention, as powerful as my intention has been to bring healing to what caused me to believe in suffering. When I began writing these concluding remarks, I had no idea that this is what my soul had been leading me to do, right here, right now, as this second book is completing the writing of itself. I know that I do not have to continue suffering until I finally heal everything.

Releasing suffering is not an angry act, nor is it a planned act; it is the bubbling up of knowing that *suffering does not define me*. Just writing that last statement has caused a rush of excitement in my body. My heart has opened and feels like a child waking up on a special day when something wonderful is about to happen without having to know or plan any of what it will be.

***

For years, when I found myself in places of suffering brought on by confusion, depression, grief, feeling separated from the world and even from myself, or feeling lost without having answers as to how to be found, I would experience a craving for warm homemade fudge. A few years ago, I made a connection of the longing for fudge with one particular childhood experience that happened when I was about eight years old. In a little log cabin hidden away in the wilderness of Alaska, one late summer's night, after my siblings and I had settled down in our sleeping bags, my father returned home from a business trip. His business must have been successful because he was in an upbeat mood. He was tap dancing around the living room, beaming with happiness and delight. The fireplace crackled, creating swaying images of firelight and shadows on the walls and ceiling that seemed to be dancing with him, while sending waves of warmth and the aroma of burning pine logs throughout the rustic spaces of our cabin.

Later that night, my father stood in front of the old wood-burning stove, stirring ingredients until they congealed to perfect consistency, which he then beat with a wooden spoon wafting the aroma of fudge throughout the cabin. At exactly the right moment, he poured the wonderful confection into a buttered pan, and while it cooled, he emptied a bag of corn kernels into a pan that he covered and placed on the fire; soon the kernels began to pop. The aromas of the popcorn, together with the sweetness of the fudge, and the smell of pinewood burning in the fireplace filled every cell of my body. Not long after the popping was finished, each of us was given our own wooden bowl filled with buttered and salted popcorn.

With pride for the perfection of his creation, my daddy made slices and moved from child to child, slipping a piece of the soft, still-warm fudge in each mouth. I can viscerally feel the anticipation of my turn, waiting like a baby bird in a nest, with mouth open, ready to receive the delight he carefully placed on my waiting tongue. And the wonder of that night, the safety of the sleeping bags, the comfort of the aromas of fudge, popcorn, and crackling pine from the fireplace, along with the gentleness of the starry night, the smile on my father's face, and the joy and peace of that moment that made me feel as if all was right with the world, were all stirred together into the taste of that small, succulent piece of warm fudge.

For a few days following the completion of the chapters in *Behind the Mask*, I had been longing for warm fudge, and for the first time in at least twenty years, I decided to make some for myself…but having changed my eating habits, I didn't have any of the ingredients. Several days passed without taking out time to go to the store, and finally the day before yesterday, I ventured out to buy a container of Hershey's Cocoa, and the ingredients, but to my disappointment, there was no recipe on the back of the can as there had been in my childhood. So I returned to my little "cabin" in the Rocky Mountains, went on the Internet, and found the recipe for old-fashioned fudge.

The directions called for the use of a heavy pan and a wooden spoon, neither of which I owned, so the day before this writing, I returned to the store and bought the ingredients, as well as a big heavy pan and wooden spoon. The cooking, stirring, and beating time consumed about an hour, and at just the right moment, I poured the confection onto a buttered plate and waited for it to cool. While it was still warm, I slipped a piece of soft, delicate fudge into my mouth.

As soon as I tasted it, I was aware of how sugary and chocolaty my creation was, and the two flavors had lost their zing for me. The truth was, the fudge didn't taste so good, and it didn't carry any comfort that some part of me longed to feel. The connection of warm fudge with peace, joy, safety, and love was a thought in my head, not a truth I could feel or taste in my body. Just to make sure I hadn't missed something, I tried a couple more pieces, but it was clear the magic was gone. I threw out the remainder of the fudge because it actually was too rich and eating it made my stomach feel slightly nauseous.

Instead, I decided to find the little girl who felt lost and alone, the child part of me who was not sure where she was or what she should be doing next in her life, the little one who thought the fudge might provide her comfort. She was the child who had curled up quietly in her bed after that wonderful fudge and popcorn night had ended and, again, became aware of her deep, unquenchable loneliness, separated from all that was around her and in her, a child who held no hope for any goodness in the life that was ahead of her.

In a deep state of inner visualization, she and I lay together on the little bed in my tiny mountain carriage house, as I shared the joys in my life now: my sweet 4-legged Jenny with eyes so big you can't help becoming enraptured by them, my very old cat, Rachael, who purrs with delight most of her waking time, hummingbirds outside my window in the day, and starry, starry nights in the forest of my adult life. I let her meet the loving friends I have collected around me, that have become my family of choice. I, also, let her see my imaginings of the future she and I are in process of creating, filled with teaching and healing so needed on our planet, today.

Now, she knows where she is; she is with me. She knows what she is doing in her life; she is trusting, both the Universe and me to provide the path that she will be walking with me. The little girl from so many years ago no longer needs to hold on to that memory of one night in her past; instead, she dreams of the future while embracing today, where she is connected, where she belongs, and where she has been healed by love.

She came to the forefront of my feelings at the completion of the writing *Behind the Mask,* because nearly my whole life that particular pattern would be reactivated when something that held my attention with such intensity and passion was finished. The fear-based belief, which controlled me for too long, was *when something good is over, bad things will begin all over again.* But today, I know that I can hold the expectancy that *good can follow good,* if I choose, and I do.

***

The Universe continues to work in mysterious ways, which is a thought that always has a way of bringing a smile to my face, a sparkle in my eyes, and great wonderment to my heart. I had turned in the manuscript for *Behind the Mask,* feeling good it was finally finished. As I boarded my flight for Florida in mid August of 2009, and settled into my seat, ready to reconnect with my home, with friends, and get in a movie or two in between catching up on personal business, I decided to turn on my computer and review the manuscript one more time. I couldn't believe that I found mistakes that I had not seen in the many previous readings. I knew I would have to call the publisher to explain that I needed to resubmit the document, but not until the next day did I know why. If I had not found the errors, I would not have called the publisher to hold off on their design work, nor would I have considered including what I added as a postscript to chapter seven about the film *Inglorious Basterds*. But more significantly, I would not have discovered one more piece that belonged here. So what looked like mistakes were really just messages from the universe that I had a chance to polish what I had written and include what had not yet happened.

In my dealing with the damage little Sandy endured, I discovered how to release the pain and the anger, and had come to understand my reluctance to surrender and trust the universe and my place in it. But I had not noticed another piece that needed to be healed. Near the end of the Tarantino film, *Inglorious Basterds,* the woman who survived a Nazi attempt on her life in childhood, became a part of the Jewish revenge team to kill Hitler, as well as other Nazi's. She had made a connection with the enemy in the form of the young hero who was actually playing himself in the film within the film. After she shot him, she heard his cry and reached out to help him. But as she reached for him, he shot her. In her reaching, I saw the reach of my child self in the forest, who lifted her arm to connect with her father just before he raped her, something I had not seen before, and I saw Rebecca reaching out to her brothers and Jeff to plead with them not to fight, but they didn't pay attention to her reaching and ended in the death of both Jeff and her brother.

In these experiences, reaching ended in great damage or death for me when I was four, for Rebecca in that past life, and for the young woman in the film. I was split between the part of me that believed in reaching out, and the part that believed death happens if you reach out. It was Mooka's story that hung on to me for all these years because she reached out and was rescued, an act that sent a message to my terrified self who had been so hurt. The new message was reaching can have a good outcome and can be beautiful. The old and deeper message, embedded behind my mask, had been that bad would follow good. Combining these messages created a meaning that said it is dangerous to reach out for good, because even if you get it, bad will follow.

In my previous work, I had brought healing to the part of me that feared surrendering but had not noticed the part of me that feared reaching out. So, it was time to reach out to my child self and let her see how reaching out could be so very good. I helped her to see that I had grown into a woman who was capable of discerning energies, and I could trust the knowing that exists inside me. It lets me sense danger, as in the case when another is possessed with rage even if he or she covers it with a convincing mask. It also lets me know that I don't have to fear what is in other people's universes even when they are right next door to mine. I can be thoughtful and aware of what might draw me into fear. I can now use any fear response I might feel as a message for me to notice I have disconnected from the unique mystery that is in me and is forever one with the Great Mystery. In connection, I can know I am safe, secure, and wise. And, in *this* Universe I have co-created with the Great Mystery, the Universe in which I have chosen to live, I am free to reach out to those open to the reaching and release the need to reach out to those who are not open. I can be me with all my flaws, all my vulnerabilities, all that I still hide, even if I don't know I am still hiding anything, and I can experience love and acceptance without needing to suffer because of my imperfections. And it can be safe to discover my imperfections, or for that matter, for other people to know or discover them, too. Suffering does not have to follow something that is good, and I don't have to be punished with suffering for not being perfect or doing something perfectly. And this is the truth.

When I know anything from a place of truth, such as *good can follow good*, and *reaching out can be safe, and beautiful,* as well as *I can be perfectly imperfect, flawed with things still hidden and I can be loved,* I experience a knowing inside me that is both wonderfully relieving, as well as empowering. In this space there is an expectancy that whatever I *know* is going to happen, will take place, and whatever that is will be exactly as it should be. This expectancy was connected to my knowing from the time I was 13 years old that I would be a teacher, and it was connected to my knowing that the German Sheppard, Pal, would survive the back breaking accident. Expectancy was connected to my knowing that I needed to live in China in 1990 and that I had to move to Florida two years later. And, again, the knowing drew me to enroll in graduate school to get my PhD in psychology. Even when completion of the 7-year program felt horribly blocked, I knew I would finish. And in 2006 that knowing returned when there was no doubt I needed to live in the Rocky Mountains of Colorado, the backbone of the US. This knowing, also, arose in me at the end of the summer of 2007 that I would write three books that would, in turn, write my life as the trilogy took form in this three-dimensional world. There is, also, expectancy that the messages included in this book and the other two will reach out to the world, and that the world will reach back in receiving the messages. I also knew that I would not curl up and let myself die, that dreadfully cold winter when I sat out by the fire pit and contemplated releasing the journey to heal my body when the pain felt too encompassing to heal.

This expectancy can be found in my knowing that healing happens, if we choose it; and I knew that I had chosen it. Expectancy fills my heart with a feeling of expansion, of peaceful excitement, and of joy that makes my cells smile, and this is what I feel now, as I know that good is unfolding in my life, following the goodness of writing *Behind the Mask*.

I open to a life filled with expectancy while releasing expectations. I have come to trust the process that has allowed the writing that flows through me to write itself into my life and into this book, and then is released out into the world for the essence of the writing to write itself into those who are waiting for their own discoveries and transformations. And all is as it should be.

AN UNEXPECTED POSTSCRPT

Sometimes you might think you are finished with a chapter in your life, when a discovery happens that lets you know everything is not finished. Like chapters in our lives that seem complete, I thought I had finished *Behind the Mask,* first with the completion of chapter eighteen, and then with the epilogue that needed to be included after my trip to Florida where I saw the *Inglorious Basterds* and knew what I had learned had to be a part of this writing. Finally, after all the changes, I resubmitted the manuscript including the epilogue mid August of 2009. But when the galley was sent from the publisher for my review on August 31, I found I had overlooked far more mistakes than I had ever made in this book than in all of my years of writing despite all the editorial reviews prior to submitting it. I spent several days making the corrections in the galley and when I found so many, I decided to do another review of the manuscript. I was shocked to find even more mistakes I'd missed in the post-galley review.

As a result, I decided I'd better withdraw the manuscript and go back through it carefully, line by line, to be sure it was clear of mistakes that somehow I had been unable to see before. Instead of having the finished product off to the publisher by the first week in September, as I was sure would be possible, so many things kept getting in my way, and I was barely half way through the review when it was the middle of September and the day for a cranial therapy session I had scheduled over a month before.

I had reviewed everything, up to the section on grieving the losses of my life, just before the passage about the wind dancing with the pine trees, something that made my heart delight, when I stopped my review and left for the appointment with a gifted Tibetan Cranial therapist in Longmont, Colorado about an hour and a quarter from my mountain place. The experience was so profound and there was no question this book, which has been writing my life, was waiting for me to experience what was still on the horizon before it was finished with me, so it stalled itself with mistake after mistake, long enough for me to include what it wanted to be written before I completed it, not just in this book, but also in my life.

After completing the session and all that happened that afternoon, I was too exhausted to do any more reviewing of *Behind the Mask*, so I went to bed without writing about the session in Longmont, and without doing any additional editing. The cursor had been stopped on page 209 with the statement, *"I know something very important is in process. It will be interesting to see where all this leads."* and I stopped, as well. What I didn't know at the time I wrote those words, and didn't know the night I had to go to bed because of the exhausting day with the cranial therapist, was what happened that day was where all of my understanding about grieving and releasing grieving was to lead. All through the night I processed what had happened that day, and in that Mid-September morning of 2009, I wrote an email message to my dear friend, Oregon David.

Dear David, Yesterday was one of those unexpected, strange days that I certainly didn't plan to have happened. I tried to write to you last night, but was not able to get beyond a paragraph and I had to go to bed without getting to what I wanted to tell you.

Yesterday morning began with feeling very concerned for Rachael. I think she needs to have a growth on her neck removed. It has grown from a small, almost flat mole the size of the nail on my little finger to a round bump the size of a thumbnail. She has had a dark mammary for years, but my vet told me to wait to see how it affected her before taking it off because she is getting up there in years and the concern is that she might not be able to survive being put under for an operation. She could die under anesthesia, but she could die if I don't do anything. This kind of decision tears me apart inside. So I don't know what is in her best interest and I am still torn. The vet was supposed to call with an estimate yesterday, but I had to leave for a therapy appointment before the call came.

I left early to have enough time to get to the appointment with Shar, the woman in Longmont who holds the Tibetan legacy for this procedure that uses cranial balancing of the rhythms to release old patterns stuck in the body that too often negatively impact our life process. It is so very powerful and has been exactly what I have needed at this juncture in my life. Though when I thought about the session, I had no idea what I would need to work with because I felt so good, and I wasn't aware of any concerns.

Before leaving, I turned on my new Magellan GPS, the first time I have used it, which gives directions based on real traffic situations, and the directions it gave me were to bypass the most direct route, I-70 to I-25, to take another route. The bypass would be like going on Hwy. 99 filled with traffic lights and a speed of 45, instead of taking I-5 to go from Seattle to Mt. Vernon. Of course, it only said bypass without telling me what was going on with I-25. I almost decided to disregard the message and take the left side exit further down the road, but acquiesced to the GPS directive as I approached the bypass exit to the right. Since the readout told me I had plenty of extra time, and I was driving on what was more like a city thoroughfare instead of a freeway, I decided to fill up with gas even though I had enough to make it to Longmont, and at least part way back. But before I stopped, I double-checked my gage and I glanced at the dashboard meters. To my surprise, three warning lights had come on as I was exiting the I-70 freeway. I didn't have a clue what the icons meant. At the gas station, I opened my glove box where I have my manual, but it was missing, so I called a Toyota dealer from Denver who looked up the icons and told me my stability was not functioning, my tracking ability was turned off and I needed to have my engine checked. All I wanted to know was whether my car could blow up or if I would be okay to drive to my appointment or not. I was assured that as long as I bought the car in within the next few days, I should be fine. But so much of my time had been eaten up in searching for numbers and getting answers that it was clear instead of being early, I would be late.

I continued my drive north, stopping at nearly every light, giving me a chance to breathe and release the distress over being late as the arrival time advanced from being 20 minutes early when I left home to being 3 minutes late, 8 minutes late, and then 20 minutes late for my appointment. As I drove off from my place, I remembered I had left my appointment book, and paused to go back to get it, but chose not to. That decision came to me when I realized I would be late and needed to let the therapist know, but the only place I had Shar's number was in my appointment book. I used my cell to call information, but hey had no listing for her in Longmont, which really distressed me, because I so dislike being late and dislike even more not being able to tell someone I wouldn't be on time.

The dash lights continued to tell me that my stability was compromised, that I was off track, and that my engine needed checking.

I arrived feeling lots of "stuff" going on inside, and gave my apologies for not being on time, but Shar was pleased that she had had time to eat a relaxed lunch, and indicated that all was as it should be. I climbed onto the table and she began her work. We chatted for a couple of minutes while she took my pulses, and I apologized, again, saying I so disliked being late. I told her I even left early to have time to rest before the session, but that I was also aware that an event like this, not unlike a dream, is filled with messages that are important. Shar indicated since she knew I was not avoiding the work, perhaps the ancient monks had created the difficulties for a purpose, something she has noticed when people need to be primed for what is about to happen in their cranial therapy process.

As soon as she told me about the monks, I felt waves of emotion moving through me, though I had no idea what it all meant. And then I asked Shar if she believes it is possible for a person to be born at the wrong time. I asked the question because I have been so focused on being exactly on time, neither too early nor too late, and I get very upset if I can't walk in at exactly the right time. If early, I wait in my car until a few moments before an appointment. After saying this, I began to sob. I explained to Shar my mother told me all my life that I had come too early, and had ruined my sister's birthday. But something even deeper was going on, I wondered if somehow, I had missed the right portal and had entered the wrong womb. I wondered if my birth into that family had been a mistake. That thought put me into great heaving sobs; if I had gone into the wrong womb, that meant the right one had been waiting for me, and I hadn't come... I was feeling the mournful sadness of a mother somewhere, out there so long ago whose child did not arrive. I ached for my real mother who had so wanted me to come, but I failed to show. And I ached for myself coming into the world through the woman who was angry that I arrived when I did. I wondered if somehow I had not timed my entry properly and my mistake made me miss the place I was supposed to be and the life I was supposed to live.

Images flashed through my mind of having missed the mark at times in the past and as a result missed important experiences. I have spent my whole life fearing making decisions because if I made the wrong choice I would miss the opening that had been prepared for me and what would follow would be a lifetime of living a mistake. I asked her if she was familiar with Frost's *The Road Not Taken*...that said, *"Two roads diverged in a yellow wood, and sorry I could not travel both, and be one traveler...long I stood and looked down one as far as I could..."* The first time I ever read that poem was when I was in grade school. It is about making a decision in life, knowing once the decision has been made, it is unlikely to ever go back, and reading it when I was so young caused me to cry deeply, grieving without knowing why I was so devastated. Now I know. I believed I had made the wrong choice and the result was a mistake that has been my life. But I also know that if one stands frozen and does not make a decision for fear of making the wrong choice, not deciding is a decision, which could be wrong, too. A wrong choice could be riddled with devastating results. Even though I had dealt with this very dilemma in earlier writing and believed I had come to know the truth, something was still missing in the earlier work.

I asked Shar if she believed it was possible that a person could miss the portal, miss that moment when everything in the universe opens for the entrance of a soul. She answered that the Tibetan monks believe that such a thing is possible. She told me many Tibetan monks have tried to die sitting up, by tying themselves into an upright position when they feel death is near so their spirits can leave without spiraling. They believe in the spiral, their souls are off balance and can easily be sent off into a wrong direction and wombs may try to snatch them while they are ascending in a spiral. But the bottom line, was that *yes*, there can be births at the wrong time, but, she said, what would be important was how the soul chose to respond to the problem. She asked me to look at what I had done with my life, and notice how much I moved through, perhaps dealing with much more Karma than I could have ever done in any other life.

More and more tears and grieving overwhelmed me...I was feeling the pain of the thought that my life has been a mistake...and my car was telling me that I was off track and unstable just before I was to go into a session where I seemed to be touching a deeply embedded belief that my life was off track, and I was unstable, unable to remain grounded. I wondered what I must have lost by making the wrong choice decades ago; perhaps, by coming too early I was snatched by my mother's womb. I thought maybe that is why I never

371

have really felt connected. As hard as I have tried to feel otherwise, I have always believed that my coming into this world was a mistake and what was real for me was somewhere else, not here. Maybe this is why my life has felt like a dream, at times a nightmare, and not something real, and why I have never become a part of anything, not really. I have participated in so much in my life, but I have not become absorbed by anything, with the possible exception of my writing. I have not felt that deep commitment, which comes with total surrender to something or someone else. I know this isn't how I always feel, but it was how I was feeling while in the session with Shar.

You mentioned something to me on a drive to one of the rivers when you were visiting about my resistance to surrender. I felt sadness for what you were telling me about my never having fully surrendered and, yesterday, I allowed myself to feel the depth of the sadness of living a life disconnected from living life. Even as I write this, I am feeling such deep sorrow.

How do you embrace life when at the core, you believe it was a mistake? If this life has been a mistake, then everything in it must be a mistake, as well. I must really not have had any important contribution to make; that idea must have been a mistake, as well. I began to wonder about all the people I thought I helped, and questioned everything I believed was good as being so much less than I thought. It seemed reasonable to believe all those people would be living their lives, basically the same whether or not I was ever here because my being here was a mistake, so my existence really didn't matter. Being here didn't matter! That was so very difficult to embrace, but it seemed true in that place of deep anguish about having made a mistake, which made me become a mistake, as well.

I looked at my inability to make decisions, like with what to do for my cat, Rachael. I remembered RB, my beautiful Great Dane that died of a broken heart after her mother died. Rome and RB had been indoor dogs until Jake did a major remodeling of the house, and then he made them outdoor dogs. They lived in a cold doghouse and ran in a muddy pen. They often stood at the kitchen sliding door, with very sad eyes, begging to be let in, but I couldn't. My heart was torn in pieces because they were forced out of their loving home, and I didn't have the courage to stand up to Jake to tell him he couldn't do such a cruel thing to them. Rome died very soon after becoming an outdoor dog, and sweet RB went into mourning. Her body broke down.

She began getting awful skin infections that I couldn't heal for her because my own heart was breaking. I am sure the outdoor living had a lot to do with it, as well. The vet saw her once and gave me antibiotics but wouldn't renew the prescription without seeing her again, and I was so ashamed to have him see the extent of the infections, which I believed would prove how much I had neglected her. My shame created even more neglect. Much later I found on the Internet that such skin disease is common in Danes. I tried to convince myself that her illness was not my fault, but I knew she didn't have to suffer as she did. Feeling inhibited from giving her what she really needed made me feel her death was my fault. She really needed to come in and be loved. But I couldn't do that when Jake required she be an outside dog.

Then I remembered my very special dog, Pal, from my childhood. He had gotten sick, and I knew I could heal him by touching him, but my mother would not let me go near my dear dog. Then one night, several men came to the door with guns. They went into the back yard where Pal had been tied up and shot him. I saw them carry him away. His feet were tied to a long stick and his head hung down swinging back and forth with each step they took. I was in shock. I felt great pain remembering my sweet dog that didn't have to die if my mother could have just understood, but she refused. Maybe that was when I really began to believe that somehow I had been born into the wrong family. The right family would have known about healing, would have allowed me to touch him with healing energy, and would not have had Pal shot.

Shar asked if I felt I had more anger toward my mother than my father, which was something I acknowledged. I told her about how my mother made any show of affection out to be something ugly, something dirty and sexual, so that even when I hugged my sister just a couple of months earlier, my mom became tight jawed and angry saying that was my sister, not my lover. I was so, so angry...and then I remembered how she had that same anger when my dog Pal, the one I found along side the road who had been hit by a car, and how his healing brought us so close. I named him after my dog from childhood that I had lost so tragically. My mother became livid when she saw him jump up and lick my face. She said he was acting like he was my husband and it was clear she was very angry.

I told Shar that I had come to realize how *the wicked witch of the north* had made any expression of love or affection seem dirty, and how deeply sad I was that I protected myself by pulling back into myself, withdrawing me from the world. Everything ached as I could see more how that feeling added to my core belief that I was here by mistake.

When Shar suggested that no one has ever really known me, not even the people who know me, everything broke open inside. I think I have never cried so deeply or grieved so profoundly as when I realized that the people I love most don't know how much I love them...even you, my dear David. It was then something even deeper cracked open. I asked myself how this life could have been a mistake when I met you? How could loving you and loving all the other people in my life be a mistake? And I thought of my clients and all the people who have crossed my path, some of whom I helped and some who helped me. How could all that have been a mistake? Something major shifted inside.

Perhaps, I had been a Tibetan Monk in a past life and had embraced the teaching that a person's soul could be snatched by a womb and forced to live an unintended life. Maybe that is why I was so open to the idea that my birth and my life were mistakes. As I reconsidered that belief, it seemed so clear that someone tying themselves upright to avoid being snatched by an uncaring womb sounded more like an age old fear of women and their perceived evil-intended power over men's souls. It was time to release that fear.

I was extremely weak after all the releasing of so many fear-based beliefs at the core level during that session. Afterward, I sat out in Shar's garden for a while watching the coy and taking in the beauty of the waterfall, and then I left.

I decided to get the oil changed, since it was close to the time it was needed, anyway. So instead of driving back up to my mountain home, I went to Lakewood near Denver and had the oil changed. When they finished, the icons were still on the dash display, so I asked if there was a way they could find out what was wrong. The young man said for $20, he could perform a diagnostics test. I asked him to check it out. After plugging the diagnostic device into my car, the attendant told me that when I got gas last I had not tightened the cap properly, which set off the emergency messages. I went back, unscrewed the lid and re-tightened it...and all the warning lights went out. The diagnosis did not explain why the icons had appeared prior to my putting in gas that morning, and why they were not there following my previous fill up. It seemed so strange that something so little made it look like something really terrible had happened. The warning did not come until taking that trip north to deal with the issues around my life being a mistake, a thought that I believed since I was such a tiny child. It was a belief that caused me to experience my life as if it were off track and unbalanced, which led to experiencing my life as unstable. What a major metaphor and how untrue!

I wanted to share all this with you last night, but after all that work, I was simply too exhausted. All night long, my body was pouring out heat. I felt like I was on fire, burning up from the inside out. I think that old lies were burning away from my core. Regardless of what Monks might have believed about mistakes of birth and of lifetimes, I now know, from the inside out, both from thinking and feeling places, that my birth and my life were not mistakes. I had patterns that needed to be released and that is what yesterday allowed. My being alive was not a mistake. Even my life with my family was not a mistake. If there is an aspect of me that went to another womb and lived her life with a mother who embraced her, a mother with whom it was safe to surrender, and this aspect of me lived a beautiful storybook life falling in love with a wonderful man and they weaved a perfect life together of great happiness, that is okay. Whoever I am as in the consciousness I hold here in this world, has been weaving a life as well, which is not a mistake. And the hummingbirds are still here, enjoying the nectar and they will move on when it is their right time. In all of this, I remembered something I wrote in one of the chapters of *Behind the Mask:*

Years ago, Oregon David and I began writing a book together on the process of releasing, but both of us had so much that we, ourselves, hadn't released that we didn't finish the book. But despite the fact that it has not, yet, been finished, the conversations we had around it were meaningful. David's words came back to me, reminding me that if we don't like the universe we are in, the only way we can move beyond what we don't like is to accept where we are and embrace it. Otherwise some part of us is denying the truth of where we are, which, also, denies the part of us that lives in the place we have denied. We cannot take a part of ourselves that we deny somewhere else. That part remains in what exists in the present universe, while we, also, remain stuck there, longing to be in another universe.

I had no idea I still had so much to learn from what you had told me. Deep inside, hidden behind my mask, though most of me knew the truth, a part of me believed I didn't belong here and that not only had I made a mistake, but I, myself, was a mistake. Whenever I fell into the pain of that belief, I disconnected from the truth and experienced the emotional distress from feeling off track and unstable. My car helped me to put words on a pattern I had lived my whole life without conscious awareness until something would trigger feeling the pain that caused me to disconnect from all the positive experiences and fall into the belief that I was a mistake. An unhealthy obsession about being on time was the pattern I created to protect me from experiencing a "time" mistake that would open into the belief that my birth, and therefore my life, had been a mistake. What an amazing discovery that really strange day allowed! A much deeper truth has emerged, and that is that I am not a mistake…I AM, and that is the only truth that matters.

My dear David, Have I told you lately that I love you?

With much love, Sandy

So ends the postscript following the epilogue to the book that has been writing itself in me for the last few months of my life and wasn't quite finished with me when I thought I was finished with it. I had worked with the part of me that believed I didn't belong in the Universe, and the part of me that had learned to be afraid to reach out to the Universe, but I had not worked with the little Sandy who believed she had made a mistake that brought her into the wrong life. Perhaps the deepest core wound I carried my entire life, without even knowing it was my belief: I was a mistake because I had made a mistake by being born at the wrong time to the wrong mother. When I wrote on page 249 about my mother reminding me every year that my birth ruined my sister's birthday, I thought this first-level abuse my mother inflicted on me throughout my life was minor. But all of what happened around arriving late to my appointment let me see that the pain I felt by my mother's reminding me of the mistake, over and over, was, in fact, major. I can now see how this belief impacted every aspect of my life until I was finally able to feel it and release it during a Tibetan cranial session. And, most importantly, I finally embraced the truth for the first time in my entire life that I am here because I was meant to be here. I am not a mistake. My life began as an intention and I am in process of living that intention each day of my life. While confronting the belief I held since I was born was a painful process, in retrospect, I can see the humor of the Great Mystery that used mistakes to present me with my belief in mistakes. It is so clear, now, that I wouldn't have been ready to truly experience what is *Under the Mask* without having taken the time for this deeper look at what was still behind my mask.

***

I believed everything was finished with this postscript—with this book—and I was ready to move on to writing *The Meaning of Three: Under the Mask,* so I resubmitted the manuscript to the publisher. When the galley came back, I began looking through it, and found mistake after mistake, again! It seemed impossible that I could have read through the chapters, line-by-line as many times as I had, with the number of mistakes still there, some very glaring, yet, I missed them.

I knew I had to do another review, and the process of having to go through it all again felt monumental. So, I gave myself a timeline to complete the project, and began to do the work of editing, yet another time. I read to page 85 and began to feel very depressed. No matter what I tried to do, I couldn't move past the paragraph that read:

The angry young man began to sob with a grieving that shook his entire body. He was sitting on the boulder, totally engulfed by the emotions that poured out of him. I walked over to the rock and I put my arms around the young man. Seeming to be more like a little boy than an angry man, he raised his arms and wrapped them around me as if to seek comfort from the pain of a wound that appeared to be so deep it could never heal. My embrace was what this broken and sobbing, angry, boy-man needed.

The place I couldn't get beyond was the passage about the processing I did with Atlanta Bill when he helped me with a dream I called the *Maniac Masculine.* You might recall that within that dream, I woke and found myself in a place that was supposed to be mine, but didn't look like it. All through the dream, I was wearing a bathrobe and was in search of my clothes so I could go to a photography class. Very soon into the dream, a man who didn't look like my former husband, but I had identified him as that in my dream, entered and began to act sexually rude. I was disturbed by his actions, and told him to stop. I, then, asked him to help me find my clothes, and I began a long search into many rooms in this big mansion. At one point, the man became violently angry, slammed down a computer, on which he had been writing something that I could not see. After his angry outburst, he ended up demolishing everything with a forklift. I woke feeling very disoriented.

Not until this writing, did I finally figure out what I had not done after the dream or in the processing of it. In the effort to work with the "dirty girl" and all the profound understanding I gained from taking that road, I had neglected to bring comfort and understanding, beyond the hug, to the part of me Bill had identified as the *dirty boy*, the angry man who had piercings all over his body and scars on his lips, which looked like they were cut in some kind of tribal coming of age ritual. He also had a piece of wood piercing his lower lip. I neglected to talk to him at that time, to ask him what was the cause of his deep sobbing or about that pain he believed could never heal.

In the dream, I shut him down by telling him to stop what he was doing because it felt so rude and inappropriate. He, certainly, seemed disconnected from anything loving and he truly felt unapproachable, perhaps like the young men wearing hoodies that I worked with in dealing with cancer. But I also allowed him to be shut down in my processing of the dream by quickly moving to the needs of the *dirty girl*, after which I decided that whatever was still remaining with these two parts of me would not be a part of this book, but would be in another book. Though this seemed like a reasonable decision, the boy-man, sitting on the rock wouldn't let me pass him by.

I, myself, in my waking life was so wounded in the area of sexuality and sensuality, that I couldn't remain with him long enough to find the meaning for everything he was showing me in the dream or in the visualization process that followed. He forced me to stop at the place in my writing that revealed much about him and he simply would not let me move on with the completion of this book until I faced what he came to show me.

I am convinced that this part of me, who sat at the computer in the dream writing something I could not see, made all sorts of mistakes and blocked me from seeing them in my reviews, knowing that the perfectionist part of me would not allow the galley to be approved if there were still mistakes, especially glaring ones. Each of the previous times I reviewed what I'd written, I stopped at the same place, knowing that there was still something calling for me to work with it, but I chose to go ahead without processing any more of the dream, with the decision to come back to it at another time.

This time, I began to study the dream, and deeper understandings of the images came to me, as never before. I could see this angry man was the shadow side of my inner romantic, the amazing Jon aspect of Jon-Luke that I wrote about in *The Mask*. The angry *dirty boy* was the very immature part of me that split off in the rape in the forest and remained separated in all the later rapes and misuse of little Sandy's body. He was unable to connect with my protector masculine self, whose job it was to be my defender, something that little children should never have to do for themselves; that is why they have fathers. But my daddy couldn't fulfill that role; *he* was the reason I needed protection.

In the process of growing from protected child to powerful adult, whether man or woman, the defender-self plays a profoundly significant roll in making sure the self is safe in the world. However, my assertive, protective self had been broken and defeated by my father when he raped me and buried me in the box, making it impossible for me to know how to defend myself. This problem was reiterated throughout my life and was most recently repeated when I couldn't tell the doctor I wanted her to change gloves after she had touched all sorts of unsanitary surfaces before beginning to look into my body.

The dream image, which began as Jake, soon became a man with piercings all over his body, scars from ritual cuttings on his lips, and a piece of wood rammed through his lower lip. For the first time I could see that my child self was showing me the damage she experienced, something I had never allowed myself to see. In all the memories of the abuse in my childhood, I had never seen images of the penetration, only the horror of the ripping apart after the penetration. So this dream was letting me see the scars and the wood—a slang word for a hard penis—that penetrated the lower lip. This image was significant because women have two sets of lips, the upper ones on the face, and the lower lips that open to the vagina. Because I simply could not look at the lower ones, the dream had to show me another way to see the damage by showing it in the lower lip.

The romantic, sexual, sensual aspect of my self had been so badly damaged in childhood that I was afraid to allow this part to have any form of expression, either in its masculine or feminine forms. Instead of opening to feeling sensual energies when they first emerged in me, I shut them down, just as I shut down the maniac masculine in my dream. Though this was coming from my unconscious, I was terrified if I allowed my sexuality to be expressed from my wounded self, it would have included violent and angry energies, as exhibited in sexual abuse or in sadomasochistic sex, so as a protection, I stopped both aspects of myself from feeling anything.

After I shut down the maniac masculine in the dream and stopped his sexual feelings, by judging them as rude, he directed me into the red velvet room, which I later discovered was connected to the prostitute's house where I had been taken as a child. It is no surprise to find that many women, who become prostitutes in their adult lives, were sexually abused as children. It is possible that if I hadn't shut her down, the *dirty girl* may have taken that path and put on the cloths of a prostitute, who would find her clothes in one of the houses like the red velvet one both in my dream and in a prostitution district of some town like Seward. That was one of the options I had to choose from for an identity, but in the dream, I walked through that space because my clothes were not there.

While I continued my search for my clothing, a computer became the focus of the man I identified as the *dirty boy* in the dream. I know that all people in my dreams are aspects of myself, so I knew the man at the computer and the Sandy looking for her clothes, along with her identity, were both me, and so were the dirty boy and dirty girl. For the past 30 years, ever since I got my first computer, I have been obsessed with writing, and much of my life force has been directed into writing instead of into my whole self, including my sexual, sensual aspects. I have tried to find my identity through what I express in my writing instead of finding it in the one I am in my essence expressed in my body. Even though I have known and written about the need for what we do in the world to come from who we are, instead of identifying who we are by what we do, I am aware that I really had not gotten that my focus has been backward, at least not as deeply as I am getting it now. Who I am in the world does not come from my writing, my photography, my teaching, my healing of myself or supporting it in others, or anything else I do, but rather, what I do comes into the world as an expression of who I am. There is a huge difference.

The man in my dream became angry when I interrupted his focus on the computer, and he attacked the driver of the emasculated forklift moving Victorian furniture in the warehouse. The *dirty boy* man could no longer distract himself with his writing, and was confronted with the part of me maintaining the metaphoric Victorian furniture, which was clearly represented in asexual Victorian attitudes of the 1800s that identified sexuality as immoral, and in the part of me that assumed those same attitudes by shutting down my own very normal sexual and sensual feelings for fear that the *dirty boy* and *dirty girl* would get me in trouble. I woke feeling dizzy and disoriented.

As I studied the dream further, I realized that the part of me sitting at the computer had another agenda. He was determined to prevent me from moving forward until I discovered who he was. I began to see that he was not the same aspect of me that was sitting on the rock, sobbing for all that had happened in his life, but he was the part that had felt so deeply judged for having been sexually damaged. I believe he is the one who was making all the mistakes and preventing me from seeing them when I did the previous reviews. It is even possible that he intentionally made the glaring mistakes after I had done the reviews. Not only did I hide him behind my mask because I believed the world would judge him for what had happened to him, to me, in childhood, but I judged him, too.

When I allowed myself to feel his presence, he gave me his name. It was Daniel, which was a surprise, since I thought he was Vincent. As is my usual response, when I hear a name like this, I look it up to find the meaning. To my amazement, Daniel means Judged by God. This was a very clear message to me that no one, but the One had the right to judge me for what happened to me, not even me. Even the names, dirty boy and dirty girl were judgments. And in that moment, I found myself standing in the oneness of the One, and felt only love. Just like the princess whose essence that danced, withdrew, fell to her knees, and embraced her lover-prince was beautiful in all that she did, so was Sandy in all of her responses to what had happened to her in her life.

No wonder I woke from this dream feeling dizzy and disoriented! In the dream, I was moving around from the intense feelings of one aspect of myself to another at a dizzying speed. I thanked Daniel for preventing me from moving forward until I discovered this very important understanding, one that allowed me to bring the truth of who I am even deeper into the wounded places within me.

And what I discovered about me is true about you, as well. You are not what happened to you; you are not what you tried to do to cover up or to reveal what happened to you. You are the beloved of the One and it is possible that you, too, might be blocked from moving forward until you embrace the aspects of you that have been split off like little shards of glass in a fallen mirror, judged, and rejected as not you and reflected back to you by the mirror of your life and those who you have drawn into your life. Once free from the blockages, you can waken from the dream, put down the script, step out of the play, and begin living a life from your true self, your essence, free of debilitating fear of what is behind your mask. Perhaps, for the very first time, you can feel life flowing through you from authenticity and spontaneity, enjoying being a stream or a river in the ocean, and at times recognizing that there is no difference between the river and the ocean.

And…as a postscript to this postscript, if there are any more errors in *The Meaning of Three: Behind the Mask*, so be it…they must be flaws that simply belong!

***

The last words I wrote in *The Meaning of Three: The Mask,* were, *'We have arrived at the point in human history where we must decide what we will do with our consciousness and with truth. It is time to choose whether or not we will face the fear to bring healing to ourselves, and in the process, bring healing to the planet.*

Though the problem is universal, the decision to find your true self is personal. It is up to you to decide. These concluding remarks are just as true now, as when I wrote them in book one. You can decide you don't want to do whatever it takes to bring healing to the parts of you that live in dungeons, and you may choose to continue to do what you can to keep them locked up there, so as not to disturb your life, but I guarantee you, they will find a way to disturb your life.

If you do decide to choose to face your fears and bring healing to your self and your life, you will discover so much more than you ever imagined was possible. You will discover the most magnificent being that you always have been and always will be, right there, waiting for you under your mask.

***

And so, begins the next chapter in my life, one that will be formed within the pages of what I write next as whatever it is writes what it needs me to know in me…and in you, if you choose to read it.

I have enjoyed spending time with you, while in some mystical reality we have worked our way through the months of bringing into being the pages and chapters contained between the covers of this book. In some very real way, you and all the energy you have added to the Universe by reading and responding to what is behind your mask has been mixed into these pages and has been a part of this whole process. Thank you for your contribution.

Perhaps, we will meet again in the pages of the last book in this trilogy, when *The Meaning of Three: Under the Mask,* decides what it will write into me, into us. Or, possibly, we will meet someplace while I am conducting a workshop or giving a presentation, finally free of all the beliefs that held me back from being who I came into this life to be, expanding more and more into my true self and moving forward in my life, unafraid of flaws or what might still be there hiding *Behind the Mask.* Be sure to say hi when our paths cross someday, as I know they will. My best wishes go with you.

About the Author

Dr. Sandy Sela-Smith has a Ph.D. in psychology. She has a practice as a mind, body, spirit, psychotherapist, and is licensed as a mental health counselor in Florida and Washington State and is a licensed professional counselor in Colorado. She is nationally certified by NBCC as a mental health counselor, and has been certified by ACHE as a clinical hypnotherapist. Sela-Smith is a part time faculty member at two graduate schools, is a published, author, and has recently enjoyed her work as a professional photographer. Her home is in Florida, and she lives part time in the mountains of Colorado where she writes. She hopes to have the third book in the trilogy, *Under the Mask,* completed early in 2010. Check her web site to find out when it will be published or to order any of her books.

Sela-Smith speaks and presents workshops on the healing processes presented in the trilogy, *The Meaning of Three,* related to the three aspects of the Great Mystery, which is eternally connected to the unique mystery that resides in each of us.

More information about Sandy Sela-Smith and her work is available on her website:

http://www.infiniteconnections.us

Purchase this book and the others Dr. Sela-Smith has written on her websites:

http://www.infiniteconnections.us

http://www.authortree.com/infinite1111

The Trilogy can be purchased from the publisher, Authorhouse:

1-888-728-8467

And it can be purchased online from:

www.barnesandnoble.com/ and www.Amazon.com